CONSCIENCE, EQUITY AND THE COURT OF CHANCERY IN EARLY MODERN ENGLAND

Finally, I want to thank my family: my daughters Mary and Jen, just for being who they are and for their tolerant (although sometimes bemused) understanding of my intellectual preoccupations, and my wife Anne, for all kinds of support, ranging from helping to translate Latin to appreciating my rather eccentric sense of humour. It is hard to imagine what working on a project like this would have been like without a companion so deeply sympathetic to and herself so involved in the scholarly enterprise.

Chapter 1
Introduction

That conscience played an essential role in the development of English equity is a commonplace. C.K. Allen observes that 'a philosophical and theological conception of *conscience*' was the 'one general principle which more than any other influenced equity'.[1] A.W.B. Simpson similarly says that 'the primary principle of decision' in the 'fifteenth- and early-sixteenth-century court of Chancery was *Conscience*',[2] and W. Barbour refers to conscience as a 'juristic principle' proper to at least the early Chancery.[3] Helmut Coing points out that the 'prominence of conscience is peculiar to English equity,' and finds 'no parallel ... in Aristotle's doctrine of equity or in the civil law'.[4] Jurists of the early period clearly declared that conscience was central. Christopher St. German (c. 1460–1540/41), whose work 'set the tone' for 'almost all' English legal reflection on equity in the sixteenth century, 'preserved the teaching of the canon law of the medieval church and its philosophical ideas of conscience';[5] Edward Hake (c. 1545–c. 1604) distinguished Chancery equity from

---

1 Carleton Kemp Allen, *Law in the Making* (6th edn, Oxford, 1958), p. 389.

2 A.W.B. Simpson, *A History of the Common Law of Contract: The Rise of the Action of Assumpsit* (Oxford, 1975), p. 397.

3 Willard Barbour, 'Some Aspects of Fifteenth-Century Chancery', *Harvard Law Review*, 31/6 (1918): 834–59, p. 838. D.E.C. Yale uses this same expression in the 'Introduction' to his edition of *Lord Nottingham's Chancery Cases* (2 vols, London, 1957), vol. 1, p. xxxvii.

4 Helmut Coing, 'English Equity and the *Denunciatio Evangelica* of the Canon Law', *Law Quarterly Review*, 71(1955): 223–41, p. 224. This observation requires qualification. Joseph Story, for example, speaks of the 'settled distinction' in the civil law 'between natural obligations, upon which no action lay, but they were merely binding in conscience, and civil obligations, which gave origin to actions' (*Commentaries on Equity Jurisprudence* (Boston, 1836), vol. 1, p. 3). Elsewhere, quoting Cicero, he suggests that the Roman Prætor judged 'according to equity and conscience' (ibid., p. 7n.). Similarly, Lord Nottingham (1621–82) tells us that civilians divided rights into '*jus precarium*, for which no remedy, *jus fiduciarium*, for which a remedy but in conscience, and *jus legitimum*' (*Lord Nottingham's 'Manual of Chancery Practice' and 'Prolegomena of Chancery and Equity'*, ed. D.E.C. Yale (Cambridge, 1965; reprinted Holmes Beach, 1986), p. 239). Francis Bacon makes essentially the same observation in his *Reading on the Statute of Uses*, in *The Works of Francis Bacon*, eds J. Spedding, R.L. Ellis and D.D. Heath (14 vols, London, 1857–74), vol. 7, p. 401. This does not, of course, indicate that any general jurisdiction based on conscience existed in the civil law, but it does suggest that the concept was not alien to it.

5 'Introduction' to Edward Hake, *Epieikeia: A Dialogue on Equity in Three Parts*, ed. D.E.C. Yale (New Haven, 1953), p. xiii.

or sincere, but in some sense a matter of *knowledge*.[21] An objective account of conscience, although perhaps paradoxical to us, would ostensibly be easier to reconcile with its status as a juristic principle, a measure of law.

So, one possible answer to the apparent rift between the subjectivity of conscience and the necessary objectivity of law is that, at the time when conscience was the informing principle of equity, it was itself an objective notion and therefore not incongruous with law. Apart from the obvious objection that, while this might justify the prominence of conscience in early equity it cannot justify its continuing invocation today—a point which is only by implication part of my study—this explanation raises other difficulties. Notably, as we have seen, there were complaints about the perceived subjectivity of conscience at least as long ago as the sixteenth century. At a time when the 'science of jurisprudence' was ostensibly still in an 'infant state' and when conscience was still seen as intimately a part of equity, it was viewed by some as problematic.

Any rationalization of conscience as a juristic principle that depends upon the argument that the concept has changed, perhaps radically, over time cannot rely on the crude dichotomy of 'medieval' *versus* 'modern'. Rather, even accepting the idea of conscience as objective in, say, the late fifteenth century, we must address how that concept might have evolved in the period which is the main focus of this study—essentially the sixteenth and seventeenth centuries. Indeed, it is largely because this period is transitional—heir to medieval ideas, womb of modern ones—that it is both challenging and potentially illuminating.

At this stage, I wish merely to flag two of the ways in which this transition, particularly relating to conscience, has been described. The first is the ostensible change in emphasis from 'conscience' to 'equity' as the focus of Chancery's judicial activity. Typical are Sir John Baker's account of the 'shift from "conscience" to "equity"'[22] and J.L. Barton's opinion that we are largely indebted to Christopher St. German for the fact that 'we have courts of equity rather than of conscience at this day'.[23] Such observations might suggest is a supersession of 'conscience' by 'equity'—a proposition that must be carefully scrutinized.

---

21 Potts, pp. 20, 41.

22 J.H. Baker, *An Introduction to English Legal History* (4th edn, London, 2003), pp. 106–8. Timothy S. Haskett, 'The Medieval English Court of Chancery', *Law and History Review*, 14/2 (1996): 245–313, p. 268, referring to an earlier edition of Baker's book, writes: 'Baker sees conscience as the hallmark of the medieval chancellors in their court and equity in the Court of Chancery as something significantly different, a product of developments in the Tudor age'. W.J. Jones, *The Elizabethan Court of Chancery* (Oxford, 1967) appears to draw the line at a somewhat different point, 'conscience' being the appropriate descriptor 'before the seventeenth century' and 'equity' for 'that modern and distinct kind of case law of which Nottingham was the greatest exponent' (p. 419n.).

23 J.L. Barton, 'Equity in the Medieval Common Law' in R.A. Newman (ed.), *Equity in the World's Legal Systems* (Brussels, 1973), pp. 139–55, p. 154.

Another way in which the change has been described, one not unrelated to the first, is suggested by D.E.C. Yale who, while observing that the earlier concept of conscience had a continuing influence on the development of Chancery equity, says that 'canonist conscience' was superseded 'by what may be called, for want of a better phrase, the Protestant conscience'.[24] That is, the Reformation effected changes in the conception of conscience and the locus of its authority which almost certainly impacted its position as a juristic principle. My object at this point is not to give an elaborated account, but merely to suggest the broad contours of the change the Reformation wrought. Meg Lota Brown, fairly typically, identifies the main difference as between 'authoritarian' Catholic casuistry, 'based on precedent and canon law', and the Protestant emphasis on individual conscience and direct engagement with scripture.[25] One can imagine how a developed casuistry based on Latin authority and administered by professionals according to established rules would be more congruent with law than is the isolated individual conscience, left to its own resources, or to those resources animated by faith. Baylor suggests that while in medieval scholasticism the 'object of the action of the conscience is restricted to particular moral actions' for Luther at least conscience definitively concerned itself 'with the individual or person as a whole'.[26] Conscience as concerned with specific actions, rather than with one's overall moral condition, appears more relevant to the legal sphere, focused as it is on instances of conduct.

One must, of course, be extremely wary of such generalizations. This may be no more starkly illustrated than by considering Benjamin Nelson's assertion that, by contrast with the Catholic 'pattern', '[t]he Court of Conscience and the Court Christian disappeared in the Protestant lands, and with them the historical notions of a law of conscience, human judges of conscience, a casuistry'.[27] In England, indubitably a 'Protestant land', the court of conscience emphatically did not disappear, nor did the notion of a branch of law somehow informed by conscience.[28] The seventeenth century in England has, not inappropriately, been

---

24 'Introduction' to Hake, p. xiv.

25 *Donne and the Politics of Conscience in Early Modern England* (Leiden, 1995), pp. 25, 30, 36. See also Camille Wells Slights, *The Casuistical Tradition in Shakespeare, Donne, Herbert and Milton* (Princeton, 1981), p. 35. Alexandra Walsham makes the somewhat different but related point that the more frequent post-Reformation occasions for people to assert conscientious objections to religious conformity of whatever stripe contributed to 'relativising and internalising the concept of conscience' ('Ordeals of Conscience: Casuistry, Conformity and Confessional Identity in Post-Reformation England' in H.E. Braun and E. Vallance (eds), *Contexts of Conscience in Early Modern Europe 1500–1700* (Basingstoke, 2004), pp. 32–48, p. 33.

26 Baylor, pp. 201–2.

27 Benjamin Nelson, 'Conscience and the Making of Early Modern Cultures: the Protestant Ethic Beyond Max Weber', *Social Research*, 36/1 (1969): 5–21, p. 16.

28 John Witte Jr., *Law and Protestantism: The Legal Teachings of the Lutheran Reformation* (Cambridge, 2002), pp. 160–61, outlines the importance of conscience in

called 'the Age of Conscience';[29] there developed a distinctive and influential Protestant casuistry. And, albeit that casuistry emphasized the engagement of the individual conscience, it was far from endorsing the idea that what was concordant with conscience was simply a matter of personal moral preference.

One strategy, therefore, for addressing the 'subjective conscience *versus* objective law' conundrum is to say that, 'historically', conscience as understood *was* objective, or more objective. But for the sixteenth and seventeenth centuries this does not resolve the difficulty. It identifies the difficulty. An important issue is the persistence of conscience, or talk about conscience, in relation to equity in the face of its ostensible subjectivization or even relativization after the Reformation.

A second conventional response to the conundrum is to narrow the claims of conscience as a juristic principle by subdividing it broadly into the non-justiciable and the justiciable. That is, the distinction is not simply between 'strict law' and conscience comprehensively; rather, within the concept of conscience itself there is a distinction between those matters which are susceptible to regulation by a court of equity and those which in any case must be left to the person himself. As Story points out, '[t]here are many cases against natural justice, which are left wholly to the conscience of the party, and are without any redress, equitable or legal'.[30] The ways in which the demarcation is described vary, but they do illustrate a theme, a theme which implicitly recognizes the tenuousness of invoking conscience comprehensively as a principle of legal judgment.

The distinction pre-dates the period which is my main focus here. As Simpson for example notes, canon law distinguished between the internal forum, which related to 'the individual's spiritual health, and the avoidance of sin', and the external forum, the ecclesiastical courts, where the 'concern was with the welfare of the Church and its members generally'.[31] He points to at least one case in which this distinction was a matter of contention in Chancery and in which, indeed, the Chancellor, Archbishop John Morton (1420–1500), apparently regarded himself as being *in foro conscientiæ* just by virtue of his being in his own court.[32] This might indicate some blurring of the distinction at that, pre-Reformation, time. By contrast, Baker cites a dictum attributed to Fitzjames C.J. (d. 1539)—'Two maine principles that guide Humane nature are conscience and law; by the one we are

---

the legal theory of the influential German Lutheran jurist Johann Oldendorp (1486–1567), albeit that theory did not involve a separate jurisdiction.

[29] K. Thomas, 'Cases of Conscience in Seventeenth-Century England' in J. Morrill, P. Slack and D. Woolf (eds), *Public Duty and Private Conscience* (Oxford, 1993), pp. 29–56, p. 29. Compare Max. Radin, 'The Conscience of the Court', *Law Quarterly Review*, 48 (1932): 506–20, p. 508.

[30] Story, p. 16. See also p. 203, where he remarks that many things that 'may be reproved in sound morals … are left without any remedy, except by an appeal *in foro conscientiæ* to the party himself'.

[31] Simpson, p. 381.

[32] Ibid., p. 399.

obliged in reference to another world, the later in relation to this'—which he, Baker, sees as implying that conscience might be 'exclude[d] ... from human law entirely'.[33] Perhaps another early variation on the theme is the *denunciatio evangelica* as described by Coing: at first a 'purely penitentiary' procedure, it later appeared in a severable version which aimed at 'redress of a material wrong as well as at penitence', becoming a *denunciatio judicialis privata*.[34]

Concern to make the distinction persisted, and perhaps became more urgent, during the sixteenth and seventeenth centuries. Of St. German's time, Baker says that the 'essence of the debate over equity and law ... lay in the difficulty of deciding which questions of conscience should be left entirely to the party's conscience'.[35] In his *Reading on the Statute of Uses*, Francis Bacon quotes Sir Edward Fenner J.'s (d. 1611/12) observation that uses are 'ordered and guided by conscience, either by the private conscience of the feoffee, or the general conscience of the realm, which is Chancery'.[36] In this instance, the operation of the two kinds of conscience may be concurrent, but Fenner J. does differentiate private from public conscience. Perhaps most famously, Lord Nottingham, who wrote 'God forbid, a man should use no better conscience than the Chancery can compel him, however the rule must always hold, that 'tis not fit for a court of equity to do everything that is fit to be done',[37] in more than one place distinguishes between *conscientia politica et civilis*—the proper focus of equity—and *conscientia naturalis et interna*[38]—the latter comprehending matters 'which cannot be reformed by the regular and political administration of equity'.[39]

Just as one might attempt to resolve the ostensible incongruity between conscience and law by dividing the concept of conscience temporally and saying that at a particular time conscience was understood objectively and therefore could be coherently assimilated to law, so one might divide the concept atemporally and say, in effect, 'we are not talking about conscience *tout court*, but about one segment of it, which is "public" and therefore (in some way) subject to agreed criteria'. But just as the temporal distinction, at least for the early modern period, is problematic, so is this attempt to divide the substance of conscience. Saying that there is an objective, public conscience, distinguishable from private or personal conscience, and that the former alone is the proper sphere of equity,

---

33 'Introduction' to *The Reports of Sir John Spelman*, ed. J.H. Baker (2 vols, London, 1978), vol. 1, p. 40n., citing Brit. Lib., MS Sloane 1523, f. 31.

34 Coing, pp. 225, 227.

35 'Introduction', *Reports of Sir John Spelman*, p. 40n.

36 Fenner J. cited in Bacon, *Reading on the Statute of Uses*, p. 401. The editor's note states that Bacon is the only source for these observations by Fenner J.

37 *Prolegomena*, p. 194.

38 *Cook* v. *Fountain* (1676) in *Lord Nottingham's Chancery Cases*, ed. D.E.C. Yale (2 vols, London, 1957), vol. 1, p. 371.

39 *Prolegomena*, p. 194.

is one thing. Identifying the criteria for making the distinction is quite another, perhaps especially for the period in question, which was probably less prone than we are to drawing distinctions between law and morality, between the secular and the sacred, and so on. As John Donne said in a sermon in 1621, although our activities may 'seeme but *Morall*, or *Civill*, or *domestique*, yet they have a deeper tincture, a heavenly nature, a relation *to God*, in them'.[40] Just as the temporal development of the concept of conscience will be a central focus of my inquiry, so will be the exploration of the distinction between those matters of conscience which are properly cognizable by judicial equity and those which are not.

Donne's observation should remind us not only that separating the 'civil' from the 'heavenly' may be an intractable enterprise, but that from a certain perspective it may not ultimately be crucial. Probably most of the commentators, religious or legal, I shall be considering would have believed that there was a sanction beyond the temporal for violations of the imperatives of conscience. In the end, it is not one's conscience that judges, but God, whose judgment is perfect and infallible, however awkwardly calibrated the assessments of human institutions may be. Thus, for example, James Forsyth, far from fortuitously, entitles his sermon about God's final judgment *The Great Day of Chancery*, explaining that, at that time, 'the iust Iudge of all the world, will according to the euidence of euery mans conscience, distribute righteous Iudgement'.[41] What this means is that it may not be critical for the temporal Court of Chancery to define precisely the distinction between conscience that is properly justiciable and conscience that is not, since a higher 'court' will ultimately put everything right.

A number of other dimensions of my subject warrant mention at this stage, in anticipation of their arising later.

One of these is the obvious, but sometimes overlooked, point that considerations of conscience were not exclusive to equity. This aggravates the difficulty of discerning the sphere of conscience as something separate from law. Norman Doe, for example, makes at some length the point that, certainly during the medieval period, 'conscience was ... extensively employed as a moral authority fundamental to the common law'.[42] Indeed, much of St. German's project involved showing how the common law was conformable to conscience. This is not to suggest that every

---

40 *The Sermons of John Donne*, eds George R. Potter and Evelyn M. Simpson (10 vols, Berkeley and Los Angeles, 1953–59), vol. 3, p. 366.

41 'Epistle Dedicatorie' to *The Great Day of Chancery* (London, 1619), sig. A5r; EEBO image 5944:3.

42 Norman Doe, *Fundamental Authority in Late Medieval English Law* (Cambridge, 1990; reprinted Holmes Beach, 2000), p. 132. See generally chapter 6, 'Conscience in the Common Law', in Doe. See also L.A. Knafla, 'Conscience in the English Common Law Tradition', *University of Toronto Law Journal*, 26/1 (1976): 1–16 and L.O. Pike, 'Common Law and Conscience in the Ancient Court of Chancery' in *Select Essays in Anglo-American Legal History*, ed. Association of American Law Schools (3 vols, Boston, 1908), vol. 2, 722–36.

rule of the common law was motivated by considerations of conscience, but many were. Even though law and juridical conscience are regularly set in opposition to each other, we should not think of them as mutually exclusive categories. Rather, we should probably think of much of law as embodying conscience and the 'conscience' of equity as being a kind of residue which the law has failed to embody—apart, of course, from that part of conscience which is in any case merely a matter for the confessional. If the line between conscience justiciable in equity and purely private conscience is blurred, so is the line between the former and law *per se*. One implication of this is that there is no radical discontinuity between law and equity, the latter being a more complete fulfilment of what is already implicit in the former. Another is that observations about conscience as it inheres in the law may be transferable to conscience in equity.

A second further dimension relates to what might be our tendency to think of conscience in equity as just yielding substantive principles or rules. Doubtless it does. But an important aspect of Chancery conscience involves procedural and evidentiary issues. Zofia Rueger observes that much of the early chancellors' task involved 'establish[ing] the truth of [a] complaint in accordance with conscience—*secundum conscientiam* ...'.[43] As late as the nineteenth century, Story could write that 'Courts of Equity … address themselves to the conscience of the defendant, and require him to answer upon his oath the matters of fact stated in the bill', so that 'every bill in Equity may be said to be, in some sense, a bill of discovery …'.[44] This suggests that the chancellor, in deciding a cause, was not so much looking for or enunciating a new principle as he was considering more facts, or facts in a more searching way, including, typically, examining litigants under oath, which bound them in conscience to speak the truth. Thus, Barbour cites a case from about 1470[45] in which the chancellor says that his decision proceeds '*secundum conscientiam et non secundum allegata*' and comments that this means 'that the truth is to be discovered by any means within his power'.[46] Baker emphasizes that the conscience of equity relieved against the common law's 'inflexible system of pleading and proof',[47] and that '[c]onscience was more within the realm of fact than law ...'.[48]

Recently, Mike Macnair has argued forcefully that the 'technical' meaning of conscience in equity should be understood primarily or even exclusively in these procedural or evidentiary terms.[49] Thus, 'conscience' would refer to means

---

43 Zofia Rueger, 'Gerson's Concept of Equity and Christopher St. German', *History of Political Thought*, 3 (1982): 1–30, p. 26.

44 Story, pp. 29–30.

45 Y.B. 9 Edw. IV, 14.9.

46 Barbour, 'Some Aspects of Fifteenth Century Chancery', p. 854.

47 'Introduction', *Reports of Sir John Spelman*, p. 39. See also Baker, *Oxford History*, p. 47.

48 Ibid., p. 43.

49 'Equity and Conscience', *Oxford Journal of Legal Studies*, 27/4 (2007): 659–81.

of accessing facts other than those authorized by strict legal rules of proof. These would include matters within the judge's private knowledge as well as information that could be extracted from parties by way of confession under oath. On this view, the distinction between justiciable and non-justiciable conscience would be marked by the availability of such evidence. As Baker observes, those facts that could not be known, even by these extraordinary means, would remain within the 'court of conscience' of 'the party's own soul'.[50] *Conscientia civilis et politica* would comprehend those matters which the Chancery could access; *conscientia naturalis et interna* would be those matters that remained concealed in the litigants' breasts.

Unquestionably, this procedural dimension was an important aspect of conscience in equity, and I shall refer to it throughout this study. At the same time, however, conscience in this context had a substantive dimension. It was commonly portrayed, at least in non-legal discourse, as having a tripartite function: it was *law[giver]*, *witness*, and *judge*. 'Whosoever … understands … these three Latine words, *Lex*, *Index* and *Judex*, or these three English words, a *Law*, a *Witnesse*, a *Judge*', writes one commentator, 'is in a good way … to understand the nature and essence of Conscience'.[51] Another observes that the book of conscience consists of two volumes, the first "a Law-booke, wherein are set downe the grounds and principles of truth, and equity', and the second 'a *Chronicle*, or a *Register*, wherein all our workes are written'; when conscience gives judgment, 'it first reades ouer the Law booke … then it turneth over the records …'.[52] Conscience tells one what the rule should be, discloses relevant facts, and then judges by applying the rule dictated to the facts revealed. Macnair disputes that this general, or 'non-technical' meaning of conscience was the meaning in the context of *legal* equity. But, as we shall see, legal writers, when they define or describe the conscience of equity often refer to authors who adopt this view, and judges regularly seem to think in terms of the norms that conscience sets. When, for example, Lord Nottingham says that private conscience dictates what is *fit to be done*, beyond what Chancery will enforce, he is, I believe, speaking normatively. This study will address both the evidentiary and the normative aspects of the conscience of equity.

One further dimension that should be mentioned now might be called 'rhetorical'. Put simply, the word 'conscience' might have continued a part of the discourse of equity as a result of, or partly as a result of, rhetorical inertia or its rhetorical force. By rhetorical inertia, I mean the tendency for language to retain words after their original significance is attenuated—perhaps something like what is suggested by Bertrand Russell's observation that 'ordinary language

---

50 'Introduction', *Reports of Sir John Spelman*, p. 40.

51 John Jackson, *The Booke of Conscience Opened and Read* (London, 1642), p. 13; EEBO image 103990:12.

52 John Hughes, *St. Pavls Exercise, or, a Sermon of Conscience* (London, 1622), pp. 7–8; EEBO images 4483:7–8. Compare, for example, Anthony Cade, *Conscience, its Nature and Corruption* (London, 1661), pp. 2–3; EEBO image 54332:6.

is shot through with the fading hues of past philosophic theories'.[53] In the fifteenth century, 'conscience' as a juristic principle might have had a coherence, albeit a coherence based ultimately on untenable premises; long after this *raison d'être* had become obsolete, people continued, as a matter of habit, to speak of the 'court of conscience'. While such an argument may contain some truth, it seems to me to be too facile as an explanation. For one thing, there was too much deliberate attention paid to conscience in the judicial context for it merely to have been perpetuated subliminally: St. German, for example, wrestled with the concept and, a century and a half later, it was still a matter to which Lord Nottingham was addressing his mind.

By rhetorical force I mean the positive power that particular formulations might have to elicit certain responses. Arguably, 'conscience' is an evocative word of this kind that was more or less deliberately preserved for the role it could play in social ordering. Lowell Gallagher has explored this aspect of 'conscience' in relation to a number of discursive contexts—from the conflict between Queen Elizabeth and Mary Queen of Scots to Spenser's *Faerie Queene*—in the sixteenth century.[54] Broadly—and I am mindful of the pitfalls of paraphrase here—he maintains that 'official' discourses of conscience, such as casuistry and some legal discourse, were part of a 'stabilizing, normative' process by which 'marginal [presumably, subjective] psychological and moral states' could be absorbed into socially 'sanctioned or legitimized modes of thought and behavior'.[55] I take this to mean that human experience evinces idiosyncrasy of 'psychological and moral states', tending to militate against a stable, or at least uniform, social order. Practices like casuistry, which address particularities in institutional terms, are efforts (conscious or otherwise) to normalize or regularize such states. Like casuistry, equity—being the official discourse of conscience in the legal sphere—attempts to accommodate the particular, the aberrant, within a system, and thus to assimilate it to the system. This process is 'rhetorical' in at least two senses. First, 'conscience' has a heavy cultural resonance. To take just one example from the period, Henry VIII repeatedly invokes conscience in his questioning the legitimacy of his marriage to Katherine of Aragon: '[t]he special cause that moved me in this matter, is a certain scruple that pricked my Conscience ...'.[56] How disingenuous this appeal might be I do not know, but it is significant that he appeals to conscience as a kind of ultimate authority. Second, the exploitation of this resonance permits the managing of behaviour by the construction of whole discourses involving it. On this view, equity's attempt to portray conscience within a structure of ruledness involves taming it. Gallagher argues, however, that this discursive practice contains the

---

53 Bertrand Russell, *Wisdom of the West* (London, 1959), p. 309.

54 Lowell Gallagher, *Medusa's Gaze: Casuistry and Conscience in the Renaissance* (Stanford, 1991).

55 Ibid., pp. 2, 6.

56 George Cavendish, *The Life and Death of Thomas Woolsey, Cardinal* (London, 1667), p. 89; EEBO image 64261:53.

seeds of its own subversion: since the discourse of conscience keeps coming back to the particular, or even the subjective, it has a destabilizing effect. While, say, the institutional power of the Church in medieval times might have been sufficient to keep the destabilizing tendencies of conscience in check, the fragmentations associated with the Reformation, including the questioning of church-as-authority-or-mediator, compromised such power. On this view, expressions of concern about 'legal uncertainty' attendant upon retaining conscience as a juristic principle themselves might mask the more radical possibility that the release of conscience threatens uniform social order itself, a possibility complicated by, or manifested in, the growing pressure for allowance to be made for diversity of conscience, associated particularly with the religious and political dislocations of the seventeenth century.

While a thesis such as Gallagher's is intriguing, I am not simply reiterating it as my own. But it is an aspect of the issue which should be borne in mind. It is always possible that the elusiveness of the juridical meaning of 'conscience' arises from the fact that what it entails is little more than 'words, words, words'. Perhaps inevitably, conscience is a concept that pulls in opposite directions and whose rhetorical weight can be invoked to buttress either of its divergent tendencies.

Recently, Mark Fortier has developed the thesis that early modern England was, among other things, importantly 'a culture of equity'.[57] He argues that this equity was not confined to the realm of the law, but encompassed as well 'the world of letters' and 'private morality and religion'.[58] My project, though related, is narrower. My primary focus is on equity as a concept in law, and my concern is with essentially just one feature of that equity, namely, conscience. As I have already intimated, I shall be exploring how conscience was, or could have been, understood as an informing principle of legal equity. Inevitably, however, in pursuing that inquiry, I shall regularly have to refer to contexts such as 'morality' and 'religion'—and perhaps at least implicitly to 'the world of letters' of which each of these discursive spheres is a dimension. In other words, I shall be situating the juristic principle of conscience within a more general culture of conscience.

---

[57] Mark Fortier, *The Culture of Equity in Early Modern England* (Aldershot: 2005) at 11.

[58] Ibid.

Chapter 2
Conscience and the Medieval Chancery

Introduction

Although my concern in this study is primarily with conscience in early modern equity, it is necessary to take account of what it arose from, and perhaps grew in reaction against—the notion of conscience as it might have been understood in the medieval Chancery. That understanding was perpetuated, and modified, in the sixteenth and seventeenth centuries.

As we have seen, conscience, perhaps even more than in the later period, was the hallmark of the medieval Chancery, certainly after a particular point in time. Simpson notes that, if one were to ask a late-fifteenth-century lawyer for the title of a book about 'what went on before the court of Chancery, he would without doubt have said "Conscience", *not* "Equity"'.[1] Thus, one petition from the period asks the Chancellor to summon the defendants 'to come before you in the King's Chancery, which is the Court of Conscience, there to answer thereto as reason and conscience demand …',[2] and the petitioners' replication to the defendants' answer in a case from 1456 claims to be sufficient 'after the lawe of consciens, which ys lawe executory in this courte for defaute of remedy by cours of the common lawe'.[3]

What exactly is 'medieval' in this context deserves some consideration. Robert Palmer suggests that 'the chancellor's court of conscience ... began around 1370' and was given impetus by the Black Death.[4] J.L. Barton claims that conscience was first mentioned in connection with Chancery in 1391.[5] A quick glance at the cases reported by Baildon suggests that, although some version of the formula 'for the love of God and in way of charity' was common throughout the period

---

1 A.W.B. Simpson, *A History of the Common Law of Contract: The Rise of the Action of Assumpsit* (Oxford, 1975), p. 398.

2 *Select Cases in Chancery A.D. 1364 to 1471*, ed. William Paley Baildon (London, 1896), case 123, p. 121.

3 Ibid., case 143, p. 146.

4 Robert C. Palmer, *English Law in the Age of the Black Death, 1348–1381* (Chapel Hill, 1993), pp. 130, 131.

5 J.L. Barton, 'Equity in the Medieval Common Law' in Ralph A. Newman (ed.), *Equity in the World's Legal Systems* (Brussels,1973), pp. 139–55, p. 146, citing *Rot. Parl.*, iii, 297, nos. 1 and 2 'where two petitions are referred to the Chancellor with an order to do not merely what is required by law and reason (the traditional phrase), but by good faith and conscience'.

covered, appeals to conscience became more frequent as the fifteenth century progressed.[6] This is not to say there is no evidence that conscience was understood to be integral to the Chancellor's function in the early decades of that century. Apart from the references that do occur in Baildon's collection, there are several examples in documents relating to Chancery from before 1450 included in the University of Virginia's *An Anthology of Chancery English*.[7]

All the cases Simpson cites in support of the proposition that 'in the year-book cases the argument is directed to deciding what conscience requires' are from the reigns of Henry VI, Edward IV and Henry VII.[8] Thus, the medieval Chancery to which I am referring is essentially the fifteenth-century Chancery, and probably the later fifteenth-century Chancery.[9] The difficulty of setting meaningfully precise boundaries is suggested by comparing observations such as Nicholas Pronay's that, by the beginning of Henry VII's reign, Chancery was being much more influenced by 'trained lawyers',[10] and, conversely, Franz Metzger's that the chancellorship of Cardinal Wolsey (c. 1473–1530) was the last phase of the medieval Chancery.[11]

---

6 Compare the earlier cases, 121 (1420–22), 136 (1432–43), 137 (1441), 138 (1441), 139 (1443–50), 141 (1456), 143 (1456), 145 (1464), which refer to charity, with the later cases, 140 (1454), 144 (1460–65), 146 (1465–67), 147 (1471), which refer to conscience. On the other hand, the *caveat* has been suggested that, because so many petitions are lost or were never recorded, we should not 'make too much of the paucity of references to conscience in the early bills' (P. Tucker, 'The Early History of the Court of Chancery: A Comparative Study', (2000) 115 *English Historical Review*, 115/463 (2000): 791–811, p. 806.)

7 Electronic version, University of Virginia Library Electronic Text Center. See Texts numbered 39 (1418), 62 (1419), 73 (1420-1), 89 (1420), 127 (after 1432), 168 (1423), 189 (after 1432), 197 (1433-50), 128 (after 1432), and 157 (1446).

8 Simpson, p. 397.

9 Nicholas Pronay, 'The Chancellor, the Chancery, and the Council at the End of the Fifteenth Century', in H. Hearder and H.R. Loyn (eds), *British Government and Administration* (Cardiff, 1974), pp. 87–103, pp. 89, 92. Pronay suggests that Chancery 'settled into its stride' as a court during the Yorkist period (1461–85). Compare M.E. Avery, 'The History of the Equitable Jurisdiction of Chancery Before 1460', *Bulletin of the Institute of Historical Research*, 42 (1969): 129–44. Avery suggests that much of the development was complete during the Lancastrian period (that is, before 1461). See also J.A. Guy, 'The Development of Equitable Jurisdictions 1450–1550', in E.W. Ives and A.H. Manchester (eds), *Law, Litigants, and the Legal Profession* (London, 1983), pp. 80–86, p. 81.

10 Pronay, 'Chancellor', pp. 91–2. See also M. Beilby, 'The Profits of Expertise: the Rise of the Civil Lawyers and Chancery Equity' in M. Hicks (ed.), *Profit, Piety and the Professions in Later Medieval England* (Gloucester, 1990), pp. 72–90.

11 Franz Metzger, 'The Last Phase of the Medieval Chancery' in Alan Harding (ed.), *Law-Making and Law-Makers in British History* (London, 1980), pp. 79–89, p. 79.

The Content of Conscience

Saying that conscience was the hallmark of medieval equity is one thing; giving content to the notion of conscience is quite another. As more than one commentator has observed, 'the reasoning of the chancellors has not been preserved'.[12] One of these commentators, Helmut Coing, has surmised what the Chancellor's reasoning might have been in enforcing uses: 'here is a promise, which ought to be exactly performed; there is a moral and reasonable duty towards the beneficiary ...; its performance is a question of "fides" and "confidence"'.[13] While plausible in general terms, such an account remains somewhat speculative and leaves certain questions unanswered. For example, how is it that the duty arises towards the beneficiary, to whom the promise has not been made and who ostensibly has not given any value for the benefit he is claiming? As Pronay has said with respect to another putative element in the Chancellor's reasoning—the application of civilian doctrines—the search for specific forms of analysis based on conscience may be 'a hopeless quest'.[14] By contrast, Simpson, while acknowledging the challenges involved in identifying the principles upon which the medieval Chancellors proceeded, does say that 'the task is not … hopeless'.[15] But this more sanguine view just takes us back to our starting point. The principle he identifies is the 'conscience' so often referred to, but almost never elaborated, in petitions to the Chancellor and in the Year Books. Principles derived from conscience and operating at a lower level of abstraction are considerably harder to locate.

Intimations from the Legal Record

One noteworthy exception to the general absence of evidence of equitable reasoning in medieval courts is the summary report under the caption 'Conscience' of an Exchequer case from 1453 in Nicholas Statham's (d. 1472) *Abridgment des libres annals*.[16] The case, in which Sir John Fortescue C.J. (c. 1394–c. 1476) explicitly

12 Timothy S. Haskett, 'The Medieval English Court of Chancery', *Law and History Review*, 14/2 (1996): 245–313, p. 263.

13 Helmut Coing, 'English Equity and the *Denunciatio Evangelica* of the Canon Law', *Law Quarterly Review*, 71 (1955): 223–41, p. 235. A more authentic indication of the tenor of the Chancellor's reasoning appears in a letter of Henry Beaufort, Bishop of Winchester (himself Chancellor from 1413–17) to John Stafford, Bishop of Bath and Chancellor (1432–50) referring to a case involving feoffees to uses who have excluded the feoffor/cestui que use: it is an 'open wroong', 'full odieux and aggregeable', raising 'a matere of conscience' that requires the attention of Chancery (*Chancery English*, Text 127).

14 Pronay, 'Chancellor', p. 102.

15 Simpson, p. 397.

16 1490. Available in a modern edition as *Statham's Abridgment of the Law*, trans. Margaret C. Klingelsmith (Boston, 1915), pp. 392–4.

and famously said 'nous ne sum[us] a arguer ley en ce cas mez la conscience',[17] contains at least indications of what the lower-order principles informing conscience might be.

The case involved what we would now call a trust—a feoffment of land to the use of one of the feoffor's daughters. When the daughter refused to marry according to her father's wishes, 'nor be well governed',[18] he attempted to revoke the trust and substitute another daughter as beneficiary. Different judges—generally referring their reasons to conscience—advanced various arguments. For example, Illington J. said that, since the feoffor had received no *quid pro quo*, he should be able 'conscientiously'[19] to change his mind. In his view, a want of mutuality in the transaction meant that the father was not bound to it in conscience. Further, he appears to have regarded the daughter's obstinacy as compromising her claim in conscience. Presumably, underlying this concern is some notion of an obligation to honour one's parents, or at least one's father. Further, Illington J. posits the hypothetical of the father's having fallen into poverty after having made the feoffment: 'is it not in conscience that the feoffee would re-enfeoff him?' Here, it appears that the feoffee's conscience, not the daughter's, is in issue, and that the need of the feoffor should somehow supersede the mere bounty that he was bestowing on another. Fortescue C.J., again very much in the context of conscience, argues that the feoffor 'can change his will for a special reason, but otherwise not'. Such a reason, he suggests, might be where the feoffment to uses is made in contemplation of death, but the feoffor subsequently recovers and has a son: 'it is conscience that the son shall have the land for he is [the] heir …'. The underlying rationale here may be that a man is not presumed to intend to disinherit his son, or (as Fortescue C.J. suggests) that he would not have so disposed of his land if at the time he had known that he would have an heir, or perhaps that he has a natural obligation to provide for his heir.[20]

---

17 Statham, sig. G3v; EEBO image 9984:53. Willard T. Barbour, 'Some Aspects of Fifteenth-Century Chancery', *Harvard Law Review*, 31/6 (1918): 834–59, p. 838 understands this to be an instance of judicial recognition of the distinctiveness of Chancery thinking. The distinction occurs in non-judicial contexts as well: see for example the claim by William Paston, in a letter written in 1436, that he is able to show that a certain manor 'by trewe title in lawe and conscience is his owen trewly' (*The Paston Letters, A.D. 1422–1509*, ed. James Gairdner (6 vols, originally published London, 1904; reprinted New York, 1965), letter 30 (1436), vol. 2, p. 41).

18 *Statham's Abridgment*, p. 392.

19 Ibid., p. 393. All the following quotations from the case appear on this page.

20 The hypothetical was invoked in the notorious *Shelley's Case* (1581) 1 Co. Rep. 93b at 99b–100b, 76 ER 206 at 225–6, where a connection is made between Chancery as a 'Court of conscience' and a concern with discerning the feoffor's intent, perhaps suggesting that that court had a special competence respecting 'internal' matters. The feoffor's intent appears, however, to be inferred just from the fact that the later-born son is his heir.

Fortescue C.J. then goes on to make some more general comments about conscience. The word, he says, 'comes of *con* and *scioscis*. And so together they make "to know with God" to wit: to know the will of God as near as one reasonably can'. This observation is significant for various reasons—notably that it makes judgment in conscience an effort to discern and do God's will. This fairly firmly places the measure of conscience in the law of God, and suggests that the judge in conscience is attempting, in some sense, to know as God knows.

Certain other inferences—although not really about the substantive parameters of conscience—can be drawn from the materials Simpson mentions and other fifteenth-century documents. As we have seen already, Chancery was referred to as a 'Court of Conscience' and conscience was said to be the 'lawe executory' in that court. The conscience invoked appears not to have been particularly that of the litigant nor that of the Chancellor, but rather a somewhat disembodied or impersonal notion. This is consistent with a meaning of 'conscience' that was more prevalent in the medieval period than it is now, that is, a concept of 'our respective shares ... of the common quality *conscience*' as opposed to 'distinct individual *consciences*, mine and yours'.[21] So, the common complaint is that a person has acted 'against conscience', not 'against *his* conscience'.[22] Similarly, what the Chancellor is typically asked to do is to give a remedy 'as conscience requireth', not specifically according to his conscience.[23] To the extent that anything can be drawn from such formulations, they appear to suggest that what is in issue is not any particular person's subjective sense of right and wrong. A similar inference might be supported by the association of conscience with, or even its substitution for, such concepts as 'law',[24] 'reason',[25] and 'justice'[26]—although probably less so by its very common linking with 'good faith'.[27] So, for example, when Henry V directs his Chancellor[28] to show a supplicant 'all the fauour and ese þat may be don by lawe and conscience'[29] or to do 'what may be doon by Lawe conscience and

---

[21] *Oxford English Dictionary*, 2nd ed., *s.v.* 'conscience'.

[22] See, for example, *Select Cases in Chancery*, cases 121 (1420–22), 136 (1432–43), 142 (1456).

[23] Ibid., cases 121 (1420–22), 137 (1441), 138 (1441), 139 (1443–50), 140 (1454), 141 (1456), 142 (1456), 144 (1460–65), 145 (1464), 146 (1465–67), 147 (1471). See also John Paston's draft petition to the Chancellor in *Paston Letters*, letter 530 (1462?), vol. 4, p. 56.

[24] *Select Cases in Chancery*, cases 121 (1420–22), 136 (1432–43).

[25] Ibid., cases 123 (no year), 138 (1441). 147 (1471) refers to right and conscience.

[26] Ibid., case 141 (1456).

[27] Ibid., cases 137 (1441), 139 (1443–50), 140 (1454), 141 (1456), 143 (1456), 144 (1460–65), 146 (1465–67), 147 (1471).

[28] Thomas Langley, Bishop of Durham (1417–24).

[29] *Chancery English*, Text 39.

reson'[30], or when Queen Margaret enjoins Henry VI's[31] to proceed 'by lawe trouth & gode conscience'[32], we can infer that these are coordinate concepts. As I have intimated in Chapter 1, it is hardly surprising to find conscience treated at that time as transcending personal moral sensibilities.[33]

Other Cultural Documents

Other features of conscience as then appreciated may be illustrated, if not from strictly legal records, at least from other contemporary sources.

One such source is what might be called 'popular literature'. Some well-known examples are not very useful in the present context. The thirteenth-century *The Pricke of Conscience*[34] contains a description of hell, purgatory and heaven and a graphic account of the corruption of human nature as a reminder to its audience to think on the destiny of their souls, but contains no analysis of conscience as such. Similarly, the fourteenth-century *Ayenbite of Inwit*[35] involves an elaborate description of the seven deadly sins and an invocation to avoid them in all their manifestations. There is quite a lot about righteousness, which the editor sometimes renders as 'equity',[36] in this work, but there is little indication that this is a particularly juristic notion. At one point a connection is made between personal righteousness and the judicial function: the person who has the virtue of righteousness will be a 'guod iustise and wys'; he will inquire closely into matters 'ase ssel do þe guode demere [i.e. judge]'; the first requirement for such a person is that he be a 'guod demere of his oyene herte', who will go 'in-to him-zelve/ and y-sy his inwyt and wel examin his þoȝtes/ and his wylles ...' (p. 153). However, it is not clear that the 'justice' or 'demere' here is anything more than a metaphor for a person making personal moral assessments. Conscience plays a similarly central role in the fourteenth-century allegorical works *The Abbey of the Holy Ghost* and *The Charter of the Abbey of the Holy Ghost*[37] in that conscience is depicted as

30 Ibid., Text 73.

31 John Stafford, Bishop of Bath (1432–50).

32 *Chancery English*, Text 157.

33 Sometimes the impersonal conscience of Chancery appears simultaneously with 'conscience' as a person's spiritual condition. Thus, Henry V asks Chancellor Langley to confirm the title of certain lands he (the king) has granted. He is concerned that the title be 'cler yn lawe and conscience' (that is, Chancery conscience). The reason for this, however, is that he wants to 'eschewe þe peril yn conscience' that might affect him for giving the land and the grantee for taking it (*Chancery English*, Text 62).

34 Richard Rolle, *The Pricke of Conscience*, ed. Richard Morris (Berlin, 1863).

35 *Dan Michel's Ayenbite of Inwit, or, Remorse of Conscience*, ed. Richard Morris (London, 1866). 'Inwit' is roughly equivalent to 'conscience'.

36 Ibid., 'Table of Contents'.

37 Both in *Yorkshire Writers: Richard Rolle of Hampole and his Followers*, ed. C. Horstmann (London, 1895–96).

the abbey itself or the foundation of the abbey, but, again, there is no hint that conscience is understood as a juristic principle.

A notable example in which 'Conscience' does figure prominently specifically in relation to law is William Langland's *Piers the Plowman* which, though composed in the latter part of the fourteenth century, remained 'very much a "living" text' into the fifteenth and sixteenth.[38] Conscience appears in more than one context in the book—for example, in places it is described as one of 'the surgeons for deadly sin' (p. 169) or as that faculty of the soul which 'consents [to] or refuses' certain actions (p. 179). My concern here is with its depiction as an appurtenance to the administration of justice, although perhaps understandably at this early date, it is not explicitly linked to the Chancellor's jurisdiction.

Early in the book, when Fraud, Flattery and their cohort set out for Westminster, apparently to 'go to Law,' it is 'Sir Conscience' who informs the King of their imminent arrival. The King vows to make them 'feel the full force of the Law' (p. 43). Then, when the King proposes that Lady Fee, who had been betrothed to Fraud, should marry Conscience ('recently come from overseas'), the latter reacts vehemently: 'she chokes up the course of justice' (p. 49). Later, the King instructs Conscience to go and fetch Reason who, the King says, 'from now onwards … alone shall direct my kingdom and be my Chief Counsellor', in consultation with Conscience (p. 56). Conscience, having found Reason, guides him back to the King; en route they have to evade the pursuit of Worldly Wisdom and Cunning 'who had certain matters to clear up in the Courts of Exchequer and Chancery' (p. 56). Subsequently, when Worldly Wisdom and Cunning try to persuade Reason to allow Crime, who has been committing numerous violations of Peace, to escape merely by paying compensation, Reason refuses. After hearing a debate on the issue, 'the King, calling Reason and Conscience to his side, gave his verdict in favour of Reason' (p. 60). Thereafter, Reason agrees to stay with the King 'forever', but insists that Conscience must be allowed to 'remain here as our advisor' (p. 60).[39]

Conscience here is not depicted as being characteristic of a separate jurisdiction, but rather as something that is necessary so that the law itself shall go aright. Indeed, at one point it appears that Conscience is what directs the King to govern his subjects 'strictly according to justice' (p. 60), that is, ostensibly, to make sure that the law is applied free of the blandishments of Lady Fee and her ilk. But Conscience is certainly presented as a necessary complement to law, and its function here is consistent with that aspect of Chancery jurisdiction which provided recourse to petitioners whose adversaries were too rich or powerful to

[38] 'Introduction' to William Langland, *Piers the Ploughman*, trans. J.F. Goodridge (Harmondsworth, 1968), p. 10. For simplicity's sake I shall refer to this modern English version of the work, except where the middle English text has significantly different connotations.

[39] We may recall the quite common pairing of conscience and reason in the Chancery documents.

allow them to get a remedy at law, although less clearly with that aspect of the jurisdiction which involved qualification of 'strict law'.

John Alford offers a suggestive account[40] of how parts of the harrowing of hell episode in *Piers the Plowman* might track the law/equity distinction, although neither equity nor conscience is explicitly mentioned. The legal question, being debated by the devils in hell, is whether Adam (and by extension all humankind) might be redeemed from 'death'. Lucifer argues that God 'hymselfe seide, þat Sire is of heuene,/If Adam ete þe Appul alle shold deye', and that mankind is his by right, so that if God is to deprive him of his right, 'he robbeþ me by maistrie [i.e., force]'. That is, God can do anything, because of His power, but if He releases humankind, He will be breaking His own law. In other words, Lucifer makes an argument based on strict legal right. He reinforces this by observing that man is also his by right of long possession: 'siþen I was seised seuene þousand winter/I leeue þat lawe nif nyl noȝt lete him þe leeste'. *Law* is on his side.

Alford points out, though, that in response to this strictly legal argument, a lesser devil named Goblin makes an argument concordant with canon law: 'We haue no trewe title to hem, for þoruȝ treson were þei dampned'. That is, man's fall, and hence Lucifer's 'seisin', were obtained through treachery or fraud. Although common law might leave undisturbed a right so acquired, canon law 'affirmed the Roman principle' that time for adverse possession or acquisitive prescription ran only 'if the possessor had acquired under a *justus titulus* … and was in good faith at the beginning of his possession'.[41] I make no comment on the theological implications of these views or, indeed, of the fact that what is said is said by devils, whose words should probably be regarded with circumspection. But what Alford says is telling: the position at 'law' may be subject to qualification by principles derived from a parallel jurisdiction. He himself makes the connection with Chancery: '[t]he doctrine of good faith became the cornerstone not only of much canonist thought … but of the law of Equity itself'.[42] And it accords with what Langland says elsewhere about 'Fraud' being one of the evils against which the King, guided by Reason and Conscience, must guard.

Another such non-legal (and this time, non-fictional) source of insight into popular medieval understandings of conscience is the Paston letters, which ingenuously record the everyday life, including engagements with the law, of a fifteenth-century Norfolk family.

Several of these provide some indication of the distinction between personal conscience and justiciable conscience, not in terms of actual analysis, to be sure, but in terms of examples. Thus, in 1454, John Paston writes to the Earl of Oxford on behalf of Agnes Denyes, whose ill-fated marriage Paston and Oxford had

40 'Literature and Law in Medieval England', *PMLA* 92/5 (1977): 941–51, pp. 944–5. I reproduce Alford's quotations of the original middle English here because they more vividly indicate the legal dimensions of the situation.

41 Ibid., p. 945.

42 Ibid.

promoted: 'if she be destroyd be this mariage, my conscyens thynketh I am bownd to recompense her after my pore and sympill power'.[43] Although he feels bound in conscience, it is difficult to imagine that she would have any recourse against him in Chancery, perhaps because either her misfortunes are too remote from his relevant actions or his actions did not involve confidence, fraud or force—or a combination of these two reasons. His conscience appears to be more scrupulous than Chancery's would be in this case. Similarly, Sir John Paston writes to his brother John in 1473 regarding the former's abortive engagement to Anne Hault: he is concerned to find 'the meanes to dyscharge hyr concyence'[44]—presumably by rescuing her potentially-compromised honour, or by preserving her from scandal. Again, ostensibly purely personal conscience is meant when Sir John promises in 1477 to be 'as kynde' to his brother 'as I maye be, my conciense and worshyp savyd',[45] or when the Prior of Norwich describes Agnes Paston as a woman of 'goode discrecioun and conscience'.[46] It is not, of course, saying a great deal to remark that some matters of conscience were purely personal and private, but that point is nonetheless worth making so as to qualify the possible implications of observations that, for example, the Chancellor regarded himself as being comprehensively *in foro conscientiæ*.

The merging of the personal into the social and, potentially, the legal is also illustrated by these materials. Sir John Paston's concern to effect the discharging of Anne Hault's conscience so as to obviate any moral obloquy that might affect, say, her prospects of another marriage is instructive in this respect. For one thing, although her personal conscience is referred to, it is not so much her inward disposition as her outward reputation that is at stake. Correlatively, the means of such rectification is not repentance so much as it is material recompense. Moreover, a third party might be able to provide the means for the discharge of her conscience. Conscience here, though not justiciable, is strikingly external: a social condemnation might be avoided by the provision of monetary compensation. This situation is not a legal process, but it contains elements that mimic such processes: conduct judged wrong not so much by a person's inner light as by social convention and righted by material means rather than by a change of heart.

Elsewhere the discharging of a person's conscience has distinctly legal ramifications. After John Paston Sr.'s death, his wife Margaret and son Sir John appear to have meddled with assets of his estate before obtaining proper administration. Mother writes to son: '[a]t the reverence of God, gete you a licens of my Lord of Caunterbery in dyschargyng of my conscyens and yowris'.[47] It is quite obvious that she is less concerned about her personal moral standing than she is about her possible liability in law, or in 'conscience', that what she wants is

43 *Paston Letters*, letter 240 (1454), vol. 2, p. 306.

44 Ibid., letter 831 (1473), vol. 5, p. 181.

45 Ibid., letter 912 (1477), vol. 5, p. 287.

46 Ibid., letter 1013 (1487), vol. 4, p. 97.

47 Ibid., letter 629 (1466?), vol. 4, p. 220.

an outward rectification of her conscience. In other places, whether the conscience referred to is justiciable or merely spiritual remains equivocal. William Paston, writing to several others in 1426, says that he has submitted a question to a number of 'worthy men' who 'seyn and informe me pleynly I have no maner cause in lawe ne in conscience to drede aught in this matier'.[48] The learned men Paston has consulted all seem to be ecclesiastics and the matter a quasi-religious one, so perhaps he was concerned only about Church law and his personal spiritual state.[49] At the same time, the dubiety 'ne in lawe ne in conscience' was a conventional way of saying 'neither at common law nor in equity', and his taking advice from clergymen in this context would hardly be incongruous; indeed, it might have been the obvious course of action.

Another point that these materials illustrate is that formal invocations of conscience are far from being limited to petitions in Chancery. Conscience is the criterion to which 'beseechers' resort in a variety of situations. In 1455, in a plea to the Duke of Norfolk, Sir John Fastolf used the very kinds of terms that we find in the Chancery materials: '[b]eseching your Lordchip ... of your habundant grace to supporte me in my right, that I be not fors ageyns lawe and concyence kepte from the possecsion of [my] londes ...'.[50] The following year, Sir John is contemplating seeking redress in a certain matter by a bill in Parliament, which he expects to be 'so rightfull and of conscience that it shall not be denyed ...'.[51] Edward IV, granting the foundation of Caister College to John Paston in 1464, pledges to assist him against certain of his adversaries: 'if it be found that thei were do otherwise thanne trought, lawe, or consiens woll … [the King would recompense Paston] as far as lawe and good consiens woll in that behalf'.[52] Again, in 1472, we find John Paston the younger beseeching the Duke of Norfolk 'at the reverence of God, and in the wey of charyte'—the same formula so regularly occurring in petitions to the Chancellor—to restore to his brother possession of certain lands 'acordyng to the

48 Ibid., letter 12 (1426), vol. 2, p. 27.

49 One might compare Margaret Paston's complaint that retainers of the addressee of her missive have taken goods belonging to her husband and to the parson of Brandeston. She undertakes that, if the parson has behaved wrongfully, 'I wyll helpe that he shall be chaysteysid as conciens and lawe requerith' (ibid., letter 597 (1465?), vol. 4, pp. 167–8). The context suggests that she is contemplating actual legal recourse, including, perhaps, recourse to Chancery.

50 Ibid., letter 277 (1455), vol. 3, p. 20.

51 Ibid., letter 319 (1456), vol. 3, p. 70. Compare letter 238 (1454), 'Ingham's Petition' to the King in Parliament, complaining that Thomas Denyes ambushed him 'of ful grete malice, prepensed ungodely soore agaynste gode feithe and concience' (vol. 2, p. 302).

52 Ibid., letter 571 (1464), vol. 4, p. 115. Compare letter 572 (1464), where the King, issuing an order to Sir John Markham C.J.K.B. (d. 1479), says that he has been informed that certain judgments against Paston have been obtained 'against conscience and law' (vol. 4, p. 117) and, letter 618 (1465), in which the King chastizes Sir William Yelverton (1400?–72), the judge, that it 'may not acorde with worship and consiens' for the latter 'to assiste the distruccion' of John Paston's manors and goods (vol. 4, p. 208).

lawe and good conscience ...',[53] and sometime between 1487 and 1502, the Queen writes to the Earl of Oxford, desiring him to restore lands to one 'Symon Blyant' 'as fer as reason, equite, and good conscience shall require ...'.[54]

What this shows is that appeals to conscience for some kind of official redress were not uncommon in contexts other than Chancery proceedings. Indeed, invocations of conscience in Chancery may have been no more than instances of the ordinary form in which all kinds of petitions were articulated at the time. This does not detract from the importance of conscience as a principle of justice, but it perhaps does suggest the need for caution in assuming that Chancery was somehow uniquely the forum of conscience as the rationale for redress of 'civil' wrongs.

Simpson has observed that what distinguished fifteenth-century judicial conscience from more modern conceptions is that it 'did not connote' simply 'some principle of injurious reliance or good faith. It connoted what we now call the moral law *as it applied to particular individuals for the avoidance of peril to the soul through mortal sin*'.[55]

Similarly, Metzger says that the 'judging activity' of the late medieval chancellors, who were typically but not exclusively ecclesiastics, involved to a significant degree promoting 'the eternal salvation of the parties who might be in danger of committing a deadly sin'.[56] To illustrate his point, Simpson refers to the case alluded to in Chapter 1, in which Sir John Fineux C.J.[57] had taken the position that the claim in issue was 'simply between a man and his confessor'[58] and therefore not a matter for a court. Archbishop Morton's rejoinder was that, unless the respondent made amends, 'he [would] be damned in Hell, and to grant a remedy in such a case ... is to do well in accordance with conscience'.[59] In the case previously cited from Statham's *Abridgment*, Fortescue C.J.—not, incidentally, an ecclesiastic—concludes his comments by observing that 'a man can have land by

---

53 Ibid., letter 824 (1472), vol. 5, p. 173.

54 Ibid., letter 1020 (1487–1502), vol. 6, p. 106.

55 Simpson, p. 398. Emphasis in original.

56 'Last Phase of the Medieval Chancery', p. 83.

57 Chief Justice of the King's Bench (1495–1525).

58 Simpson, p. 399 citing (1491) Y.B. 7 Hen. VII P.f. 10, pl. 2.

59 He cites another case, Y.B. 8 Edw. IV, P.f.4, pl.11, which contains the expression, as he reads it, *Deus est procurator futurorum*, meaning that God looks after the departed, 'and the Chancellor, being charged to God's will, must act appropriately and make sure that the will is performed for the good of the soul of the departed' (pp. 399–400). Robert Stillington (1420–91), Bishop of Bath and Wells and Chancellor from 1467–70, is reported to have used the formulation *deus est procurator futurus* (see George Cary, *Reports or Causes in Chancery* (London, 1665), p. 24; EEBO image 105479:21). More commonly this is read *Deus est procurator fatuorum* and is taken to mean that God, not the court, looks after fools, that is, the court will not give relief for injuries arising from the plaintiff's own folly.

our law, and by conscience he shall be damned …'.[60] He does not distinguish the conscience which may damn a person from the conscience he is applying in the case; in other words, he appears not to see judicial conscience as sharply distinct from the conscience of the confessional.

Again, one encounters this kind of sentiment in non-Chancery, or perhaps 'pre-Chancery', contexts. Sir John Fastolf, enjoining his executors to do 'as wysdam, justice, and conscience' direct, exhorts them 'that for the more hasty delyveraunce of my soule from the peynefull flawmes of the fyre of Purgatory' to 'dele and departe my goodes feithfully'.[61] Here, the soul expressly in issue is the testator's, not those of his executors, but the implication seems to be that the burden on their consciences is even greater since not only their souls, but his too, will be affected by how they carry out (or fail to carry out) their duties. Acting on his behalf, their actions are attributable to him.

This tendency to formulate conscience, even as a juristic principle, in spiritual terms means that, at least for this early period,[62] we must try to take account of the religious dimension. I propose to do this by adverting to two matters: first, the ostensibly confessional role of the Chancellor, including the likelihood that his practice was affected by the principles and procedures of canon law, and, second, theoretical or theological accounts of conscience, which probably constituted the perhaps unenunciated framework for the Chancellor's understanding of the concept.

The 'Confessional' Role of the Chancellor

The argument that the medieval Chancellors, as ecclesiastics (and hence, as confessors) were influenced by Church law has often been made. Simpson's observations in this regard are typical. Given 'the identity and careers' of these early Chancellors, he says, 'it is hardly conceivable' 'that as judges in conscience

60 *Statham's Abridgment*, p. 393.

61 *Paston Letters*, letter 385 (1459), vol. 3, pp. 159–60. Compare letter 407 (1460), vol. 3, p. 219, where Abbot Langley similarly sees the executors' function as involving the disposition of the testator's goods 'for the well of hys soule', and letter 508 (1462), vol. 4, p. 31, where John Paston asks the addressees of his letter to clear up an allegation that Sir John Fastolf had, during his lifetime, conveyed land in breach of trust, 'so that thorowh your defaute your seid maisters soule ther for lie not in perell ...'. It is not entirely clear to me why, if the allegations are false, the condition of Sir John's soul should depend upon their being refuted; presumably, if he is actually innocent, what slander might report of him should not matter.

62 As we shall see, however, at least traces of this tendency persist—certainly as late as Lord Nottingham.

they could avoid deriving ideas from the canon and civil law'.[63] This likelihood is reinforced by the common identification of canon law as a law of equity. 'Late medieval canonists', we are told, referred to it variously as 'the mother of exceptions', 'the epitome of the law of love', and 'the mother of justice'.[64] Moreover, Simpson maintains, these Chancellors 'must have been perfectly familiar' with the then-popular *Summæ Confessorum*—'comprehensive manuals for confessors'—and 'in so far as they required guidance in deciding cases in accordance with conscience ... it is very likely that they would turn to the obvious books on the subject—the *Summæ de Casibus Conscientiæ*'.[65]

The Rule of Conscience?

Apart from identifying the 'spiritual' sources of the doctrines of conscience that the medieval Chancellors enforced, some of the commentators make this kind of point to highlight the *ruled* nature of what was dispensed in Chancery. As Thomas Tentler has observed, the *Summæ Confessorum*, for example, 'taught ... that morality was definable; that human authorities could define it ...'.[66] Charles Lefebvre points to the distinction between 'canonical equity' and 'cerebral equity'—the latter involving the judge's own 'vague notions of what was equitable' and the former being '*informata a jure*'—based on articulated principles.[67] Pronay emphasizes the civilian legal training of many medieval Chancellors to make the point that the justice they dispensed 'was likely to have been a great deal more precise and juristic than "common sense and common fairness"'.[68] On this view, the conscience of the medieval Chancery was arguably law-like, whether its impetus was religious

---

63 Simpson, p. 400. See also Haskett, 'Medieval English Court of Chancery', pp. 311–13, giving outlines of backgrounds of the Chancellors from Edmund Stafford (1396–99, 1401–1403) to More (1529–32) and emphasizing the training of many of them in canon and civil law.

64 John Witte Jr., *Law and Protestantism: The Legal Teachings of the Lutheran Reformation* (Cambridge, 2002), p. 39. The last of these epithets ('*mater iusticie*') was applied by at least one petitioner, Bernard de Reco, to the Chancellor himself (*Select Cases in Chancery*, case 9 (1389), p. 10).

65 Simpson, pp. 377, 401. He notes that the author of one of these, the *Summa Angelica*, explains that he has written the book mainly for the benefit of 'poor and simple confessors' (p. 380)—hardly an apt description of the typical Chancellor.

66 'The Summa for Confessors as an Instrument of Social Control', in C. Trinkhaus and H.A. Oberman (eds), *The Pursuit of Holiness in Late Medieval and Renaissance Religion* (Leiden, 1974), pp. 103–25, pp. 122–3.

67 'Natural Equity and Canonical Equity', trans. Jeanne Rodes, *Natural Law Forum*, 8 (1963): 122–36, p. 130.

68 'Chancellor', p. 92. Long before Pronay, George Spence had suggested that what saved the Chancellor's jurisdiction from subjectivism was adherence to 'the equitable doctrines and principles of the Roman Law' (*The Equitable Jurisdiction of the Court of Chancery* [Philadelphia, 1846], p. 413. See also pp. 411, 414).

(canon) or secular (civil) law. Whether, at that time, many would have explicitly argued that in order to justify what the Chancery dispensed as being a kind of law it must be based on canon law is doubtful.

There are dissidents from the probably predominant position[69] that Chancery principles were based on, or influenced by, canon law. J.B. Post argues that 'the links between canon law and Chancery's equity were tenuous',[70] and suggests that what distinguished Chancery from the many lower-level forums making decisions on the basis of common sense and discretion was its 'central bureaucratic power' and not the type of justice it dispensed.[71] Haskett reminds us that Maitland admitted 'only minimal civilian and canonical influences' on Chancery,[72] and D.E.C. Yale attributes to Maitland the caution that 'the medieval churchman was not necessarily a canonist any more than he was a saint'.[73] One must exercise caution in advancing the 'medieval Chancellor equals ecclesiastic equals canonist equals expositor of conscience in canonist terms' argument.

A possible fifteenth-century vindication of Maitland's skepticism appears in Margaret Paston's admonition to her son Sir John in 1469 to proceed expeditiously to deal with his father's will while 'my Lord of Caunterbury', Cardinal Bourchier (1404–86) was still alive, 'for he is an old man and he is now frendly to you', but if he were to die, there is no way of knowing who his successor might be 'and if he wer a nedy man, in asmych as your fader was noysed of so greet valew he wull be the mor straunge to entrete'.[74] This apparently indicates an 'ordinary' perception—perhaps exemplified in *Piers the Plowman*—that these high churchmen were not above being affected by considerations of affinity and lucre. The 'court of conscience' may have been a part of medieval political calculation.

---

[69] See, for example, Willard T. Barbour, *The History of Contract in Early English Equity*, ed. Paul Vinogradoff (New York, 1974), pp. 167–8, Paul Vinogradoff, 'Reason and Conscience in Sixteenth-Century Jurisprudence', in *The Collected Papers of Paul Vinogradoff* (Oxford, 1928; reprinted London, 1964), vol. 2, pp. 190–204, and C.C. Langdell, 'The Development of Equity Pleading from Canon Law Procedure', in Association of American Law Schools, ed., *Select Essays in Anglo-American Legal History* (Boston, 1908), vol. 2, pp. 753–78.

[70] 'Equitable Resorts Before 1450', in E.W. Ives and A.H. Manchester (eds), *Law, Litigants and the Legal Profession* (London,1983), pp. 68–79, p. 78.

[71] Ibid. p. 68.

[72] Haskett, 'Medieval English Court of Chancery', p. 257.

[73] 'Introduction' to Edward Hake, *Epieikeia: A Dialogue on Equity in Three Parts*, ed. D.E.C. Yale (New Haven, 1953), p. xiiin. Yale does not reference this quotation. T.F.T. Plucknett says something similar: 'It must not be supposed that every clerk in minor orders was a canonist, any more than he was a theologian—or a saint' (*A Concise History of the Common Law* (Boston, 1956; reprinted Union, N.J., 2001), p. 236).

[74] *Paston Letters*, letter 701 (1469), vol. 5, p. 11. She adds that if Sir John had been more sedulous 'whill my Lord of York [George Neville, Archbishop of York] was Chanceller' the whole matter would already have been settled (p. 12).

The Denunciatio Evangelica

Coing's discussion of parallels between Chancery procedure and the Church process of *denunciatio evangelica*[75] provides a treatment, more specific than most, of the possible influence of canon law on English equity. This influence, Coing maintains, had both a procedural and a substantive dimension.

The biblical warrant for the *denunciatio evangelica* is Matthew 18:15–17, which outlines a procedure for Christians whose 'brother' has offended them. First, speak privately to him; if that does not avail; speak to him in the presence of one or two witnesses; if he still will not listen to you, then you may complain to the church. The *denunciatio*, properly, involved this third stage, whereby a person's sins might be 'brought to the attention of the ecclesiastical authorities so that they might take measures to reform the sinner and save his soul'.[76] We will recognize in this strong similarities to how the Chancellor's function was sometimes described, notably by Simpson. Coing notes that, in its pure form, the judgment of the Church was a decree ordering the offender to 'go out of his sin'.[77] However, sometimes going out of one's sin involved not merely penitence and reformation, but some kind of material restitution.[78] As we have previously noted, it was at this point that the 'purely penitentiary' procedure 'acquired a legal character'.[79] As we have also noticed, a possible line of demarcation between a purely confessional procedure and one which will engage Chancery's conscience is where such restitution, or some other material remedy, might be ordered. What distinguishes matters of purely private conscience from matters of justiciable conscience might be not so much the intrinsic character of the 'sin' as its remediable impact on other people.[80] It is worth noting, of course, that material restitution might be made concurrently with continuing inward stiffneckedness. Thus, if a person makes only grudging restitution for fear of temporal punishment he has probably not 'gone out of his

---

75 Coing cites De Luca, 'Aequitas canonica ed equity inglese alla luce del pensiero di C. St Germain', *Ephemerides Juris Canonici*, 3 (1947), pp. 46–66. Barton appears to endorse at the least the general tendency of Coing's argument: see 'Equity in the Medieval Common Law', pp. 144, 147. See also 'Introduction' to *St. German's Doctor and Student*, eds T.F.T. Plucknett and J.L. Barton, (London, 1974), p. xxxiv.

76 Coing, '*Denunciatio Evangelica*', p. 225.

77 Ibid., p. 229.

78 Tentler, 'Summa for Confessors', p. 119. For example, Tentler points out that ecclesiastical authorities 'looked on the obligation to restore damages ... as an absolutely binding condition for the remission of sins'.

79 Coing, '*Denunciatio Evangelica*', p. 225; compare Barton, 'Equity in the Medievial Common Law', p. 144.

80 Again, one must be cautious about such generalizations. We will recall the example of John Paston's pangs of private conscience in respect of an action that certainly had an impact on another, Agnes Denyes. The emphasis probably has to be on *remediable* impact.

sin', and, for all the rhetoric of, say, an Archbishop Morton, that person's soul might still be in jeopardy.

Substantively, as Coing points out, the question was 'whether the defendant was committing a sin',[81] which had to be determined according to 'the moral teaching of the Church, based on the "lex divina" and "lex naturalis"'.[82] So, again, the criterion applied was theoretically at least not the moral intuitions of the judge but articulated principles or rules. As examples of the kinds of principles upon which an 'obligatio naturalis' might be based, Coing, referring to Bartolus de Saxoferrato (1313–57), identifies consent and unjust enrichment.[83] Here we have principles which, though general, are at a somewhat lower level of abstraction than 'conscience', and which may account for many of the particular doctrines of early equity. To recur to an example I have already mentioned, Coing (still following Bartolus) relates promises given for the benefit of a third person to the 'consent' rationale and explains the enforcement of uses in these terms. Obviously, 'consent' will often have to be qualified. So, in the case of uses, it is not the feoffee's mere consent that binds his conscience; it is that consent coupled with the reliance involved in making the feoffment. It might be possible to analyse these situations in terms of unjust enrichment as well. The feoffment to uses is a kind of gratuitous conditional transfer; if the feoffee purports to retain the land without carrying out the condition, he will be unjustly enriched. On this analysis, however, it appears that conscience would require restitution of the land to the feoffor—since at least a volunteer beneficiary will not have given any *quid pro quo* which would make the withholding of the land unconscionable *vis-à-vis* him.

Tentler's treatment of the *summæ confessorum*—arguably a source of the substantive rules—emphasizes a rather different point: that these processes were an important mechanism of social control. Clearly, it needs no ghost come from the grave to tell us that law, even the law ostensibly applied by the Chancellors, is an instrument of social control. But the point is the imposition of law in cases of conscience—individual persons' moral dilemmas in particular circumstances. So Tentler observes that the object of the 'prominent' 'exposition of legal cases' in the *summæ* 'was to represent law in the forum of penance and make conformity to the regulations of the hierarchy a strict matter of conscience'.[84] In this regard, Lowell Gallagher's argument that the reduction of conscience to official discourses was a way of managing potentially destabilizing subjective psychological and moral states may be telling.[85]

---

81 '*Denunciatio Evangelica*', p. 230.

82 Ibid.

83 Ibid., p. 234.

84 'Summa for Confessors', p. 117.

85 Lowell Gallagher, *Medusa's Gaze: Casuistry and Conscience in the Renaissance* (Stanford, 1991), p. 6.

Conscience as Knowledge of Facts

One thing that the emphasis on the *denunciatio evangelica* and the *summæ confessorum* entails is the idea of scrutinizing the facts closely, and especially examining what a person knows, or can be induced to call to mind. As Tentler points out, the *summæ* required the confessor to 'inquire distinctly and methodically' into the alleged sin.[86] This has a parallel in Chancery practice. As we have noticed in Chapter 1, while the common law was conventionally said to proceed *secundum allegata et probata*, Chancery proceeded *secundum conscientam*, inquiring at large into the facts and particularly probing the consciences (bound by oaths) of the parties to make them come to terms with what they inwardly know to be the truth.

This distinction must be seen in the context of the medieval debate about what judicial assessment of facts, with reference to the judge's conscience, involved.[87] The problem typically addressed was that of the judge having purely personal knowledge that might go beyond or contradict what was presented to him formally in his official capacity, that is, *secundum allegata et probata*, according to the ordinary rules of evidence. If the judge was to proceed according to conscience, did this not necessarily mean that he had to incorporate his personal knowledge of the facts into his decision? One response to this conundrum was to separate the judge's public *persona*—which would require him 'to take cognizance only of those facts which, during the course of the proceedings, have been publicly proved and established',[88] and his private character, which might involve 'privately acquired knowledge … of no concern to his judicial activity'.[89] In effect, with respect to the facts, he would have two consciences, one public and one private.[90]

Variants of the distinction come up quite regularly, not just in the medieval materials, but throughout the period of this study. Spence cites the case in which Chancellor Robert Stillington repeats the formula that he is to judge 'according to conscience and *non secundum allegata*', and on this basis would rely on his own appreciation of the truth, nothwithstanding that a defendant did not answer an allegation of wrongdoing.[91] In another case, Beresford C.J. urges the defendant's counsel 'in the name of good faith' to admit a fact that had not been proved; the lawyer's response was '[y]ou must not allow conscience to prevent your doing

[86] 'Summa for Confessors', p. 115.

[87] See, for example, Walter Ullmann, *The Medieval Idea of Law as Represented by Lucas de Penna* (London, 1946), pp. 126–31, and Mike Macnair, 'Equity and Conscience', *Oxford Journal of Legal Studies*, 27/4 (2007): 659–81, pp. 672–5.

[88] Ullmann, p. 127.

[89] Ibid.

[90] As Ullmann notes, this was not an uncontroversial solution to the question.

[91] Spence, p. 375, citing Y.B. 9 Edw. IV, 14, no. 9.

law'.[92] The implication is that law allows judgment only on the basis of regularly-proved facts.

While it is clear that proceeding *ad conscientiam* involved a more wide-ranging inquiry into the facts, we must be cautious about suggesting that this inquiry was unrestricted. That is, while Chancery procedure might have been looser, that does not mean that there were no limits at all on the basis of establishing or inferring facts. Certainly, Lord Nottingham's distinction—made much later, of course—between public and private conscience suggests that, though the conscience of the Chancellor may be informed by more liberal means, those means might not extend to the merely personal knowledge, or 'imagination' of the Chancellor himself.

Thus, a regular feature of petitions to the Chancellor was a plea that he should *examine* the defendant: one petitioner asks the Chancellor 'to search out the truth of this matter';[93] another asks him 'to examine [the defendants] to tell the truth';[94] another asks the Chancellor 'to ordain due remedy upon whatever may be found before you by examination or confession';[95] another case tells us that 'the said Philip was examined in the Chancery by the venerable Father, Thomas, Archbishop of Canterbury, Chancellor of England ... and was sworn upon the Holy Gospels to speak the truth ...';[96] another asks that the defendant 'be examyned of the articles ..., as faith, reason and conscience requireth'.[97] It appears almost as if, once the facts are revealed by careful examination (of the party's conscience), the applicable rule becomes self-evident. Certainly this indicates that conscience was engaged in the factual inquiry as well as in discovering the relevant 'law'.

Again, the Paston letters may afford some insight into what was involved in such examinations, in a quasi-legal context—the matter of the much-disputed will of Sir John Fastolf. In 1467, John Paston the younger wrote to his brother Sir John Paston relating what a 'Freyr Mowght's' testimony in the matter might be. Friar Mowght was the confessor of a Master Brakley, a witness to the will:

> He seyth at syche tyme as he had shryven Master Brakley, and howsyllyd hym [given him Communion] bothe, he let hym wet that he was enformyd by dyvers personys that the seyd Master Brakley owt for to be in gret consyens for syche thyngys as he had doone and seyd ... To whom the seyd Mastyr Brakley answerd

[92] *Year-Books of Edward II, vol. 1, 1 and 2 Edward II, A.D. 1307–1309*, ed. F.W. Maitland (London, 1903) , p. xix. Of course, judicial conscience was concerned not only with getting at the facts: in the case from Statham's *Abridgment*, for example, the facts are not in issue, and the conscience the court argues involves normative considerations.

[93] *Select Cases in Chancery*, case 8, p. 9.

[94] Ibid., case 45, p. 49.

[95] Ibid., case 42. p. 46.

[96] Ibid., case 95, p. 89.

[97] Ibid., case 138, p. 132.

> thus agayne: 'I am ryght glad that it comyth to yow in mynd for to meve me with thys mater in dyschargyng of my consyens ayenst God.[98]

Here we have a confessional situation; allegations are laid before (here) the witness; and he is urged to relieve his conscience by telling the truth. In respect of the same case, Thomas Howys makes a declaration (not in the confessional, to be sure) 'of trouth in this processe and mater, and for the discharge of my conscience'.[99] It seems likely that, as far as the fifteenth-century Chancery was concerned, a litigant could discharge his conscience first by disclosing the truth and second by doing what thereby became almost self-evidently right.

The Theory of Conscience

Tentler says that the *summæ* were 'reference books designed to give answers, not philosophical inquiries designed to evoke debate'.[100] Presumably this was true of Chancery practice as well: it was probably concerned to reach decisions, not to engage in theoretical inquiry. Nevertheless, the concept of conscience it employed had a context which doubtless informed the Chancellor's thinking, whether explicitly or not. As Timothy Potts notes, the medieval period saw considerable philosophical and theological reflection on conscience,[101] providing at least 'conventional' terms in which it was understood. Not only because these accounts almost certainly provided the framework in which the ecclesiastical Chancellors understood conscience, but because afterimages of these accounts appear in later writers such as St. German, Hake, and the Protestant casuists, it is important to outline them here.

My intention is not to give a detailed explanation of these analyses, but to refer to them to make three points. First, they again consistently illustrate the fact that, to the medieval mind, conscience was largely an objective matter. Second, they provide accounts of the theoretical structure of conscience which, in general terms, was widely accepted, and which, in some measure, persisted throughout the sixteenth and seventeenth centuries. This looks back to the first point in so far as these accounts seek to explain quite precisely in what sense conscience is objective. Moreover, they look forward to the third point in so far as the structure described revealed conscience to have both a normative and a fact-apprehending dimension. The third point, to which I have already adverted, is that a crucial element in the operation of conscience, in addition to identifying appropriate rules, was the witnessing of the relevant facts.

98 *Paston Letters*, letter 666 (1467), vol. 4, pp. 275–6.

99 Ibid., letter 672 (1467), vol. 4, p. 285.

100 'Summa for Confessors', p. 108.

101 T.C. Potts, *Conscience in Medieval Philosophy* (Cambridge, 1980), p. 1.

That conscience for the scholastics was an objective concept is clear. M.G. Baylor asserts that they all 'agreed that a divinely ordained and objective moral order exists'; this is 'the genuine criterion of right and wrong, rather than a subjective conviction or belief'.[102] Moreover, it is not conscience as conviction *per se* that has authority; it has authority 'in virtue of its correctness', its 'conformity with divine law'.[103] The standard for conscience is something outside itself, but accessible to it. Again, as we have seen, the relevance of this point to conscience as a juristic principle is that it renders it coherent with law: it is not subjective, variable, or arbitrary.

Elements and Operation of Conscience

The basic components in terms of which almost all the scholastics described conscience were *synteresis* (or *synderesis*) and *conscientia*.[104] *Synteresis* is the human faculty or disposition[105] corresponding to the external, objective moral law. It is what allows humans to apprehend that law. Thus, says Aquinas, the human mind 'has a natural disposition concerned with the basic principles of behaviour, which are the general principles of natural law. This disposition relates to *synderesis*'.[106] Or, in Potts's paraphrase, *synderesis* is for Aquinas 'an innate rational disposition by which basic deontic premises are known to us without reasoning'.[107] Among the key terms here are 'innate' (inherent in human nature), 'rational' and 'known' (relating to the understanding), and 'without reasoning' (the basic premises are 'just there', not the result of a deliberative process). Crudely, one might say that on a modern subjectivist account conscience *dictates* the basic precepts, whereas on the medieval account *synteresis* apprehends them.

By way of qualification, I should mention that, while Aquinas and others placed *synteresis* in the understanding, emphasizing that it was a *rational* disposition or faculty, not all scholastics did so. Potts says that Bonaventure, for example, regarded

[102] Michael G. Baylor, *Action and Person: Conscience in Late Scholasticism and the Young Luther* (Leiden, 1977), p. 107.

[103] Ibid.

[104] See Potts, p. 32. The seminal use of the term in this context appears to be St. Jerome's commentary on Ezekiel 1:6–10, where he posits a fourth part of the soul 'which the Greeks call *synteresin*: that spark of conscience which was not even extinguished in the breast of Cain …' (ibid., pp. 79–80). See also T.C. Potts, "Conscience" in *The Cambridge History of Later Medieval Philosophy*, N. Kretzmann, A. Kenny and J. Pinborg (eds) (Cambridge, 1982), pp. 687–704, p. 687.

[105] One focus of debate among the scholastics was whether conscience was a faculty (potentiality) or a disposition (habit); the distinction is not crucial for my discussion.

[106] Thomas Aquinas, *Debated Questions on Truth 16–17*, trans. T.C. Potts, in Potts, *Conscience in Medieval Philosophy*, p. 124.

[107] Potts, *Conscience in Medieval Philosophy*, p. 46.

it (although not consistently) as 'a desiring potentiality',[108] 'an innate tendency to want to do what is honourable rather than useful ...'.[109] And, in one of the 'popular' works alluded to earlier, *The Charter of the Abbey of the Holy Ghost*, *synderesis* seems to be associated more with will than with reason: there is, we read, 'a lytel preciouse place þat is clipid Conscience, þat lieþ in here soules by-twixten a place þat is clepid Resoun, þe whiche knoweþ good & wikke, on þat o sydde, and a place þat is I-clepid Synderisys, þe whiche steriþ a man to good and grucciþ agaens wykke, on þat oþere sydde …'.[110] According to Baylor, 'an affective or volitional *synteresis* was not unknown among late medieval thinkers',[111] prominent among whom was Jean Gerson. As we shall see in the next chapter, Gerson apparently heavily influenced St. German's thinking on this topic. Baylor notes as well that, early in his career, before essentially abandoning the idea of *synteresis*, Martin Luther posited a 'double *synteresis*', combining an 'innate knowledge ... of the first principles of morality' with an 'inherent desire to do good'.[112] Although one must be extremely cautious about postulating links between these early volitional accounts and the modern notion of conscience as a sincere desire to do the right thing (whatever that might be), they do indicate an alternative, arguably more subjective, emphasis. As we shall see, there are indications, certainly by the end of the seventeenth century, that conscience was becoming increasingly identified with sincerity of intent rather than with accuracy of understanding.

Conscientia, in contrast with *synteresis*, involves the application of the knowledge afforded by *synteresis* to actual, particular situations. In Aquinas's terms, *conscientia*, unlike the disposition which is *synteresis*, is an act or an 'actualization'. As Potts puts it, 'we might say that *synderesis* consists of *rules* [or, more strictly, our apprehension of rules], whereas *conscientia* is concerned with

---

108 Ibid., p. 32.

109 Ibid., p. 42.

110 *Yorkshire Writers*, p. 339. Indeed, in some popular works, *synderesis* is portrayed as being, essentially, remorse of conscience. Thus, in Guillaume Deguileville's *Pèlerinage de l'Ame* (1355–58), ed. J.J. Stürzinger (London, 1895), which was translated into Middle English, *synderesis* is the worm of conscience, whose teeth are worn away from gnawing at the soul of man and who acts as prosecutor on Satan's behalf. See Hope Traver, *The Four Daughters of God* (Philadelphia, 1907), pp. 71–2, J.B. Drewes, 'Zinderises, Hell's Public Prosecutor: Origin, Name and Function', *Neophilologus*, 53/1 (1969): 257–60, pp. 257–8, and Robert A. Greene, 'Synderesis, the Spark of Conscience, in the English Renaissance', *Journal of the History of Ideas*, 52/2 (1991): 195–219, p. 202. In his translation of the second version of Deguileville's *Pèlerinage de la Vie Humaine*, John Lydgate was moved to add a gloss to the depiction of *synderesis* as remorse of conscience, describing it in more orthodox terms as 'The hiher party of Resoun;/ Whereby A man shal best discerne/ His conscience to governe' (John Lydgate, *The Pilgrimmage of the Life of Man*, eds F.J. Furnivall and Katherine B. Locock [London, 1899–1904], p. 130).

111 Baylor, p. 161.

112 Ibid., p. 157.

their application (including misapplication)'.[113] Similarly, C.S. Lewis speaks of *synteresis* as a kind of internal 'lawgiver' and *conscientia* as a 'witness', referring especially to its fact-discerning and fact-appreciating role.[114]

What follows from this basic structure is that the operation of conscience is, as Baylor notes, and as was to become a commonplace, syllogistic, having generally the following form:

1. 'a universal moral precept' given by *synteresis*[115] (major premise);
2. 'factual knowledge provided by the senses in the case of proposed action (or presumably by memory in the case of past action)'[116] (minor premise);
3. 'a particular moral conclusion of judgment'.[117]

Facts and Norms

From this account we can see that conscience has both a normative (major premise) and a factual (minor premise) component. Conscience provides not only the governing rule, but also the facts (past, present, or anticipated) to which the rule must be applied. This complex use of 'conscience' meaningfully supports its being used to refer both to the principle of right applied by the Chancellor and to the process of getting at the facts by requiring a party to call them to mind, or to confess, and of requiring that those facts be sufficient to satisfy the conscience of the court.

Potts expresses surprise that the medieval philosophers did not make a more sustained effort 'to identify the basic deontic propositions' given by *synteresis*'.[118] Indeed, some of the examples that occur are very general: 'Love your neighbour'; 'Do not injure others'. Baylor observes that in fact these very general primordial

---

[113] Potts, *Conscience in Medieval Philosophy*, p. 18.

[114] C.S. Lewis, 'Conscience and Conscious', in *Studies in Words* (2nd ed., Cambridge, 1967), pp. 181–213, pp. 190–91.

[115] Subject to the qualification below that, while Aquinas 'associated the major term of the practical syllogism with the *synteresis*', he did not identify it with what *synteresis* immediately apprehended.

[116] Aquinas, for example, distinguished between 'consequent' conscience, relating to actions in the past, and 'antecedent' conscience, relating to proposed or future actions (see Baylor, p. 42). According to C.A. Pierce, *Conscience in the New Testament* (London, 1955), p. 111, in early Christian thought (essentially, St. Paul's) conscience related exclusively to past actions or present actions begun in the past.

[117] Baylor, pp. 47–8. As we shall see, the process is sometimes presented as more complex than this, so that in many—perhaps most—accounts there is a first syllogism in which reason derives a lower-order moral precept from *synteresis* and this derivative precept becomes the major premise in a second syllogism in which factual knowledge provides the minor.

[118] Potts, *Conscience in Medieval Philosophy*, p. 60.

propositions did not really constitute the major premises for the syllogism of conscience. 'The conscience', he says, 'is not immediately dependent upon the content of the *synteresis* in its operations'; rather, the 'major term' in the syllogism is 'more accurately viewed as a precept derived from or supplied indirectly by the *synteresis*'.[119] The point perhaps may be illustrated as follows. Presumably, the commandment 'Honour thy father and thy mother' would be a basic deontic proposition, part of both divine and natural law. But, in a particular set of circumstances, some kind of derived or second-order precept might be the rule of conscience. This could be something like: 'Obey your father and your mother' or 'Do what is prudent in the interests of your parents, regardless of what they tell you to do'. So, there may be several more specific derivative norms; moreover, these might not be mutually compatible. Furthermore, there may be a reflexive relationship between fact and norm: that is, the factual circumstances (for example, parents' dotage) may dictate which derivative norm should in conscience be applied. And, of course, apprehension of the facts may be problematic—for example, because of the apprehender's self-interest or lack of perceptual acumen.

From this account, Baylor (referring mainly to Aquinas) identifies three points in the structure of conscience where problems might arise. By hypothesis, *synteresis* itself cannot be one of them. As Potts explains, the medieval classification (generally) of *synteresis* as 'a form of knowledge' meant that it could not be wrong. If a person thinks he knows something, but in fact does not, he does not have knowledge, but belief. If he has knowledge, it must by hypothesis be true.[120] That leaves three possible *loci* of error: ignorance of the correct derivative moral precept, ignorance of the factual circumstances of the case, and faulty reasoning in applying the precept to the facts. So, presumably, when the Chancery was engaged in correcting conscience, that activity could have related to any one of these areas of possible error.

Regarding the facts, there were two kinds of potential error: invincible or incorrigible error, and culpable error. Invincible error 'is that which unavoidably remains after a determined effort to discover the nature of the morally relevant facts in a given case'.[121] This kind of error is the only error of conscience that, at least in the view of Aquinas and some others, excuses. Culpable error, on the other hand, is error that remains in the face of neglectful efforts to discern the truth. It is clear, therefore, that a crucial aspect of the activity of conscience is getting at the truth via 'a careful inquiry as to the factual circumstances of a particular case'.[122] Thus, Spence cites another fifteenth-century case in which Chancellor Stillington, observing 'Jeo adjugera sure ceo come Judge de Conscience', allows the objection of an executor who is the only one of three being sued on the basis that 'one ought

---

119 Baylor, p. 52.

120 Potts, *Conscience in Medieval Philosophy*, p. 16. See also p. 59, respecting Aquinas's view. Compare Baylor, p. 36.

121 Baylor, p. 90.

122 Ibid., p. 89.

not in conscience to be sued alone, lest by his ignorance of what has been done he may be damnified'.[123]

In a letter to his mother in 1482, John Paston the younger complains that she has clandestinely solicited his wife to intercede with him to ensure that certain relatives are provided for after her death. He says that he wishes she had asked him directly for he will do anything she commands 'if I may have knowlage of it; and if I have no knowlage, in good feyth I am excuseabyll bothe to God and yow'.[124] In terms of the framework I have just outlined, one can identify the elements of conscience (several of them implicit only) in his complaint. First, he knows that he owes his mother a duty; this may be a basic deontic proposition given by *synteresis*. Further, from this he derives the second-order proposition that he is to obey her wishes, at least in so far as they involve the disposition of her property and she is competent. If, for example, he had taken the position (as his mother perhaps thought he might) that he could best honour her by exercising his own judgment about what should be done with her estate, this might have been an error at the level of derived precept which would be correctible in Chancery. His difficulty, however, is that he does not know the facts. In other words, he has a major premise to direct his conscience; but he lacks the minor premise that knowledge of the facts (her wishes) would provide. Presumably because the only way he can discover those facts is from what she tells him, and she might not be telling him what he needs to know, his factual error may be 'invincible'. Apparently this is how he sees it, since 'in good feyth' (conscience?) he prays to be excused.

A Medieval Bishop's Account

As we have noticed, a fundamental difficulty in characterizing the conscience of the medieval Chancery is the absence of direct evidence. We do not have an example of a Chancellor working through an argument based on conscience by referring to an established framework. No Chancellor says, explicitly, 'I am applying the procedure of the *denunciatio evangelica* or the rules elaborated in one of the *summæ confessorum*'. Nor do they expressly refer to the structure of conscience elaborated by the scholastics: perhaps the closest we have to something like this is Fortescue C.J.'s etymological observation about *con* and *scio* and his suggestion that conscience means to know with God.[125] We must rely on accounts of conscience apparently prevalent in the ecclesiastical culture at the time to infer—or conjecture—what the Chancellors likely thought.

---

123 Spence, p. 373, citing Y.B. 8 Edw. IV, 5.

124 *Paston Letters*, letter 979 (1482?), vol. 6, p. 54.

125 Etymological arguments about the meaning of conscience are quite common. Baylor points out that Aquinas thought that *conscientia* derived from *cum alio scientia*—'knowledge applied to an individual case' (pp. 29–30), and as we shall see in a later chapter, many Protestant casuists characterized it as 'knowing together' or 'knowing with another'—generally, with God.

One other example of such a 'source,' and one closer to home, so to speak, might be Reginald Pecock's (1395–1460) *The Reule of Crysten Religioun*, written in 1443.[126] Pecock was, of course, never Chancellor, but, like so many medieval Chancellors, he was a bishop and he was a privy councillor. Perhaps aspects of his thinking are representative of his fellow ecclesiastics' mindset, and he does give an account of conscience.

His particular preoccupation is with the 'doom [roughly, law] of oure resoun'. There are, he says, two sources of the doom of reason: 'doom bi natural liȝt, which doom is callid lawe of mannys kynde [nature], or bi sure reuelacioun ..., which doom is callid lawe of feiþ'. These two dooms 'euereiþer is callid lawe of conscience' (p. 227). We have, as human beings, the power to know these laws. 'And siþen what euer þing is of power forto knowe a lawe, is þerby of power forto knowe defautis and synnys doon anentis þilk lawe, apart from those things only known by faith, reason allows us to fynde and knowe ... alle maners of synnys aȝens lawe of kinde' (pp. 24–5). In applying the doom of reason, all the particular circumstances of an action must be considered:

> Siþen þe doom of resoun bi whiche a dede ouȝte be reulid, muste strecche ... not oonli vpon þe mater into which þe deede passiþ ... but also into circumstauncis of ... tyme and place ..., þe maner of doying þe deede and þe meenys or helpis, þe knowing or vnknowing of oþere folk, and þe eende wherfore þe deede is entendid and purposid ... (p. 230).

In other words, moral judgment involves a doom or law, a human faculty capable of discerning that law, an examination into all the circumstances of the facts in question, and a judgment about the nature of the default or sin involved. And, because of the 'darking of resoun bi fal fro ynnocensie into synne in paradise',[127] moral truths are not easily apparent to reason and people 'muste haue now labour to encerche and fynde þe trouþis of þi lawe', resorting, for example, to authority (p. 463).[128] This is very much what we have seen in other accounts of the processes of conscience.

---

126 Reginald Pecock, *The Reule of Crysten Religioun*, ed. W.C. Greet (London, 1927).

127 This idea was conventional among commentators on conscience. For example, Philip the Chancellor, whose treatise appeared around 1235, writes that 'the original righteousness of man's powers' was radically compromised by the Fall, but 'not completely taken away' and what remained 'can be called *synderesis*' (*Treatise on Conscience*, trans. T.C. Potts in *Conscience in Medieval Philosophy*, p. 100.

128 For Pecock, though, authorities were themselves subject to correction by reason—a controversial position at the time.

'Wiþynneforþ' and 'Wiþoutforþ' Actions

Before leaving the medieval period, it is important to recur to the distinction, when considering 'sin', between outward acts such as material restitution and the inward moral dispositions that accompany them. As Pecock says, all the deeds we do are 'wiþynneforþ or wiþoutforþ' (p. 227) or have an inner or an outer dimension. This distinction is important both for the account of conscience *per se* and for the relationship of conscience to law.

Conscience is, of course, concerned with both what one does and the mind with which one does it. But one or the other of these may be emphasized in any moral assessment. Tentler points out that a common criticism of manuals of cases of conscience is that they can tend to make sin, and hence morality, more a matter of external actions than of internal dispositions.[129] Thus, Sir Thomas More is reported to have said of 'the Casuists of his time'—still Catholic casuists—that 'by their too particular resolutions of Cases, did not teach men *non peccare, not to sin*, but did show them *quàm propè ad peccatum liceat accedere sine peccato, how near men might come to sin, and yet not sin*'.[130] Conscience on this view becomes a fine calculation of what one can get away with, and what one cannot. In reaction, at least in part, to this tendency, it is sometimes said that the Protestant emphasis was more on the internal than on the external—an emphasis that would be consistent with the notion of justification by faith rather than by works. So, for example, Baylor tells us that, for Luther, 'it was with the practice of ... interior qualities that the conscience ought to concern itself'.[131] Again, of course, one must be very wary of large generalizations. Thus, Pecock—who might have anticipated Protestantism in some respects—writes that 'whanne euer an outward werk is bifore wiþynnforþ considerid', 'certis þan in þe willing and chesingis of þilk outward werk is more holynes and goodnes þan is in þe outward parfoormyng of þe same werk'.[132] Arguably, though, some time between the end of the medieval period and the period which is my main concern in this study the emphasis of conscience shifted from the outward to the inward. I shall revisit this issue in greater depth in due course.

For the moment, I wish simply to indicate that this putative shift has at least two related kinds of relevance for conscience as a juristic principle—one substantive, the other evidentiary. Substantively, the law is—and, in its early stages certainly was—more concerned with outward acts. To be sure, the mental disposition accompanying such acts is often crucial to the law's assessment of them, but,

[129] 'Summa for Confessors', pp. 123–4. He himself disagrees with this criticism.

[130] John Tillotson, 'Wherein lies that exact Righteousness, which is required between Man and Man?' in Samuel Annesley (ed.), *The Morning-Exercise at Cripplegate or, Several Cases of Conscience Practically Resolved, by sundry Ministers, September 1661* (London, 1664), p. 235; EEBO image 105033:12.

[131] Baylor, p. 198.

[132] Pecock, p. 487.

ultimately, the law is concerned with the manifestation of internal states in actual conduct. Certainly, the law rarely, if ever, occupies itself with internal states alone; as far as the law is concerned, 'thought is free'[133]—although its expression may not be. To the extent that matters of conscience are mainly internal and therefore 'extra-legal', conscience ostensibly becomes less relevant to the law. Correspondingly—and this is the evidentiary point—if what makes an action good or bad in terms of conscience is the internal disposition that accompanies it, the conscientious nature of that action becomes harder to prove. If, as Fortescue C.J. suggests—and as is often repeated elsewhere—conscience is essentially 'knowledge with God' or knowledge that only the subject him or herself, together with God, has, it tends not to be accessible to others. If conscience can be measured by a fine calculation of actions in their circumstantial context, it is more amenable to the law's competence than if it involves internal states accessible only to the person experiencing them. To be sure, the medieval theory of conscience emphasized that a third party, the priest, could reach a person's conscience and, correspondingly, the Court of Chancery had a 'confessional' aspect—it purported to be able to get at what only the parties themselves could know. But, as we have also seen, if that remained unconfessed, the power of the Chancery ended there. Even in seeking this confessional information the Chancery appears to have been more interested in what the parties knew about external facts than about their own internal dispositions. For example, in discerning the existence of a use, the concern would have been more with the feoffee's manifestation of his undertaking to hold the land for another's benefit than with his sincerity in making the undertaking. The point is that conscience, understood as relating mainly to internal things, is inherently more 'private'.

Conclusion

Referring to the early Chancery, Joseph Story has observed that '[e]quity ... acted upon principles of conscience and natural justice, without much restraint of any sort'.[134] The implication of such an observation might be that the early Chancellors 'did what they felt like'. One should not dismiss this possibility. At the same time, as we have seen, Allen suggests that the concept of conscience they relied on was

[133] Macnair, 'Equity and Conscience,' p. 678, reminds us that Bryan C.J., in 1477, observed that 'the intent of a man cannot be tried because the devil himself does not know the intent of a man' (citing YB P 17 Edw. IV fo. 1a pl. 2). Macnair opines that the confessional aspect of the early Chancery facilitated access to such internal dispositions. This access would, in turn, have facilitated adding the mental element to the substantive requirements of legal liability.

[134] *Commentaries on Equity Jurisprudence* (Boston, 1836), p. 23, referring to James Kent, 'Lecture 21: Of Reports of Judicial Decisions' in *Commentaries on American Law* (2nd ed., 4 vols, New York, 1832), vol. 1, 471–98, pp. 490–92.

'philosophical and theological'.[135] If it was, there would have been theories of conscience ready to hand, in both the standard accounts involving *synteresis* and, more practically, in the *summæ confessorum*. I do not wish to be taken as suggesting that, when the Chancellors applied 'conscience', they began by saying, 'this is the primary principle given by *synteresis*, from which I derive the second-order rule "X", which I shall apply in this case'. What they did was almost certainly much more implicit. But also implicit in what they would have done was something like this theory. I suspect that, if pressed, they would not have said 'conscience directs each person to do what, subjectively and sincerely, is according to his best lights'. I suspect that they would have elaborated conscience as an objective notion, referable ultimately to a determinate moral law, and accessible to human reason. They would, I suspect, have maintained that it was, to co-opt Lord Nottingham's expression, a 'certain measure', though not promulgated in any positive human law. And they would, in some way, have understood themselves to be authoritative speakers of conscience—not just because they had the power, but because they could apprehend what was *right*.

135 Carleton Kemp Allen, *Law in the Making* (6th edn, Oxford, 1958), p. 389.

Chapter 3
The Early Sixteenth Century and Christopher St. German

Introduction

Two regularly recounted anecdotes, involving, respectively, two of the best-known chancellors of the sixteenth century, serve to highlight the fact that the relationship of conscience to law continued to be a live issue during this period.

The first concerns Cardinal Wolsey.[1] At the end of his career and in disfavour, he was visited by Shelley J. with a commission from the King demanding that he execute a recognizance granting York House, which belonged to the Bishopric of York, to the King. Wolsey, appealing to the King's 'Royal spirit', 'not requiring more than reason shall lead him to by the law', admonishes Shelley J. and the other members of the Council,

> to put no more into his head than Law, that may stand with Conscience; for when you tell him that although this be Law, yet it is not Conscience, for Law without Conscience is not fit to be ministred by a King nor his Council, ... for every Council to a King ought to have respect to Conscience before the rigour of Law.[2]

Law, Wolsey maintains, expressing a view that we have encountered at least as early as *Piers the Plowman*, must be governed by conscience. He goes on to make the connection between conscience and the Chancery to emphasize that this point

1 I take this account from George Cavendish, *The Life and Death of Thomas Woolsey, Cardinal* (London, 1667), pp. 114ff.; EEBO images 64261:66ff.

2 Ibid., p. 115; EEBO image 64621:66. Similar rhetoric occurs (in a different context) in an incident reported by Lord Herbert of Cherbury, *The Life and Reign of King Henry VIII* (London, 1741): when the question of Henry's divorce from Katherine of Aragon was being discussed in his Council, 'one who much favour'd the Papal Authority' wondered 'who shall mitigate the Rigour of Laws in those Cases, which may admit Exceptions, if the Pope be taken away?' 'For', he continued, 'his [the Pope's] Court is a Kind of Chancery to all other Courts of Justice in the Christian World; so if you take it away, you subvert that Equity and Conscience which should be the Interpreter of all Laws and Constitutions whatsoever' (p. 285; ECCO image CW100151570: 284). The relating of papal authority to Chancery is interesting, anticipating a perceived connection that was exploited by some anti-Chancery polemicists in the seventeenth century.

has an institutional *imprimatur*: 'therefore in his Princely place he hath constituted a Chancellor, to order for him ['to mitigate the rigour of the law'], and therefore the Court of Chancerie hath been commonly called the Court of Conscience ...'.[3] That is, the Court of Chancery is a formal manifestation of the integral importance (and, indeed, the pre-eminence) of conscience *vis-à-vis* the law.

Wolsey sees what is being asked of him as against conscience since it involves giving 'that away which is now mine for me and my Successors'.[4] In other words, he regards himself as a trustee for himself for the time being and thereafter for his successors to the Archbishopric and balks at giving away what in conscience is not his own. He asks Shelley J. what he thinks and receives the reply: 'there is no great Conscience in it', because the King 'is sufficient to recompense the Church of *York* with the double value'.[5] True, Wolsey replies, but he finds no such offer in the demand made of him, 'but only a bare and simple departure of others rights'.[6] Still, because he is 'his Highness['s]' 'most faithful Subject and obedient Beadsman', he will obey the command. But he charges Shelley J.'s conscience 'to discharge me', and he asks him to remind the King that, there is both Heaven and Hell'.[7]

Besides the two points already mentioned—that law should be mitigated by conscience, and that the Court of Conscience was integral to the administration of justice—this exchange illustrates a number of other dimensions of what 'conscience' implies. One is the tendency to formulate such issues in terms of conscience; another is the question of the subject's obligation to obey even the unconscientious command of the sovereign—or, in other words, the extent to which the subject is bound in conscience to obey the King; yet another is the possibility that the decrees of human magistrates are subject to a higher, supernatural tribunal and that, ultimately, breaches of conscience are subject to 'eternal' sanctions.

The other anecdote involves Sir Thomas More, Wolsey's successor as chancellor. More, of course, was notoriously devoted to the dictates of his conscience. When Henry VIII made him Chancellor, he made it clear that, while 'he would serve his majesty … he *must* obey his God: he would keep the king's *conscience* and his *own*',[8] and when exhorted by leading churchmen, one of whom, Archbishop Cranmer, described conscience as '*that* Lesbian *rule which was* uncertain', to obey the king or 'to yield to the wisdom of the kingdom', More refused to compromise his conscience in the name of political expediency.[9] The anecdote is that More invited the common law judges to dine with him and offered that, if they 'would upon reasonable considerations by their own discretion, as

---

3 Cavendish, p. 115; EEBO image 64261:66.

4 Ibid., p. 116; EEBO image 64261:67.

5 Ibid.

6 Ibid.

7 Ibid.

8 David Lloyd, *State-worthies, or, the Statesmen and Favourites of England Since the Reformation* (2 vols, London, 1766), vol. 1, p. 62; ECCO image CW104918924:75.

9 Ibid., p. 64; ECCO image CW104918924:77.

they were as he thought in conscience bound, mitigate and reform the rigour of the law themselves', he would refrain from granting further injunctions pursuant to the equitable jurisdiction.[10] The judges declined the offer.

This story illustrates, among other things, that (unsurprisingly) conscience in More's mind was associated with the Chancellor's jurisdiction, that that jurisdiction might be exercised in the common law courts (and, indeed, that common law judges were in some way bound in conscience in exercising their functions), and that, for some reason,[11] some members of the judiciary preferred that judicial 'conscience' should continue to be administered in a separate court. Moreover, Cranmer's comment, invoking the 'Lesbian rule', raises the concern that conscience might be a rather inconstant standard.

So, for Wolsey and for More, conscience remained front-and-centre as far as Chancery was concerned. One problem with drawing inferences about the status of conscience at this time is the paucity of recorded decisions.[12] Another is that these two chancellors, at least, might have been *la fin de leur race*. As we have seen already, Franz Metzger describes Wolsey's tenure as the 'last phase of the medieval Chancery';[13] and Timothy Endicott calls More the last chancellor 'to cleave to a pre-Reformation vision of conscience'.[14] These observations suggest that Wolsey and More marked the end of an era, that a transformation occurred around or just after their time. Metzger's observation suggests that *Chancery* changed, while Endicott's suggests that the view of *conscience*, specifically, changed. However, neither commentator says that conscience disappeared: Metzger seems to suggest that conscience continued to play a role,[15] and Endicott says only that the vision

10 William Roper, *The Life of Sir Thomas More*, in R.S. Sylvester and D.P. Harding (eds), *Two Early Tudor Lives* (New Haven, 1962), p. 222.

11 More's explanation for their recalcitrance was that they did not want to take responsibility for ultimate decisions, but rather preferred to 'cast all scruple from themselves upon the poore jurie'—that is, to leave the final assessment of the facts to the consciences of others (ibid.).

12 Lord Campbell observes that 'there is no trace of any of the decisions' not only of Wolsey or More, but also of William Warham (1450–1532), Thomas Audley (1488–1544), or Thomas Wriostheley (1505–50), so that 'the rules by which they guided their discretion remained vague or unknown' (*Lives of the Lord Chancellors and Keepers of the Great Seal of England*, ed. J.A. Mallory (10 vols, Toronto, 1876), vol. 2, p. 138.

13 Franz Metzger, 'The Last Phase of the Medieval Chancery', in Alan Harding (ed.), *Law-Making and Law-Makers in British History* (London, 1980), pp. 79–89, p. 79. Compare J.A. Guy,,'Introduction' to *Christopher St. German on Chancery and Statute* (London, 1985), p. 65: 'The final consolidation of Chancery in its classic late-medieval format was accomplished under Wolsey ...'.

14 Timothy A.O. Endicott, 'The Conscience of the King: Christopher St. German and Thomas More and the Development of English Equity', *University of Toronto Faculty Law Review*, 47/2 (1989): 549–70, p. 565.

15 'Last Phase of the Medieval Chancery', p. 84.

of conscience changed, that of Christopher St. German supposedly displacing that which More represented.[16]

Others too have identified this as a transitional period, in which the character of what the Chancery was doing changed. J.H. Baker remarks a change of emphasis from 'conscience' to 'equity'.[17] That the emphasis might have shifted does not necessarily mean that conscience was obviated as a factor in Chancery—although Endicott (somewhat implausibly, since a separate court which continued to be referred to as in some sense a 'court of conscience' persisted) says that '[i]t can be argued that [Christopher St. German's] *Doctor and Student* reduces the role of conscience to insignificance, and makes equity into an internal mechanism of the common law'.[18] So the question arises: what sea-change, if any, did the concept of conscience as a juristic principle undergo at this time?

Christopher St. German

Whatever assessment different writers make of this issue, they appear to agree that St. German is a, if not the, key figure. Endicott argues that *Doctor and Student* was the central text in the reconceptualization of conscience *vis-à-vis* equity and law. And Barton claims that we probably owe to St. German the fact that we have courts of equity rather than courts of conscience today.[19] That St. German was very influential is uncontroversial. J.A. Guy calls him 'equity's most learned defender in the sixteenth century'[20] and Paul Vinogradoff is just one modern writer who reminds us that *Doctor and Student* 'was reprinted over and over again' and was accepted as substantially authoritative by subsequent jurists.[21] It is therefore

16 Endicott says that More was a 'proponent of a form of conscience that St. German had rejected' ('Conscience of the King', p. 549)—although he also says that More 'did not theorize on the nature of equity' (ibid., p. 565), so it might be a little hard to know exactly what More's 'vision' of conscience was. As we shall see below, St. German's own vision had distinctly medieval, and, indeed, 'Catholic' roots—as one might assume *a fortiori* did More's.

17 J.H. Baker, *An Introduction to English Legal History* (4th edn, London, 2002), pp. 105–8. See also Timothy S. Haskett, 'The Medieval English Court of Chancery', *Law and History Review*, 14/2 (1996): 245–313, p. 268.

18 'Conscience of the King', p. 559. This is, as I hope will become clear, a misreading of what St. German is saying, and perhaps involves Endicott's failure to recognize that 'equity' had at least two well-recognized meanings.

19 J.L. Barton, 'Equity in the Medieval Common Law', in Ralph A. Newman (ed.), *Equity in the World's Legal Systems* (Brussels, 1973), pp. 139–55, p. 154.

20 J.A. Guy, 'The Development of Equitable Jurisdictions 1450–1550', in E.W. Ives and A.H. Manchester (eds), *Law, Litigants, and the Legal Profession* (London 1983), pp. 80–86, p. 85.

21 Paul Vinogradoff, 'Reason and Conscience in Sixteenth-Century Jurisprudence', in *The Collected Papers of Paul Vinogradoff* (2 vols, Oxford, 1928; reprinted London, 1964),

appropriate—indeed, essential—to focus on St. German in considering the status and role of conscience as they were understood during the post-medieval early Tudor period.

Aspects of the Context

Before turning to a more detailed consideration of St. German's treatment of conscience, I should mention two contextual matters. The first of these is what might be termed the equivocal nature of equity, and the second is the continuity of medieval conceptions into the Tudor period—notwithstanding what some commentators see as something of a revolution.

The ambiguity of "equity"

One aspect of the first, the equivocal nature of equity, is whether its status in English law changed in the early sixteenth century. We have seen that more than one commentator credits St. German with a shift in emphasis from conscience to equity. Certainly, equity is a central concept in *Doctor and Student*, and Barton might be justified in suggesting that St. German 'introduced English lawyers to the theological doctrine of equity, or *epikeia* …'.[22] At the same time, as G.H.M. Posthumus Meyjes points out, after Aquinas, 'the concept of epikie/*aequitas* was soon naturalised in moral theology and canon law' and '[a]ll theologians and canonists made use of it'.[23] One would therefore expect at least the ecclesiastical chancellors to have been familiar with it. This is not necessarily to say that English lawyers knew much about it—although observations such as Sir John Fortescue's that 'justice begets law, justice and law produce equity, and law and natural equity are at one with justice'[24] indicate that it could hardly have been unknown to them. So, just how aware English jurists were of *epieikeia* before St. German's work is unclear. At least one commentator suggests that his views were readily accepted at least in part because they embodied 'familiar and conventional notions concerning the relationship between law and equity'.[25]

---

vol. 2, pp. 190–204, p. 191. See also W.S. Holdsworth, *A History of English Law* (16 vols, Boston, 1924), vol. 5, pp. 267–9.

22 'Equity in the Medieval Common Law', p. 152. Different writers spell this word differently: *epikeia*, *epikie*, *epieikeia*. Except where I am quoting, I shall use the last of these.

23 G.H.M. Posthumus Meyjes, *Jean Gerson Apostle of Unity: His Church Politics and Ecclesiology*, trans. J.C. Grayson (Leiden, 1999), p. 243.

24 *De Natura Legis Naturae* (1463), c. 36; cited in Norman Doe, *Fundamental Authority in Late Medieval English Law* (Cambridge, 1990, reprinted Holmes Beach, 2000), p. 103.

25 Stephen A. Siegel, 'The Aristotelian Basis of English Law', *New York University Law Review*, 56/1 (1981): 18–59, pp. 43–4.

Just as we must be chary of the contention that St. German introduced English lawyers to the concept of equity, we must recall that, although equity is unquestionably foregrounded in *Doctor and Student*, most of the book is focused on conscience, and, more specifically, on how English (common) law accords with conscience and, indeed, how that law often (but not exhaustively) offers 'good direction of conscience in this realm'.[26] That is, the book might be said to be *about* conscience, rather than equity, in spite of the prominence equity might have in it. Moreover, St. German's concern is more with conscience in the common law than with conscience in the Chancery. If Norman Doe is to be credited, the importance of conscience to the common law was not a new development: as we have seen in Chapter 2, he argues that conscience informed medieval common law. These observations are just by way of issuing a *caveat* against too literal an acceptance of observations suggesting a sharp demarcation between medieval concern with conscience and post-St. German preoccupation with equity—a demarcation that may disguise continuing overlap and interplay between the two concepts.

But to return to my more central point about the equivocal character—or characterization—of equity, not just in St. German, but elsewhere. Barton remarks this ambiguity when he says that, in *Doctor and Student*, there are times 'where the equity of the Chancellor is part of "conscience"' and other times when 'equity changes sides, and becomes a part of "the law"...'.[27] This seems to suggest that equity is sometimes outside the law, located in a separate place, so to speak, while sometimes it is intrinsic to the law.

This kind of ambiguity is, however, longstanding. It is probably implicit in Aristotle's observation that the presence of equity in law is sometimes intended and sometimes not intended by the legislator: the former where the legislator finds it impossible to express itself exactly; the latter where the legislator unintentionally leaves gaps.[28] He further complicates the matter by saying that '[e]quity bids us be merciful to the weakness of human nature' and that it should be concerned 'less about what [the legislator] said than about what he meant' (p. 1374b). The former comment associates equity with mercy, ostensibly an extra-legal consideration, and the latter suggests that equity is a principle of interpretation of the law, based on sensitivity to intent rather than on a literal reading of the text. Thus, within a few pages, we see several possible meanings—or dimensions of meaning—of 'equity'.

Commentators have remarked the persistence of such ambiguity. Meyjes, for example, contrasts Aristotelian *epieikeia* (whose internal ambiguity we have

---

[26] *St. German's Doctor and Student* , eds T.F.T. Plucknett and J.L. Barton (London, 1974), p. 3.

[27] 'Equity in the Medieval Common Law', p. 151. Compare Plucknett and Barton, 'Introduction' to *St. German's Doctor and Student*, p. xlix: 'Equity has changed sides, and has become part of the law'.

[28] Aristotle, *Rhetorica*, trans. W. Rhys Roberts, in *The Works of Aristotle Translated into English*, ed. W.D. Ross (12 vols, Oxford, 1908; reprinted 1946), vol. 11, p. 1374a.

just noticed) with the *æquitas* of Roman law: the former is 'concerned with a correction of the law'; the latter is 'a matter of the quality of the law or of its interpretation'.[29] Myron P. Gilmore, referring to the oft-repeated Ciceronian maxim *summum ius summa iniuria*, queries whether, in the Roman theory of equity, the concept 'could be drawn on to remedy the course of justice or was it the actual embodiment of justice'.[30] Again, the issue is whether equity is intrinsic to the law or an extrinsic, corrective principle. Moreover, as some have observed, the problem has been further complicated by the admixture of Christian influences. For example, Gilmore says that 'the *æquitas* of the canon law was throughout that of the Roman law but infused with the spirit of Christianity, a sense of *benignitas* and *misericordia*' (p. 494).[31]

Thus, 'equity' could refer to the justice or reason which was regarded as essential to law, or to a mode of interpretation whereby the true spirit of the law was discerned. Both these meanings emphasize that equity is already *in* the law. Or equity could mean the adjusting of the ordinary law—already 'just' in its general application—in response to particular circumstances, or even the merciful application of the law. These latter meanings tend to make equity something that is added to the law.

Most commentators characterize St. German's view of equity as making it intrinsic to the law. For St. German, Guy says, equity 'is not outside the law, but resides implicitly in ... every human law'.[32] This, he asserts, is by contrast with Aquinas, who 'maintained that *epieikeia* could be used in exceptional cases only'.[33] Sharon Dobbins says that St. German portrayed equity 'primarily as a canon of legal interpretation, tempering the letter of the law to perfect its just intention'—in contrast with Hobbes's approach, which emphasized the aspect of equity which involves 'the discretionary dispensing power of an absolute sovereign'.[34]

---

29 Meyjes, p. 242.

30 Myron P. Gilmore, 'The Jurisprudence of Humanism', *Traditio*, 17 (1961): 493–501, p. 493.

31 Endicott, 'Conscience of the King', p. 554, notes that St. Cyprian, in the third century, wrote '*æquitas est iustitia dulcore misericordiæ temperata*' ('equity is justice tempered by the sweetness of mercy'), a characterization repeated by early modern writers such as St. German himself (p. 95) and William West, 'Of the Chauncerie', in *Three Treatises, Of the Second part of Symbolæographie* (London, 1594), sig. A2v; EEBO image 29131:139. But, as we have already seen, some notion of mercy or clemency seems to have been present even in certain versions of Aristotle's account.

32 'Introduction', *St. German on Chancery and Statute*, p. 71.

33 Ibid., p. 73, citing *Summa Theologica*, II.i, q. 96 (art. 6). See also Zofia Rueger, 'Gerson's Concept of Equity and Christopher St. German', *History of Political Thought*, 3/1 (1982): 1–30, p. 14.

34 Sharon K. Dobbins, 'Equity: The Court of Conscience or the King's Command, the Dialogues of St. German and Hobbes Compared', *Journal of Law and Religion*, 9/1 (1991–2): 113–49, p. 114.

Famously, St. German himself described equity as follows:

> Equytye is a [ryghtwysenes] that consideryth all the pertyculer cyrcumstaunces of the dede / the whiche also is temperyd with the swetnes of mercye. And [suche an equytye] must alway be obseruyd in euery lawe of man ....[35]
>
> And it is called also by some men epicaia. The whiche is no other thynge but an excepcyon of the lawe of god / or the lawe of reason / from the generall rewles of the lawe of man ... the whiche excepcion is secretely vnderstande in euery generall rewle of euery posytyue lawe (p. 97).
>
> ... and so it apperyth that equytie rather foloweth the intent of the lawe / then the wordes of the lawe (p. 99).

I do not propose to analyse these passages, but only to point out that they contain an amalgam of ideas. Equity looks at all the particular circumstances in which the law is to be applied; it is tempered with mercy; it is an exception to the general rules of positive law—but an exception which is already understood as implicit in those rules; it looks to the intent of the law rather than to the letter, and so is a principle of interpretation. Equity for St. German seems to be a mixed notion, comprehending several of the ambiguities we have remarked.

The difficulty of pigeon-holing is illustrated by the fact that, while Meyjes contrasts Aristotelian *epieikeia* with Roman *æquitas* and regards the latter as more intrinsic to the law than the former, Rueger says that Jean Gerson's (1363–1439) view of equity—on which St. German's 'intrinsic-to-law' account is supposedly based—was itself Aristotelian.[36] This could suggest a 'trichotomy' or a continuum of equity, rather than a duality: Roman *æquitas* (the principle of justice inherent in the law and governing its interpretation); St. German (the principle of implied exception or correction, taking into account particular circumstances); Aquinas (resort to sovereign discretion in extraordinary cases only).

The difficulty is further highlighted by the fact that different rationales can support the same result in the same case. As Guy notes, both Aquinas and St. German present the example of a law prohibiting the opening of the gates of a besieged city. The gates are opened to admit citizens trapped outside. Aquinas justifies this apparent contravention of the law in terms of extraordinary, 'extrinsic' circumstance—that is, necessity. On the other hand, that same necessity can be understood as an exception implicit in the law, so as to fulfil the inner criterion of justness. Or, as a matter of interpretation, one could argue that the intent of the law is to safeguard the citizenry and so those who have opened the gate are within the spirit or intent, if not the letter, of the law.

In adverting to the equivocal meaning of the word 'equity', I want to make several points. For one thing, we cannot assume that St. German is much clearer in making the relevant distinctions than are other commentators. Moreover, of the

---

35 *St. German's Doctor and Student*, p. 95.

36 'Gerson's Concept of Equity', pp. 8–10.

types of equity that we can identify, only one might be proper to, or really distinctive of, Chancery jurisdiction. Thus, we could say that one kind of equity is 'the equity of the statute'—the principle of what today might be called 'liberal' or 'purposive' interpretation. Then, there might be the equity that is supposed to be intrinsic to any law; that is, all laws are taken to incorporate justice, or equity, and are to be applied consistently with that internal principle. But, beyond that, there are cases for which ordinary law simply does not provide, which may not be contemplated by the *ratio legis*. So, for example, Baker presents an account of *æquitas* as being the idea of abstract justice, implicit in all law, and as an interpretive principle. But, specifically with regard to the 'classical' English notion of equity, he says that '[e]quity of that kind, or "conscience", involved the relaxation of known but unwritten rules to meet the exigencies of justice in particular cases ...'.[37]

Certainly, St. German does seem to assume—and, indeed, to assert—that there is a kind of equity, or perhaps conscience, that is peculiar to the Court of Chancery. He envisages that in at least some cases 'where any thynge is exceptyd fro the generall customes or maxymes of the lawes of the realme / by the lawe of reason the partie must haue his remedye by ... sub pena',[38] and, when asked by the Doctor whether a person who 'may be holpen by conscyence' is to 'be holpen in the same courte or in another', the Student replies, with a qualification, that '*[o]ne can never be aided by an equity of this sort in the same court*, unless that equity is reinforced by some subsidiary maxim of the law' (p. 79).[39] Rueger notes St. German's position that separate courts remain necessary—the common law courts applying equity understood as a principle of interpretation, and an alternative forum admitting at least a different procedure where the judge actually has to 'leave the words of the law'.[40] Indeed, the editors of *Doctor and Student* suggest, somewhat inconsistently,[41] that St. German 'does not venture to treat the exclusive jurisdiction of the Chancery as a form of *epikeia*, but prefers to base it upon conscience'.[42] Paradoxically (given the fairly common view that St. German promoted the displacement of conscience by equity), such an observation might be taken to indicate that St. German actually contributed to the continuing identity of Chancery as a court of conscience.

---

37 'Introduction' to *The Reports of Sir John Spelman*, ed. J.H. Baker (2 vols, London, 1978), vol. 2, p. 37.

38 *St. German's Doctor and Student*, p. 103.

39 Note his specifying 'an equity of this sort'—that is, one kind of equity.

40 'Gerson's Concept of Equity', p. 25. Compare Georg Behrens, 'An Early Tudor Debate on the Relation Between Law and Equity', *Journal of Legal History*, 19/2 (1998): 143–61, p. 145, pointing out that, elsewhere, St. German sought to justify 'the institutional separation of law from equity'.

41 In view of their crediting St. German with our having courts of equity today rather than of conscience.

42 'Introduction' to *St. German's Doctor and Student*, p. xlviii.

There is some force in the argument that, if equity in all its forms is part of the ordinary law, then a separate court is otiose.[43] Indeed, there are contemporary judicial pronouncements that could support just this conclusion. In a case in the Court of Common Pleas in 1522, Broke J. justifies his position that uses might be enforced there by saying 'Conscience does not make uses, but common reason, which is common law and is indifferent to all laws as well spiritual as temporal'.[44] He appears to be saying that reason is the ultimate criterion for law and it supports the recognition of uses, and that would justify the intervention of the common law.[45]

That St. German appears not to address the specific features of Chancery equity in a developed way perhaps leaves this argument unanswered. But, at least with respect to *Doctor and Student*, some explanation is possible. Perhaps most importantly, St. German's project was not to explain Chancery equity, but to show that some kinds of equity and conscience are consistent with the ordinary law. Moreover, it may be significant that some of his examples, particularly respecting equity, involve *public law* issues—hence, the statute prohibiting opening of the city gates, or the statute proscribing the giving of alms to 'valyant begger[s]' (able-bodied beggars capable of working).[46] Statutes particularly lend themselves to 'equitable interpretation'. Further, unlike the kinds of private law issues governed largely by common law, these statutes do not engage conscience as a basis of legal *obligation*. Conscience may be in play in each case: that is, those who opened the gates might argue that they should be exonerated because they were acting in accordance with 'moral' conscience, just as the person giving alms to a stranded sturdy beggar might claim to be relieved from the legal penalty on the basis that conscience binds him to be charitable. 'Typical' equitable obligations or qualifications arise where conscience makes more onerous positive demands than the strict law. It may be that the 'rule of exception' is more amenable to the former, exculpatory situations than to liability-enhancing situations. Or, as Rueger's observation that the need for separate courts arises from the need for a different *procedure* suggests, St. German may have simply been making what we have seen to be the common assumption that the trial of conscience requires a forum where formalities are less strict. This, of course, is not a radical rationale for the existence of distinct courts.

---

43 See, for example, Endicott, 'Conscience of the King', p. 559.

44 M. 14 Hen. 8, 4, pl. 5. cited by Baker, 'Introduction', *Reports of Sir John Spelman*, p. 197.

45 A more common rationale for the cognizance of uses by common law courts is that uses have been recognized by statute. See, for example, *Re Lord Dacre of the South* (1535) in *Reports of Sir John Spelman*, pp. 228–30. The qualification that St. German places on his 'no aid by an equity of this sort in the same court' is that it does not apply if the equity is '*reinforced by some subsidiary maxim of the law*' (*St. German's Doctor and Student*, p. 79). If a subsidiary maxim of the law will suffice, *a fortiori* a statute will.

46 *St. German's Doctor and Student*, pp. 99–101.

Continuing medieval influences

Apart from the matter of the equivocal nature of equity, the other preliminary contextual point is that, although many have treated St. German as the harbinger of a new age of equity, his position is hardly an abrupt departure from medieval concepts. Various commentators have made this point. For example, Dobbins opines that St. German's view of conscience was 'very much a medieval canonist view'[47]—an observation that is generally valid, although it needs to be nuanced. Similarly, C.K. Allen calls St. German's treatment of conscience and related concepts 'plainly canonical and somewhat pietistic in conception',[48] and Doe observes that St. German 'follows the traditional medieval outlook'.[49] A.W.B. Simpson notes that the 'immediate sources' of the Doctor's view of promises are two of the *summæ confessorum*, although he does not follow them exactly.[50] The point is worth reiterating because it reminds us that St. German was as much the inheritor and perpetuator of an old tradition as he was the progenitor of a new one.

As is well known, the major specific medieval influence on St. German was probably Jean Gerson.[51] Although, as we shall see, St. German was influenced by Gerson's account of conscience,[52] it is Gerson's account of *epieikeia* that he appears to have found particularly congenial. Meyjes relates Gerson's view of equity to his criticism of what he took to be the canon law's excessive positivitism: '[h]e accuses [canonists] of introducing a purely juridical way of thought into the Church'.[53] One can understand how St. German, given his anticlericalism and his project of vindicating the common law, might be attracted by such a critique of the canonists. One can also understand the appeal of an account that presents law in terms of more fundamental concepts, as opposed to 'collections of rules'. One might be tempted to see in St. German's invocation of these deeper concepts, or perhaps processes, the introduction of a different way of thinking about, say, conscience.[54] Thus, instead of the rather programmatic 'manuals for confessors,'

---

47 Dobbins, 'Equity', pp. 126–7.

48 C.K. Allen, *Law in the Making* (6th edn, Oxford, 1958), p. 390.

49 Doe, p. 134.

50 A.W.B. Simpson, *A History of the Common Law of Contract: The Rise of the Action of Assumpsit* (Oxford, 1975), pp. 377, 395–6.

51 See Rueger, 'Gerson's Concept of Equity' for a detailed discussion. See also Guy, *Christopher St. German on Chancery and Statute*, pp. 72–3, Richard Janda, 'Legal Architecture, Equity and Christopher St. German', in J.E.C. Brierley *et al.* (eds), *Mélanges offerts par ses collègues de McGill à Paul-André Crépeau* (Cowansville, 1997), pp. 373–416, p. 396, and Dobbins, 'Equity', p. 117.

52 Plucknett and Barton call the Doctor's description of conscience a 'shortened version' of Gerson's *De Natura et Qualitate Conscientiæ* ('Introduction' to *St. German's Doctor and Student*, p. xxvn).

53 Meyjes, p. 220. See also pp. 220–23.

54 Plucknett and Barton suggest that the conscience of the medieval chancellor, to the extent that it was influenced more by the canonists than by Gerson, might have been

giving standard answers, St. German presents this process of moral inquiry as being dialogic, not just in the form of *Doctor and Student* as a conversation, but in the wider sense of involving rational discourse rather than just 'rules'. Hence it is more philosophical and searching. Such a position is broadly reminiscent of Meg Lota Brown's general distinction between Catholic and Protestant casuistry.[55]

One must be wary of overstating the case, however. St. German's general theory of conscience is very medieval; he does invoke the *summæ confessorum*; he does try to reach definitive answers to the questions of conscience he poses. Moreover, if his programme was simply a more open, morally-based approach to legal conscience, he would have been out of step with the growing demand that Chancery equity should be more certain and precedent-bound—that is, more 'law-like'. Indeed, in making the case that the common law often provides a reliable guide to the conscience of cases, he may be in part just replacing one system of rules of conscience (canon law) by another (common law). Indeed, as we shall see, some of his examples involve a rather positivistic approach to determining issues of 'conscience'.

One further point should be made about Gerson's concept of equity: it may not be as cohesive as it is sometimes portrayed. Thus, Meyjes notes that Gerson uses the word *epikie* in the Aristotelian sense as the correction of the law, but also 'equates it with *discretio*, the power of distinction' or 'with the power of dispensation and exception', and he says that it interprets laws 'not according to the letter but according to the spirit'.[56] This again suggests the ambiguity of 'equity'. But to impose our own ideas of consistency in these circumstances may be a precarious strategy.

St. German's Concept of Conscience

As I have already intimated, St. German's theoretical account of conscience is very reminiscent of the medieval accounts that we have seen.

First, unsurprisingly, his account quite insistently depicts conscience as 'objective'. As Plucknett and Barton point out, he tells us more than once that conscience 'must always be founded upon some law'.[57] I shall return presently to what that law, in his view, comprehends, observing for the moment that although it can comprehend human positive law, it gives precedence to what might be termed, generally, natural law.

uncongenial to St. German ('Introduction', *St. German's Doctor and Student*, pp. xxviii–xxix).

55 Meg Lota Brown, *Donne and the Politics of Conscience in Early Modern England* (Leiden, 1995), p. 25.

56 Meyjes, p. 244.

57 'Introduction', *St. German's Doctor and Student*, p. xxvi.

Second—and this is a related point—he portrays conscience in terms of *synderesis*.[58] What *synderesis* is for him is equivocal. He defines it initially as 'a naturall power *or motive force* of the *rational* soule sette *always* in the hyghest parte therof / mouynge and sterrynge it to good / & abhorrynge euyll'.[59] On this definition, synderesis is not an intellectual power that discerns first principles, but it is an affective power which moves us to follow such principles. This description is close to Gerson's: '[s]ynderesis is an appetitive power of the soul that comes immediately from God. It takes on a certain natural inclination to the good. Through this proclivity it is drawn to follow the movement of the good on the basis of the understanding presented to it in the simple intelligence'.[60] St. German's opting for an affective account of *synderesis* is rather paradoxical: one would have thought that a cognitive or intellective account would have been more congenial to a consideration of law; moreover, the latter would appear to be more congruent with objective conscience. This latter concern is, of course, met by Gerson's account on the basis that the good is known in another way—that is, by 'simple intelligence'. And, indeed, Gerson also admits descriptions of *synderesis* which seem to make it more a cognitive power: '[w]e call synderesis by other names, such as ... a spark of intelligence on whose basis there are movement and attraction toward the good'.[61] This description makes *synderesis* what allows us to distinguish good from evil, and it makes 'movement' or motivation something else. It seems to equate *synderesis* with 'simple intelligence'.

A similar ambiguity emerges from St. German's discussion of reason. Reason is man's 'inwarde iye',[62] 'that power of the *rational* soule / that *deliberates and* dyscerneth bytwene good and euyl'.[63] We will recall that, for Aquinas, *synderesis* is cognitive and non-deliberative, but that there are other cognitive faculties that

58 J.H. Baker, *The Oxford History of the Laws of England Volume VI 1483–1558* (Oxford, 2003), pp. 43–4 observes that St. German 'presented conscience as an objective ideal implanted in man by the mysterious workings of synderesis'.

59 *St. German's Doctor and Student*, p. 81.

60 Jean Gerson, *On Mystical Theology: The First and Speculative Treatise* (1408), in *Jean Gerson: Early Works*, trans. and ed. D.P. McGuire (New York1998), pp. 262–87, p. 279. As we have noted previously, Gerson was 'the chief espouser' of 'an affective or volitional *synteresis*' among late medieval thinkers (Michael G. Baylor, *Action and Person: Conscience in Late Scholasticism and the Young Luther* [Leiden, 1977], p. 161).

61 Gerson, p. 280. This kind of terminological ambiguity appears to have a long pedigree. Thus, for example, when quoting the passage from St. Jerome which introduced the term into discussions of conscience, Peter Lombard 'ignored *synteresis* altogether and substituted *superior... scintilla rationis* for Jerome's *scintilla conscientiæ*' (Robert A. Greene, 'Synderesis, the Spark of Conscience, in the English Renaissance', *Journal of the History of Ideas*, 52/2 (1991): 195– 219, p. 199).

62 *St. German's Doctor and Student*, p. 83. See Reginald Pecock, *The Reule of Crysten Religioun*, ed. W.C. Greet (London, 1927), p. 225: 'þe resoun of men, which is þe iȝe of þe soule and þe ynner iȝe of þe soule'.

63 *St German's Doctor and Student*, p. 85.

do deliberate. For St. German, it appears that *synderesis* is affective, and reason is cognitive and deliberative—that is, that it does not immediately apprehend the basic precepts of the law.

But St. German goes on to identify that faculty which does immediately apprehend these precepts, that is cognitive but non-deliberative:

> Reason and intellect are not distinct as two separate powers, but as two activities of the same power; for 'intelligere', 'to understand', is simply to apprehend an intelligible truth; but 'to reason' is to proceed from one thing that is understood to another, so as to reach the knowledge of intelligible truth (p. 85).

Understanding is thus a state of knowledge of some truth; reason is a process that starts from such knowledge and can eventuate in further knowledge or understanding. The ambiguity arises when St. German says that '*reason is concerned with principles which, as soon as their terms are apprehended and known, cannot fail to be known, and cannot be disputed, it may then be called sinderesis* ...' (p. 87). On this account, *synderesis* is cognitive. It is perhaps less significant to point out the awkwardness of St. German's account[64] than to observe that, in one way or another, it does contain the idea of the power of apprehending objective, certain, truth.

As for conscience *per se*, while some might emphasize that it 'says and imports knowledge by itself'', and although it 'is conjoined with that higher light of reason which is called sinderesis', it is to be distinguished from synderesis. Synderesis is 'concerned with the universal aspects of things to be done' whereas conscience 'says and imports ... knowledge with something else, that is to say, with some particular act',[65] so that conscience is 'no thynge els / ... but an applyenge or an ordering of any scyence [or knowledge] to some partyculer acte of man ...' (p. 89). In terms of what we have already seen elsewhere, this is unremarkable: conscience involves assessing the moral quality of particular acts in terms of already-apprehended basic deontic precepts.

Equally unremarkably, St. German characterizes the process involved as syllogistic, giving the example: 'No evil is to be done.' 'This is evil.' 'This is not to be done.' The major premise is given (here) by *synderesis*, which 'mynysteryth a vnyuersall prynciple that neuer erryth' (p. 91).[66] This premise is very general indeed—perhaps reflecting again the difficulty that we have encountered before with the basic precepts—not only in identifying them, but in distinguishing them from lower-order derivative principles. Thus, 'Do not kill' might be taken to be a basic precept, given by *synderesis*; at the same time, it is a derivative principle of 'Do no evil', an even more fundamental or general precept. The minor premise is

64 Others—notably the earlier Luther—posited the co-existence of a cognitive and a volitional *synderesis* (Baylor, p. 157).

65 *St. German's Doctor and Student*, p. 87.

66 Recall Aquinas and other scholastics regarding the inerrancy of *synderesis*.

perhaps even more problematic, or more complex, because it appears to involve a factual apprehension ('This') as well as a moral assessment ('is evil'). Again, we must go back to Aquinas's position that the major premise of the syllogism of conscience is not given immediately by *synderesis*, but rather consists of some more specific moral precept deduced from what *synderesis* apprehends. Thus, embedded in St. German's 'This is evil' is probably a second syllogism, of the form: 'Killing is not to be done (derived normative premise); what I am doing is killing; this (what I am doing) is not to be done.' But, again, it is probably not necessary for my present project to delve too compulsively into such issues.

As we have seen, Aquinas identifies as possible loci of errors of conscience the defective derivation of lower-order principles from what *synderesis* tells us, the misapprehension of facts (either by memory, perception or prediction), and faulty reasoning in applying the principles to the facts. Apparently, ignorance—at least if it is in some sense unavoidable—of both relevant facts and lower-order deontic propositions may excuse in conscience.[67]

St. German offers a rather different account of the ways in which 'errour in conscyence commeth', outlining seven: ignorance of what to do, negligence, pride, singularity (obstinacy), inordinate affection, pusillanimity, and perplexity (the belief that one must sin, whatever choice one makes).[68] It may be worth remarking that many of these modes (or causes) of error are affective, which may accord with Gerson's and St. German's affective *synderesis*. But I do not find the list logically coherent: for example, the 'affective' causes may simply lie behind the more cognitive ones. Thus, ignorance (obviously cognitive) may be the result of negligence or pride or obstinacy or 'desire'—all except 'negligence' apparently affective. Presumably, all these sources of error except for the first and perhaps the last would be culpable and therefore unconscientious.

Elsewhere, St. German does say that conscience may err '*because it has to deal with particular things by means of knowledge or research in which there is often chance of error*' (p. 79). Presumably, this error could arise in determining the particular rule to apply to a situation or in ascertaining the relevant facts. He does give as an example of an erroneous apprehension of a particular rule the simple assertion that oaths are unlawful, and distinguishes this from a precept given by *synderesis* which, again, 'neuer erreth'. He also allows that not only 'ygnoraunce of the dede' but also 'inuyncyble' 'ygnoraunce of the lawe excusyth' (p. 162), at least as far as conscience is concerned. For St. German, an error of law is 'inuyncyble' when 'they haue done that in them is to knowe the trouth as to counsel with lernyd men'—that is, they have sought advice as to what the law is. Of course, the law here is not the basic precepts of *synteresis*, but rather derived norms. In his treatment of unavoidable ignorance of facts or even of the law as excuses, St. German displays affinities, if not exact congruity, with Aquinas.

---

67 Timothy C. Potts, *Conscience in Medieval Philosophy* (Cambridge, 1980), p. 59.

68 *St. German's Doctor and Student*, p. 91.

From all this it is clear that the general theoretical framework of St. German's account of conscience is essentially 'medieval'—albeit not entirely orthodox or consistent.[69]

Conscience Founded on Law

As we have already noticed, St. German repeatedly makes the point that conscience 'must alway be groundyd vpon some lawe'.[70] Being thus law-governed, conscience is objectively-based. The three kinds of law that St. German identifies as possible grounds of conscience are the law of reason, the law of God, and—particularly significant for his project—the law of man, so that 'conscyence muste be orderyd by that *human lawe / (as long as it remains in strength and force) in every way*[71] *as it muste be in the proper cases* vpon the lawe of god / and vpon the lawe of reason' (p. 111). These in fact appear to be the three ways in which the overarching 'law eternal' is made known to us (p. 11). But St. German's point is that the basis for any deduction of conscience must be one of these laws. The law of reason '*is nothing else than the participation or knowledge of eternal law in a rational creature, revealed to him by the natural light of reason*' (p. 13). Presumably, this is closely related to *synderesis*, as we have seen. The law of God is 'gyuen by reuelacyon to reasonable creatures', and conduces to 'optaynynge of the felycytie eternal' (p. 21), a point that we shall see elsewhere. The qualification that, strictly, the law of God relates only to matters involving eternal felicity means that some laws ostensibly emanating from God—including much of the canon law—may be merely 'human', 'civil', or 'political (p. 11)'.[72]

Regarding human law, St. German suggests that 'in euery lawe posytyue well made is somwhat of the lawe of reason / and of the lawe of god' (p. 27). One expects, or hopes, to see the image of those other, more fundamental, laws in human laws. However, while any human law that contravenes the law of reason or the law of God 'is no lawe / but a corrupcyon [& a manyfest errour]' (p. 113), being positively based on one of these laws seems not to be a prerequisite for the validity of human law. The law of man may be merely 'superaddyd vnto them for the better orderyng of the common welth' (p. 111). That is, there may be human laws which are merely 'indifferent' *vis-à-vis* the other laws, but which do not contravene them. Such human laws, 'not contrary to the lawe of reason nor the lawe of god', are an independent ground for conscience (p. 111). A possible rationale for this may

---

[69] As we have seen in Chapter 2, the scholastics were not all *ad idem* as to the characterization of conscience.

[70] *St. German's Doctor and Student*, p. 163.

[71] Perhaps an early acknowledgment by a Chancellor of this relationship is Sir Thomas Wriostheley's that his court 'gave law to the kingdom; his constant and exact rules, to the court; and his conscience guided by the law of the kingdom, to his rules' (Lloyd, vol. 1, p. 124; ECCO image CW104918924:137).

[72] See also Meyjes, p. 233. Meyjes makes the same point about Gerson.

be found in St. German's rather cryptic observation that 'because since the law eternal is the reason of government in the supreme governor, then necessarily all reasons of government in inferior governors must be derived from the reason of the supreme governor' (p. 11).[73] Moreover, there is no positive obligation on human law to cover every situation that the other laws cover: the fact that human law does not address everything that is against conscience does not mean that the law is unconscientious, although it may need reinforcement from elsewhere.

From the foregoing, we can infer (or re-iterate) the following. First, positive human law, either concurrently with or independently of the other laws, will often be the ground and guide of conscience. This, in fact, constitutes much of St. German's thesis. Second, there are matters of conscience which the positive law simply does not address. This means that there are areas in which the law of reason and the law of God must supplement conscience as indicated by the positive law, or provide separate grounds of conscience. St. German thus points to the error of those people who think that they can do, conscientiously, whatever is not forbidden by the positive law. That law can itself be a sufficient ground in conscience for acting or forbearing to act, but it is not the comprehensive ground of conscience.

St. German thus identifies three areas in which conscience arises: conscience—or perhaps equity—may be already in the ordinary law; or 'where any thynge is exceptyd fro the generall customes or maxymes of the lawes of the realme / by the lawe of reason the partie must haue his remedye by ... sub pena'; or, 'in some case there is no remedye for suche an equytie by waye of compulsyon [either at law or by subpoena] / but all the remedye therin muste be commytted to the conscyence of the partye' (p. 103). In other words, sometimes concerns of conscience are adequately addressed by the positive law—either because it is congruent with the law of reason or the law of God, or because it deals with matters that are morally indifferent. However, sometimes the 'generall customes or maxymes of the lawes' are not sufficiently congruent with the law of reason to satisfy conscience. In these cases, resort to Chancery (that is, explicitly, 'remedye by ... sub pena') is necessary. It may be worth noting that it is only general customs and maxims—not, say, statutes—which St. German identifies as amenable to this kind of equity.[74] This may imply that the 'equity of the statute' is always a matter for the common law courts. Finally, there are matters of conscience which cannot be redressed in any court other than the *forum internum* of a person's private conscience. Throughout *Doctor and Student* St. German makes reference to these three categories, giving

[73] We shall see in other contexts that there are three kinds of rationales making human laws binding on the conscience: first, that they are congruent with the law of reason or of God; second, that the law of God (and probably the law of reason as well) dictates that we are to obey our rulers; and, third, that rulers have God's mandate to govern. St. German's observation may be an amalgam of these last two.

[74] The Student identifies six principal grounds of the law of England: law of reason, law of God, general customs, maxims, particular customs, and statutes (p. 31).

many examples but unfortunately not elaborating cogent general principles for assigning cases to one category as opposed to another.

'Ordinary' Law and Conscience

Because his main concern is with how the law of the realm—essentially, the positive law—stands with conscience, his main focus is on the first category. How is the ordinary law consonant with conscience? The Doctor and the Student explore this question with regard to a large number of cases. I shall refer to only a few representative ones, to illustrate the kinds of analysis involved, and to raise some questions about that analysis.

One of the most straightforward of these is the example of a law that is apparently neutral *vis-à-vis* the laws of God and of reason. St. German instances the variable rules respecting the devolution of property: under the common law, the eldest son inherits; under boroughenglish, the younger son does; and under gavelkind, all sons share in the inheritance. All of these, St. German says, are equally consonant with conscience and each, as it is law, is binding in conscience. One might, of course, question the assumption. Arguably, the law of reason might say that a father has an equal responsibility to provide for all his children, and therefore the law that excludes other children in favour of one is contrary to this law of reason.[75] On the other hand, there is no doubt biblical authority for primogeniture, which may also be supported on the basis of a putative law of reason that mandates maintaining the integrity of the inheritance by having it devolve upon one person only.

Another of the 'dyuers cases where conscyence is to be orderyd after the lawe' involves the question whether an older son born before his parents' 'spousals' should inherit in preference to a younger son born after them. St. German explains the 'Silogisme of conscyence' operating here as follows:

> sinderesis mynystreth the maior thus. Ryghtwysenesse is to be done to euery man: vpon which maior the law of Englande mynystreth the minor thus: the inherytaunce bylongeth to the sone borne after spousellys ... then conscyence maketh the conclusyon & sayth therfore the inherytaunce is [in conscyence] to be gyuen to the sone borne after spousellys (p. 129).

One may be pardoned for being not entirely satisfied with this. For one thing, it involves the statement of two rules, one ('Ryghtwysenesse is to be done to euery man') at a greater level of abstraction than the other (that respecting inheritance). But the more specific rule does not clearly follow from the more general one, although it is arguably a plausible instantiation of the more general one. But, if righteousness is to be done to every person, why should the 'accident' of premarital birth deprive the older son? Certainly it is not self-evident to a modern sensibility

[75] I realize that what is involved here is not the father's act, but different legal rules for the taking of estates in land by descent.

that it should. There seems to be a further, unexpressed, premise or assumption here. Moreover, the conclusion, in relation to the minor premise, seems merely tautological. Indeed, both the minor premise and the conclusion are stated in the same words—which may, in fact, be St. German's point, namely, that the legal rule is conclusive of the conscience of this matter.

No doubt St. German thinks that this case, like 'infynyte' others, involves 'the ryght Iugement of conscyence', but this appears debatable. An explanation that St. German gives is that 'they that be lernyd in the law of the realme say that in euery case where any lawe is ordeyned for the dysposycion of landes & goodis / wiche is not agaynst the law of god / nor yet against the law of reason / that yt law byndeth all them yt be vnder the law in the courte of conscyence / [that is to say inwardly in his soule]' (pp. 129–31). Again, though, this simply begs the question: might not this law be contrary to the law of reason or of God?

An element in St. German's approach may be his argument that, since property is a creature of the positive law, the positive law may order it more or less as it sees fit. '[A]t the begynnynge', he writes, 'all goodes were in comon / but after they were brought by the law of man in to a certayne propertye ... and than whan suche property is gyuen by the lawe of man the same law may assygne suche condycyons vppon the property as it lysteth ...' (p. 183). Assuming that the allocation of things is not a matter for the laws of God or of reason, the positive law of man is the measure of conscience.

A similar position seems to be taken regarding contracts. Another question posed is whether A, a fully-competent twenty-year-old 'infant' who sells his land to X and with the proceeds buys land of greater value, may avoid the first transaction on the basis of the legal rule that contracts made by minors are not binding. First the Student ventures an opinion that, as a matter of conscience, A should not be able to avoid the contract, because the rule of voidability is grounded in a presumption of incapacity that 'fayleth in this infaunte' and therefore he may not 'with conscyence aske the lande agayne ...' (p. 131). The Doctor responds by asking: 'What is the law of England?' The Student says, in effect, 'Infants' contracts are voidable'. The Doctor reiterates that, for conscience to be invoked, it must be based upon some law. The law in question here cannot be the law of God or the law of reason, because '[feffementes nor] contractes be not groundyd vpon neyther of tho lawes but vpon the lawe of man' (p. 133).[76] Since the source of the rule does not lie outside human law, human law is determinative of conscience; hence A may void the contract and require a reconveyance of the land. But, having done so, A would have to refund the purchase price and pay X's costs since, apparently, restitution *is* dictated by the law of reason.

If both the law of property and the law of contracts are effectively the creatures of human law and therefore whatever human law decrees about them determines what is conscience, this radically curtails the range of situations in which

---

[76] See also Plucknett and Barton, 'Introduction', *St. German's Doctor and Student*, p. xxvi.

considerations of conscience based on the other laws can qualify the positive law. But St. German clearly does not go this far.

This is illustrated by his treatment of the stock example of the debtor who repays his debt without taking the acquittance required by the law. The Doctor asks how it may be said 'that that lawe standeth with reason or conscyence' because 'vpon the law of reason ... *and conscience* that when they be payde that he that payeth them shuld be dyshcargyd [*sic*]' (p. 77). In other words, this seems to be a case in which the law of man directly contravenes the law of reason. Using the argument previously mentioned, one might say that, since contracts are an invention of human law,[77] whatever that law determines is what conscience is in these cases. But the Student does not make that argument here. Indeed, he agrees that, if the law positively required the second repayment such a law would be 'bothe agaynst reason & conscyence' (p. 77), and, as St. German puts it elsewhere, the common law judges know full well that '*the paymente suffycyently dischargith the det in reason and conscience*'.[78] Since the law 'commaundyth not that the money of ryght ought to be payde agayne', there is no repugnancy to reason.[79] The Student goes on to make a point that seems to be based on a substance *versus* procedure distinction. The common law does not require the second repayment; it simply precludes the pleading of the first repayment without a particular kind of proof—that is, the acquittance. But, St. German says in the *Little Treatise*, the common law judges do not suppose that 'ye maxysmes and custumes of ye lawe' regarding what is a 'suffycyent ple' extend to other courts.[80] Thus, the debtor 'maye be holpen *in equity* by a sub pena'.[81]

In terms of the framework St. German adopts, then, we have a maxim of the common law that cannot determine what conscience requires in this case because there is a law of reason that dictates that. Yet this is not a case where, because it directly contradicts the law of reason, the common law maxim is no law at all but a corruption of law. Rather, it is a case where the common law, because of

---

77 A rather implausible position, if one considers the centrality of promises, or more ponderously, 'covenants', in the Bible.

78 *A Little Treatise Concerning Writs of Subpoena*, in *Christopher St. German on Chancery and Statute*, ed. J.A. Guy (London, 1985), pp. 106–26, p. 111.

79 The author of *The Replication of a Serjeant at the Laws of England*, in *Christopher St. German on Chancery and Statute*, p. 100, offers another theory: the second repayment would not be unreasonable because the debtor 'hath hurte hym self by his owne necligence and by his owne follye'. That is, the second repayment is not against reason, because the debtor has failed to inform himself of an easily-accessible law. He is not a victim of 'invincible' ignorance—ostensibly the only kind of ignorance that excuses in conscience. The thrust of the Serjeant's argument may be implicit in the maxim '*Deus est procurator fatuorum*'—that is, 'only God can help fools'—which we have encountered before and shall again.

80 St. German, *Little Treatise*, p. 111.

81 *St. German's Doctor and Student*, p. 79.

procedural limits, fails to do all that reason and conscience demand. As we have seen, that the common law does not meet all the demands of conscience does not make it unconscientious. So the full realization of conscience requires another forum. Alternatively, one might say (problematically) that the rules of evidence are morally indifferent, and emphasize that the Court of Chancery's procedures equip it better to examine all the facts of particular cases, as they might engage conscience. As St. German says, the 'no plea of repayment without an acquittance' maxim is 'a general rule', conducing to the convenience of 'all the people' in most cases, and extraordinary circumstances must be examined elsewhere. This is, of course, not fully convincing, if only because the 'extraordinary circumstance', the first repayment, seems to be the very situation that the maxim addresses. Moreover, it must be remarked that this appears to be an instance in which the exception, based on reason, is not understood as inhering in the law itself. The law must be corrected, or completed, from outside.

In another question, ancillary to the one we have just been considering, the Student asks 'whether may a man with conscyence be of counsayle with the playntyfe in an accyon at the comon lawe knowynge that the defendaunt hath suffycyent matter in conscyence wherby he may be dyscharged by a subpena in the chauncerye whiche he can not plede at the comon lawe?' (p. 189). The example given is once again that of a debt repaid, but an acquittance not taken. Note that, here, the issue is not whether the law itself is in accordance with conscience, but what is conscientious for a lawyer to do. Indeed, the word 'conscyence' is used in both senses in the question asked. So there is some semantic slippage here. But St. German seems to assume that this question is relevant to his broader concerns.

This may be because the answer involves the question of the ambit of the lawyer's oath: he is sworn to give counsel according to the law. So it is not just a matter for his private conscience, but of what a more disembodied conscience might say about the extent of his obligations. What that conscience comprehends comes down to a determination of what the word 'law' means in this context. The Student suggests a narrow meaning—essentially, the common law and statute, so that the lawyer is fulfilling his oath in advising on these matters. But the Doctor judges the Student out of his own mouth, reminding him that he had previously said that 'the law of god and the law of reason be two especyall groundes of the lawes of Englande', and therefore a lawyer 'may gyue no counsayle (sauynge his othe) neyther agaynst the law of god nor the law of reason' (p. 189). An implication is that all law—including Chancery law—is part of the 'ordinary' law of the land, and that a common lawyer's knowledge should be understood to include the law of reason not pleadable in the common law courts. Another implication is that conscience has the dual aspect—substantive and procedural, normative and evidentiary—that we have seen before. Chancery will take cognizance of facts not admissible in the ordinary courts; but what those facts relate to is given by the law of God and the law of reason.

One of the cases put regarding the ostensible congruity of the common law and conscience vividly illustrates the cultural or historical relativity of the content given to the notion. A villein is granted to X for life; the villein purchases for himself land in fee simple; the law permits X to appropriate his villein's fee simple estate in the land: what is the case in conscience? The Doctor raises a preliminary objection, which to a modern sensibility would seem to be the glaringly fundamental issue of conscience: 'whether it may stande with conscyence that one man may clayme an other to be his vylleyn / & that he may take fro hym his landes & goodes & put his body in pryson yf he wyll / yt semeth he loueth not his neyghbour as hym selfe that doeth so to hym' (p. 213).[82] Indeed, if there is ever a case where the law of God or of reason should be the measure in conscience trumping the positive human law it is where that positive law purports to make one person effectively another's property. But the Student replies, in effect, that villeinage has been an institution in the law for so long that it is not to be questioned now. Oh, well, says the Doctor, in that case this is another situation where 'conscyence must folowe the lawe of the realme' (p. 214). This is a blatant instance of the phenomenon I alluded to previously: St. German's deference to one programmatic system of rules (the law of the realm) instead of another (canon law), in spite of some of his descriptions of *epieikeia* which suggest that laws must be understood in terms of searching moral or philosophical inquiry.

It is perhaps perverse to make the kind of criticisms that I have been making. St. German's main point, after all, is not that his account of conscience in each situation is unassailable, but that, in general, the common law is accordant with conscience and that, apart from unusual cases, it is a reliable guide for conscience. Still, if many of his examples are doubtful, this does tend to call into question the overall thesis.

Conscience and Chancery

Although St. German's focus in *Doctor and Student* is on vindicating the common law as a site of conscience, he consistently acknowledges that there are some matters of conscience that can be pursued only in Chancery. That is, he nowhere (as I read him) says that Chancery, as a court of conscience, is redundant.

Insufficiencies of the common law

Again, perhaps because this is not really his theme, he tends not to offer useful *general* guidelines to distinguish the conscience adequately recognized by the common law courts from that which is cognizable only in Chancery. Rather, he gives examples, without really articulating the general principles. He does say that, in some cases, 'the lorde Chaunceller must ordre his conscyence after the

[82] Note that, regarding the previous case I discussed, the Doctor says that 'do unto others as you would have them do unto you' (not a direct quote) is a law both of reason and of God (p. 190). The 'Golden Rule' arises regularly in discussions of equity and conscience—customarily being presented as *the* basic moral precept as far as interpersonal relations are concerned.

rewles and groundes of the lawe of the realme' (p. 105). This implies, *a contrario*, that there are other cases where his conscience is not restricted to the ordinary rules and grounds of law. At one point the Doctor does say that (apart from the case where 'the law of man is in it selfe dyrectely agaynst the law of reason or else the lawe of god') there are two types of situations where conscience might go beyond human law: 'where the generall groundes of the law of man worketh in any pertyculer case agaynst the sayd lawes' and 'where there is no lawe of man prouyded for hym that hathe ryghte to a thynge by the lawe of reason or the law of god' (pp. 207–8). He goes on to note that in some, but not all, of these cases there will be recourse by subpoena; in some cases, 'it shall be referred to the conscyence of the partye' (p. 208). This latter point, of course, refers to matters of conscience cognizable in Chancery as opposed to those which must be left entirely to the internal forum.

The possibly equivocal relationship of these two scenarios in which conscience goes beyond the law is perhaps illustrated by the acquittance case. On the one hand, we might say that it is an instance of the generality of the law working injustice in particular cases—that is, where repayment has already been made. On the other hand, it could be conceptualized as a case for which the law simply does not provide. This latter seems to be St. German's take on it: the law does not say that the debt is repayable twice; it simply says that the unattested repayment may not be pleaded. Regarding the 'right' of the debtor, it says nothing. Conscience fills this gap by recognizing that double repayment is inconsistent with the law of reason. Incidentally, the remedy sought may vary with the rationale offered for the intervention of conscience. Thus, we might argue that an injunction would be the appropriate remedy on the basis of the first rationale: since the general terms of the law here would in this particular case work against the law of reason, it would be proper to prevent the second repayment. On the basis of the second rationale, it might be more coherent to allow the law to operate, but to allow the debtor to recover one of the repayments on the basis that it would be unconscientious for the creditor to retain the second payment. Of course, St. German does not say this, and it may be an overly nice distinction.

Another example of a case in which St. German acknowledges that there will be relief in Chancery involves a contract for the sale of land. The Doctor posits that the law might ordain '*that contracts shall not be made without certain witnesses*' and '*then if anyone should sell his land without witnesses against the form of the statute and even receive the purchase money, there would remain for him in conscience no other duty than to return the purchase money ...*' (p. 135). It is not clear that it is the law that will require this refund, or only Chancery. It seems somewhat analogous to the double repayment of a debt for want of observing certain formal or evidentiary requirements situation. The Doctor goes on to say, however, that 'yf a man sell his lande by a suffycyent [and lawfull] contracte thoughe there lacketh lyuerye of season ... yet *the contract holds in conscience and* the seller is bounde in conscyence to performe the contracte (p. 137)'. Presumably the 'suffycyent … contract' involves both the payment of consideration and the presence of the formal requirements mentioned above. This obligation to perform is enforceable in Chancery. Again, this appears to be a case of omission by the common law, which will not order specific performance. Chancery, in ordering the performance of the contract, is not opposing the common law, but supplementing it so as to give more complete effect to the requirements of conscience.

Another instance of something similar involves the duties of an executor, particularly with respect to paying the debts of the testator or making amends for wrongs that person has committed. The Student makes the now familiar point that, since human law creates executorship, that law (to the extent that it makes specific provision) determines what is conscience in the case. But, where human law does not make any provision, the default position is the law of reason or the law of God. So, if the executors have discretion, 'by the law of god they shalbe bounde to do that fyrst / that is to the moste profyte of the soule of theyr testatour'—that is, pay the debts and compensate for wrongs done (p. 197). Similarly, as regards the payment first of legacies or of debts, executors 'are bounden by the lawe of god to loue theyr neyghboure ... and it is better for the testatour that his dettes be payde: wherefore his sowle shall suffre payne' (p. 200). Needless to say, this is a very 'medieval' sentiment, one that we have encountered for example in the Paston letters. But it is one that we shall continue to encounter, in these terms, at least as late as the chancellorship of Lord Nottingham.[83]

A problem with all these cases is, however, that though we can say that Chancery enforces conscience in cases that the common law fails to address, the precise criterion for 'fails to address' is not clear. Arguably almost any situation in which Chancery wanted to do something more than the law does could be rationalized as a situation for which the common law had simply not made provision.

Matters of purely private conscience

If one boundary of Chancery's jurisdiction in conscience is matters that the common law has failed to provide for, then the other boundary is those matters to be left to the private conscience of the individual person. Thus, some cases of conscience are not triable in any external court, '[a]nd in such case he is in conscyence as well bounde to redresse it yf he wyll saue his soule / as he were yf he were compellable therto by the lawe'.[84] Again, while St. German recognizes that there is such a boundary, and while he offers a number of examples, he does not undertake to develop comprehensive general criteria of distinction.

Nevertheless, there are some indications of relevant principles, although it is not clear that these are meant to be exhaustive.

83 *Hickson* v. *Wytham* (1674/75), in *Lord Nottingham's Chancery Cases,* ed. D.E.C. Yale (2 vols, London, 1957), vol. 1, p. 137.

84 *St. German's Doctor and Student*, p. 109.

One of these emerges from his distinguishing the two aspects of reason.[85] The higher part conduces to the knowledge of God and things pertaining to God. The lower part, on the other hand, 'workyth the moste to gouerne [wel] temporall thynges'; 'she groundeth her reasons moche vpon lawes of man / and vpon reason of man / wherby she concludyth that that is to be done / that is honest and expedyent to the common welth …'.[86] This suggests a distinction that we will see again between what some have called 'spirituals' *versus* 'civils'.[87] Some matters of conscience involve only our spiritual well-being and do not, at least directly, engage 'temporall thynges'. Thus, St. German says, a promise to God is binding only in private conscience.[88]

Another general distinction that may help to demarcate Chancery conscience from private conscience is that between 'outward' and 'inward' things, a distinction that we have encountered for example in Reginald Pecock and which we shall see again. Thus, St. German writes, '[a]nd of the entent inwarde in the herte: mannes lawe can not Juge / and that ys one of the causes why the lawe of god ys necessary … to Juge inwarde thynges'.[89] As this suggests, there is some overlap between 'spirituals' and 'inwarde thynges', but they are not co-extensive. So, for example, '[i]f the force of a promise in conscience depend[s] merely upon the intention of the party who made it, this is a question which no court can try. It must be left to the confessional'.[90] One must be cautious, however, about inferring that inward psychological states are never relevant in, say, Chancery. Guy points out that, in responding in the *Little Treatise* to the charge that uses were an instrument of fraud, St. German distinguishes between uses where the feoffor 'conceive[d] his lord's loss of an evil will' and those where he did not[91]—apparently making something like motive a key criterion for what is unconscientious. Indeed, that God's law—a ground of conscience explicitly contemplated by Chancery—relates particularly to these inward things might imply that Chancery will be disposed to take cognizance of them. On the other hand, of course, the mere fact that an act is 'outward' does not make it justiciable, or susceptible to the conscience of

85 This distinction, at least in some versions, is probably ultimately traceable to Aristotle: see Siegel, 'Aristotelian Basis of English Law', pp. 36ff.

86 *St. German's Doctor and Student*, p. 87.

87 See, notably, John Calvin, *Institutes of the Christian Religion*, trans. H. Beveridge (Peabody, Mass., 2008), pp. 556–7 (Bk. 3, c.19, s. 15): 'let us observe that in man government is twofold: the one spiritual …; the other civil'. 'The former has its seat within the soul, while the latter only regulates the external conduct. We may call the one the spiritual, the other the civil kingdom.'

88 *St. German's Doctor and Student*, p. 229.

89 Ibid., p. 230. Elsewhere, the Doctor cites Gerson's *De vita spirituali anime*: he 'sayth that god wyll that makers of lawes iuge only of outwarde thynges & reserue secrete thynges to hym' (p. 159).

90 'Introduction' to *St. German's Doctor and Student*, p. lvi.

91 *St. German on Chancery and Statute*, p. 86.

equity. The examples are legion, but one relevant to the present context is the naked promise, which, however binding as a matter of private conscience, is not enforceable in Chancery.[92]

A third, generically different, basis of distinction is between matters which can be proven and matters which cannot. Plucknett and Barton observe that an 'example of a duty which must be left to the conscience of the party which has the rare distinction of having been unanimously accepted … is the duty which cannot be established by evidence'.[93] An example referred to by St. German is the party who lies under oath.[94] An oath, in effect being a promise to God, the party's conscience is engaged. But only that person can know about the lie. Sanctions for the breach of the obligation of conscience must be left to the divine tribunal. Again there is overlap between 'spirituals', 'inward things', and 'unprovables': what is internal to a person tends also to remain secret or unknown. So, if the enforceability of a promise depends upon the promisor's intention alone, 'yt ys secrete in [hys] owne conscyence whether he entendyd for to be bounde or naye'.[95] Indeed, it may often be that inward things are susceptible only to one's private conscience exactly because they are unknowable by others.

While these criteria may be sufficient bases for leaving a matter to the private conscience, they are not necessary or exhaustive bases. If a matter is purely spiritual, purely inward, purely secret, then it will almost certainly be left to the internal forum. But the converse is not true: that something is civil, outward or apparent does not mean that it is susceptible to a judgment in Chancery. Many of our ordinary actions, which may in some sense be unconscionable, are not therefore justiciable. This appears to be true even in the judicial context. St. German addresses the question whether a statute, such as 4 Henry IV c. 22, which in some circumstances prohibits remedies based on conscience in Chancery would itself be 'agaynst conscyence'.[96] This may relate to the case of 'a judgment given contrary to the justice of the case by a court of competent jurisdiction' of which Plucknett and Barton say that the 'successful party commits a mortal sin by relying on the judgment if he know the truth, but that is a matter between him and his confessor'.[97] The Doctor defends the statute by saying that it is necessary in order to avoid endless suits and inconvenience. Purely pragmatic considerations relating to the administration of justice might sometimes be a sufficient rationale for leaving something to private conscience. The Student goes on to say that it appears from the statute '*that it* doth not prohybyt equytie / but it prohybyteth only the examynacion of the Iugment / for the eschewynge of … inconuenyence'.[98] This

92 *St. German's Doctor and Student*, p. 229.

93 Ibid.,'Introduction', pp. xxxv–xxxvi.

94 Ibid., p. 109.

95 Ibid., p. 230. See also 'Introduction', p. lvi.

96 Ibid., p. 107.

97 Ibid., 'Introduction', p. xxxvi.

98 Ibid., p. 109.

implies that the statute is concerned only with preventing a substitute judgment on the same matter, not with preventing the ostensibly different process of examining the conscience of the successful party in respect of matters not comprehended by the judgment. As we shall see, this distinction becomes a common strategy for the argument that Chancery equity does not disturb the judgment at law—that is, it merely requires the successful party to exercise his legal rights according to conscience.

Other Concerns about Conscience

Several further points about the status of conscience for St. German and his contemporaries should be mentioned. Two of these I have already touched upon, from a somewhat different angle.

Jurisdictional Competition

The first is what might be called the competition between the common law courts and Chancery equity. This competition is implicit in the More anecdote related at the outset of this chapter, as well as in the question just discussed. It reached a kind of crisis in the Coke-Ellesmere confrontation in the early seventeenth century, but it continued to be an issue for controversialists throughout the seventeenth century. Broadly, the concern was about the effect on the common law of there being a jurisdiction that was perceived as superseding or negating it. A characteristic complaint appears in the *Replication of a Serjeant at the Laws of England*: the subpoena 'is commonly usede nowe, so that the commen lawe of the realme is taking [*sic*] for nothing, but all the lawe that nowe is usede is to determyn which is conscience, and whiche is no conscience'.[99] As we have seen, St. German at least hints at two kinds of response to this concern. One is that the common law, although largely congruent with conscience, does not extend to all justiciable cases of conscience. Chancery, in addressing these residual areas, does not conflict with the law; it merely fills gaps. The other response, which may be just a variant, is that Chancery does not overturn or negate the common law; it merely requires persons to exercise their undoubted common law rights according to what is conscientious in the circumstances. That is, it says nothing about the common law *per se*, but fixes on the conscience of the defendant.

Conscience as Fact-Determination

The second point involves the possibility that conscience for Chancery is significantly a matter of getting at the facts—all the facts, or more of the facts. I have just suggested that a possible basis for distinguishing justiciable conscience

[99] *St. German on Chancery and Statute*, p. 105.

from conscience reserved for the confessional is whether a matter is 'apparent' from evidence or 'secret'. But Chancery offers in this respect a middle ground between what is admissible as evidence by strict common law forms and what is inevitably cached in the breasts of the parties. It is perhaps significant that, in Gerson's allegorical, psychomachic *Treatise Against 'The Romance of the Rose'*, framed as a court case, '[t]he prosecutor had the name of Conscience, for there is nothing she does not know or does not report'.[100] Thus, again, J.H. Baker, in speaking about the failure to take an acquittance case, emphasizes that it is not that the common law judges did not know what was substantively in accordance with conscience, but that they were handcuffed by 'an inflexible system of pleading and proof'.[101] The common law courts were limited in what they could *see*, in informing their consciences as to all the facts, however much they might know very well the major premise of the relevant syllogism of conscience.

As we know, unlike the common law courts, the Court of Chancery had what Baker calls 'a procedure for delving into individual circumstances',[102] or what Rueger, following others, refers to as a way of establishing 'the truth of [a] complaint ... *secundum conscientiam*'.[103] The Chancery was a court of conscience not just because it had a different conception of what was right, but at least partly because it had a more comprehensive means of getting at the factual truth. These means were hardly absolute, of course. So, if on examination by the Chancellor a defendant was adamant in withholding the truth, his lie would be a matter between himself and God, or between himself and his spiritual confessor. From this perspective, the distinction between justiciable and non-justiciable conscience might be simply that what is justiciable has to be limited to what can be judicially known.

Plucknett and Barton refer to a distinction that may be relevant in this context, between formalities that constitute an act and formalities that are merely proof of an act. So, '[i]f an act derive its force merely from the law of man, it may be fairly argued that any requirements of form are part of the definition of the act itself—*forma dat esse rei*'; on the other hand, if the act is 'founded upon the Law of Nature [or reason?], any solemnity which the law of man may require is of necessity not a *solennitas formalis*, but merely a *solennitas probatoria*, imposed for the convenience of proof'.[104] How might this apply to the failure to take an acquittance case? Arguably, a debt is just a contract, and contracts are creatures of the law of man (although *promises* presumably engage the higher laws). Therefore the law of man can make a formality an essential part of the contract (or the discharging of a contract): the contract is not performed if the formalities are not observed. So the Doctor says that it is a matter of 'the law of

100 *Jean Gerson: Early Works*, pp. 378–98, p. 378.

101 'Introduction', *Reports of Sir John Spelman*, p. 39.

102 Ibid., p. 37.

103 Rueger, 'Gerson's Concept of Equity', p. 26.

104 'Introduction', *St. German's Doctor and Student*, p. xxxviii.

reason *secondary*[105] that dettes ought … to be payde'.[106] On this basis, we might say that the contract is not performed until the acquittance is taken. So the debt remains. But if there is a law of *reason* that prohibits the holding or taking of what is another's, the formality is merely one form of proof, among other possible forms of proof. In these circumstances, Chancery may intervene by looking at a wider range of evidence than the procedures of the common law permit. This justifies equity's looking at whether the debt has actually already been repaid, or whether it has been paid twice. In this inquiry, it does not restrict itself to looking only at the presence or absence of the acquittance.

The Variability of Conscience

A third point, one that I have alluded to in this chapter only in passing in Cranmer's advice to More, but which is an ongoing issue for conscience as a juristic principle, is concern about the arbitrariness, or at least variability, of conscience. An early expression of this concern is Thomas Audley's[107] reading at the Inner Temple in 1526, when he refers to '… a law called "conscience", which is always uncertain and depends for the greater part on the "arbytrement" of the judge in conscience'.[108] The point is made emphatically in the *Replication of a Serjeant at the Laws of England*: 'yn what uncertayntie shall the kinges subgiettes stande whan they shalbe put from the lawe of the Realme, and be compellede to be ordrede by the discrecion and conscience of oon man?'[109]

To this criticism, St. German offers two related kinds of responses in the *Little Treatise*. First, the conscience which the Chancellor is bound to follow is objectively based: it is 'that conscience which is groundede upon the lawe of God, and the lawe of *reason, and upon the lawe of* the realme not contrary to the saide

---

105 Harold Berman, 'The Origins of Historical Jurisprudence: Coke, Selden, Hale', *Yale Law Journal* 103/7 (1994): 1651–1737, p. 1659, explains that St. German sought to account for the 'peculiarities of English law by distinguishing between "the law of primary reason" and the "law of secondary reason"', the former consisting of 'general principles applicable at all times and places such as the elements that constitute murder', and the latter consisting of 'uniquely English laws that were the product both of reason and of particular English customs'. It is not self-evident to me why the repayment of debts should be only a law of secondary reason.

106 *St. German's Doctor and Student*, p. 77.

107 Lord Chancellor (1532–44). For his apparently unblinking support of Henry VIII in many of the latter's less creditable machinations, Lord Campbell labels Audley a 'sordid slave' (*Lives of the Lord Chancellors*, vol. 2, p. 121).

108 *St. German on Chancery and Statute*, pp. 79–80.

109 Ibid., p. 101. Behrens, on the basis of the similarity between the reading just referred to and passages like this, raises the possibility that Audley was the author of the *Replication* ('Early Tudor Debate', 161n). Guy suggests that St. German himself might have composed the *Replication* as a kind of 'straw man' for his response in the *Little Treatise* (*St. German on Chancery and Statute*, p. 57).

lawes of God nor *to ye* lawe of reason'.[110] We have seen this point developed at length in *Doctor and Student*. The essential idea is that conscience is itself firmly rooted in *law*. Second, according to St. German, the Chancellor is a particularly accurate reader of conscience: 'it is not to presume that the Chauncellor, whiche is alwaies appoyncted to his office ... as a man of singuler wysdom and good conscience, wilbe disceyvede thoroughe suche errours yn conscience'—again, at least partly because he will have 'so strayte rules to thorder of his conscience'.[111] As we have seen before and as we shall see again, the postulated ruledness of conscience *versus* its supposed unruliness is a major site of contention about conscience as a juristic principle.

One aspect of this issue is that, however ostensibly unguided decisions based on conscience might initially have been, by St. German's time 'the jurisdiction was well over a century old, and on many topics the pressure of litigation had led to the development of distinct bodies of principle'.[112] Thus, there were developing identifiable rules of conscience 'which were coming more and more to look like a part of English law'.[113] This leads to the possibility—or likelihood—that specific equitable rules continued to be referred to in terms of conscience, but no analysis relative to conscience accompanied such references, nor, really, was any such analysis necessary. Moreover, it leads to the possibility that conscience would, over time, lose its force as a generator of new doctrines.

The Rhetorical Power of 'Conscience'

A fourth point is the 'rhetorical' one, and one can detect this at this time in both the aspects—rhetorical inertia and rhetorical force—I have previously mentioned. The first of these arises from what I have just been saying: the language of conscience may have persisted as part of the inherited discourse long after conscience as a dynamic principle in the development of the law was becoming attenuated. A second aspect is the resort to 'conscience' for the power the concept had in the culture of the time. As for example Alexandra Walsham notes, '[t]he language of conscience was in constant use in early modern England'.[114] We have already noticed that Henry VIII resorted to conscience as a kind of ultimate (and perhaps disingenuous) justification for actions whose motivations may have been less than creditable. That is, conduct otherwise questionable might have been clothed in the respectable rhetorical garb of conscience. The author of the *Replication* appears to

110 Ibid., p. 123.

111 Ibid., p. 124.

112 Plucknett and Barton, 'Introduction', *St. German's Doctor and Student*, p. xlviii.

113 Ibid.

114 Alexandra Walsham, 'Ordeals of Conscience: Casuistry, Conformity and Confessional Identity in Post-Reformation England', in Harald E. Braun and Edward Vallance (eds), *Contexts of Conscience in Early Modern Europe, 1500–1700* (Basingstoke, 2004), pp. 32–48, p. 32.

make a charge of this kind: complaining about resort to the *subpoena*, he says that it is 'a wryt abusede, yn my mynde, contrary to the commen lawe of the realme, and contrary to reason and all good conscience; and *yet it is collowrede by the pretense of conscience*'.[115] Conscience associated with the Chancery is a 'pretense' for things that, in the Serjeant's view, are highly problematic. This will not be the last time that we shall see Chancery criticized for compromising the rule of law under the colour of conscience.

Conclusion

Early in this chapter, I referred to the fairly common view that the early Tudor period was a time of transition for the Chancery and that Christopher St. German was a key figure in this change. No doubt both these positions are valid, but, as I have tried to show, they have to be qualified. Without question, St. German identified the common law (especially as opposed to canon law) as at least a partial guide for conscience. But *Doctor and Student* is *about* conscience; it treats conscience as central. Moreover, St. German preserves an essential role for Chancery in the matter of juridical conscience; he explicitly, in the *Little Treatise*, defends it as a separate court. It may be, as some commentators have argued, that in spite of his defence of Chancery, St. German undermined Chancery as a distinctive jurisdiction: if conscience is in the law anyway, why should not the common law courts administer it, as far as it needs to be administered? If all that prevents a full recognition of conscience in the common law courts are certain formal or procedural impediments, surely these can be adjusted? Indeed, More's approach to the common law judges appears to acknowledge that conscience could be quite capaciously administered in the common law courts.

An answer to this might be that the common law courts must be limited to the established law in seeking the grounds of conscience. It might, in a sense, be a contradiction in terms to say that the courts of law might seek inspiration outside the law. Thus, 'logically', for the law of God and the law of reason to contribute to legal development, it must be in another forum. This assumes a rather positivistic view of the law, of course, inconsistent with St. German's account of equity—if not conscience—as an intrinsic principle.

In any event, as we have already seen and shall continue to see, *Doctor and Student* did not obviate the concern with conscience and the law, nor did it end the association of Chancery, particularly, with conscience. Indeed, as I have already suggested and as we shall see in detail, the discourse of conscience persisted, if not in exactly the terms we have been examining at least in terms more or less explicitly continuous with them, late into the seventeenth century.

---

115 *St. German on Chancery and Statute*, p. 102; my emphasis.

Chapter 4
The Later Sixteenth Century

Introduction

W.J. Jones, who has written in detail about the Elizabethan Court of Chancery as an institution,[1] treats the role of conscience in the court's jurisdiction rather variously. Thus, he observes that 'the words "equity" and "conscience" were … often used in a general rather than a narrow sense' but he does not really explain the distinction (p. 273). And, while acknowledging that the sixteenth century had a developing 'doctrine of equity or conscience' (p. 301), he also says that 'men in the fifteenth and sixteenth century failed to develop a consistent … picture of the constituent elements of equity or conscience…' (p. 418). The court records of the time, he says, 'do not appear to provide the evidence to sustain notions of an elevated theory' (p. 42); indeed, he describes declarations that decrees 'rested upon good equity and conscience' as part of a 'ritual' (p. 301). This leaves unclear the extent to which considerations of conscience were substantial or merely formulaic. Jones also suggests that '[c]onscience reflects a norm of common people' (p. 419), involving 'vague concepts' such as 'fair play' and 'justice between party and party' (p. 420). At the same time, Chancery's jurisdiction was 'cathartic', concerned 'to cleanse the conscience of the wrongdoer rather than to safeguard the excess interests of the wronged' (p. 424). One discerns in these isolated, rather disconnected, assertions some tantalizing ideas, and several conventional ones, but they scarcely offer a coherent or developed picture of the conscience of Elizabethan equity.

My objective in this chapter is to offer a more detailed or comprehensive, if not more definitive, assessment of the status of conscience in equity in the later sixteenth century, roughly to the end of Elizabeth's reign in 1603. This enterprise will involve considering a range of case law, which, if it does not evince 'high theory,' might permit us to draw some inferences about what the Chancery and courts exercising a similar jurisdiction were about in applying 'conscience'. It will involve as well some attention to such theory as there was—notably the commentaries on Chancery and equity by such writers as Robert Snagg, William West and Edward Hake.

---

1 W.J. Jones, *The Elizabethan Court of Chancery* (Oxford, 1967).

Relevance of the Time-Frame

Before moving to this examination of materials bearing on my subject, I do want to say something about why this time-frame—which I have chosen partly as a matter of convenience—might be substantively significant.

The Changing Law?

One possibility is suggested by D.E.C. Yale's observation concerning Hake, who wrote about equity near the close of the century, that 'as St. Germain had stood at the end of ecclesiastical equity, so Hake stood at the beginning of the new secular system'.[2] This could point to the end of the sixteenth century as a kind of watershed for equity. Certainly, Thomas Egerton, Lord Ellesmere, Lord Keeper and Chancellor about this time, is associated with the process of regularization, and perhaps secularization, of equity. At the same time, my reading of the materials suggests continuity, rather than a sharp break. Thus, for example, Hake explicitly adopts the work of his predecessors. He abbreviates his discussion of Chancery equity because (he says) it has recently been comprehensively treated by William West, the second part of whose *Symbolæography* includes a 'Treatise of Equitie, and the jurisdiction and proceedings of the high Court of Chauncerie',[3] and by Richard Crompton (c. 1529–99), whose work on the jurisdiction of various courts contains a section on Chancery.[4] As we shall see, West's work (and, for that matter, Hake's itself) draws heavily and uncritically on *Doctor and Student*, and Crompton's cites as authorities both St. German and medieval sources, so that the distinctions Yale's comment suggests are rather blurred. Moreover, as we have seen, *Doctor and Student* was re-published often in the seventeenth century—as, too, was *Symbolæography*. So the work that Yale sees as marking the end of an era in equity continued to be influential into the next era, and the next. And, of course, Ellesmere himself straddled the Elizabethan and Jacobean periods and, as we shall see, can hardly be said to have superseded earlier assumptions.

Reformed Conscience?

Another reason for choosing the late sixteenth century as a site for exposition is that, by this time, the Reformation was solidly established in England. Various

---

2 'Introduction' to Edward Hake, *Epieikeia:A Dialogue on Equity in Three Parts*, ed. D.E.C. Yale (New Haven, 1953), p. xvi.

3 William West, 'Of the Chauncerie' in *Three Treatises, of the Second part of Symbolæographie* (London, 1594). Indeed, one of Hake's speakers says that 'there is almost nothing more to be sayde of [equity] then a man may readily find in [West's] book' (Hake, p. 120).

4 Richard Crompton, *L'Avthoritie et Ivrisdiction des Covrts de la Maiestie de la Roygne* (London, 1594), section 3. (The dedication is to Sir John Puckering, Lord Keeper.)

authors have remarked a change in the role and characterization of conscience as a result of the growth of Protestantism. M.G. Baylor claims that, for Luther at least, 'the most important religious function of the conscience' became, instead of evaluating individual actions or choices, assessing 'the individual as a whole', and recognizing the essentially flawed condition of human nature and the need for divine grace.[5] Baylor points out that, since the scholastics' *synteresis* is located in humans' corrupt reason and will, it became irrelevant for Luther (p. 182), and so he discarded it as an element in his later account of conscience. To the extent that such an account of conscience develops, it compromises conscience as a juristic principle, since it removes the focus from particular justiciable acts and it makes it more a matter of inspiration than of reasoning. An approach that assesses specific conduct and attaches to it specific measures of discharge in the form of penance conforms more to the legal pattern of analysis than does an approach that contemplates the renovation of the whole person by means of free grace. Similarly, an account that posits a faculty of the soul that retains at least a residual capacity to apprehend the right norms of conduct fits more cogently with our concept of a juristic principle than one which posits that that faculty is radically impaired.

Concomitantly, as Harold Berman points out, the Reformation suggested a new kind of relationship between the civil and the spiritual. Luther taught that the church 'belongs to the heavenly kingdom of grace and faith' while 'the kingdom of "this world," is the kingdom of sin and death ... governed by Law. It is the secular authority alone that governs the secular society'.[6] This might imply that the realm in which conscience most typically operates—the realm which relates to the condition of one's soul—is essentially private or otherworldly, so that, as Berman says, at least initially, 'Luther's emphasis on the Biblical faith and Christian conscience ... seems ... to move in a direction away from ... law' (p. 191).

One must be cautious about generalizing from such observations. As Berman goes on to explain, the Lutheran concept of Christian conscience is not radically incompatible with secular law; indeed, he describes how Luther's follower Johann Oldendorp reconciled Protestant conscience with that law. In any case, Luther was scarcely the whole of the Reformation, especially in England, and, as we shall see in the next chapter, Protestant casuistry did not abandon the terms of reference of scholastic conscience or the preoccupation with assessing the moral dimensions of specific conduct. Indeed, West (who was not a casuist) essentially adopts St. German's description of conscience and, to take just one Elizabethan ecclesiastic as an example, John Woolton (c. 1537–94), who was to become Bishop of Exeter, discusses conscience in terms reminiscent of what we have already seen.[7] Thus, for him, *synderesis*, located in the contemplative understanding, is 'the keeper and

5 Michael G. Baylor, *Action and Person: Conscience in Late Scholasticism and the Young Luther* (Leiden, 1977), pp. 196, 200, 252–3.

6 Harold Berman, 'Conscience and Law: The Lutheran Reformation and the Western Legal Tradition', *Journal of Law and Religion*, 5/1 (1987): pp. 177–202, p. 180.

7 John Woolton, *Of the Conscience* (London, 1576).

conseruer of notices, or understandinges, which are bredde with vs by nature', and '[i]n the second place of the minde is Intelligence practicall, which consisteth in accion' and 'therin is the Conscience properly placed'.[8] The process of reasoning in conscience is syllogistic, the *synderesis* providing the major premise, the practical intelligence providing the minor premise and the conclusion—a 'Judgement, pronouncing of all accions, whether they be worthy of prayse or disprayse …'.[9] Here, clearly, it is not the whole person, but rather 'all accions', which conscience regards, and this is certainly consistent with much later Protestant casuistry.

As we have previously noted, another way of seeing the change for conscience (and for casuistry) wrought by the Reformation has been proffered, for example, by Meg Lota Brown. While Catholic casuistry, she says, posited set answers and ostensibly claimed to be authoritative, Protestant casuistry emphasized the *process* of moral self-examination and made it a matter for the 'individual conscience and reason'.[10] Thomas Pickering's complaint that Catholic casuists and priests regarded themselves as 'made by Christ himselfe' as '*iudges of the Cases of conscience*, hauing in their owne hands a *iudicarie power* and authoritie *truly* and *properly* to binde or to loose …'[11] captures the concern.

Moving the authority for moral assessments from a uniform, external authority to the individual person would appear to make conscience more subjective. Theoretically, of course, it was not subjective, for decisions of conscience, as the Protestant casuists regularly remind us, are referable to the laws of God (or perhaps other laws). But making every person a judge in conscience will certainly tend to fragment the edifice. Paradoxically, the Catholic practice of casuistry, as Brown describes it, displays more characteristics of 'law' than the Protestant version. Thus, there is an authoritative judge (as Pickering disparagingly notes); decisions are based on 'precedent and canon law'.[12] Indeed, Brown refers to the 'legalism of Catholic case divinity'.[13] One could speculate, then, that the Protestant approach to conscience was less compatible with the concern of the Chancellors (at least from Ellesmere to Nottingham) to make equity more regular, law-like, and consistent. Thus, as Chancery law became more systematized and rule-governed, and conscience became more a matter of internal, individual dialogue (a possibility that I shall consider in detail later), a divergence would have developed.

---

8 Ibid., sigs. B4v–C1r; EEBO image 6659:9.

9 Ibid., sigs. C1r–C1v; EEBO images 6659:9–10.

10 Meg Lota Brown, *Donne and the Politics of Conscience in Early Modern England* (Leiden, 1995), p. 30. See also Camille Wells Slights, 'The Conscience of the King: *Henry V* and the Reformed Conscience', *Philological Quarterly*, 80/1 (2001): 37–55, pp. 42–3.

11 Thomas Pickering, 'Epistle Dedicatorie' to William Perkins, *The Whole Treatise of the Cases of Conscience* (Cambridge, 1606), sig. ¶4r; EEBO image 14434:4.

12 Brown., p. 25.

13 Ibid., p. 46. See P.J. Holmes, *Elizabethan Casuistry* (Catholic Record Society, 1981) for two 'English' Catholic casuistical texts from the sixteenth century.

One aspect of Catholic casuistry that several writers have identified (again rather paradoxically in view of its ostensibly greater coherence with 'law') as associating it with relativism and, indeed, disingenuousness, and thus bringing it into disrepute, was the development of the school known as 'probabilism', notoriously associated with the Jesuits. Brown offers a somewhat tendentious description of the probabilists' basic approach: the doctrine holds, she says, that 'if one has the support of authority, one may disregard a law, even though conceivably there are stronger arguments and more authorities in favour of the law'.[14] Similarly, Lowell Gallagher discerns a 'drift' in the development of casuistry from the earlier 'rigorous adherence to the law' and 'objective morality' that guided the first casuists, the 'tutiorists',[15] to the 'gradual development of a subjective morality' implicit in probabilism, which 'turned all secure, authoritative readings … into provisional, unstable ones' (p. 7). One must again treat such large generalizations warily. But, to the extent that popular perceptions of some kinds of moral inquiry associated them with sophistry and self-interest, their creditability, and that of their focus, conscience, might be eroded. Thus, both Protestant individualism and perceived Catholic relativism would have rendered conscience more tenuous as an objective touchstone.

Apart from the putatively distinctive features of Protestantism or of particular schools of casuistry, the Reformation might have contributed to the relativization of conscience simply by the proliferation of religious sects that accompanied it.[16] Because of the diversity of belief, coupled with the pressure to conform, individuals were increasingly faced with the issue of conscientious religious objection, and with it greater awareness that non-conforming consciences could be sincere. This is not, of course, to say that many—or any—of the disputants would have said simply, 'Whatever a person's conscience tells him or her is right for that person, so long as s/he is sincere'. These dissenting consciences, in whatever context, were customarily reprobated as erroneous. But the diversity of conscience no doubt became more insistent, which again would have tended to destabilize conscience

---

14 Brown, p. 58. For a recent argument that probabilism has got an undeservedly bad reputation, see M.W.F. Stone, 'Scrupulosity and Conscience: Probabilism in Early Modern Scholastic Ethics' in Harald E. Braun and Edward Vallance (eds), *Contexts of Conscience in Early Modern Europe, 1500–1700* (Basingstoke, 2004), pp. 1–16. Stone gives the less pejorative description of probabilism as deferring to authority where two or more positions are probable, even if the authority supports a position that turns out to be less probable. A Protestant response to probabilism was *probabiliorism*, which requires one to choose 'the most probable solution to a case of conscience' (Brown, p. 60).

15 Lowell Gallagher, *Medusa's Gaze: Casuistry and Conscience in the Renaissance* (Stanford, 1991), p. 6. The tutiorists emphasized choosing the safest course, thus insisting upon caution in case of doubt.

16 See, for example, Alexandra Walsham, 'Ordeals of Conscience: Casuistry, Conformity and Confessional Identity in Post-Reformation England', in Harald C. Braun and Edward Vallance (eds), *Contexts of Conscience in Early Modern Europe, 1500–1700* (Basingstoke, 2004), pp. 32–48.

as the kind of uniform rule-giver that could serve as a juristic principle. Moreover, it might have accentuated the divide between the religious and the secular, tending to make the latter more the domain of law while simultaneously altering the balance between conscience and public convenience.

A wide-ranging recent treatment of conscience in Elizabethan England is that of Gallagher, who confronts head-on the paradox of conscience. Noting as we saw in Chapter 1 that the discourse of conscience was a 'privileged' one in the period,[17] he argues that, while it was regularly invoked to reinforce social, political, and cultural conformity, it carried in its very nature a destabilizing potential. That is because conscience, as reflected in casuistical practice (and like equity), involved engagement with particular 'circumstances of time, place, and person' (p. 133). Although casuistry can be seen as a way of assimilating the particular or anomalous case to a form of approved institutional discourse, a way of taming the aberrant, its very practice militated against this: it constantly engaged the variety of human moral experience. As Gallagher points out, although the conventional view was that equity could be measured 'out along,/According to the line of conscience',[18] that line may turn out to be far from a straight measure, and may be equivocal, fragmented, or multiple. If such a tendency is inherent in the examination of conscience, conscience becomes problematic, to say the least, as a juristic principle.[19] In fact, Gallagher makes the connection with law, saying the 'the action of equity in relation to the law virtually replicated that of *conscientia* in relation to *synteresis*'[20]—*synteresis* in this context being a 'privileged, authoritative discourse' and *conscientia* being 'a host of subordinated, not to say suppressed, discourses … that contextualized what *synteresis* held up as indisputable …' (p. 142). Although the analogy is not without its awkwardness,[21] the main point is clear: equity, understood in terms of conscience, has a potentially 'roguish' (to use John Selden's term) quality which *may* render it unsustainable as a juristic principle. This is assuming that there is such a thing as a stable, certain juristic principle with which equity can be contrasted. Arguably, hiving conscience and its apprehended anarchic tendencies off by relegating them to a different institutional

---

[17] Gallagher, p. 1.

[18] Edmund Spenser, *The Faerie Queene*, Bk. 5, Canto 1:7 (*Edmund Spenser: The Faerie Queene*, eds Thomas P. Roche, Jr. and C. Patrick O'Donnell, Jr. [New Haven 1978]).

[19] I am of course mindful that the discourse of certainty within a system of legal rules may itself partake of the illusory, but the (perhaps inevitable) indeterminacy of legal rules is at most tangentially my concern here.

[20] Gallagher, p. 145.

[21] For example, equity is often—as by St. German—characterized as the perfection of the law, as itself containing the authoritative principles that may be imperfectly realized in the forms of law. Moreover, equity is described—again, say, by St. German—in terms of conscience, which conceptually contains *synteresis*. So, to equate *synteresis* with law, rather than equity, is a little awkward.

container—Chancery—was a way of saving the appearance of ordinary law as determinate.[22]

There are thus a number of ways in which the second half of the sixteenth century might have been transitional for conscience (and equity) and which could justify making this period a discrete focus. These possibilities notwithstanding, however, much of the conventional discourse about the conscience of equity does appear to assume that it could provide a 'line', or at least that it was a necessary complement to the law. Certainly, conscience continued to be referred to as somehow key to equity, and it is not easy to discern a radical or even a clear change in how its role was described.

The Continuing Role of Conscience

One need not look far to confirm this continuing centrality of conscience. West's 'Treatise of Equitie' includes many, many sample Chancery pleadings. Those I have looked at I would say *ordinarily* contain expressions claiming that the defendant has acted 'contrarie to all right, equitie, and good conscience' and/or asking for an order that will 'stand with right, equitie, and good conscience'. Conventional practice appears to have assumed the operation of conscience, or at least to have adopted the (perhaps formulaic) discourse of conscience uncritically.

Similarly, Crompton's treatment of Chancery contains regular allusions to conscience as part of the ordinary discourse in this context: the Chancellor is the 'chiefe Judge … de matters de conscience', although in matters 'de common ley il les doit adiudger, & proceder accordant al common ley, & nemy per conscience';[23] if X is holding goods to the use of Y and Z interferes with them, X 'est tenus in consciens de mainteiner actiõ de trespas';[24] 'pur ceo que le Plaintife ne poit auer *quid pro quo, ideo in* conscience lobligour doit releas le Obligation';[25] a feoffor to uses 'na remedie per le cõmon ley, mes il auera remedie en le Chancerie per conscience';[26] 'quant al matters de conscience, [the Chancellor] eux determinera

[22] This point, as we shall see, was advanced by some writers in the seventeenth century in response to agitation to dissolve the Chancery and allow the ordinary courts to dispense equity. The need to isolate discretionary judicial activity by limiting it to a distinct tribunal was also a justification put forward by Lord Hardwicke in the mid-eighteenth century for maintaining a separate court of equity (see his letter to Lord Kames reproduced in Philip C. Yorke, *The Life and Correspondence of Philip Yorke, Earl of Hardwicke, Lord High Chancellor of Great Britain* (3 vols, New York, 1977), vol. 2, p. 550).

[23] Crompton, fol. 41v; EEBO image 9565:47.

[24] Ibid., fol. 43r; EEBO image 9565:48.

[25] Ibid., fol. 44v; EEBO image 9565:50.

[26] Ibid., fol. 45v; EEBO image 9565:51.

solonque conscience';[27] 'le rent est extinct en ley, et nemy en conscience';[28] and so on. A good number—but not all—of these allusions are to fifteenth-century materials, but Crompton adopts the language without demur, making no effort to confine it to its earlier historical context or to suggest it has become obsolete.

Conscience in the Cases

A survey of equity cases from the period collected by W.H. Bryson[29] reveals many references to conscience in contexts with which we are familiar. A Common Pleas case from 1594 describes the Chancery as 'an ancient court of conscience'.[30] Several cases juxtaposc 'law' and 'conscience' in ways that make clear that the latter term describes the jurisdiction of equity: 'the lord keeper [Sir John Puckering] says that the justices were of opinion that neither by [the common] law nor [in] conscience [did] [the plaintiff] have a right';[31] '[t]he Lord [Keeper] BROMLEY [was] of opinion ... that the land should go as the [common] law had settled it and conscience should be supplied with money';[32] although a widow with only a life estate who had joined her husband in granting, for consideration, a lease for three lives to the plaintiff was not bound in law, 'the court thought [that] it should be helped in conscience'.[33]

Similarly, conscience is often invoked as the court's criterion in determining cases. In the *Earl of Shrewsbury's Case*, a copyhold was held to be good as a matter of conscience.[34] In *Morris* v. *Morris* one of the parties contends that there is 'no conscience' to aid his opponent,who had not acted in good faith.[35] Sometimes,

---

[27] Ibid., fol. 46v; EEBO image 9565:52.

[28] Ibid., fol. 50r; EEBO image 9565:55.

[29] *Cases Concerning Equity and the Courts of Equity 1550–1660*, ed. W.H. Bryson (2 vols, London, 2001).

[30] Ibid., case 70, vol. 1, p. 139.

[31] *Witham* v. *Waterhouse* (1596), ibid., case 80, vol. 1, p. 244. [All but last set of brackets in source.]

[32] *Crudge* v. *Lower* (1581–82), ibid., item 118 ('Cases and Notes [Ch. C. 1580–c. 1600]'), case 98, vol. 1, p. 244. [All but first set of brackets in source.]

[33] *Damery* v. *Woston* (1594), ibid., item 118, case 152, vol. 1, p. 252. [Brackets in source.] And see *Stone* v. *Withepoole* (1588) Owen 94, ER 924, where Egerton, counsel for the plaintiff, argues that although an executor in the circumstances is admittedly not chargeable by law, yet in equity and conscience he is chargeable in Chancery.

[34] (c. 1573), *Cases Concerning Equity*, case 11, vol, 1, p. 100.

[35] (After 1580), ibid., case 25, vol. 1, p. 109. See also *Cotton* v. *Causton* (1579) Cary 79, ER 42, where the court thinks an outcome 'in conscience to be meet'; *Lacy* v. *Anderson* (1581–82) Choyce Cases in Chancery 155–6, where 'the Court thinks it no conscience' that a widow should have dower in freehold lands as well as copyhold lands devised to her in lieu of dower; and *Corbet's Case* (1600) I Coke's Reports 83b, p. 87b, ER 187, p. 198, where we are told that the Chancellor would oblige a litigant 'according to conscience and the intent of the parties'.

specific equitable doctrines are referred to conscience: thus, in *Finch's Case*, the principle (which we have seen elsewhere and will encounter again) that a testator's debts are to be paid before his ward or other legatees is said to be 'according to the civil law and good conscience'.[36]

Sometimes, even where conscience is not explicitly mentioned, other language makes it evident that equity judges are thinking in terms of the morality of a party's conduct. In *Smallman* v. *Pollard*, for example, a creditor's 'crafty and false dealings' in taking double repayment of a debt are condemned;[37] in *Pomery* v. *Ford*, it was held that if A reposes a trust in B to defraud C, and B breaks the trust 'it is not in equity to be helped';[38] in *Orrell* v. *Eccleston*, Egerton refuses to enforce a trust made to protect land from forfeiture on the anticipated attainder of the feoffor 'because the practice was lewd and dishonest …'.[39] And, in another type of case, he warns that he will not countenance a claim if 'there be usury or patching or paltering chevisance in the case'.[40]

Some cases go further, suggesting that the Chancellor is still thinking in the religious terms historically associated with Chancery. Egerton, in one case, denies a plaintiff's claim on the basis that, in previous dealings with the defendant, the former had falsified accounts and 'untrue accounts … do never before God nor in good conscience work the debtor's release'.[41] In another, he says that 'he would not trust a corporation of all [the] persons in the world with the performance of his will … or any charitable act committed to them in trust for the soul's health of the testator; for he said a body politic had no soul to lose but private men had'.[42] Possible peril to the soul of the testator or trustee is a powerful persuasive. Although Egerton may not be going so far here as to say (as, for example, Archbishop Morton had a hundred years earlier) that it is the business of Chancery to cure defendants' souls, concern for this spiritual dimension is clearly part of his intellectual framework.

In yet another case, Egerton upholds a testamentary trust in favour of 'certain recusants and obstinate papists', because 'they [are] men and ought to be pitied and relieved', and because alms-giving is meritorious irrespective of whether the recipients are good or bad.[43] Here what is at stake is the spiritual condition of the alms-giver, the testator. Egerton appears to be giving legal recognition to the 'relenting heart' and the 'merciful and tender compassion' of the testator. These

36 (1579–87), *Cases Concerning Equity*, case 22, vol. 1, p. 107.

37 (1600), ibid., case 91, vol. 1, p. 159.

38 (1600), ibid., item 118, case 341, vol. 1, p. 275.

39 (1601), ibid., item 119 ('Cases in Tempore Egerton [Ch. C. 1598–c. 1602]'), case 222, vol. 1, p. 307.

40 Ibid., item 119 case 179, vol. 1, p. 299.

41 *Hayward* v. *Trumble* (1596), quoted in Jones, p. 439.

42 *Cases Concerning Equity*, item 119, case 123, vol. 1, p. 290. [Brackets in source.]

43 Ibid., item 119, case 150, vol. 1, p. 290.

will 'entreat' for him 'before God',[44] but they also (and for that reason) apparently affect the conscience of equity. The Chancellor may no longer be in the business of positively saving souls, but Egerton here is not prepared to gainsay the testator's provision for his own spiritual well-being.

If equity judges at this time took into account the moral quality of parties' conduct, they seem to have been less sympathetic to litigants' foolishness—that is, situations where one's bad judgment put one at a disadvantage.[45] The issue has, potentially, two dimensions. Foolishness or improvident conduct *on the part of the plaintiff* could be a reason for precluding a claim in conscience. This would be analogous to, but not quite the same, as the 'clean hands' doctrine, precluding a person who has acted unconscientiously from making a claim in equity. Perhaps something like this reasoning lies behind the position taken by the author of the *Replication of a Serjeant at the Laws of England* that a debtor who has failed to take an acquittance when he repaid the debt should not be relieved in conscience: his own folly was the reason for his remaining liable on the obligation.[46] 'Folly'—or neglect, or inattentiveness—fits rather awkwardly with the clean hands doctrine because it arguably does not entail the kind of moral failing that conscience ordinarily addresses,[47] although it might engage issues of diligence, or lack thereof.

The other dimension involves a focus on the defendant: is it unconscientious for him or her to retain a benefit arising from the plaintiff's foolish or improvident act? While, say, Christian charity might dictate restitution of such a benefit, the conscience of equity appears not to have been so indulgent. We have already noticed the maxim *Deus est procurator fatuorum*: God is the advocate of the foolish. This suggests *a contrario* that a human court—even Chancery—is not such an advocate. Egerton and others appear to have adopted this position. In one case, invoking a variant of the maxim—*Deus protector fatuorum*—he observes that he will not 'meddle' with a foolish bargain.[48] In another case, a wife is not given relief because the judge 'accounted [it] her foolishness that she has taken

44 Ibid.

45 Although J.H. Baker, *The Oxford History of the Laws of England, Volume VI 1483–1558* (Oxford, 2003), p. 41, intimates that Chancery might have been rather more indulgent towards 'personal weakness' or 'folly' than was the common law.

46 *Christopher St. German on Chancery and Statute*, ed. J.A. Guy (London, 1985), p. 100.

47 Of course, the debtor's failure may involve different scenarios: lack of awareness of the legal requirement, lack of concern or attention, or mistake based on a misleading representation by the creditor, etc. Each of these scenarios would lead to a different calculus of conscience.

48 *Tufton* v. *Waller* (1598), *Cases Concerning Equity*, item 119, case 12, vol. 1, p. 279. The issue is not uncomplicated, however. As Jones, for example, points out, one of the things conventionally helped 'in conscience' was mistake—which would often involve a litigant's imprudence (p. 416).

such a husband'.[49] And in a case in which a woman had transferred some of her husband's assets to a third party on trust for her, the ascerbic Egerton says that he does not sit there 'to relieve fools and buzzards that cannot keep their money from their wives'.[50] In the latter two instances one senses that the plaintiffs' folly is being treated almost as a bar to an equitable claim, so that the two dimensions of the issue run together. If one's foolishness creates a benefit for another, the court appears disinclined to entertain the first person's claim that retention of the benefit by the other violates conscience. If one were to apply the rule—routinely said to be a precept given by *synteresis*—'do unto others as you would have others do unto you' to its full extent, one might say that conscience requires a person to attend to others' interests and lack of sagacity in bargaining.

It may be worth reflecting further how conscience is or is not engaged in such cases, taking the failure to obtain an acquittance case as an example. Again, we will recall that the author of the *Replication* insists that the debtor's folly should preclude relief. But Chancery does give relief in such cases. Does this mean that the Chancellor is adopting the position that he is the protector of the foolish, that an aspect of his enforcement of conscience involves protecting people from their own improvidence?

Almost certainly not. One can usually identify other factors that engage equity's conscience. If, for example, the creditor leads the debtor to believe that he will not sue on the debt in the absence of an acquittance, the creditor is not benefiting just from the debtor's foolishness; he is making a fraudulent representation, and this affects his conscience. Of course, this is not the typical situation, which supposes an absence of active fraud like this—although Hake for example does rationalize equity's intervening on the basis that the debtor's repayment 'was or might be deemed to have byne by his over greate truste and confidence in the obligee'.[51] But even in the 'pure' situation, a characterization that more evidently engages the creditor's conscience is possible. By hypothesis, he has been repaid. Repayment of the debt is something that is due to him. He has received exactly what is his. To purport to take it again would be to take what is another's. This may be distinguished from the case of a person paying an excessive price for something, or even paying a usurious rate of interest. Misvaluing something is ostensibly different from taking something for nothing.

So, in granting relief in such cases, equity was identifying something beyond the plaintiff's folly to bind the defendant's conscience. Of course, the failure to judge prudently must be distinguished from defects compromising a person's *capacity* for discernment. Thus, when relief is granted in a case like *Kettleby* v.

---

[49] *Cases Concerning Equity*, item 117 ('Richard Powle's Reports [Ch. 1579–1600]')', case 29, vol. 1, pp. 175–6.

[50] Ibid., item 120 ('Cases in Tempore Egerton [Ch. c. 1599–c. 1604]', case 91, vol. 1, p. 334.

[51] Hake, p. 123.

Kettleby because there was 'fraudulent practicing with an old doting man'[52] it is because there are two kinds of factors affecting the defendant's conscience: his own fraud and the compromised capacity of the other party. In the absence of 'conscience factors' such as these, equity appears not to have been willing to intercede to save people from their own foolishness.

Most of the cases I have cited involve the normative dimension of conscience. But the other aspect of conscience, fact determination, appears quite regularly as well. As I have remarked more than once in this study, a significant part of what it meant for the Chancery to be a court of conscience was that the Chancellor had a greater latitude to examine parties and witnesses as to what they in conscience know and, correspondingly, to inform his own conscience, so as to make a more fact-sensitive determination. Egerton refers to this latitude when he says that Masters in Chancery 'may examine witnesses *ad informandum conscientiam* [*judicis*] … or [proceed] to minister an oath to the plaintiff or defendant himself, or [proceed] by any other way to know the truth even as amply as he himself might'.[53] Examinations *ad informandum conscientiam judicis* were a specific procedure exceptionally available,[54] but the name of the process reminds us, first, that gathering facts was an aspect of the operation of judicial conscience and, second, that it was ultimately the Chancellor's conscience (and not, say, a jury's) that was being informed. Egerton more than once refers the admission of evidence to conscience. He cannot 'send for any to appear before him to certify him of anything whereof his conscience doubts'; nor will he 'give faith to a Londoner's shop book nor receive it for any manner of proof, for he said it was no evidence to bind a lord chancellor's conscience'.[55] I am not here concerned with the cogency of the particular rulings, but rather with Egerton's general concern that, in the Court of Chancery, his conscience should be fully and correctly informed.

Related to Chancery's aspirations to obtain comprehensive information is equity's greater willingness to consider 'inward things'—that is, not only to admit a greater range of evidence, but evidence relating to a wider range of facts regarded as material. Egerton does say that '[c]onditions or contingent things that will alter uses … must be grounded upon overt acts that can be known to others, and not upon secret intentions or meanings that cannot be known to anyone

---

52 (1599), *Cases Concerning Equity*, item 118, case 319, vol. 1, p. 272.

53 Ibid., item 119, case 210, vol. 1, p. 305. [Brackets in source.] Jones quotes the following form of an interrogatory: 'Item, do you not know or have you not credibly heard or are you not fully persuaded in your conscience that …?' (p. 238, citing *Pulter* v. *Bristowe* [C24/293, no. 64]).

54 Thus, on a point already examined, a witness *ad informandum conscientiam judicis* will be heard only if he 'be a man without all colour of exception' (*Willoughby* v. *Paramore* (1596), *Cases Concerning Equity*, case 78, vol. 1, p. 147); and such evidence may (or may not) be received after publication of the initial interrogatories and answers (ibid., item 119, case 46, vol. 1, p. 284).

55 *Matthews* v. *Askwill* (1604), ibid., item 120, case 67, vol. 1, p. 329.

except God and the party himself'.[56] That is, he recognizes that juridical acts must depend upon evidence, and that some things are knowable only by the person him or herself and by God. However, he says elsewhere that, when he can, he will consider inward things: he 'would ever judge according to the intention of the parties but with this [exception], that if the intention be not apparent, then [he will judge] as the [common] law will';[57] where such an intention appears, he will not be affected because some 'nice strain' or 'nice caption' of the common law has not been observed.[58] At one level this attitude appears to instance the maxim that equity regards the intention, not the form. But it also suggests that the Chancellor might be prepared to delve deeper to acquire evidence of that intention.

The last point arising from these cases that I want to mention at this stage is, again, how determinations in Chancery are rationalized as not interfering with or negating the common law on the basis that they are concerned only with the defendant's conscience. In *Hurd* v. *Dodington*, we learn that '[a] judgment [is] no let to examine [the] equity, so [long as] the truth of the judgment not [be] examined … '.[59] The case once again involves a repaying debtor's failure to take an adequate acquittance. Conscience is not explicitly mentioned here; the rationale appears to comprehend anything that does not directly challenge the judgment at law—that is, consideration of facts that the law is precluded from taking into account. The connection with conscience particularly is made elsewhere, however. In *Ward* v. *Fulwood*, we are told that '[t]hough the court [will] examine not a judgment [at common law], yet they will examine the corrupt conscience of the party'.[60] This is not the first time we have encountered this strategy of reconciling the operation of equity with the law; nor will it be the last. The reporter of the 'Cases in Tempore Egerton' directly addresses this issue, and what he says suggests that what we have just seen is the standard answer:

> I did very diligently inquire of men of good report and experience in Chancery how it comes to pass that judgments are so often examined in Chancery, yet the danger of the statute avoided which ordains that no judgments given in the king's courts shall be examined in Chancery …. And all the answer that could be made me was this, that the Court of Chancery does not use to examine the judgments themselves directly but by what conscience the plaintiff came to that judgment, so that they do not examine the judgment directly but by a circumstance, but as it were *a longe et a latere*.[61]

56 *Peck* v. *Davis* (1600), ibid., item 117, case 366, vol. 1, p. 229.

57 Ibid., item 120, case 49, vol. 1, p. 326. [Brackets in source.]

58 Ibid., item 120, case 87, vol. 1, p. 333.

59 (1598), ibid., item 118, case 273, vol. 1, p. 266. [All brackets but first set in source.]

60 (1598), ibid., item 118, case 201, vol. 1, p. 258. [All brackets but first set in source.]

61 Ibid., item 119, case 152, vol. 1, pp. 294–5.

It is not clear whether the expression *a longe et a latere* comprehends more than conscience itself, but presumably these other circumstances, beside or beyond those considered at common law, are all referable back to conscience. I shall return to this issue of collateral matters later, partly because Hake makes much of it. But the possibility does arise that the persistence of the epithet 'court of conscience' for the Chancery is partly explicable in terms of the need of a characterization which facilitated the argument that equity was not interfering with the law.

Speaking of cases on equity during this period, Mark Fortier expresses disappointment that they do not really offer much in the way of explanation of equity generally; they tend to be unelaborated examples of its application.[62] The same is true of conscience: it is often mentioned, but rarely explicitly explored.[63] That it is often mentioned evidences its centrality in the legal discourse of the time. That it is rarely explored requires that somewhat conjectural inferences be drawn about the general criteria of its application. We know, for example, that the Chancery does not like fraud and that it will enforce confidences, and we can fairly easily discern the issues of conscience involved. But elsewhere generalization is more difficult.

The difficulty may be illustrated by looking at two cases involving the kind of knowledge that will affect a transferee of a property interest affected with some kind of prior burden. One case is that of a conveyance in which there is 'some slip which by general conscience the party that conveyed the land may be relieved in to avoid his own conveyance or some imperfection in law in the conveyance which notwithstanding the party that conveyed the lands ought to make good in conscience'.[64] Note that there seem to be two kinds of conscience here. One is the 'general conscience' which would allow the grantor to rely on a slip to avoid the conveyance. The other is the kind of conscience that ought to make good an 'imperfection in law'.[65] These seem to operate in opposite directions, the first apparently justifying the grantor's repudiating the conveyance, the other not. The case then postulates another person who, 'knowing of this slip or imperfection does *bona fide* and for good consideration buy the same lands, yet this shall never grieve the purchaser'.[66] It is somewhat unclear whether this second conveyance is from the original grantor or the original grantee. Assuming the latter—a grantee whose title is imperfect—it appears that the second purchaser is allowed to rely on

---

[62] Mark Fortier, *The Culture of Equity in Early Modern England* (Aldershot, 2005), p. 60.

[63] Recall Jones, p. 420.

[64] *Cases Concerning Equity*, item 119, case 172, vol. 1, p. 298.

[65] This may be the kind of situation described by Egerton in *Omer* v. *Ashley* (1599), ibid., item 118, case 298, vol. 1, p. 269, where, having said that equity will afford no help where there is 'no livery at all … upon a deed', he does allow that 'if it [the livery] were made in some sort and be sought to be avoided by a quirk or slight' then equity will intervene.

[66] Ibid., item 119, case 172, vol. 1, p. 298.

the first grantee's flawed title. This makes more sense where the original grantor would be required in conscience to make good the imperfection than where the slip is such as to justify the grantor's repudiating the conveyance.

In any event, this case is contrasted with one where 'the purchaser takes notice of a secret trust or a secret promise ... which is a particular case of conscience ... he shall be ordered and become subject to the trust, whatsoever good consideration he gives for the lands'.[67] Certainly, we can understand the dimensions in conscience of this hypothetical, which illustrates a central doctrine of equity. Awareness of the prior equity binds the purchaser's conscience as, for example, Francis Bacon explains: 'the chancery looketh farther than the common law, namely, to the corrupt conscience of him that will deal with the land knowing it in equity to be another's ...'.[68] The difference in outcome appears to lie, at least in part, in the 'general conscience' *versus* 'particular conscience' distinction. But that distinction is not clear. Is 'general conscience' the general or legal rule that permits avoidance of such conveyances, or is it the fact that, unlike the secret trust postulated, the flaw in the conveyance does not bind the grantee's conscience—because, by hypothesis, conscience would have completed the defective conveyance? The difference would be between knowledge of a full-fledged equitable interest and knowledge of a legal flaw remediable in conscience.

A related case illustrating the difficulty of generalizing about the location and character of conscience is that of a person about to take a conveyance of land who is told by a third party, 'take heed [that] you buy not such land of such a one for he has it but upon a trust'.[69] We are told that the prospective purchaser 'is not forced to believe it' unless he is told so by the feoffee in trust himself.[70] This point is reiterated in the later case of *Lister* v. *Lee*, where Lord Ellesmere says that 'yet may [the purchaser] safely buy the land and this shall be no such notice ... of a trust as shall charge [the purchaser] in equity, admit that such a trust be *in rei veritate*'.[71] Here we might recall that Aquinas says that only an incorrigible error of fact will excuse in conscience, and others say that, to be protected in conscience, a person must take steps to ascertain the truth. Ellesmere's position seems a radical departure from that kind of exigency, in that the purchaser has been alerted to the possible existence of the trust and might verify this by further inquiry. Admittedly, Ellesmere does not say that there is independent evidence corroborative of the allegation of trust. He does say that if the feoffee in trust tells the purchaser this, he is (not surprisingly, since the feoffee is in the best position to know) fixed with notice. So, perhaps the situation envisaged is one where the third

---

67 Ibid.

68 *Reading on the Statute of Uses* (1600), in *The Works of Francis Bacon*, eds J. Spedding, R.L. Ellis and D.D. Heath (14 vols, London, 1857–74), vol. 7, p. 405.

69 *Ragland* v. *Wildgoose* (1596), *Cases Concerning Equity*, item 118, case 199, vol. 1, p. 258. [Brackets in source.]

70 Ibid.

71 (1604), ibid., item 120, case 71, vol. 1, p. 330.

party alleges a trust and the vendor insists, 'No trust'. While an adherent of the tutiorist school of casuistry might say 'take the safest way; don't take the risk', a probabiliorist might justify the purchaser's decision to buy anyway on the grounds that the vendor is better placed to know the state of his title than the third party is. In *Lister* v. *Lee*, Ellesmere advances what seems to be a much more pragmatic rationale: '[i]f words shall amaze men, who should then buy land but one or other willing to hinder the bargain would stop it upon such suspicions'.[72] The need to foster commerce countervails strict considerations of conscience. This not the first instance we have encountered of the conscience of equity being qualified by prudential or pragmatic considerations. It is unconscientious to deny a prior equitable interest of which you are aware; it is impractical to make mere suspicion a basis for assigning such awareness.

Elizabethan Commentators on Equity and Conscience

If the cases (as they have come down to us) afford limited insight into how courts conceived of the actual criteria for and operation of conscience, the commentators offer somewhat more. Certain of these commentators—Robert Snagg, William West and Edward Hake—are more instructive in this regard than others such as William Lambard and Richard Crompton, who nevertheless deserve brief notice.

In his *Archion*, written by 1591, Lambard does assert that 'all our Higher Courts at this day, be either Courts of *Rights* and *Law*, or else of *Equity* and *Conscience*', and he does use the general descriptor 'Courts of *Conscience*',[73] but his main concern is not to explore the nature of juridical conscience. Rather, it is to justify the existence of the Court of Chancery *vis-à-vis* the common law courts. He does not do this in the conventional way by saying that equity does not challenge the law, but acts only on a party's conscience; rather, he emphasizes the moderation ostensibly arising from the interaction of law and equity. He does allude to some of the themes we have been considering—for example, the problem of seemingly 'absolute' judicial power, the challenge to lawyers or litigants of not knowing 'before hand what will be the *consciences* or *discretion* of the *Judges*'[74] and whether equity or conscience should be bound by 'certaine *Rules* and *Limits*'.[75] But he regards some of them at least as matters 'of more difficulty then that I may with modesty take upon mee to determine'.[76]

Similarly, Crompton offers very little in the way of general analysis of the conscience of Chancery. Rather, he presents a list of Chancery doctrines, often mentioning conscience, without much elaboration, as he does so. But the very

---

72 Ibid.

73 Willam Lambard, *Archion, or, a Comentary upon the High Courts of Ivstice in England* (London, 1635), pp. 24, 26; EEBO images 8665:16, 17.

74 Ibid., p. 137; EEBO image 8665:74.

75 Ibid., p. 84; EEBO image 8665:48.

76 Ibid., p. 85; EEBO image 8665:48.

form of his treatment of Chancery is significant. That is, rather than exploring the character of conscience, he appears to regard it as sufficient to enumerate the kinds of determinations that have been made in Chancery, often in the name of conscience. In other words, the reach of Chancery's conscience can be described in terms of precedent. Unlike St. German, who feels compelled to wrestle with what conscience involves, Crompton tends to take it as a given. To be sure, he does give some indication of the underlying preoccupations—as, for example, when he suggests that the absence of a *quid pro quo* precludes relief in conscience—but what he offers suggests that the conscience of equity is defined by what the cases have decided. Thus, his work may illustrate implicitly the tendency to regularize and fix the substance of conscience: its content tends to be given by, and limited by, what has previously been done, and what has been previously done becomes increasingly comprehensive.

Much more substantial and therefore germane to my project are the writings of Snagg, West and Hake.

Robert Snagg's 'Reading'

In 1581, Robert Snagg (d. 1605) delivered a reading in the Middle Temple discussing, among other things, the office and authority of the Lord Chancellor. Subsequently, in 1587, he reduced part of his discourse to writing and presented the manuscript[77] to Sir Christopher Hatton (1540–91), said to have been the first holder of the Great Seal to describe himself as keeper of the sovereign's conscience,[78] on the latter's accession to the Chancellorship.[79] The special problem that concerned

---

[77] Published as *The Antiquity & Original of the Court of Chancery, and Authority of the Lord Chancellor of England* (London, 1654). On the title page, the author is designated 'Serjeant Snagg', although in his dedication he describes himself as 'an Apprentice of the Common Laws'. The only Snagg listed in Sir William Dugdale's *Origines juridiciales* (London, 1666) as having been made a serjeant-at-law in the Elizabethan period is Thomas Snagg, in 1580 (p. 95, EEBO image 58205:206). J.H. Baker, *Readers and Readings in the Inns of Court and Chancery* (London, 2000), p. 611 notes that the editor of the 1654 version has confused Robert Snagg (or Snagge) with his brother Thomas, and has mistakenly dated the reading to the 13th year of Elizabeth's reign.

[78] Samuel E. Thorne, 'Preface' to Hake, *Epieikeia*, p. viiin. His words were that it is 'the holy conscience of *the Queen*, for matter of equity that is in some sort committed to the Chancellor' (George Spence, *The Equitable Jurisdiction of the Court of Chancery* [2 vols, Philadelphia, 1846], vol. 1, p. 414, citing Reg. Lib. B 1516, fol. 661). Jones calls the notion of the Chancellor's 'keepership of the sovereign's conscience … false in history and false in practice …' (p. 44).

[79] Joseph Parkes, *A History of the Court of Chancery* (London, 1828) quotes Camden's somewhat apologetic tribute '*quod ex juris scientiã defuit, ex æquitate supplere studuit*', suggesting that Hatton's sense of equity much exceeded his knowledge of the law (p. 69), and tells us that Hatton relied on the advice of a civilian, Sir Richard Swale, 'in all his judicial business' (p. 70). More positively, Jones calls Hatton's reliance on advice from the Masters in Chancery 'a canny humility' (p. 42).

Snagg, as for Lambard, was how resort to Chancery could be squared with chapter 28 of *Magna Carta*, which appeared to guarantee that no one was to be tried except according to 'the Law of the Land'. The difficulty is that the Chancellor appears on the one hand to 'examine Witnesses as he pleaseth, to inform his Conscience, & also examine the parties by Oath or otherwayes, and to proceed as it shall seem best to his Wisdom, to beat out the Truth, as it seemeth good to him in his privat judgment' and, on the other, to 'Order & Decree the Cause, as it seemeth to him to agree most with Equity and Conscience, howsoever the Law is in the Case …'.[80] In responding to this familiar concern, Snagg addresses many of the themes relating to conscience as a juristic principle that we have seen already and shall continue to see.

One of these is the rationale for a court of conscience in the first place. Snagg offers a fairly conventional account. 'For that the … Law of the Land … standing of General Grounds, Rules, and Maxims', he writes in his dedication to Hatton, 'it was impossible but some particular Cases must fall out, that either the General Rule whereon it lighteth should be too hard for it, or too short to reach it'; therefore it was necessary 'to have one under the Prince, above the rest, to have such an Authority that might judge *secundum æquum, & bonum, & sanam conscientiam* … and to mitigate where the Rule of Law would light too hard, and to supply where it came too short …'.[81] It is important that there be general rules, he notes later, so that judges might not make 'of the Golden Rule of the Law, a Leaden Rule, to bend at [their] will'.[82] But such general rules of Law, which do not regard person or circumstance, will sometimes prove inadequate and will be exploited by some so that they 'might get more by subtilty, or the others simplicity, than Conscience would [allow]'.[83] This is not surprising, he observes, because 'there is no Law in any Nation, but particular mischiefs have grown upon it'; even Moses sometimes had doubts about the application of the laws he himself had delivered.[84]

So, the common law, while just in general, is flawed. Still, how does this justify intervention by the Chancellor? Snagg offers the conventional explanation: 'his Lordship by his Absolute power cannot stay the Course of Law, but onely bindeth the person not to follow the Law in any Unconscionable Course'.[85] That is, the Chancellor does not deny, negate or cancel the law, but merely restrains the

---

80 Snagg, p. 32; EEBO image 152381:20.

81 Ibid., pp. 21–2; EEBO image 152381:15.

82 Ibid., p. 38; EEBO image 152381:23. Unlike Aristotle, but like Cranmer and others, Snagg here uses the image of the pliable leaden rule with a pejorative connotation.

83 Ibid., pp. 40–41; EEBO image 152381:24. Incidentally, this suggests that, sometimes, a person's simplicity or folly might involve the conscience of someone who benefits from it, or takes advantage of it.

84 Ibid., pp. 41–2; EEBO images 152381:24–5.

85 Ibid., p. 46; EEBO image 152381:27. Here the Chancellor's power is 'absolute' only in contrast with his 'ordinary' judicial power.

defendant *in personam* from exercising his legal rights contrary to conscience. Untoward effects of the law are thus remedied while the law itself remains intact.

Snagg also alludes to the Chancellor's flexibility in getting at the truth in matters of conscience. As I have just intimated, the Chancellor was said to have two kinds of judicial powers: the '*Potentia ordinata*, which is in process, in pleading, and in judgement, according to the course of the Common Law', and the *Absoluta potentia*, his specifically equitable power, 'which is in process according to the Law of Nature, to send for the party to Answer, and receive his Answer if he will make it, & then proceed to examine the truth of the matter'.[86] In exercising the latter (unlike the former), the Chancellor is 'to judge for him for whom Equity serveth … for that he is to judge as he shall find the matter to be in Conscience good or bad, and not as he shall find the pleading to be formal and good …'.[87] Whatever 'the precise Rule of Law requireth, if his Lordship perceive by his Wisdom that the cause in Conscience is good on his side, his Lordship is to adjudge with him' because 'judgement is to proceed *Secundum Conscientiam & Veritatem*, and not in *Forma Juris*'.[88] So the Chancellor's inquiry in conscience—both to inform his own conscience and to elucidate the conscientious dimensions of the case—is much less circumscribed than that of a common law judge. The inquiry in conscience is not limited by 'artificial' rules of proof and pleading.

Snagg also discusses two matters—both of which we have previously encountered—related more directly to the substantive content, as contrasted with the procedural dimensions, of conscience as an element in the determinations of Chancery.

One is that not all matters of conscience will be vindicated in Chancery. He repeats the point—made by St. German and often reiterated—that 'many things that a good Conscience would will a man to doe in Charity to his Neighbour, his Lordship by his Conscience cannot compell him to do, by the course of that Court'.[89] Like others (notably St. German) he presents examples of apparently unconscionable cases with which the Chancellor will not deal. He offers one which 'seemeth in every Mans particular Conscience to be unconscionable', and yet it goes uncorrected on the basis of the legal maxim that it is 'Better to suffer a Mischief than an Inconvenience'.[90] As I have mentioned before, such a pragmatic rationale seems anomalous in the context of concerns about conscience, and it makes it very hard to pin down when a Chancellor's moral insight (even when virtually universally shared) will yield to 'convenience'. What Snagg says here

86 Ibid., p. 60; EEBO image 152381:34.

87 Ibid., pp. 61–2; EEBO images 152381:34–5.

88 Ibid., p. 64; EEBO image 152381:36.

89 Ibid., p. 74; EEBO image 152381:41. See also Sir Christopher Hatton, *A Treatise Concerning Statutes, or Acts of Parliament* (London, 1677), p. 27; EEBO image 98014:21 (citing St. German). Hatton's authorship of this tract has been questioned.

90 Snagg, p. 70; EEBO image 152381:39.

suggests that Chancery's conscience does not extend to enforcing altruism, or even to mitigating 'inconvenient' mischief.

Snagg does suggest one criterion for distinguishing between justiciable and non-justiciable issues of conscience, observing that 'that Conscience whereby his Lordship is to judge, is not to be understood *simpliciter*, and to be *Simplex Conscientia*, but *Regulata Conscientia*'—that is, 'to take order in such Cases as by the Course of the Court hath been ordered before-time, and in Causes of like Equity, or greater'.[91] This is reminiscent of some of my comments about Crompton. The Chancellor does not apply conscience at large, but conscience as the court has defined it. At one level, this is a process-based definition of conscience, but it implicates substance in so far as what has been previously ordered presumably defines the content of conscience ('like Equity'). Snagg's somewhat question-begging distinction suggests that, in his estimation anyway, equity or conscience was by this time precedent-bound or at least precedent-regarding—although, as we shall see presently, this cannot be asserted (as he might say) *simpliciter*.

He elucidates the distinction he is making. Although, for example, 'it is against Conscience that a rich father should suffer an honest son to begg', the Chancellor will not intervene because what 'that *Regulata Conscientia* relieveth, is not when one keepeth his own unconscionably, but when one seeketh an other mans Goods or Lands, or to trouble his person unconscionably; either by colour of Law, or extorted power, further or otherwise than in good Conscience it ought to be'.[92] This distinguishes between positive and negative obligations: Chancery will not enforce the conscience that calls for one to relinquish his own (because, say, charity or natural affinity requires it), but it will enforce the conscience that decries the taking of what is another's. This apparently asserts an exclusively substantive criterion for conscience (equity will not take away what is one's own) as compared with the more procedural *regulata conscientia* (equity should do what has been done previously). Moreover, it does not directly acknowledge that, in many instances, equity effectively defines what is another's more expansively than the common law does—so that equity is not applying a different principle, but applying the principle in a greater range of cases.

The second substantive matter Snagg confronts just how the Chancellor is to determine what is unconscientious. This engages the putative subjectivity of judgment according to conscience. Snagg's explanation is rather inconclusive. Like others, he does say that conscience is objectively based, in divine law: God's will 'is the Rule of the Lord Chancellors Conscience'.[93] As to how the Chancellor accesses that 'perfect rule of Righteousness',[94] Snagg counsels faith: 'God never faileth to give wisdom and means to perform those Offices and Callings, that

---

91 Ibid., p. 65; EEBO image 152381:36.

92 Ibid., pp. 65–7; EEBO image 152381:37.

93 Ibid., p. 76; EEBO image 152381:42.

94 Ibid., p. 79; EEBO image 152381:43.

his Majesty placeth men in'.[95] The Chancellor 'without limitation referred to his own Gifts, and the Grace of God, that giveth Wisdom to find out the Truth, and Conscience to judge accordingly'.[96] It is worth foregrounding (and treating with caution) the words 'without limitation'—an express acknowledgement that the Chancellor has (in Snagg's view) a rather free hand in inquiring into the facts of a case, and in determining what conscience demands normatively. This, of course, is exactly what others found objectionable.

This excursus into Snagg's reading is intended to highlight several points. It shows that, during Elizabeth's reign, an extended 'academic' treatment of the Chancery regarded it as quintessentially a court of conscience. Moreover, it is a justification of such a jurisdiction. If the court had its detractors, it appears that they had not undercut the mainstream account of the role of Chancery. Moreover, Snagg's discourse continues many of the themes that we have seen as accompaniments of the construction of Chancery as a court of conscience: the factual and normative dual personality of conscience in equity, the attempt to mark off justiciable from non-justiciable matters of conscience, the problem of stipulating criteria for conscientiousness, and so on. Worthy of emphasis, but unsurprising, is the continuing close linking of conscience with God's law, and hence the intermingling of the legal and the religious, which persists throughout the period this study considers.[97]

William West on Chancery

Early in his discussion of Chancery, West announces that the first thing he will do is 'to vnfolde the nature of equity, conscience, and the rigor of the common Lawes'.[98] He does this more or less satisfyingly, his treatment of equity, which he acknowledges to be equivocal or 'diversly termed in the Law',[99] in relation

95 Ibid., pp. 75–6; EEBO images 152381:41–2.

96 Ibid., p. 75; EEBO image 152381:41.

97 For a late sixteenth-century example, consider Hatton's treatment of the stock case of a statute prohibiting giving alms to 'valiant beggars'. If such a beggar is in extremity of cold or hunger, and unlikely to reach any town where he might find work, the alms-giver will not offend the law. We might say that the rationale for this is that the purpose of the law—encouraging those able to work to work—would be frustrated by applying it in this instance, or we might invoke 'necessity'. But Hatton identifies the equity of the law as involving 'an inward dispensation by the bond of Christian Charity and Compassion' (Hatton, pp. 32–3; EEBO image 98014:24). Although he is speaking of equity here, and not 'conscience' specifically, he is essentially invoking the law of God as the ultimate criterion for human law. Of course, here charity is what justifies the putative offender in legally-cognizable conscience; we do not know that equity would compel this person to be charitable.

98 West, sig. A1r; EEBO image 29131:137.

99 So, he says, it is variously characterized as 'a ruled kind of Justice, allaied with the sweetnesse of mercie', 'a Conveniencie', 'plain dealing', 'natural Justice', 'Law that is opposite to forged & deuised law', or even 'Religion'. His definition is 'the correction or

to strict law or *summum jus* perhaps being more complete than his treatment of conscience as such. Besides this introductory discussion of the general nature of equity and conscience, his 'treatise' on Chancery contains two other main parts. First, there are two lists of typical cases: those in which an aggrieved party will obtain relief in conscience, and then those where, in spite of there apparently being an issue of conscience, equity will not intervene. These two lists are largely summaries of cases examined more searchingly in *Doctor and Student*, so they are of limited use in characterizing the conscience of equity. They do illustrate St. German's continuing influence, and their very brevity—even perfunctoriness—may suggest that allusions to conscience by this time had become rather formulaic, as Crompton's approach also illustrates. Second, West offers a great number of precedents of pleading in Chancery (bills, answers, replications, etc.), which illustrate the kinds of assumptions—or forms—upon which Chancery litigants proceeded. Taken together, these three elements—the introductory commentary, the case lists, and the sample pleadings—do provide some insight into the status and character of conscience as understood by a late Elizabethan lawyer.

Once again, West portrays conscience very much as the focus in Chancery. He observes that Chancery suits are 'for the most part occupied' with conscience in relation to the law's rigour.[100] At the beginning of the part entitled 'Cases remediable in Chauncerie', he emphasizes that it is upon conscience that 'suits in this court do chiefly relie'.[101] As I have previously noted, the sample bills he presents regularly allege that the defendant's conduct is 'contrarie to all right, equitie, and good conscience'.[102] Similarly, the relief asked for is regularly some 'order and direction … as to your honourable Lordshippe shall seeme to stand with right, equitie, and good conscience'[103]

A second point, evident in all three elements of the 'treatise,' is that conscience relieves where the strictness of the common law precludes a remedy. West develops this point in his introduction, and it is the first of his 'cases' illustrating the requirements for relief in Chancery: '[a] *Subpena* lieth in no case but where the common law faileth, so as the partie who in equitie hath wrong, can haue no

---

amendement of a good Law, which is defective in some part, by reason of the generality of it' (sig. A2v ; EEBO image 29131:139)

100 Ibid., sig. A1r; EEBO image 29131:137.

101 Ibid., sig. B2r; EEBO image 29131:142.

102 See ibid., for example, sig. E1v, sigs. E6v, E7r, sig. F3r, sig. F4r ('unconscionably … contrarie to all humanitie, equitie, and right'), sig. F8v, sig. G2r, sig. G3v, sig. G7r ('contrarie to all equitie, good conscience and true dealing'), sig. G8r, sig H3r, sig. H8v, sig. I1v (EEBO images 29131:168, 171, 175, 176, 181, 182, 184, 187, 188, 191, 197, 198, respectively).

103 Ibid., sig. F3v. See also sig. F8v ('shall bee thought to stand with right equitie, and good conscience'), sig. G2r, sig. G2v, and sig. G4r (EEBO images 29131:176, 181, 182, 183, 184, respectively).

ordinarie remedie by the course and rules of ye common law'.[104] A common feature of the sample bills is the plea that the petitioner has no recourse at law. Sometimes that is all that is said;[105] often, however, there is explicit reference to the rigour or strictness of the common law.[106] While this does not tell us substantively what conscience is, it does make clear that it is more flexible and expansive than the law.

In his introduction, West offers a description of conscience based not on his own analysis but on largely unelaborated quotations from other writers. Thus, he quotes the original Latin version of Justus Lipsius's (1547–1606) definition, which occurs very much in a religious context and, rendered in a contemporary translation, is: '*Conscience is a remaine, and sparkle, of right and perfect reason in man, iudging and manifesting good or euill deeds.*'[107] From St. German he takes the observation that conscience 'is an actual applying of knowledge to some pticular act of man',[108] as well as the definition of *synderesis* as 'a naturall power of the soule, perswading, good, & disswading euill'.[109] Then—and his choice here is perhaps significant—he cites the Lutheran German jurist Johann Oldendorp to the effect that conscience is an infallible judge, inscribed in all men by God.[110] He cites Oldendorp again, making the connection of conscience to adjudication: unless he applies true conscience, a judge cannot determine a case according to equity, even if he has before his eyes a thousand witnesses and as many other proofs.[111]

Here in rather unorganized form, we have many elements of the conventional description of conscience: its coming from God, its being in every person, its being in some sense infallible, its involving 'perfect reason', its being rooted in *synderesis*, and its involving a factual as well as normative assessments. What is absent, however, is the presentation of a coherent structure or an exploration of implications. So, for example, he cites the neo-Stoic Lipsius and the Lutheran Oldendorp without noting their ideological differences. And, while he quotes Oldendorp, it is far from evident how far he would accept this jurist's developed theory of law and conscience. As John Witte observes, Oldendorp regarded equity

---

104 Ibid., sig. B2r; EEBO image 29131:142.

105 Ibid., for example, sig. E8v, sig. G2v ('without … remedie by the due order and course of the Common lawes'), sigs. G3v–G4r ('no remedie by the vsuall course of the common Lawes'), sig. G7r, and sig. G8r (EEBO images 29131:173, 183, 184, 187, 188, respectively).

106 Ibid., for example, sig. F3r, sig. F4r, sig. F8r, sig. G1v, sig. H3r, and sig. H5v (EEBO images 29131:175, 176, 180, 182, 191, 194, respectively).

107 Justus Lipsius, *Sixe Bookes of Politickes or Civil Doctrine*, trans. William Jones (London, 1594), p. 8; EEBO image 9028:12.

108 West, sig. B1r; EEBO image 29131:141.

109 Ibid., sig. B1v; EEBO image 29131:142.

110 Ibid., sig. B1r; EEBO image 29131:141.

111 Ibid., sig. B1v; EEBO image 29131:142.

as involving 'a judgment of the soul', 'consultation and application of the natural law of conscience' in *every* case.[112] Therefore, his theory 'effectively merged law and equity'.[113] West, by contrast, apparently does not question the separation of the two jurisdictions.

In the next section, where he lists some cases in which Chancery will act and others in which, though they engage conscience, Chancery will not act, West implicitly distinguishes between justiciable and non-justiciable conscience. However, since he presents only lists of examples, it is difficult to extract general criteria of distinction. I have already alluded to one of these: presumably, in many cases, the common law vindicates conscience, so that those cases are excluded from the purview of Chancery. Following St. German, West appears to accept that where the only basis for a rule is the 'law of man', that is the exhaustive criterion for conscience. Thus, '[e]uery Law ordeined for the disposition of lands or goods, contrary neither to the Law of God, nor to the law of Reason, bindeth in the Court of Conscience'.[114] But this begs the question: at what point is a law ordained for the disposition of property contrary to the law of God or the law of reason? Take the prototypical case of the trust. Certainly it is about property. Why is the common law not conclusive? One could say that a basic common law rule that requires feoffment with livery of seisin to effect a conveyance of land is not contrary to the laws of God or reason. There nothing in those laws that dictates the necessity of some other form—say, a deed. Whether a deed or livery of seisin is mandated does not engage conscience, beyond observance of what the law requires. So the legal conveyance stands and human law is not contrary to the other laws. But in the case of a trust there is an additional element which the ordinary law of man does not address—that is, the confidence reposed in the feoffee and the concomitant unintended enrichment which would arise from the feoffee's claiming absolute ownership. Human law does not contravene the other laws here; it simply has nothing to say about this other factor that engages them. As we have seen in our discussion of St. German, this kind of explanation, while it may reconcile the positive law with these additional demands of conscience, does not tell us when there will be additional factors that cause the law of God or the law of reason to become engaged.

Moreover, like other authors we have seen, West does seem to allow that matters of expediency may override moral factors or themselves amount to sufficient considerations of conscience in some cases. Again citing St. German, West observes of a certain law that 'by Conscience also as it seemeth, because thereby the right & title is made certain, & therby the common wealth more

---

112 John Witte, Jr., *Law and Protestantism: The Legal Teaching of the Lutheran Reformation* (Cambridge, 2002), p. 166.

113 Ibid., p. 175.

114 West, sig. B5r; EEBO image 29131:145.

quiet'.[115] Arguably, what conduces to the quiet or peace of the commonwealth is not merely expedient, but consonant with (or even a dictate of) God's law, and therefore according to conscience in that higher sense. But elsewhere West explicitly does defer potential issues of conscience to what might be characterized as considerations of convenience, or at least the pragmatic demands of the administration of justice.[116]

Regarding a case where a lawyer has given a client defective counsel, West says 'it is good to aske the advise of none but such as be learned in the Lawes, and of good conscience'.[117] This formulation is curious in so far as he does not say 'learned … in good conscience', but 'of good conscience'. Perhaps this suggests that one should consult only lawyers of integrity. Or perhaps it suggests that knowledge of the conscience of equity requires that one have a good conscience. This would accord with Oldendorp's insistence that a judge in equity must have a refined conscience.[118]

Commenting upon 'the power absolute of the Chauncerie', West says that it 'is not tied to the rules of the common Law, but by that, matters may bee examined *omnibus vijs & modis quibus rei veritas melius sciri poterit*', and repeats the common observation that '[n]either is such precise forme of pleading vsed in the Chauncerie … nor any aduantage be taken for mispleading, or want of forme, so as the substance of the matter be sufficiently disclosed in conscience'.[119] Again, it is very significant that the 'absolute power' of the Chancery—its typical equitable power—should be defined in terms of fact-finding and procedure. West does not say that this absolute power lies in the Chancellor's authority to make or discern new law, but in his having at hand much more comprehensive means of getting at the truth. Moreover, it is not the form of proof, but what is 'disclosed in conscience' that is critical in Chancery. This is another instance of what I have often referred to before: Chancery was a court of conscience largely in the sense that it was a court characterized by special modes of fact-gathering, modes that purported to give the tribunal direct access to the consciences of litigants. Another way of putting this might be to say that the Chancery was concerned with conscience not so much at the level of the major premise (the rule derived from *synderesis*) but at the level of the minor premise (assessing the facts to which the self-evident principles apply).

As I have suggested, this matter of closer inquiry into the facts has two dimensions. One of these is that equity takes a wider range of facts to be material

115 Ibid., sig. B5v; EEBO image 29131:146. Compare Crompton, fol. 51r; EEBO image 9565:96.

116 West, sig. B5r, sig. C1r (EEBO images 29131:145, 149).

117 Ibid., sig. B7r; EEBO image 29131:148.

118 Berman, 'Conscience and Law', p. 198.

119 West, sigs B1v–B2r; EEBO image 29131:142. Compare Crompton, who says that, when the Chancellor is acting *secundum potestatem absolutam*, "[h]ome ne serra preiudice.. pur mispleder, [ne pur default de forme,] mes sil poet prouer son matter que serue pur luy in consciens, *vijs, & modis* cest sufficient ...' (fol. 42v; EEBO image 9565:48).

than does the common law. West gives the example of two 'strict rules': 'keepe thy word' and 'hurt no man'.[120] He then comments: '[b]ut here you see no respect had to any circumstance, of your word or hurting, for this point belongeth to equitie, or the Court of Conscience'.[121] Elsewhere, not innovatively, he observes that equity is 'sometime … very significantly called a Conueniencie, because it ministreth amongest men, a fit proporcion, answerable to the persons, the matters, the places, & the times'.[122] It is not so much that equity is administering different *principles* from the common law, but that it is regarding more facts as significant to the application of the principles.

The other dimension of this more comprehensive approach to the facts is that equity is more lax about the modes of establishing facts. I have noted already that a typical feature of the sample petitions is a plea that the plaintiff can get no remedy by the strict course of the common law. But it is often not so much that the common law lacks an applicable substantive principle. In a high proportion of cases, the obstacle at common law is parsimony respecting the modes of proof. Frequently, the problem is that some sort of evidence is unavailable: relevant documents have 'by casuall meanes' 'gotten into [the] hands' of others;[123] an agreement has been made 'secretly … by & betweene' the parties themselves, the 'few witnesses being priuie thereunto' now being dead or unknown to the petitioner;[124] the defendants, relying on possession of documents of title 'have contriued and made diuers and sundry feyned & secret estates of the … premises, to diuers persons to your said Orator vnknowen, so that your said Orator knoweth not against whom to bring' an action at common law,[125] and so on. More specifically, the petitioner often lacks the only kind of proof that the common law recognizes and accepts. So, for example, in the case of a contract, the petitioner is unable to proceed by 'the strict course of the common lawes' 'for want of such proof as is requisite';[126] another petitioner is unable 'to make any such due proofe … as the strict course of the common Lawes … requireth';[127] another is precluded from going to law because he does not know where certain documents are, whether they be 'conteyned … in box, bagge, or chist locked, sealed, or open'.[128] It is not that the common law does not recognize

120 West, sig. A1v; EEBO image 29131:138.

121 Ibid.

122 Ibid., sig. A2v; EEBO image 29131:139.

123 Ibid., sig. E7v; EEBO image 29131:172; compare sig. E1r–E1v and sig. G2r (EEBO images 29131:165–6, 182).

124 Ibid., sig. F8r; EEBO image 29131:180; compare sig. G1v EEBO image 29131:182.

125 Ibid., sig. G2v; EEBO image 29131:183.

126 Ibid., sig. H3r; EEBO image 29131:191. Compare sig. F4r and sig. G1v (EEBO images 29131:176, 182).

127 Ibid., sig. F3r; EEBO image 29131:175.

128 Ibid., sig. G2v; EEBO image 29131:183. Here, of course, he is asking Chancery to help him get the evidence which would be necessary at law.

the obligations, but rather that it has a rather narrow view of what will suffice as proof of those obligations.

Where that is lacking, the only way to get at the facts is by examining the person[129] who might have knowledge of those facts—and this is a procedure peculiar to Chancery or analogous forums. Many of the petitions envisage that, if the defendant is brought before the Chancellor, a confession will be forthcoming. One petitioner observes that 'the trueth and certaintie of all these matters do rest in the priuate and proper notice of [the defendants]',[130] and expects that if they are brought into Chancery, 'no doubt, vpon their corporall Oathes [they] will dysclose and set downe the trueth and certaintie of all these matters'.[131] Another notes that, lacking other evidence, the only way of proving his allegations is 'by the answeres' of the defendants.[132] Another says that the only evidence possible is 'the parties own confession vpon his oath in this Honorable court' and expresses confidence that the confession will be forthcoming.[133] Yet another envisages that he will suffer great damages in the common law action pending against him 'vnlesse it please God … to moue the harts of [the defendants] vpon their awnsweres on othes in this honorable Court, to discouer and disclose the trueth of their euill dealing …'.[134] On this basis, then, Chancery is a court of conscience not just because it applies a different variety of substantive law based upon more demanding moral criteria, but because it is more sedulous in seeking the truth of a matter. In this respect, it is a court of conscience in two senses. First, it is a forum in which the truth is sought by examining the consciences of those, bound by their oaths, who are in a position to have special knowledge. Second, the 'conscience' of the Chancellor is informed by the revelation of such facts. He makes a determination based not only on superior normative insight also upon more exhaustive information.

West makes another, rather tantalizing, observation that merits comment before we leave him. In his introductory lucubrations, explaining 'How the Chauncerie is termed the Court of Conscience', he says that 'the common people terme the Chaũcery the court of conscience'.[135] This seems to imply that it is 'the common

[129] Jones points out that by this time both interrogatories in Chancery and answers to them were ordinarily written, although *viva voce* examinations were sometimes conducted (p. 252).

[130] West, sig. I2r; EEBO image 29131:198.

[131] Ibid.

[132] Ibid., sig. I1r; EEBO image 29131:197.

[133] Ibid., sig. H3r; EEBO image 29131:191; compare sig. F3r; EEBO image 175.

[134] Ibid., sig. E8v; EEBO image 29131:173. This process is reflected in judicial decisions as well. In *Cotton* v. *Causton* (1579) Cary 79, ER 42, the reason the court thought an outcome to be 'meet' 'in conscience' was that 'the defendant by answer, confessed the trust and receipt of two hundred pounds'.

[135] Ibid., sig. B1r; EEBO image 29131:141. West is not the only Elizabethan observer to have made this kind of comment. Sir Thomas Smith, a 'Doctor of the ciuil lawes,' in *De Repvblica Anglorum* (London, 1583) says that 'the court of the chauncerie is called of the

people', and not legal experts, who call Chancery a court of conscience. This, of course, is patently not the case: we have seen many lawyers and judges, and will see many more, who apply this epithet to Chancery. It is rather hard to fathom West's attributing the term particularly to the usage of laypersons. It may be a kind of indirect deprecation of 'conscience' as an adequate way of summing up what Chancery is about. West may be suggesting that it is a rather simplistic way of describing Chancery's jurisdiction. Lawyers, he might be implying, have a much more complex and technical appreciation of that jurisdiction and know that 'conscience' is a compendious term for a whole panoply of specific equitable doctrines beyond the ken of the nonspecialist. This could imply that West thought of equity as involving a system of rules, rather than a broad moral approach. Indeed the fact that his work is really about providing many, many technical precedents may be the best evidence of his real attitude, so that his introductory references to conscience are rather *pro forma*.

Edward Hake on Equity

Hake's general project—not unlike St. German's—is to argue that all laws partake of equity, that equity is essentially *in* the law. Thus, he observes that 'neyther the Common lawe is withowte *Equity*, neither yet that *Equity* is a distincte and severed thing from the lawe, but is (as it were) the very life, sowle and spirit of the lawe …'.[136] Having portrayed law and equity as thus integrated, he is confronted with the challenge of saying what is distinctive about the equity administered by Chancery. This issue he faces perhaps more squarely than St. German: indeed, the very structuring of his work into separate sections on 'The Equity of the Common Law' and 'The Equity of the Chauncery' reflects his intention to make the distinction. In insisting on the one hand that equity is 'the very life, sowle and spirit of the law', and on the other that Chancery equity is somehow distinctive, he does create a conundrum for himself, which he resolves only somewhat satisfactorily.

Not unexpectedly, at a fundamental level Hake says that what typifies Chancery equity is its connection with conscience: 'in the said highe Courte the decrees, iudiciall actes, ought not to be lymitted by rules or guided by exposition of textes, as ye judgements of the Common lawe are, but sholde be deryved upon Conscience, even the conscience of the judge there …' (pp. 2–3).[137] Having made this general connection, Hake raises a number of points with which we have become more or less familiar.

One of these is the tripartite account of conscience. This is significant because, once again, we find a lawyer, when he actually purports to give a theoretical

common people the court of conscience, because that the chauncellor is not strained by rigour or form of wordes of lawe to iudge but *ex æquo* and, and according to conscience …' (p. 54; EEBO image 18192:30).

136 Hake, p. 121.

137 Compare p. 122: 'the *Equity* of that highe courte is drawne owte and deryved allonly from the conscience of the Lord Chauncellor or the Lord Keeper …'.

account of conscience, resorting to 'theological' concepts. For the details, Hake simply refers us to St. German (p. 130).[138] He also offers us, by way of paraphrase, another account, that of Johannes Rivius[139] which, though not exactly congruent with those we have seen, evinces a similar pattern:

> … for the parts of Conscience, … they are three, namely, Synderesis, Monition and Conscience. Synderesis is that which is said to be the doome or pure parte of the Conscience, which is as much to say as an universall rule of things to be done …. Monition, which they call *Dictamen Rationis* or the principle of Reason, is that which giveth a Reason wherefore things shold be done, and it is twoe maner of wayes, namely, prescripte of Reason superior and prescripte of Reason inferior. Prescripte of Reason superior perswadeth heavenly and everlasting things; prescript of Reason inferior perswadeth worldly, temporall … things. And this it is that either letteth or furthereth Synderesys. Conscience (which is the thirde) is that which bringeth the consequent into a conclusion.[140]

Apart from presenting a version of the familiar threefold structure of conscience, this account merits comment for other reasons. One is that it does not explicitly mention the apprehension of facts as an element in the operation of conscience. Rather, it appears to present a picture of moral reasoning involving precepts only. That is, conscience involves deriving secondary principles by the application of reasoning to what is given by *synderesis*. Moreover, it involves two objects of such reasoning: 'heavenly and everlasting things' and 'worldly, temporall … things'. This corresponds, roughly, to the distinction between 'spirituals' and 'civils' which is one plausible basis for distinguishing between conscience generally and Chancery conscience. Also, it contemplates that the two kinds of reason might either further or hinder ('let') *synderesis*, apparently implying that errors might occur at the stage of 'monition'—a point we have noticed before. Perhaps most important, for our purposes, it makes *synderesis* the *sine qua non* of conscience.

Hake offers an example that, in my view, reveals the awkwardness of this theoretical structure more than it illustrates its usefulness. The issue is whether a person might swear an oath. The precept given by *synderesis* is 'no unlawfull thing is to be done'. This is so general, not to say tautological or question-begging, as to

[138] Given Hake's heavy reliance on St. German—not only for the account of conscience, but also for equity in general (see, for example, pp. 13–14) and for guidance as to when the Chancellor 'must order his conscience after the growndes and rules of the lawes of the realme' (p. 129)—one might again want to question Yale's identifying of the two with discrete points in the development of equity.

[139] Johannes Rivius, *De conscientia* (Leipzig, 1541).

[140] Hake, pp. 130–31. See also Hake's , *A Touchstone for this Time Present* (London, 1574), where he refers to 'the infallible doome of our conscience (which of the learned is called *Synteresis*)' (p. 1; EEBO image 6276:5).

be virtually meaningless. In Hake's hypothetical, the prescript of inferior reason ('to sweare in any case is unlawfull') is in conflict with the prescript of superior reason ('a subiect ought to sweare his allegiance unto his Prince'). Conscience requires that the prescript of superior reason be followed. Part of my difficulty is why the 'no swearing' rule is a prescript of inferior reason. We will recall that Jesus himself—presumably pretty hefty authority for an Elizabethan Protestant like Hake—said 'Swear not at all' in the Sermon on the Mount.[141] Far from being a precept of inferior reason—or, for that matter, of superior reason—this could plausibly be characterized as a divine law. Similarly, although I can see that *giving* allegiance to the sovereign might be a precept of superior reason, I am less sure why the formality of *swearing* allegiance should be. Indeed, my sense is that equity should emphasize actual loyalty, rather than the outward forms of loyalty. My point is that, when one actually applies the theoretical structure of conscience, a large measure of arbitrariness remains: the basic principles are broad enough to contain inconsistent lower-order precepts; not only the content but the very classification of such precepts may be rather unpredictable. While the standard accounts of conscience depict it as objective, it may be that the actual application of those accounts entails substantial discretion.

Another point that Hake makes, and which may follow inexorably from his description of Chancery equity as deriving solely from the conscience of the Chancellor, is that 'the essentiall parte required to be in the Lord Chauncellor is a good and sownde conscience' (p. 130)—or, indeed, that a judge in equity should be 'adourned & beautifyed with the sweete ornaments of clemency & mercy, patterned by the lenitye of the mylde Sauioure of mankynde …' (p. 3). Whether this requirement of sound conscience is to make the Chancellor incorruptible or to enable him to appreciate accurately the conscience of the case—or, probably, both—Hake does not make explicit.

Relative to this issue, he considers whether a Chancellor might be trained in the common law or whether, as formerly, he should be an ecclesiastic. Hake gives a typically 'Protestant' response to this. Whereas in earlier times, 'spirituall persons' might have been presumptively 'of better conscience than were any of the laytie or temporalty', now laypersons have ready access to Scripture, the ultimate source of the rules of conscience, so 'to alledge any such reason or difference of meliority of Conscience betweene spiritualty and temporalty … were … no lesse scandalous then ydle and frivolous' (pp. 141–2). That is, after the Reformation 'everyone' has access to the source of authority in matters of conscience. But, of course, Hake would not have said that this democratization of conscience made it any less subject to the criterion of correctness.

Although he does not develop the point, Hake offers essentially the standard rationalization of Chancery's appearance of conflicting with the law: 'the helpe which the Chauncery gyveth, the decree or sentence thereof is compulsory *ad*

[141] Matthew 5:34. I appreciate that the lawfulness of 'swearing' was a topic of debate during the period.

personam and not *ad rem*, as at the Common lawe it is' (p. 126). And, as well as sending the reader to St. German to know when the Chancellor must order his conscience according to the ordinary law, he suggests the kind of general principle that we have encountered previously: when the law of the realm 'doth concurre with the lawe of God', so that, in following it the Chancellor is acting 'according to Conscience' (pp. 129–30). This is a somewhat more restrictive criterion than St. German's that conscience is dictated by the ordinary law as long as it is not inconsistent with the law of God or of reason. If pressed, Hake would, I suspect, agree with St. German on the criterion, because so many matters are 'indifferent'.

Once again, Hake regards Chancery as distinctive in respect of both the kinds of facts it will consider and the modes of establishing them. Thus, unlike the common law's proceedings which are 'wont to be *stricti juris* and (as it is said) *secundum allegata et probata*' (pp. 47–8), Chancery 'hath so greate regard unto circumstances as that it admitteth the examination of causes *omnibus viis et modis quibus rei veritas melius sciri poterit*' (p. 122).[142] Thus, too, Hake makes the point that it is not so much that the common law fails in substance, or in the kinds of actions it permits, but that 'oftentymes the party who is to bring the action fayleth of his proofes' (p. 127). But he also presents two important qualifications to the platitude that, while the common law is insensitive to particular circumstances and rigid in its procedure, equity takes cognizance of time, place, person, etc., and is lax in its admission of evidence. One of these is that 'a judge of the lawe'—and presumably a judge in equity—has 'two knowledges, the one a private, the other a iudiciall knowledge', and that the Chancellor as much as any judge must still judge according to 'iudiciall knowledge' (p. 33), albeit what constitutes such knowledge may be more expansively defined in Chancery. We have encountered this distinction before, and it at least partially anticipates Lord Nottingham's distinction between private and civil conscience, in so far as that distinction has an evidentiary dimension.

The other qualification—which requires him to take his analysis a step further—is that the assertion that the law is indifferent to particular circumstances is incorrect. Hake repeatedly insists that the common law does take circumstances into account; it does allow 'severall pleas, as *infancy*, *coverture*, *non compos mentis*, *threates*, *dures*, *nient lettred*, *averment de fraude*, &c' (p. 51).[143] Whence, he asks rhetorically, 'are these circumstances but of the very *Epieikeia* of the lawe?' (p. 122).

If the common law, like Chancery equity, is responsive to circumstances, does this mean that the only distinctive feature of Chancery is its more flexible procedure? Is this what "conscience" is ultimately reduced to—greater leniency in admitting proofs?

Although he does not raise the question in this form, Hake's answer would appear to be 'No'. Chancery, he argues, is responsive to a different *kind* of circumstance from that which the common law recognizes. The distinction, he says, is that, while 'the circumstances of the Common lawe's *Equity* ... are not circumstances collateral

---

142 Recall that West and others use the same formula.

143 See also p. 122.

or owte of the case, … but … circumstances which may stand with the case', those which Chancery particularly regards are 'circumstances … merely collaterall and from the case, and so owte of or beside the case' (pp. 123, 122).[144] For Hake, the fact that the conscience of Chancery takes cognizance of 'collaterall' circumstances is what makes it distinctive.

Unfortunately, Hake provides sparse analysis to help us distinguish the two kinds of circumstances. Rather, he offers some examples, from which we can glean something of his meaning.

One which illustrates the common law's approach involves the maxim that, if a party claims land in a certain real action, but enters the land before judgment, the writ will abate. This maxim, says Hake, 'wee may call the generality of the lawe' (p. 124). But, if there is a special circumstance in the case—that is, 'that the entry of the demaundant was not to make clayme to the land or to gayne the possession thereof by his entry'—then the law will judge according to that circumstance and not according to the general maxim. How is this circumstance 'altogither within the facte' (p. 126)? One could answer by saying that 'entry' has a technical meaning here—not simple coming onto the land, but taking possession of the land. In this case, the situation would not even be within the general maxim. Or one could say that 'entry' is to be read literally, but implicit or 'secretly understood' (as St. German might say) in the rule is that it contemplates only entries in relation to the action brought, which is an action for recovery of possession. The circumstances here take this case out of the *ratio legis*, which may be that self-help anticipates and thus vitiates the action at law.

What kinds of circumstances, then, might be 'beside the facts' or merely collateral in this kind of case? A possible answer is suggested by the example Hake gives of a plaintiff who enters premises pursuant to a dinner invitation from the defendant. Assuming that an intention to take possession was not implicit in the legal notion of 'entry', one might say: 'Yes, there was entry here, but it was induced by the defendant so that he could take advantage of the strict law.' The defendant's *bona fides* is not part of the abatement plea; all that is relevant—within the case—is the entry. But because of the defendant's representation, his conscience is engaged, and the plaintiff can go to Chancery on this basis. Hake does not, however, take the analysis this far; I am merely supposing that such circumstances would be relievable only in Chancery.[145]

He does suggest something like this when he discusses the 'common and ordinary case' of the debtor who pays his debt without taking an acquittance. Here, where the law specifically requires an acquittance, it may be hard to argue that, implicitly, the law does not require an acquittance where the debtor does not ask

[144] Recall that the compiler of 'Cases in Tempore Egerton' uses the expression 'a circumstance … as it were *a longe et a latere*' (*Cases Concerning Equity*, item 119, case 152, vol. 1, p. 295).

[145] I am assuming as well that this scenario would not come within the legal circumstance of *averment de fraude*.

for one. That would be 'every' case. In order to justify Chancery's intervention, one must find collateral circumstances affecting the creditor's conscience. Hake suggests that, in these cases, the debtor's failure 'was or might be deemed to have byne by his over greate trust and confidence in the obligee' (p. 123), this being the reason for relief '*per obliquum*, that is to saye, by reason of a circumstance of *Equity* collaterall or owte of the case' (p. 127). So, either the creditor actually induced the debtor to trust him that no acquittance was necessary (a fact which might be established by examination of the creditor by the Chancellor), or such trust will be deemed to be present. The former account seems more consistent with Chancery's ostensible concern with getting at the actual truth in the particular case. It would also mean that the debtor would not succeed in every case—at least (in the latter account) if the presumption were not overcome. I have suggested previously that another possible approach would be to allow the law to take its course, so that the creditor recovers a second time. Then the debtor could prove the earlier repayment—not by way of negating the need for an acquittance as an answer to the claim in debt, but by way of establishing the double receipt or unjust enrichment of the creditor, by evidence admissible in Chancery. It would presumably be substantively unconscionable for the creditor to retain the double payment, and he would have to disgorge. Again—apart from being rather sophistical—this approach would have the 'disadvantage' of requiring the defendant to refund half the money every time. That is, in every case the common law would be thwarted. In effect, the rule would be changed.

Another of Hake's examples merits mention. This is the case of a person who makes 'a deed of feoffment unto J.S. and dye[s] before livery of seisin [is] made thereupon' (p. 127). J.S. has no remedy at law, or 'in Conscience'. Hake says that the reason for this is apparent. Presumably, it is that there are no 'collaterall circumstances' for Chancery to fix upon. There is the deed, which may be required but is not sufficient to effect the conveyance at common law. But there is nothing else. For Chancery to intervene in these circumstances would involve making the feoffor give up what is still his, not to return what is another's. What other factors might be present appears when Hake alters the hypothetical—'if J.S. had payed any money for the land, then in Conscience he oughte to be relieved at the least for the restitution of his money' (p. 127). The common law would still say that the transaction is ineffective. But here, consideration has passed. It would be unconscionable for the feoffor to have received J.S.'s money when he has given nothing for it. Arguably, for there to have been a circumstance within the case justifying relief at common law there would have to be facts which, though non-standard, amounted to livery of seisin within the *ratio legis*.

Before leaving this distinction, it should be remarked that many—but not all—of the kinds of circumstances Hake says the common law courts will recognize go to capacity: infancy, coverture, *non compos mentis*, involuntary ignorance—even perhaps necessity. One might be inclined to think of these as collateral. But Hake seems to be assuming that any act requires volition, and where that is lacking, the very act itself is vitiated. Although he does not clearly say this, it is implicit in his treatment of the stock case of a bailment of a sword in which the bailee refuses to re-deliver the weapon after the bailor becomes *non compos mentis* or 'starke staring madde' (p. 18). One might be tempted to say that the madness is 'merely collateral', a circumstance outside the case, involving personal characteristics of one of the parties. The obligation of the bailee is clear: he must return the chattel that is the subject-matter of the bailment. He has not done so. Therefore, there should be no relief from his obligation at law. But Hake explains that, by virtue of his madness, the bailor is no longer the same man that he was; he is, almost literally, beside himself. This is a circumstance that compromises the nature of the actor, and, by implication, of the act. On this rationale, the bailor's capacity is a matter that appears to be 'within the fact', and therefore a circumstance that the law will take into account.

Conclusion

As we have seen, some commentators suggest that St. German, in spite of his concern to preserve Chancery equity by emphasizing that equity is intrinsic to the law and that the ordinary law is often the criterion for what is conscionable, in fact promoted the absorption of equity into the law. One might see in Hake's approach a similar phenomenon. Again intent on discerning the essential unity of equity and its presence within the law, he creates for himself the problem of then identifying the point of distinction between Chancery equity and the equity that pervades the law. He says that it has something to do with the former being somehow cognizable by the conscience of the Chancellor. Some of what he says tends to suggest that the distinction is merely procedural, which would then raise the question why the common law might not just modify its procedure. But he does propound a substantive difference when he makes the distinction between 'intrinsic' and 'collateral circumstances'. While one can attempt to rationalize many of his examples in terms of this distinction, there may be real practical, if not theoretical, problems with saying that a particular circumstance in within as opposed to beside the facts of the legal case. The law incorporates facts into cases by extending its definition of what is material—as, for example, whether a party was *compos mentis*. Similarly, by taking cognizance of additional circumstances, equity makes them material—in other words, brings them within the case. So the distinction remains slippery. It may be that, with Hake, the tenuousness of the distinction between 'conscience' and 'law' is not far below the surface of his argument, and that any kind of careful scrutiny reveals that tenuousness. One has the sense of being in what Snagg would describe as a 'Laborinth', which, in spite of picking up many suggestive threads, one leaves pretty much as one found it.[146]

---

[146] Apparently the labyrinth image was not uncommonly associated with conscience. See, for example, Gallagher, p. 224 (re Spenser) and Brown, p. 46 (re Donne).

Chapter 5
Protestant Conscience One: The Early Seventeenth Century

Introduction

We have already encountered the observation that the 'canonist conscience' of the medieval period was superseded, at least in England, by 'what may be called, for want of a better phrase, the Protestant conscience'.[1] This notion warrants much closer examination for the purposes of the present study, especially in so far as that 'Protestant conscience'—itself undoubtedly a complex concept[2]—presumably reflected how conscience was commonly understood during the period with which I am concerned.

Pervasive Conscience

As is well-known, there is a massive body of literature on conscience from the early modern period, especially the seventeenth century. In 1642, John Jackson (1600–1648) wrote that '[a] man would thinke there were much Conscience in the world, to consider all the books, that are written of the nature and cases of Conscience', and that, 'if all were printed that hath been said, talked, disputed, preached [and written] of Conscience', 'the world would scarce contain the books'.[3] And, in the 1680s, John Sharp (1643–1714), who was to become Archbishop of York, could

---

1 D.E.C. Yale, 'Introduction' to Edward Hake's *Epieikeia: A Dialogue on Equity in Three Parts* (New Haven, 1953), p. xiv

2 Thus, for example, the moderate Anglican Richard Hooker writes of the Puritans' disparagement of reason that it implies an abrogation of the law of nature, 'which is an infallible knowledge imprinted in the minds of all the children of men, whereby both the general principles for directing of human actions are comprehended, and conclusions derived from them …' (*Of the Laws of Ecclesiastical Polity*, ed. Christopher Morris [2 vols, London, 1907; reprinted 1963], vol. 1, p. 310). However, as Thomas Wood, *English Casuistical Divinity During the Seventeenth Century* (London, 1952) observes, whatever their differences, Anglicans like Joseph Hall, Robert Sanderson, Jeremy Taylor and John Sharp and Puritans like William Perkins, William Ames and Richard Baxter shared a resolve to inculcate moral living (pp. x–xi). Generally, my project will not involve exploring the varieties of Protestant opinion on conscience.

3 John Jackson, *The Booke of Conscience Opened and Read* (London, 1642), p. 12; EEBO image 103990:12.

still say, '[t]here is nothing more in our Mouths than *Conscience*'.[4] A modern writer notes, uncontroversially, that the seventeenth century 'can justly be called the Age of Conscience'.[5] Wood reminds us that interest in the subject of conscience was not just the purview of professionals: 'casuistical divinity' was a topic of 'popular interest',[6] many of the leading casuists giving 'their most extensive and systematic teaching on the subject in public lectures and sermons' (p. 48).

As the foregoing suggests, the vast preponderance of this literature is religious, concerned, for example, with instructing the individual as to the likelihood of his or her salvation. Much of it is 'political', in that it is concerned with issues of liberty of conscience. Little of it directly or explicitly addresses conscience as a concept in Chancery. Nevertheless, non-equity accounts of conscience should afford insight into the cultural understanding of the concept, and hence about at least the context of its apprehension as a juristic principle in the Chancery.[7]

Moral Conscience and Equity

The perceived connection between conscience in general and Chancery conscience is evidenced in a number of particular ways. Writers on conscience sometimes explicitly highlight its relationship to justice: William Perkins (1558–1602) says that 'iustice and conscience haue alwaies bin friends';[8] Richard Bernard (1568–1641) observes that '[c]onscience is the chiefest maintainer of iustice and equity among men';[9] and Edmund Calamy (1600–1666) notes that 'a good conscience is, as Aristotle saith of Justice, a Synopsis and Epitome of all virtues'.[10] Moreover,

---

4 John Sharp, *A Discourse Concerning Conscience: The First Part* (London, 1687), p. 1; EEBO image 37553:3.

5 Keith Thomas, 'Cases of Conscience in Seventeenth-Century England', in J. Morrill, P. Slack, and D. Woolf (eds), *Public Duty and Private Conscience* (Oxford, 1993), pp. 29–56, p. 29. See also Camille Slights, 'Ingenious Piety: Anglican Casuistry of the Seventeenth Century', *Harvard Theological Review*, 63/3 (1970): 409–32.

6 Wood, p. 36.

7 In asserting this, I am taking a position rather at odds with that of Mike Macnair, 'Equity and Conscience', *Oxford Journal of Legal Studies*, 27/4 (2007): 659–81, who argues that 'conscience' in legal contexts should be understood as a technical term of art, like 'fee simple', with a meaning discontinuous from the common meaning.

8 William Perkins, 'Epistle Dedicatory' to *A Discourse of Conscience* (Cambridge, 1596); EEBO image 10898:3.

9 Richard Bernard, 'The Epistle Dedicatory' to *Christian See to Thy Conscience* (London, 1631), sig. A5v; EEBO image 14165:13.

10 Edmund Calamy, 'The Epistle to the Reader' in William Fenner, *The Sovles Looking-glasse ... With A Treatise Of Conscience* (Cambridge, 1640), sig. ¶2v; EEBO image 15425:3. This connection continues to be made: see Henry Carpenter, *The Deputy Divinity or Inferiour Deity and Subordinate God in the World, Conscience* (London, 1657), pp. 2–3; EEBO image 170295:8.

some of these writers explicitly discuss legal topics in terms of conscience—sometimes in sermons on the subject addressed to judges.[11]

A number of writers on conscience dedicate their works to judges exercising equitable jurisdiction and remark on their common enterprise. Perkins dedicates *A Discourse of Conscience* to Sir William Piriam (1534–1604)—not indeed a judge in Chancery but Chief Baron of the Court of Exchequer, a court exercising equitable jurisdiction—hoping that since Piriam is '*set apart for the execution and maintenance of civill justice*' he '*will approoue and accept a Treatise propounding rules and precepts of conscience*'.[12] William Worship dedicates his *The Christians Iewell* to Francis Bacon, Lord Keeper, exhorting him to '[g]oe on … to be a *Sanctuarie* to *Conscience*'.[13] Both John Hughes's (*fl.* 1622) *St. Pavls Exercise* and Bourne's (1590–1672) *Anatomie of Conscience* are dedicated to Lord Keeper John Williams (1582–1650), the former apostrophizing Williams as '*a Paterne of equity and Iustice …, and a principall agent in these vnconscionable dayes, to restore and recouer conscience againe*',[14] and the latter calling him '*the* Lord-protector *of* Conscience' and referring to his '*graue and Conscionable Iudgment in matters of* Equity'.[15] And Henry Mason (c. 1573–1647) dedicates *The Tribvnall of the Conscience* to Lord Keeper Sir Thomas Coventry (1578–1640), noting that by his office he is 'IUDGE of the Court of Conscience'.[16]

Moreover, it was common to characterize conscience in terms of legal metaphors. We are told that 'Conscience … is the invisible Iudge that sits upon the Tribunall of our Soules',[17] that 'the *Conscience* is whole in the whole soule, keeping a Court in the whole',[18] that conscience 'is like a iudge, causing malefactours to

---

11 See, for example, Robert Sanderson, 'Ad magistratum' in *Twelve Sermons* (3rd edn, London, 1637); Immanuel Bourne, *The Anatomie of Conscience* (London, 1623); Samuel Garey, *Ientaculum iudicum: or, a Breake-fast for the Bench* (London, 1623); Richard Carpenter, *The Conscionable Christian* (London, 1623); Robert Harris, 'St. Paul's Exercise' in *Sixe Sermons of Conscience* (2nd edn, London, 1630); and Thomas Scot, *God and the King* (Cambridge, 1633).

12 Perkins, 'Epistle Dedicatory', *Discourse*; EEBO image 10898:3. Richard Eburne dedicates his *The Royal Law: or the Rule of Equitie* (London, 1616) to one of the Masters of Requests, observing that 'Equity *and* conscionable dealing' are apt to his 'Honorable place' (sig. A3r).

13 William Worship, *The Christians Iewell, or, the Treasvre of a Good Conscience* (London, 1617), sig. A3v; EEBO image 14830:4.

14 John Hughes, *St. Pavls Exercise, or, a Sermon of Conscience* (London, 1622), sig. A2v; EEBO image 4483:3.

15 Bourne, sig. A2r; EEBO image 7186:2.

16 Henry Mason, *The Tribvnall of the Conscience: or, a Treatise of Examination* (London, 1626), sig. A3v; EEBO image 12751:4.

17 Alexander Ross, *The Picture of Conscience Drawne to the Life, by the Pencell of Divine Truth* (London, 1646), p. 1; EEBO image 119965:12.

18 Bourne, p. 8; EEBO image 7186:7.

be arraigned at the barre of his iudgement seate',[19] that we should 'hearken to the councels, to the urgings, and to the injunctions which come out of the Court of Conscience',[20] or that 'the Court of Conscience is always open, Equity hath no Non-Term, written Laws may be interrupted, but this *Lex non scripta sed nata* is always of force'.[21] Sometimes this kind of metaphor is part of the title of a work, and thus forms the organizing idea of the whole discourse, as in Mason's *The Tribvnall of Conscience* or in Thomas Barnes's *The Court of Conscience*.[22]

Sometimes, indeed, the metaphors invoked involve conscience and Chancery specifically—that is, the 'tribunal' of conscience is explicitly an equitable forum. Hughes, who describes his subject as '*meere* Chancery',[23] urges a personified conscience to '[s]peake to those that are towards the Law … specially in those Courts that are of thy Iurisdiction, and haue their Denomination from thee …'.[24] Bourne observes that conscience is '*Priuata lex*' which begins where 'the Ciuill Law, and Common Law haue done': '[i]t is the *Lord-Keeper*, the *Chancellor* … who keepeth a Chancery in the soule of man'.[25] Like equity, conscience goes beyond the ordinary law. Robert Harris (1581–1658), addressing the judges of assize at Oxford, likens the three parts of the soul to three courts: 'the sensitiue part hath its court of Common plea's [*sic*]; the intellectuall, of the Kings Bench; the spirituall … a Chancery'. In the last 'sits the Conscience as Lord Chancellor,

---

19 John Howesoun, *A … Discourse of Conscience* (Edinburgh, 1600), sig. C2v; EEBO image 17063:20.

20 Jeremiah Dyke, *Good Conscience, or, a Treatise Shewing the Nature, Meanes, Markes, Benefit, and Necessitie Thereof* (6th edn, London, 1635), p. 62; EEBO image 17557:37.

21 John Goodman, *The Golden Rule, or, the Royal Law of Equity Explained* (London, 1688), p. 40; EEBO image 60390:23.

22 Thomas Barnes, *The Court of Conscience* (London, 1623). For a political example, see 'Theophilus … Decius', *An Answer ... Put into the Great Court of Equity, otherwise Called the Court of Conscience* (London, 1643). Later in the century, see Andrew Jones, *The Black Book of Conscience Or Gods High Court of Justice in the Soul* (6th edn, London, 1658).

23 Hughes, sig. A2v; EEBO image 4483:3.

24 Ibid., p. 23; EEBO image 4483:14.

25 Bourne, p. 11; EEBO image 7186:8. Compare Goodman, p. 11; EEBO image 60390:8: 'we have a *Chancery* and Court of Equity in our own Bosoms'. Michael Wigmore, in an assize sermon dedicated to Bishop John Williams, likens human faculties to courts or court officers, observing that one's '*Tender-conscience* [would be] his *Court of Chauncerie*, whose *Judge* should be *Charity*' (*A Dissection of the Braine* [London, 1641], p. 3; EEBO image 93539:4). Later in the century, John Tillotson will similarly speak of 'the Equity and Chancery of our own breasts' ('Wherein lies that exact Righteousness, which is required between Man and Man?' in Samuel Annesley (ed.), *The Morning-Exercise at Cripplegate or, Several Cases of Conscience Practically Resolved* (London, 1664), p. 235; EEBO image 105033:12).

the *Synteresis* as master of the Rolles …'.[26] This conceit seems to have acquired a continuing currency.[27] And Jackson urges people with drowsy consciences to rouse them: '[c]ry aloud, and say, Hoe Conscience, conscience, *up and be doing* …. To day is a Chancery day …'.[28] As we have already noticed, Forsyth's *The Great Day of Chancery*—dedicated, incidentally, to Francis Bacon as Chancellor—is so named because it is about the last judgment when 'righteous Iudgement' will be meted out according to the evidence of every person's conscience.[29]

One should not ask such particular instances and verbal conceits to carry too heavy a burden. Nevertheless, they are indications of the linking of general conscience and Chancery in the non-legal mind and they reinforce the intuition that treatments of conscience in the religious context should be relevant to the particular context which concerns us here.

Protestant Conscience, pre and post Civil War

In this chapter and in Chapter 7, then, I propose to consider 'Protestant conscience', on the basis that what is said about it will afford insight into, first, how conscience was understood at the time, and, second, how that conscience (by contrast with 'canonist conscience') is more or less reconcilable with the requisites of a juristic principle. I am devoting two separate chapters to this topic partly for pragmatic reasons: it is simply very large. More substantively, it makes sense to consider what might be called pre-Civil War Protestant conscience and post-Civil War Protestant conscience.

Although there is no definitive break between the two and there is considerable continuity in the consideration of the topic, there are reasons to suppose that the character of discourse about conscience, or perhaps more accurately the concept lying behind that discourse, might have evolved during the course of the century. For one thing, controversy about the role of Chancery evinced a shift in emphasis. As we have seen, Chancery as a court of conscience had long been criticized for being too subjective or arbitrary, and, indeed, for second-guessing the Common Law courts. The issue came to a crisis in the dispute between Coke and Ellesmere early in the seventeenth century. At that time, the controversy tended to be formulated in essentially legal terms: the jurisdiction of Chancery was questioned on the basis of *Magna Carta*, or other statutes ostensibly insulating judgments in the Common Law courts. To be sure, a fundamental political question—the role of the prerogative *versus* the ordinary law—lay at the bottom of the dispute,

[26] Harris, 'St. Paul's Exercise', p. 5; EEBO image 6263:8.

[27] See Henry Carpenter, pp. 38–9; EEBO image 170295:26, and Samuel Clarke, *Medulla Theologiæ or the Marrow of Divinity* (London, 1659), p. 430; EEBO image 64694:239.

[28] Jackson, p. 49; EEBO image 103990:30.

[29] James Forsyth, *The Great Day of Chancery* (London, 1619), sig. A5r; EEBO image 5944:3.

but it was nevertheless formulated largely in terms of legality. During the Civil War the terms of reference became much more explicitly political. So defence of the Chancery—which, indeed, came close to being abolished during the Commonwealth period—had to be made in, if not different, then more energetic terms, and the pressure on Chancery to become more like an ordinary court was more intense. A further consideration of Protestant conscience becomes expedient in reference to these developments.

Moreover, the quality of even mainstream Protestant writing about conscience arguably changed. For example, James Tully speaks of the ethical 'voluntarism'—as opposed to the 'intellectualism' of earlier writers—of Jeremy Taylor (1613–67) and Robert Sanderson (1587–1663), and opines that the *Ductor Dubitantium* of the former is 'remarkably sceptical and unsure'.[30] And, of course, the question of liberty of conscience—and, hence, the diverse, if not subjective, nature of conscience—became increasingly insistent.

In this chapter, I shall consider Protestant conscience as it was elaborated from about the end of the sixteenth century to roughly 1640, and in Chapter 7 I shall return to the topic for the period following 1640, always mindful of the fact that specifying this year is not intended to mark a definitive watershed.

Remnants of Canonist Conscience

Before considering this matter in detail, one general caveat must be entered. The distinction 'canonist conscience' *versus* 'Protestant conscience' tends to suggest a clear-cut difference, or at least a discontinuity. However, Protestant writers did not break sharply with their Catholic predecessors—at least in describing the general structure of conscience. So, for example, Calvin speaks of 'that internal law [that is, natural law], which ... is in a manner written and stamped on every heart' and of conscience as acting 'as an inward witness and monitor' which 'points out the distinction between good and evil'.[31] As Thomas Merrill suggests, although the Protestant casuists[32] rejected much of especially *Jesuit* casuistry, they 'availed themselves of the rich heritage of Roman Catholic casuistry for the general patterns

30 James Tully, 'Governing Conduct', in Edmund Leites (ed.) *Conscience and Casuistry in Early Modern Europe* (Cambridge 1988), pp. 12–71, pp. 37, 28. I shall return to this characterization in Chapter 7.

31 *Institutes of the Christian Religion*, trans. H. Beveridge (Peabody, Mass., 2008), p. 234 (Bk. 2, ch. 8, s. 1).

32 James F. Keenan argues for a strict definition of casuistry, distinguishing it from, say, 'spiritual directories' or summaries of cases ('Was William Perkins' *Whole Treatise of Cases of Conscience* Casuistry?: Hermeneutics and British Practical Divinity', in H.E. Braun and E. Vallance (eds), *Contexts of Conscience in Early Modern Europe 1500–1700* (Basingstoke, 2004), pp. 17–31. I use the expression to refer more broadly to 'writings about conscience'.

of their practical divinity' and hence regularly refer to Aquinas, among others.[33] Similarly, Wood remarks 'the extent to which they adopted, or adapted, the general principles, terminology, categories, and distinctions' of scholastic writers.[34] What the Protestants tended to object to was not how Catholic theorists adumbrated the basic framework and processes of conscience, but the attributing of authority to confessors over penitents' consciences[35] and the reliance on what they regarded as 'weake and vnstable Grounds' in resolving specific moral or spiritual dilemmas,[36] or, more broadly, to what has been described as 'the legalistic and authoritarian emphasis in Roman [Catholic] moral theology'.[37] Even respecting solutions to particular cases, William Ames (1576–1633) acknowledges that '[t]he Papists have laboured much this way, to instruct their Confessors: and in a great deale of earth and dirt of Superstitions, they haue some veines of Silver ...'.[38] Thus, while a writer like Richard Carpenter (1575–1627) might protest that, in his treatment of conscience, he is not aiming at 'an exact Scholasticall Discourse' and that he is eschewing 'the nicities and curious speculations of Schoole-men', his 'generall notions'[39] and those of his co-religionists are specifically reminiscent of frameworks of thought that we have already encountered.

---

33 Thomas Merrill, *William Perkins 1558–1602, English Puritanist* (Nieuwkoop, 1966), pp. xii–xiii.

34 Wood, p. 57.

35 As usual, one must be cautious about assuming a uniform Protestant, or even Anglican, position. For example, in a sermon preached at Cambridge University in 1637, Anthony Sparrow (1612–85; later Bishop of Norwich) argued, citing St. Gregory the Great, that 'Priests were made God's Vicegerents here on Earth, in his Name to retain and forgive Sins, not *declaratively* only, but *judicially: Animarum judices sunt* …' (*Confession of Sins, and the Power of Absolution* [London, 1704], p. 16; ECCO image CW122804330:17). Wood points out that Anglicans, generally, 'approved of the confessional when used wisely and judiciously' (p. 54).

36 See, for example, Thomas Pickering, 'Epistle Dedicatorie' to William Perkins, *The Whole Treatise of the Cases of Conscience* (Cambridge, 1606), sig. ¶6v; EEBO image 14434:7.

37 Wood, p. xviii.

38 William Ames, *Conscience, with the Power and Cases thereof* (Leyden and London, 1639), sig. A4v; EEBO image 15139:5. At the end of the seventeenth century Thomas Barlow (1607–91) in *Autoschediasmata, de studio theologiæ, or, Directions for the Choice of Books in the Study of Divinity* (Oxford, 1700) could say of 'the *Schoolmen* (and of *Popish Casuists* and Commentators too, especially those before *Luther*) that when they speak of Moral Duties, and those things which are within the compass of Natural Reason … we shall find many things well, and some very accurately said', although in specifically religious matters their errors are 'many and great' (pp. 40–41; EEBO image 17143:26).

39 Richard Carpenter, p. 40; EEBO image 8100:26.

Objective Conscience

One important difference to which I have already alluded is the Protestant assigning of responsibility for making determinations of conscience to the individual person him or herself. Not only, in Perkins's words, does 'euery particular man [have] his owne particular conscience',[40] but, in Merrill's, and more tellingly, 'every man [is] his own casuist'.[41] However, Protestantism's celebrated individualism notwithstanding, the Reformers' account of conscience remained insistently objective. Typical of the claims that one encounters are Pickering's that Perkins's doctrine of conscience 'is not founded in the opinions, and variable conceits of men … but it resteth vpon most sufficient and certaine Grounds',[42] and Bernard's that '[t]he knowledge of *Conscience* commeth not with an *If*, or *An*, as opinionatiue, resting on coniectures and probabilities' but 'is grounded on sure Principles … and speakes with authority from God ...'.[43] While ascertaining what conscience requires is the responsibility of each person, it is not a matter of opinion, probability, or conjecture, but, again, something to be measured in so far as it is *right*. That, at least, was the theory.

Among the aspects of Protestant conscience that conduce to its objectivity are its ruledness, its being a function of knowledge or understanding, and its involving a set, syllogistic form of reasoning, leading to 'inevitable' conclusions. Each of these elements—which we have certainly encountered before—warrants closer examination, including some assessment of its implications, in its Protestant form, for conscience as a principle of legal judgment.

The 'Law' of Conscience

We will recall St. German's insistence that conscience must always be based upon a law—the law of God, the law of reason, or human law. This is no less true in the subsequent Protestant writers on conscience, although, as we shall see, some of what they say makes the issue problematic when it comes to relying on positive *human* law as determinative of conscience. One need not seek far for assertions of this general point: Cornelius Burges (1589?–1665), for example, says that for a person's conscience to 'stand vpon a firme ground, it must bee guided in euery thing by *a sure Rule*';[44] Jackson, noting that '[e]very science and art proceeds by a rule', observes that this is equally true of conscience, 'which ought to be as levell-handed in her cases as the men of *Gibeah* in the book of *Judges*, who could

[40] Perkins, *Discourse,* p. 4; EEBO image 10898:6.

[41] Merrill, p. xiv.

[42] Pickering, 'Epistle Dedicatorie' to Perkins, *Whole Treatise*, sigs. ¶2v–¶3r; EEBO image 14434:3.

[43] Bernard, p. 16; EEBO image 14165:29.

[44] Cornelius Burges, *A New Discouery of Personal Tithes* (London, 1625), p. 23; EEBO image 14242:18.

throw stones at an haire-breadth';[45] Dyke (1584–1639) argues that it is 'no marvell if men have crooked wayes, and crooked conscience, when they will not live by Rule';[46] and for Bernard we 'know when we do a thing of very Conscience; when we looke to the Rule of our action ...'.[47] A primary requisite for conscience, as described by these Protestant commentators, is its being subject to a rule or law outside the will of the individual.

The source of this rule or law is variously described. For Dyke, it is simple: 'Gods Word is the Rule of conscience.'[48] Bernard presents a more elaborate picture: '[t]he Rule is but one onely, which is Gods Law and Will', but '[t]hough this Rule bee but one, it is Considerable three waies: first, as it is in nature: Secondly, as it in the Law, and old Testament: Thirdly, as it is in the Gospell, and new Testament'.[49] So, ostensibly, one manifestation of the law of God is the law of nature, or of reason. Other writers include human law. Thus, Burges (1589?–1665) identifies the rule of conscience—at least as it relates to tithes—as 'either the *expresse Word* of God; or else the *Established Law of the Kingdome* wherein a man liues ...',[50] and Jackson says that the 'law or line of conscience is foure-fold', namely, '*Divine* law', the 'law of *Nature*', the 'law of *Nations*', and '*Positive* lawes, whether they be Ecclesiasticall, or Civill ...'.[51] Putting these all together, we can identify something like the elements in St. German's account: the law of conscience may be the law of God, of nature, or of man.

However, for many of these Protestant commentators how human law could bind the conscience was problematic. Perkins is typical—or perhaps prototypical.[52] He draws a fundamental distinction between those laws that 'properly' (or 'immediately'[53]) bind the conscience and those that do so only 'improperly' (or mediately): 'God alone makes laws binding cõscience properly, & no creature can do the like'.[54] Similarly, Ames observes that 'the perfect and only rule of

45 Jackson, pp. 38–9; EEBO image 103990:25.

46 Dyke, p. 49; EEBO image 17557:30.

47 Bernard, p. 38; EEBO image 14165:41. See also Thomas Scot, 'Salomon's Puritan', in *Christ's Politician, and Salomon's Puritan* (London, 1616), p. 17; EEBO image 164:27: 'conscience neuer bindeth in it selfe, but by vertue of some commandement from God'.

48 Dyke, p. 48; EEBO image 17557:30.

49 Bernard, pp. 42–3; EEBO image 14165:43.

50 Burges, p. 23; EEBO image 14242:18. He adds the qualification that this latter does not bind in conscience if it contradicts divine law. See discussion below.

51 Jackson, pp. 40–42; EEBO images 103990:26–7.

52 Merrill says that Perkins's casuistry 'set a pattern for all later work in Protestant moral divinity' (p. xx). Compare Meg Lota Brown, *Donne and the Politics of Conscience in Early Modern England* (Leiden, 1995), p. 10. Ames credits Perkins with providing the inspiration for the study of cases of conscience (sig. A3r; EEBO image 15139:3).

53 Barnes, p. 70; EEBO image 15204:42.

54 Perkins, *Discourse*, pp. 54–5; EEBO image 10898:31.

Conscience is the revealed will of God'.[55] So, the law of God properly binds the conscience; human law does so only in some secondary, derivative, or 'improper' sense.[56] This distinction has important (though not unanswerable) implications for the notion of a human tribunal that purports to engage conscience.

Perkins goes on to offer a more nuanced analysis of the 'law of God', which I shall merely outline here. That law consists of two main subdivisions: 'the Law' and 'the Gospel', or, perhaps, the law of the Old Testament and the law of the New. The latter relates especially to spiritual righteousness and 'life everlasting'. The former Perkins analyses further. 'The law' is either (1) 'Morall', the very law of nature written in all mens hearts', and involving duties of love, partly to God and partly towards our neighbour, (2) 'Judiciall', to which I shall return, or (3) 'Ceremoniall', prescribing rites and forms for the outward worship of God.[57] Judicial laws—those given to the Jews in the Old Testament—are themselves of two kinds: (1) laws of particular equity, addressed to and binding upon only the Jews in their particular circumstances, and (2) laws of common equity, 'made according to the lawe or instinct of nature common to all men' and thus binding on everyone. Thus, in Perkins's account of the law of God is included what might be called the law of nature or the law of reason (that is, the moral law, and the judicial law of common equity recognized not only in the Old Testament, but among all nations as being 'equall, iust, and necessary'[58]).

Against these categories Perkins juxtaposes 'improper' binders of conscience, that is, those 'which [have] no power at all or vertue in [themselves] to binde

---

[55] Ames, p. 6; EEBO image 15139:8. Ames distinguishes revealing of the rule of conscience from commanding. Elsewhere, a distinction is drawn between commanding and binding conscience. While these distinctions may be significant for many purposes (for example, a human law may *show* us what the rule of conscience is even though, as we shall see, it does not properly *bind* conscience), I do not propose to develop them here, since my concern is essentially with the status of different kinds of law *vis-à-vis* conscience.

[56] This distinction appears to have been fairly commonplace, and to have been made in more 'popular' theology as well as in more formal treatises like Perkins's. See, for example, Thomas Scot's sermon *God and the King*, preached to the judges and lawyers at the Bury St. Edmund's assizes (13th June 1631), p. 12; EEBO image 141:9 ('Gods law is *immediately* seated upon the conscience, mans law is seated upon the conscience too, but *mediately*').

[57] Perkins, *Discourse*, pp. 14ff.; EEBO images 10898:11ff. In view of the fact that Perkins (and others) explicitly make this distinction, it is puzzling that, in the nineteenth century, Joseph Parkes, *A History of the Court of Chancery* (London, 1828) could suggest that it was unknown to (or not perceived by) 'the mystified intellects of our evangelical ancestors' (pp. 188–9).

[58] Perkins, *Discourse*, p. 18; EEBO image 10898:23. He gives as an example the rather startling law that not only murderers but also adulterers should be put to death, since he finds this rule in other cultures as well as in the Old Testament (pp. 19–20; EEBO images 10898:13–14).

conscience': these include 'Humane lawes', 'an Oath', and 'a Promise'.[59] Oaths are, of course, of central importance in the context of the present study, since it is the oath that binds the conscience of the litigant in the Chancellor's court. But the effect of an oath on conscience is relatively unproblematic. As Perkins observes, an oath is binding by virtue of specific biblical command.[60] Outlining the nature of an oath, he explains that it has a dual aspect: first, it is an invocation to God 'that he would become a witness vnto vs that we speak the truth', and, second, it involves our acknowledging that 'if we faile and breake our promise, [God will] take reuenge vpon vs': 'in both these petitions we binde our selues immediately to God himselfe'.[61] An oath is an obligation to God; breach of an oath is a sin, and punishable as such—in the final analysis, by God.

More complex is the question of how human laws are binding on conscience. In their effect on conscience, Perkins (and other Protestant writers) see human laws as being different not just in provenance, but in kind, from the laws of God and of nature.

Perkins adumbrates two ways in which human laws bind—or can be said to bind—conscience. First, though, he identifies two areas of human legislation: subjects that are already governed by divine law, and subjects which are 'indifferent'. Ames explains that the latter (commonly known as *adiaphora*), are things which are 'in the middle betweene morall good and evill'.[62] Respecting these indifferent matters, human laws 'have no vertue or power in themselues to constraine conscience, but they bind onely by vertue of an higher commandement'.[63] That is, conscience is involved not directly by the human ordinance, but 'because Gods law is broken which ordaineth magistracie, and … binds mens consciences to obey their lawfull commandements'.[64] Perkins apparently rejects the idea, accepted by

---

59 Ibid., p. 38; EEBO image 10898:23.

60 Ibid., p. 70; EEBO image 10898:39. He is referring to Numbers 30:2–3.

61 Perkins, *Discourse*, p. 72; EEBO image 10898:40.

62 Ames, p. 88; EEBO image 15139:82.

63 Perkins, *Discourse*, p. 62; EEBO image 10898:35. Compare Scot, *Salomons Puritan*, p. 17; 'In matters of indifferency the commandement of a Prince and a prelate, doth more binde man, then his owne conscience, because in these things the Prince … hath preheminence aboue conscience.'

64 Perkins, *Discourse*, p. 47; EEBO image 10898:27. So, for example, see Romans 13:1: 'Let every soul be subject unto the higher powers' and 1 Peter 2:13: 'Submit yourselves to every ordinance of man for the Lord's sake'. See also, for example, Bernard, p. 51; EEBO 14165:48. John Donne, in *Pseudo-Martyr*, ed. Anthony Raspa (Montreal and Kingston, 1993), identifies another possible way in which human laws bind conscience: since the object of such laws is '*The common good, and tranquility*, and to offend against that, is to offend against rectified Reason, and therefore sinne …' (p. 227). Generally, see Johann Sommerville, 'Conscience, Law, and Things Indifferent: Arguments on Toleration from the Vestiarian Controversy to Hobbes and Locke', in H.E. Braun and E. Vallance (eds), *Contexts of Conscience in Early Modern Europe 1500–1700* (Basingstoke, 2004), pp. 166–79.

some, that the authority magistrates exercise is a delegation to them by God of His 'soueraigne and absolute power … ouer all his creatures',[65] an idea which presumably would entail that governors were exercising vicariously God's own law-making power and that their ordinances would be intrinsically or 'properly' binding on conscience.

A major reason why human laws cannot, in themselves, govern conscience is that the special subject-matter of conscience is inherently not susceptible to those laws. As Perkins explains:

> Whosoeuer bindes conscience, commaunds conscience. … Now Gods laws commaund conscience in as much as they are spirituall, commaunding bodie and spirit, with all the thoughts, will, affections, desires, and faculties … As for the laws of men, they want power to commaund conscience. Indeede if it were possible for our gouernours by law to commaund mens thoughts and affections, then also might they command cõscience: but the first is not possible, for their lawes can reach no further then the outward man, that is, to bodie and goods ...[66]

Human laws cannot command or act upon the internal dispositions of persons—that which is proper to conscience. Thomas Morton (1564–1659) advances a similar point, saying that we must not 'confound the distinct Courts & *Iurisdictions*, one whereof is *Gods*, and the other is *Mans*; The first being spirituall and inuisible; the second onely ciuill and sensible'.[67] Since the act of binding a person's conscience is 'spirituall and inuisible', it can occur only in the *forum coeli*; in the *forum soli*, 'onely the outward Acts of men' may be judged and punished.[68]

Thus, Perkins particularly and emphatically rejects what he claims to be the view of 'the very pillers of the popish Church' that '*Civill and Ecclesiasticall Iurisdiction have a coactive power in the conscience, and that the lawes made thereby doe as* truly *and properly binde ... to mortall & venial sinne, as Gods law it selfe*'.[69] That is, they would say, human laws alone can bind the conscience

---

65 Perkins, *Discourse*, p. 53; EEBO image 10898:30.

66 Ibid., pp. 57–8; EEBO images 10898:32–3. Compare, for example, Ames, p. 6; EEBO image 15139:8 ('God onely knowes the inward workings of the Conscience; he therefore onely can prescribe a law unto it, or bind it by one') and Bourne, p. 11; EEBO image 7186:8 ('Conscience can no man binde; they may bind thy body and cast that into prison ...'). Donne tells us that, while Princes can only 'by reward and punishment … encline or avert our dispositions to a love or feare [,] those [Catholic] Bishops pretend a power upon the substance of our soules, which must be in their disposition, for her condition and state in the next life' (*Pseudo-Martyr*, 54–5).

67 Thomas Morton, *A Defence of the Innocencie of the Three Ceremonies of the Church of England* (London, 1618), p. 187; EEBO image 13324:104.

68 Ibid.

69 Perkins, *Discourse*, p. 38; EEBO image 10898:23.

in the sense that a transgression of them *per se* would be a *sin.*[70] If this is so, one can immediately recognize in the Protestant insistence upon a strict separation of the *forum coeli* from the *forum soli* at least a demotion of human law *vis-à-vis* conscience. The effect is not necessarily to exclude conscience from human law, but to give it a more circumscribed role. If human law, *per se*, does bind conscience, it almost certainly makes more sense (or makes sense in a different way) to speak of a court of conscience, of the Chancellor's acting upon the defendant's conscience, or, indeed, of the court binding litigants' consciences.

The other kinds of subjects addressed by human law are, of course, those which are *not* indifferent or morally neutral. Where human laws decree 'things that be good in themselues'—that is, that are already subject to some aspect of God's law—'then they are not *humane* properly but *divine* lawes', and, as such, directly bind conscience.[71] Indeed, Perkins observes, a person who violates such a law sins in two ways: first, by disobeying the direct ordinance of God respecting the action in issue and, second, by disobeying God's command that we are to obey the 'higher powers'. Another possibility is that a human law might be inconsistent with divine law. In such a case there is 'no bonde of conscience at all but contrariwise, men are bound in conscience not to obay'.[72] This is reminiscent of St. German, who, we may remember, opines that a human law that contravenes the law of God or the law of reason is no law at all.

The foregoing raises the question of what place remains for conscience as exercised by Chancery. If the law relates to morally indifferent things, by hypothesis conscience as moral judgment has no role to play. Arguably, if the alleged Catholic view were correct and human laws, even respecting things otherwise indifferent, could bind conscience, then Chancery might have a role in rendering such laws more 'convenient' (the initial criterion for legislating in respect of *adiaphora*[73]), and thus fine-tuning what conscience is bound to. But this would be rather odd—making the 'conscience' element in Chancery's jurisdiction something that follows from the exercise of that jurisdiction, rather than being the criterion upon which Chancery acts in the first place. If what is in play are morally significant matters, then the law either accords with God's law, and presumably does not need to

---

[70] Interestingly, Perkins says that the Catholics should have learned from 'their owne *Doctor Gerson*' 'that they that binde any man to mortall sinne, must be able to punish him with answerable punishment, which is eternal death' (ibid., pp. 39–40; EEBO images 10898:23–4).

[71] Ibid., p. 62; EEBO image 10898:35.

[72] Ibid., p. 63; EEBO image 10898:35.

[73] See Perkins, *Whole Treatise*, pp. 8–9; EEBO image 14434:25, where he suggests that indifferent things may be divided into those which are 'convenient' and those which are 'inconvenient'. At the time, 'convenient' had a connotation closer to 'fitting' than it does now. Even so, it is not clear whether, when Chancery judges invoke 'convenience' as a criterion, they are engaging 'conscience' or 'prudence'.

be modified to make it binding on conscience, or it contravenes God's law and therefore is not binding on conscience. So what role can conscience play?

The answer probably would be something very much like what St. German says. That is, respecting *non-adiaphora*, there is a third possibility. The argument implicit in the preceding paragraph is that human law is exhaustive—that it either accords with, or disaccords with, God's law, the law of reason, etc. But, as St. German has already told us, there will be areas in which human law is simply imperfect or incomplete. Where such law does not offend conscience, but falls short of what conscience requires, there will presumably still remain space for it to be made more accordant with conscience. So, for example, there is nothing against the law of God in requiring that repayment of a debt be evidenced by an acquittance. But that human law falls short in not providing for cases of fraud, or of unjust enrichment. This brings us back to the more or less conventional account of how and where Chancery equity operates: it purports to make whole matters of conscience which the ordinary law fails adequately to embody. Of course, this analysis again does not tell us which matters of conscience are the proper purview of Chancery. It tells us *how* Chancery can intelligibly be said to add conscience to the law, but it tells us nothing about the extent of the matters of conscience that Chancery should enforce. I shall return to this point later.

So, from the first point regarding the objectivity of conscience—its basis in some external law—we can conclude that the Protestant account attributes a less radical role to human law than does the Catholic. St. Peter, we may recall, was given the power to bind and loose not only on earth but in heaven as well.[74] The Popes were understood to be Peter's successors in this regard, as in others. Thus, to the Church was attributed the power both of making law whose transgression was sin and of imposing directly spiritual sanctions. This power was energetically denied by Protestants like Perkins. One aspect, then, of the difference between the Catholic and the Protestant positions for our purpose is that the former was more immediately consonant with the notion of human tribunals that directly engaged conscience. Perkins's position is that human law, and by implication human tribunals, can neither command nor bind conscience immediately, nor can they impose sanctions 'answerable' to the nature of conscience. At most what they can do is discern what appears to be conduct consonant or not consonant with conscience and impose outward, material sanctions that purport to correspond to those conditions of conscience. They cannot create sin, nor condemn in a manner proper to sin; they cannot directly affect conscience. Again, this does not make the invocation of conscience in a Protestant legal tribunal unintelligible, but it does render it less radically compelling.

---

[74] Matthew 16:19. For a discussion, and a Protestant interpretation, see for example Perkins, *Discourse*, pp. 40–41; EEBO image 10898:24.

Conscience and Knowledge

If examining this one locus of the purported objectivity of conscience allows us to identify one kind of difference that attenuates the force of Protestant conscience as a juristic principle relative to its Catholic counterpart, examining other loci reveals similar implications.

A second such locus is the emphasis on the connection of conscience to understanding and its involving *knowledge*. Perkins, explaining that 'God in framing of the soule placed in it two principall faculties, *Vnderstanding* and *Will*', describes conscience as 'a part of the vnderstanding in all reasonable creatures'.[75] For Hughes, conscience is what Aquinas (and St. German, following him) said it was: '[a]n *act of reason*, applying our knowledge to our works';[76] for Worship too it is '*a Part of the Practicall vnderstanding*';[77] for Harris, conscience is 'a prime faculty of the reasonable soule'.[78] Ames says that he calls conscience '*Iudgement*' 'to shew that it belongs to the Vnderstanding, not to the Will', and notes that the word itself tells us as much.[79] Rational judgment, in contrast with the movements of the will or affections, is supposedly much more 'objective'. If *desiring* to do the right thing could satisfy the demands of conscience, all persons having that desire would satisfy those demands, albeit their conclusions were at variance. Positing that conscience involves correct understanding of what is to be done entails a more exacting and invariable standard.

To be sure, some of the Protestant writers offered a more complex account of the site of conscience, but reason and understanding still tend to be given prominence. Bernard, for example, characterizes conscience as 'a distinct thing in the soule from all other faculties' which 'worketh in euery one of them'—understanding, memory, will, affections.[80] Still, he makes the common etymological point that

---

75 Perkins, *Discourse*, p. 1; EEB0 image 10898:4. Wood, p. 67, emphasizes that most of the Protestant casuists regarded the operation of conscience as 'primarily a rational activity'. Conversely, Perkins explains, it is not in the will or the 'affections' which are joined to it (ibid.).

76 Hughes, p. 4, EEBO image 4483:5, citing Aquinas, *Summa Theologiæ*, Part I, Question 79, answer 13. Donne, also quoting Aquinas as authority for the proposition that '*Conscience* ever presumes *Knowledge*', uses this connection to argue that, if we do not know something, we cannot (and should not) base our conscience upon it: 'we may not … doe any thing upon *Conscience*, if we doe it not upon *Knowledge*' (Donne, *Pseudo-Martyr*, p. 173).

77 Worship, p. 9; EEBO image 14830:15. See also Edward Reynoldes, *A Treatise of the Passions and Faculties of the Soule of Man* (London, 1640), p. 531; EEBO image 16360:246.

78 Harris, p. 5; EEBO image 6263:8.

79 Ames, p. 1; EEBO image 15139:5.

80 Bernard, pp. 6–7; EEBO image 14165:24.

the 'science' part of the word imports knowledge[81] and he insists that knowledge is essential 'for the furthering of the work of Conscience'.[82] Bourne, as we have seen, places conscience in the whole soul, not just the understanding, although the latter is 'the Throne and Palace of Conscience, where it exerciseth the principall offices'.[83] It is not part of my project to explore these nuances, but simply to make the general point that all these writers emphasize the primarily intellective, as opposed to the volitional or affective, nature of conscience—although none would deny that will and affect are involved in its operation.

Customarily they make the further point that intellectual activity involved is practical and not just theoretical. Perkins explains that there are two parts to the understanding—the '*Theorical*', which 'stands in the view and contemplation of *truth* and *falshood*, and goes no further' and the '*practical*', which applies knowledge to particular actions.[84] Conscience resides in the latter. Ames similarly makes the point that 'Conscience is not *a contemplative judgement*', but a practical one in which one's knowledge is applied to one's own circumstances and aims at providing direction for one's will.[85] So, conscience involves understanding, which imparts an objective element to it. But, at the same time, it is applied and particularized knowledge, which imparts a measure of relativity to it. In being attuned to particular circumstances, as opposed to general statements of principle, conscience resembles the conventional portrayal of equity, and the similarity is not fortuitous. At the same time, the characterization of conscience as involving particularized knowledge has a subjective dimension which, as we shall see, makes it problematic as a juristic principle.

One aspect of the understanding involved in conscience is the apprehension of the principles underlying its application. Many of the Protestant writers identify this with *synteresis*,[86] which we have already seen. Ames speaks of *synteresis* as

---

81 Ibid., pp. 9–10; EEBO images 14165:25–6.

82 Ibid., p. 35; EEBO image 14165:39.

83 Bourne, p. 8; EEBO image 7186:7. Compare Richard Carpenter who, although he gives conscience 'roome and place in the whole soule', does accept that it 'resideth … principally in the vnderstanding, as her Metropolis Palace-Throne' (pp. 41–2; EEBO image 8100:26–7).

84 Perkins, *Discourse*, p. 2; EEBO image 10898:5.

85 Ames, p. 2; EEBO image 15139:6.

86 Robert A. Greene, 'Synderesis, the Spark of Conscience, in the English Renaissance', *Journal of the History of Ideas* 52/2 (1991): 195–219, p. 208, suggests that, by around 1600, synderesis had been 'derisively' and 'satirically' rejected 'as a term of common English usage', citing a few literary occurrences of the term as evidence. As the following discussion indicates, I would question his conclusion. Moreover, his position is equivocal: although the term may have fallen into desuetude, he appears to say that the *concept* persisted under other names, notably the 'spark of conscience' (p. 210). Further, if it was 'a term of common English usage', that suggests that it was familiar to a broader public than, say, professional casuists.

'a *naturall habit* … whereby the understanding of man is fitted to giue assent unto Naturall principles'; it relates to the law of conscience as apprehension relates to its object: the law is the object; *synteresis* is the apprehension of that law.[87] *Synteresis* is our knowledge of what Bernard calls 'certaine, vnfallible' principles of truth.[88] For Richard Carpenter it is the '*treasury of morall principles, and of sacred rules wherewith the practicall understanding is furnished* ...'.[89]

If the knowledge that conscience entails ended there, it would presumably be (at least theoretically) perfectly objective. But conscience involves another kind of knowledge. Indeed, Perkins distinguishes conscience from a number of other 'gifts of the minde', including knowledge (or 'science') *per se*. Thus, it is to be distinguished from intelligence, which 'simply conceives a thing to be or not to be', science, which judges a thing 'to be certen and sure', faith, opinion, and so on.[90] He goes on to explain that, in respect of human conduct, the difference between knowledge *per se* and conscience is that the former allows us to be 'certen what an other man hath saide or done', whereas the latter permits a person 'to be certen what he himselfe hath done or saide'.[91] Or, as Bourne (following St. Bernard) puts it, conscience is '*Cordis scientia*, the science or knowledg of the *heart* … When [the heart] knoweth other things, it is called *science*; and when it knoweth it selfe, it is called *conscience*'.[92] Science, or knowledge, relates to things external to oneself—principles of right and wrong, what we can know of other persons by what words and actions communicate to us. Conscience, by contrast, is the faculty which allows us to know ourselves. That knowledge is objective in so far as it is either right or wrong, but it is 'subjective' in containing elements ultimately unfathomable by others.

This point is regularly made by the writers when they refer to the other component—'con'—of the word 'conscience'. '*Scire*', says Perkins, 'to know, is of one man alone by himselfe: and *conscire* is, when two at the least know some one secret thing.'[93] This notion, that conscience is 'a *knowledge together*',[94] is a

87 Ames, p. 5, EEBO image 15139:7.

88 Bernard, p. 45; EEBO image 14165:44.

89 Richard Carpenter, sig. B1v; EEBO image 8100:5.

90 Perkins, *Discourse*, p. 4; EEBO image 10898:6.

91 Ibid.

92 Bourne, p. 6; EEBO image 7186:6. St. Bernard's definition is frequently cited: see Richard Carpenter, p. 41; EEBO image 8100:6. There is some ambiguity in some authors' use of 'science' and 'conscience'. Sometimes these are the basis of knowledge, so for example, conscience is a faculty of understanding through which a certain kind of knowledge may be acquired. Sometimes, however, conscience is spoken of as if it were the knowledge itself, and science is similarly identified with knowledge.

93 Perkins, *Discourse*, p. 5; EEBO image 10898:6.

94 Dyke, p. 14; EEBO image 17557:13.

commonplace.[95] Indeed, it is hardly new with the Protestant writers, who regularly cite the scholastics in this regard.[96] We will recall that Sir John Fortescue, in a fifteenth-century case, made this same etymological point.[97]

But what the Protestant writers emphasize is who shares—indeed, who can possibly share—this knowledge with the individual. As Perkins explains, it is *secret* knowledge, knowable only by oneself and by God:

> Now man and man … cannot be combined; because they can not know the secret of any man vnlesse it be reuealed to them: it remaines therefore that this combination is onely betweene man and God. God knowes perfectly all the doings of man, though they be neuer so hid and concealed: and man by a gift giuẽ him of God; knows togither with God, the same things of himselfe: and this gift is named Conscience.[98]

This has significant implications for conscience as a juridical principle. If only God and the person involved can have the knowledge that conscience entails, how can a human tribunal purport to act according to conscience? To be sure, earlier writers saw conscience as involving, as Fortescue puts it, *quasi simul scire cum deo*.[99] However, Catholic doctrine, in its concepts of auricular confession and the vicarious powers of the clergy, appears to have been much more amenable to the possibility of that knowledge being accessed by another person—the priest/confessor or, ostensibly, the ecclesiastical Chancellor. For example, Fortescue gives no inkling that the 'secret' nature of the knowledge afforded by conscience precludes its application as a principle of judicial decision. At least there seems to have been a recognized procedure for revealing such secret knowledge. For Protestants, the exclusivity of this knowledge to God and a person's own heart was much more absolute.[100]

---

95 See also Bourne, p. 6; EEBO image 7186:6, Bernard, pp. 32–3; EEBO image 14165:38, Hughes, p. 7; EEBO image 4483:6.

96 So, for example, Bourne quotes Aquinas's dictum: '*Conscientia dicitur cum alio scientia*' (p. 6; EEBO image 7186:6.) See also Richard Carpenter, p. 41; EEBO image 8100:26.

97 Nicholas Statham, *Abridgment des libres annales* (1490), under 'Conscience', sig. G3v; EEBO image 9984:53.

98 Perkins, *Discourse*, p. 5; EEBO image 10898:6. Compare Dyke, p. 14; EEBO image 17557:13 ('when God and a mans heart know a thing, there is Conscience, knowledge together'), and Bernard, p. 33; EEBO image 14165:38 ('Conscience hath acquaintance with God, knowing with God, and God with it').

99 Statham, sig. G3v; EEBO image 9984:53.

100 Bourne offers a poignant picture of the essentially private nature of Protestant confessional engagement with conscience: 'Once a weeke at least … spend one *hower* in *examination* of thy selfe, in opening the *booke* of thy *conscience*, in confessing thy selfe to

While the emphasis upon conscience as involving knowledge of an objective character remains, access to that knowledge is curtailed. It is objective knowledge that is only subjectively available, so to speak. To the extent that the implications of this position were recognized, the cogency of calling Chancery a 'court of conscience' in any very literal sense would once more have been compromised.

This is not to say that, in the Protestant view, characterizing Chancery as a court of conscience would have been simply untenable. Indeed, some of the very writers to whom I have been referring say that it is a court of conscience. And the effect of being examined under oath would be that a party should disclose knowledge otherwise secreted in his or her conscience. But it appears that Chancery would have been such a court only in a secondary, attenuated, or perhaps 'figurative' way.

Bernard, rather *en passant*, suggests one way a human tribunal engages conscience:

> Conscience meddles with me, in behalfe of another, as farre as I am to thinke or speake of him, as in Conscience I take him to be. Iury-men giue in their Virdict upon others from their Conscience in this respect. Hence is it that we vse to say, of my Conscience he is an honest Man ….[101]

This in no way suggests that we are able to plumb the consciences of others, or to bind them in conscience. Rather, the conscience involved is that of the person sitting in judgment: his or her conscience becomes the measure of the act of judging. Hence the expression 'informing the conscience of the Chancellor'—that is, providing him with knowledge (albeit never comprehensive or exhaustive) that will allow *his* conscience to be satisfied respecting facts. Thus, we may still be in a 'court of conscience' in some sense, but this is a far cry from a court which is focused upon the actual condition of conscience of the litigants. I would not want to be taken to be adopting an unqualified position at this point: the conscience of the party continues to be referred to in Chancery throughout the period I am considering. But the shifts in understanding which we have seen probably made this focus less theoretically compelling than it might have been to the medieval mind.

The Logic of Conscience

Another aspect of the putative objectivity of conscience, closely related to those just discussed, is that it was understood as following logical processes. As we have seen before, and as the Protestant commentators regularly remind us, the rational operation of conscience takes the form of a syllogism, or, as Fenner calls

---

God … goe into thy closet, and shut the doore after thee, and weepe in secret for thy owne sinnes …' (p. 30; EEBO image 7186:18).

101 Bernard, p. 55; EEBO image 14165:50.

it, 'a Logicall discourse'.[102] Bernard characterizes the process of conscience as a 'concluding science'[103] and Jackson says that conscience 'can make unanswerable Syllogismes, and can out of strong premisses bring undeniable conclusions'.[104] What conscience tells us is not a matter of intuition or opinion or 'feeling', but of demonstration.[105]

Ames offers a fairly typical account of the syllogism: '[t]hat which doth dictate or giue the proposition is called *Synteresis*, by the Schoolemen *Synderesis*. The assumption especially and peculiarly is called *Syneidesis*, the conclusion is the *Krisis*, or Iudgement'.[106] Dyke uses similar terms, explaining that *Syneidesis* relates to 'a mans particular estate, or action'.[107] As we have seen previously, another common way of describing the three elements in conscience is to call them 'Law', 'Witness' and 'Judge'. As Jackson explains, 'in the *major proposition* is the *law* of Conscience, in the *minor* or *assumption* lies the evidence or *witnesse*, in the *conclusion* lies the *sentence* or *judgement*'.[108] Similarly, Anthony Cade (c. 1564–1641) says that the text of conscience is tripartite: '*De jure*', '*De facto*' and '*De krisei*'.[109] Not only do these observations make the point that conscience involves logical processes, but they indicate that those processes exactly mirror the structure of legal judgment—that is, the application of law to proven facts to reach a decision. Moreover, they remind us that conscience has normative ('*De jure*') and evidentiary ('*De facto*') dimensions; it involves both the identifying of rules and the discovery of facts.

In this account, the major premise is provided by *synteresis*—our apprehension of basic principles. Ames explains that, 'being taken after a large sense', *synteresis* includes both 'generall conclusions touching right or Law … deduced … out of naturall principles' and 'all practicall truths, whereunto wee giue a firme assent, through the revelation wee haue by faith'.[110] What is especially significant about *synteresis*, and the law to which it relates, is that they are universal; they do not vary from person to person. The law, and the correlative knowledge of the law, are

---

102 Fenner, pp. 64; EEBO image 15425:43. He refers to the operation of conscience as a 'judiciary process'.

103 Bernard, p. 40; EEBO image 14165:42.

104 Jackson, p. 24; EEBO image 103990:18.

105 See Merrill, p. xiii, observing that, as an intellectual act, the operation of conscience could be 'described in syllogistic form', and Lowell Gallagher, *Medusa's Gaze: Casuistry and Conscience in the Renaissance* (Stanford, 1991), p. 314n.

106 Ames, p. 4; EEBO image 15139:7. Compare Richard Carpenter, sig. B1v and pp. 42–3; EEBO images 8100:5, 27.

107 Dyke, p. 19; EEBO image 17557:15.

108 Jackson, pp. 13, 20–21; EEBO images 103990:12, 16. See also Ames, p. 28; EEBO image 15139:19.

109 Anthony Cade, *Conscience, Its Nature and Corruption* (London, 1661), p. 3; EEBO image 54332:6.

110 Ames, p. 5; EEBO image 15139:7.

necessarily objective. *Synteresis* discloses the *truth*.[111] As we have seen elsewhere, this is because *synteresis* is knowledge: if a thing is known, it must be so; in matters of *synteresis*, two different views cannot both be correct. This picture is, of course, complicated by the fact that, as Ames, among others, notes, the principles actually applied to questions of conscience are not just the basic concepts themselves, but more specific norms derived from them.

The second element in the syllogism—what Ames calls *syneidesis*—is theoretically more problematic in this regard. As I have already intimated, for the Protestant casuists, this element involves the appreciation of facts—of a person's actual conduct or state of mind. Hence, as we have seen, it is described as a witness, the purveyor of evidence. This point occurs repeatedly in our authors. For Perkins, this aspect of conscience, associated with memory, is 'a notarie, or a register that hath alwaies the penne in his hand, to note and record whatsoeuer is saide or done';[112] it 'beares witnesse of our thoughts, of our affections, of our outward actions'.[113] Similarly, for Dyke, this 'office' of conscience 'is the Register and Recorder of the soule', which, in 'the Court of Conscience', will be a true witness, testifying 'according to every mans deeds';[114] and for Cade, it provides '*a Record, History, or Chronicle of all our counsels, courses, thoughts, words, and works*'.[115] One of Ames's chapters is entitled *Of the attention of Conscience to its Facts*, and he again emphasizes that the minor premise of the syllogism of conscience 'is nothing else, but the *recognizing*, or considering of our action or estate'.[116]

Conscience is an excellent witness; it is 'placed in the soule, as Gods spy'; it is 'with a man at all times, and in all places, so that there is not a thought, word, or worke that it knowes not';[117] as many authors tell us, it is as good as or better than a thousand witnesses.[118] Yet it suffers from one radical limitation: it is internal to each individual. It knows everything about a person, but what it knows is accessible only to that person and to God. As Bourne observes, a defect of ordinary judicial proceedings is that 'the *Truth* is [often] hidden from' those participating in 'outward

111 Bernard, for example, gives a number of examples of 'generall Notions, and common Principles of truth' that 'neither Deuils, nor iniquitie it selfe, can blot out of Mans Vnderstanding and Conscience': '[t]hat *there is a God*, that *he knowes all things* … that *men must loue one an other*; that *we are to doe, as we would be done unto* … that *euery one haue his owne* …' (pp. 44–5; EEBO image 14165:44).

112 Perkins, *Discourse*, p. 8; EEBO image 10898:8.

113 Ibid., p. 7; EEBO image 10898:7.

114 Dyke, pp. 12, 13; EEBO image 17557:12.

115 Cade, p. 2; EEBO image 54332:6.

116 Ames, p. 2; EEBO image 15139:15.

117 Dyke, p. 11; EEBO image 17557:11

118 See, for example, Bourne, p. 11; EEBO image 7186:8, Dyke, p.13; EEBO image 17557:12, Ames, p 21; EEBO image 15139:15 and Jackson, pp. 11–12; EEBO images 103990:11–2.

Tryals', whereas 'conscience in tryall of our actions knoweth the truth'.[119] But only conscience knows that truth. While the law—and even knowledge of the law—may be infallible and objective, and while the process of drawing conclusions from the application of this knowledge of the law to the facts constituting the minor premise may be 'unanswerable', the minor premise is ultimately internal. This presents an important obstacle to the operation of an external court of conscience: that court, by hypothesis unable to judge as the conscience judges, can be a court of conscience only in an approximate sense. That is, it can judge, not according to conscience, but according to the approximation it achieves of the conscience's factual knowledge. Again, if a Catholic confessor theoretically could know what a person's own conscience knows, and if a medieval ecclesiastical Chancellor could theoretically duplicate the confessor in this respect, it makes more sense (although probably deluded sense) to refer to the earlier Court of Chancery as a court of conscience than it does so to refer to a Protestant version of that court.

The Reach of Justiciable Conscience

Thus, certain aspects of the Protestant account of conscience—notably, its objective character—are consistent with its operating as a juristic principle while others—notably, its radically private nature—are more problematic. Having considered how that account might generally impact on conscience as a basis for legal judgment, I want now to consider whether that account tells us anything about the scope of conscience's relevance to law, particularly to Chancery equity. One way of limiting that scope is the evidentiary one: the conscience of Chancery is only what can be proven, even with relaxed procedures, in the public forum. But for the moment I am concerned with the normative scope of the conscience of equity: what are the general limits on the *rules* it will prescribe? As we have seen elsewhere, not everything that conscience requires will or can be translated into legal constraint. The conscience of equity must be understood as a smaller circle within the much (perhaps immeasurably) larger circle of conscience *per se*. Clearly, the Protestant commentators (unlike such legal writers as St. German, Snagg and Hake) were not explicitly or significantly concerned with defining the bounds of conscience for Chancery purposes. But, to the extent that their treatments of the subject-matter of conscience were systematic they do at least suggest frameworks for approaching this issue.

One such possible framework is suggested by Harris's blunt assertion in his sermon to the judges of assize at Oxford: 'God speakes Law by you, Conscience by vs [that is, divines]'.[120] While it may be theoretically true that common law judges concerned themselves only with the law, Harris's distinction is too stark for our present purposes. Even assuming that only judges in equity might avail themselves

[119] Bourne, p. 11; EEBO image 7186:8.

[120] Harris, p. 19; EEBO image 6263:15.

of conscience, we know that they certainly at least purported to do so—a point acknowledged by many of the religious writers we have been considering. More useful, although requiring some circumspection in its application, is Perkins's division of spheres of human relatedness into three: 'Man Simply Considered in Himselfe without Relation to Another', 'Man as He Stands in Relation to God', and 'Man, as he stands in relation to Man', that is, as he is a member of some society.[121] Intuitively, we might feel that the first of these, concerning only the person him or herself and perhaps largely 'internal' matters, and the second, concerning a person's spiritual condition *vis-à-vis* God, are not matters for juristic conscience. This is, I believe, broadly the position that Protestant writers, both theological and legal, would have adopted, although it requires elaboration and qualification. The third sphere, that of social relations, seems eminently the domain of the law and hence the proper locus of juristic conscience. But, of course, there are all kinds of social interactions in which we would not expect the law to intervene—however much conscience is affected or engaged—and therefore we must look for some further limiting principle, even as regards 'man's relationships with man'. Broadly, that principle might lie in some kind of distinction between positive virtue and socially negative conduct, including derogations from certain kinds of undertakings, or between 'generosity' and, rather tautologically, 'justice'.

Concerning Oneself Alone

With respect to 'Man Simply Considered in Himselfe', we know that law tends to be concerned with outward, not inward things. As Perkins says, magistrates have the power to bind 'bodye & goods & outward cõversation' but not a person's 'thoughts, will, affections, desires, and faculties',[122] and other writers distinguish 'sins of the Heart'—relating to 'thoughts', 'delights' and 'desires'—from, say, 'sins of the Mouth' and 'sins of Works'.[123] As we have noticed, at least part of the reason such matters are not susceptible to legal regulation is evidentiary: ultimately, it is impossible to know what is in another person's heart.

But the 'inwardness', in the sense of not being manifested to others, of matters simply concerning persons themselves is not exhaustive of such matters. People can do outward things that ostensibly concern only themselves. Cade gives the fairly standard instance of dishonouring one's own body 'with lusts and uncleannesse'.[124] Fornication, say, does involve others, but (in Cade's view anyway) conscience condemns it not for (or just for) its possible effect on them, but, independently, for the harm it entails for oneself, for its intrinsic sinfulness. Now, whether the law should involve itself upon that basis alone, or only in so far as it poses a real or

---

121 Perkins, *Whole Treatise*. The book is structured around these categories.

122 Perkins, *Discourse*, pp. 47, 57; EEBO images 10898:27, 32.

123 Ames, pp. 94ff.; EEBO images 15139:85ff. Compare Fenner, p. 58; EEBO image 15425:40.

124 Cade, p. 12; EEBO image 54332:11.

imagined danger to society (for instance, as threatening 'legitimate' succession or just setting a bad example) is another issue. Certainly, outwardly manifested sins ostensibly involving oneself only (for example, suicide) have been visited with various legal consequences, so, at least historically the fact that one's conduct apparently harms only oneself does not automatically remove it from the reach of the law. That complex question aside, however, I want simply to make the point that, though what concerns the person only will often be internal, that is not inevitably the case.

Conversely, an inward disposition can of course be aimed at others, and this can involve conscience, apart from any material manifestations. Thus, for example, Ross suggests that 'mental' restitution of improperly detained property may go some distance towards satisfying the demands of conscience, notwithstanding that real, or material, restitution is not possible,[125] and Lancelot Andrewes (1555–1626) says that fulfilling a legal obligation such as paying taxes will not satisfy conscience unless it is done in the same spirit 'as it were a *Gift*, voluntarily, willingly, cheerfully'.[126] Our inclination in such cases would probably be to say that, as long as the material payment is made, the law should not care a whole lot whether it is made with a generous or a grudging heart. We would tend to leave the payer's internal disposition to his or her own non-legal conscience. While some matters having an outward character may concern only the person him or herself, some matters having an outward dimension very much involving relationships with others may nevertheless retain an internal dimension that is a matter of private conscience only.

This is not to say that equity—or, indeed, the law generally—never takes account of internal dispositions. Patently it does. Ames, for example, speaking of conscience in general, says that we sometimes have to distinguish 'the substance … of [a] worke, and the fault of the person'.[127] Ross makes a similar distinction between actions which are 'materially' but not 'formally' evil, giving the example of a man who has sex with his neighbour's wife believing her to be his own: 'he commiteth adultery *materially* & in effect, though not *formally* or in his conscience and intention'.[128] This primacy of state of mind in determining the quality of an act in conscience generally corresponds very nearly to the fundamental distinction in criminal law between *actus reus* and *mens rea*, and, indeed, in all those legal doctrines requiring some kind of awareness or intent as well as an overt act before conduct will have a legal effect. The correspondence is not exact, however. Private conscience, at least in the view of the authors we are considering, is more demanding. For example, for Ames 'an evill intention' by itself 'doth make an

125 Ross, p. 126; EEBO image 119965:75.

126 Lancelot Andrewes, 'A Sermon Preached at Whitehall, 26 November 1606', 'Certaine Sermons Preached at sundry times, upon severall occasions', in *XCVI Sermons* (London, 1629), p. 93; EEBO image 7203:563.

127 Ames, p. 82; EEBO image 15139:79.

128 Ross, pp. 4–5; EEBO image 119965:14.

action evill'.[129] Generally, the law as law does not condemn for *mens rea* alone. But it unquestionably does take account of internal states, albeit almost always in respect of actions involving other persons and not oneself alone.

One internal state affecting conscience that Ames discusses is ignorance, and what he says is reminiscent, on the one hand, of Aquinas, and, on the other, of certain doctrines of equitable liability.[130] Rather like Aquinas, he distinguishes ignorance of law from ignorance of fact, and, within the latter category, incorrigible (or relatively incorrigible) ignorance from corrigible ignorance. Ignorance of the law, he says, rather cryptically, 'doth never wholly excuse … yet it doth somewhat lessen the fault'.[131] This corresponds to the legal doctrine that, generally, ignorance or mistake of law is no defence, although, of course, this doctrine usually refers to positive law. Ignorance of fact, he says, will excuse a person who 'hath used such diligence as he ought', whereas failing such diligence, the ignorance 'doth not altogether excuse although it do somewhat lessen the fault'.[132] If one compares this to both early modern and modern doctrines regarding the kind of awareness that will bind a person who takes property subject to a prior equitable interest, one detects similar preoccupations. As we saw in Chapter 4, Bacon states the general doctrine that equity will fix upon the 'corrupt conscience' of such a person.[133] And much modern discussion of what binds the conscience, and how, centres upon distinctions between simple negligence, awareness of (other) facts that should have put the person on inquiry, wilful blindness, and actual knowledge. To take one judge, Sir Robert Megarry suggests that while some kind of objective notice might be sufficient to require the recipient to make simple restitution, a form of subjective knowledge is required before the recipient's conscience will be engaged so as to justify imposing upon him or her the full panoply of obligations of 'constructive trusteeship'.[134] These differences in intensity of the obligation based on degrees of ignorance perhaps correspond roughly to what Ames has in mind when he suggests that even negligent ignorance will 'somewhat lessen the fault', though not obviate it. I am not arguing here for a precise correspondence; nor am I pretending to explore the nuances of these matters. My point is simply that the inward/outward dichotomy is not a decisive basis for distinguishing matters of purely private conscience from matters cognizable by the conscience of equity.

---

[129] Ames, p. 84; EEBO image 15139:80.

[130] He also discusses, for example, fear and concupiscence as internal psychological states affecting the quality of acts in conscience.

[131] Ibid., p. 92; EEBO image 15139:84.

[132] Ibid.

[133] Francis Bacon, *Reading on the Statute of Uses* (1600), in *The Works of Francis Bacon*, eds J. Spedding, R.L. Ellis and D.D. Heath (14 vols, London, 1857–74), vol. 7, p. 405.

[134] *In re Montagu's Settlement Trusts*, [1987] 1 Ch. 264 at 277 (Chancery Division).

Concerning God

Of Perkins's second category—matters concerning 'man in his relationship to God'—we might once more be inclined to say that these are, in general, to be excluded from the purview of equity. But, again, while this is broadly the case, some qualifications are necessary.

One arises from Bernard's observation that 'Conscience is exercised in and about such matters onely, as haue some relation to God'.[135] The logical implications of this are evident. If conscience must always relate to matters involving God, how can there be any category of questions of conscience involving only, say, 'man in his relationship to other men'? This logic is reinforced by the recollection that (for these writers) the ultimate rule of conscience is the law of God: whenever conscience is in play, there must be some relation to God.

Of course, God's law as the rule of conscience does direct our relationships with other people. 'Do unto others as you would have them do unto you' is clearly (again, in these writers' terms of reference) divine law, but it directly envisages inter-human relations. Violating it certainly affects other people immediately, but it also disrupts our relationship with God. Presumably, Perkins's category comprehends something narrower than this, something perhaps suggested by the conventional categorization of the Ten Commandments into the first table, specifying people's duties to God ('Thou shalt have no other gods before me'), and the second, specifying people's obligations to each other ('Thou shalt not steal'). All these are basic ordinances of God, binding on the conscience, but the first involve man's disposition to God directly. If we understand Perkins's second category in this way, we might say that the law generally, including the conscience of equity, should leave it alone—although the early moderns might not have seen the question in exactly the same way. Indeed, there were many secular laws prescribing religious allegiance, forms of worship, and so on,[136] and these were crucial foci of disputes involving liberty of conscience and religious freedom. Such laws were normally positive state laws, that is, they would not ordinarily have been generated in the Court of Chancery on the basis of conscience.

Sometimes the distinction, or something like it, was articulated in terms of the dichotomy 'spirituals' *versus* 'civils'—the former relating exclusively to the state of a person's soul *vis-à-vis* God, the latter to questions involving the social order. One might want to say that the Chancellor should be concerned only with 'civils', leaving 'spirituals' to persons themselves and God. While this general point appears sensible and even obvious, there are complications. Not the least of these are the traditional claim that Chancery was in fact directly concerned with the state of litigants' souls, and that the line between the sacred and the profane

[135] Bernard, p. 30; EEBO image 14165:37.

[136] We might recall, for example, that the subtitle of Cade's book on conscience tells us that it is 'A Vindication of the Publick Prayers and Ceremonies of the Church of England'.

was, even in the seventeenth century, not as starkly drawn as we think we draw it today. Arguably, however, for the reasons that I have already adumbrated, the dissociation of the religious and the secular was becoming more insistent by the seventeenth century—as opposed, say, to the fifteenth.

A distinction related to the 'matters concerning man's relationship with God' *versus* 'matters concerning man's relationship with other men' dichotomy is that between 'Conscience … which is *Naturall*, and that which is *Inlightened*'.[137] I say 'related' because there appears to be a correspondence between 'relation to God' and 'enlightened' and between 'relation to other men' and 'naturall'. Cade says that even post-lapsarian natural conscience left 'light enough for performance of outward, morall, civill, and some religious duties, for preservation of humane societie and common life', but that a light of different order was necessary to allow people 'to attain to the knowledge of the mysteries of saving religion'.[138] If natural conscience tells us what is necessary for the preservation of human society and our lives together, we might again want to say that the conscience of equity should limit itself to that.

The correspondence is again not exact, however. The natural *versus* enlightened conscience distinction refers to the *faculty* of apprehension, whereas the matters concerning people's relationship to God *versus* those involving people's relationships to each other distinction refers to the thing apprehended. While there might be matters (the deeper mysteries of religion) only knowable by the enlightened conscience, there will be overlaps at a less rarified level. As Cade intimates, natural conscience may reveal to us 'some religious duties', and, indeed, he says explicitly that the laws written in 'the Gentiles hearts, concern God or our neighbour', so that, by this law alone, they know that there is a God, that he has transcendent properties, that he is to be worshipped, and so on.[139] Conversely, enlightened conscience tells us not only about divine mysteries, but also about our human relationships.

Arguably, what enlightened conscience adds to the knowledge of these relationships that we already have by natural conscience is a matter beyond the proper bounds of judicial equity. Bernard gives some examples of the differences in understanding of naturally and supernaturally-instructed conscience, respecting the same subject-matter:

> The Law in Nature saith, *Thou shalt not commit adultery*; the Decalogue goeth further, and saith, *Thou shalt not couet thy Neighbours wife:* then commeth a more spirituall exposition thereof in the Gospell, and saith, *Thou shalt not looke*

[137] Ames, p. 5; EEBO image 15139:7. Compare Fenner, p. 44; EEBO image 15425:33 ('naturall' as opposed to 'illuminated' conscience).

[138] Cade, p. 12; EEBO image 54332:11.

[139] Ibid., p. 3; EEBO image 54332:6. Compare Bernard, p. 45; EEBO image 14165:44.

> *vpon a woman to lust after her*; for he that so doth, hath committed adultery with her already in his heart.[140]

If we accept that extramarital perambulations are subject to this kind of rule, we might also say that only in its most rudimentary form need or should it be subject to legal regulation, because this suffices for the preservation of families, of social peace, and so on. Enlightened conscience involves counsels of perfection (notably addressed to internal dispositions) that the conscience of equity cannot practicably hope to realize and that are not necessary for civil order.

Concerning Other Persons

Although we cannot say simply that Chancery conscience has nothing to do with inward things or with 'spirituals', it is Perkins's third category—matters concerning relations among people—that appears most germane to that conscience. Indeed, the examples I have given of law's intervention with respect to 'internal' matters, although they relate to the subject's personal psychological state, involve almost exclusively qualifying that person's conduct in relation to others. As Perkins says, the end of all human laws—including, presumably, equity—is not 'to maintaine spirituall peace of conscience, which is betweene man and God, but onely that externall and ciuill peace which is betweene man and man'.[141]

Nevertheless, as we have already seen in more than one context, the law (including equity) is far from concerning itself even with all civil intercourse between 'man and man'. Cade reveals something of the range of such intercourse when he characterizes 'civill righteousnesse' as including 'honesty, justice, temperance, sobriety, providing for the poore, helping the distressed, speaking the truth, observing leagues, contracts, and promises, avoiding perjury, punishing vice, honouring vertue and living orderly'.[142] All of these engage conscience and, indeed, Cade says that 'the Gentiles' have made 'many excellent laws' concerning them.[143] But the question is not whether positive laws *might* be made with respect to these matters, but whether equity, on the basis of its conception of conscience, will intervene to correct such laws, or, more particularly, to fill gaps left by the positive law. Considering them superficially, we can see that they involve different sorts of things: restraining vice is not the same as 'honouring vertue'; providing for the poor and distressed involves something different from observing contracts; and contracts themselves are not the same as the simple 'promises' with which they are coupled. One kind of difference is between doing positive good (helping the

---

[140] Bernard, pp. 50–51; EEBO image 14165:48. I recognize that the proposition that natural law, if there is a natural law, prohibits adultery might be contested, and, indeed Bernard appears to be quoting the Decalogue here.

[141] Perkins, *Discourse*, p. 58; EEBO image 10898:33.

[142] Cade, p. 7; EEBO image 54332:8.

[143] Ibid., p. 8; EEBO image 54332:9.

poor) and being prevented from doing positive wrong (punishing vice); another is between 'reinforced' undertakings (contracts, and certain promises under oath) as opposed to matters of merely keeping one's word. The religious writers typically identify the Golden Rule as the fundamental precept of conscience governing our relationships with others,[144] but the Court of Chancery hardly goes so far as to require us, comprehensively, to love our neighbours as ourselves.

Regarding people's social relations, Perkins identifies a number of subcategories of what he calls 'virtues'. Those that relate particularly to other members of society are 'curtesie, as Liberality', and 'Equity', the latter subcategorized into 'Justice' and 'Fortitude'.[145] Although he is not using 'equity' in the technical sense of Chancery jurisdiction, a reasonable line of demarcation between non-justiciable and justiciable conscience is somewhere between 'liberality' and 'justice'. Liberality here seems to be essentially synonymous with charity; illustrating its purport, Perkins cites Luke 11:41, '*Therefore giue almes of those things which ye haue ...*' and, significantly, says that true charity involves not just 'outward good actions' but 'the inward syncere affection of your hearts towards your brethren'.[146] Broadly, we can say that, while the conscience of equity will not require one to be kind, generous, or merciful, it will require one to render what is justly due, at least as a matter of corrective justice, to others.[147] To take our familiar example of the failure to take an acquittance, equity intervenes not by saying to the creditor, 'conscience requires you to be merciful or charitable', but by saying that insisting upon the second payment is against conscience because is unjust. It involves taking what is another's.

Not only is there a difference in kind between obligations of charity and those of justice,[148] but there appears (at least for some purposes) to be a priority as between them. For example, Henry Jeanes (1611–62) tells us that the 'duties of justice … are of stricter obligation, than those of charity' and explains that therefore a debt

---

144 See, for example, Hughes, p. 21; EEBO image 4483:13. For both Eburne and, rather later, Goodman, this is 'the rule of equity'. William Penn (1644–1718) in *The Great Case of Liberty of Conscience* (London, 1670) says that 'the first Lesson of that great *Synteresis* … learns Mankind, *to do as he would be done to*' (p. 23; EEBO image 98352).

145 Perkins, *Whole Treatise*, p. 474; EEBO image 14434:262.

146 Ibid., pp. 596–7; EEBO image 14434:323.

147 Arguably, the law, in requiring the payment of taxes or tithes, does impose upon people the obligation to give 'something for nothing' to others. But the court of Chancery appears not to have been engaged in any kind of exercise of generally fair or humane redistribution of resources.

148 This distinction was not exclusive to Protestant writers. In a case reproduced in P.J. Holmes's *Elizabethan Casuistry* (Catholic Record Society, 1981), we are told that a tenancy contract lacking legal formalities may be 'null, even in conscience', thus allowing a person to go back on it (p. 45). This point is then qualified, the casuist saying that it 'must be understood with reference to sins against justice', for 'many have sinned against charity' by exploiting such absences of formal legal requirements (ibid.).

is 'farre more obligatorie' than the duty to give alms: '[a] man oweth money to the poore by a *morall debt*, but to his creditour he oweth them by *legall debt*, or debt *of justice*; and therefore he is more strictly obliged to pay his creditour, than to give almes'.[149] There are different intensities of obligation in conscience, and equity takes account of this. An instance of such priority in equity is the principle that a testator's debts are to be paid before legacies, because conscience requires us to be just before we are generous.[150] More comprehensively, this type of priority appears in equity's reluctance to relieve projected recipients of mere gratuities: 'equity will not assist a volunteer'.

This point is illustrated by the Protestant casuists' treatment of mere promises. For them, as perhaps for us, such promises *per se* are binding in conscience. Perkins says that a 'single' promise (or, in Barnes's terms, '*a simple promise* … distinguished from a promise, mixt and bound with an oath'[151]) 'bindes a man according as he will to whome the promise is made'.[152] In other words, the promisor is bound until released by the promisee. Perkins then asks himself what place is left for contracts, if simple promises already bind in conscience. His (not wholly satisfactory) answer is that 'the bonde of conscience is betweene man and God: but the bonde of an obligation is onely betweene man and man'.[153] So, something more is required to bind a person in the purview of human law than in the eyes of God.[154] As we know, the presence of a conscience factor recognized by God (or even moralists) in such circumstances came to make no difference. Until something was given for the promise, it apparently engaged only liberality, and not justice.

---

149 Henry Jeanes, *A Treatise Concerning a Christians Carefull Abstinence from all Appearance of Evill* (Oxford, 1640), pp. 64, 67; EEBO images 3605:35, 36.

150 As George Spence points out, however, Chancery at this time did give some preferential treatment to 'Charity Legacies for the poor', ensuring that they were paid ahead of other legacies, 'on the ground of equity and conscience' (*The Equitable Jurisdiction of the Court of Chancery* [2 vols, Philadelphia, 1846], vol. 1, p. 386). Equity did not require persons to be charitable in the first place, but it did show some favour to charity once it was expressed in a legally significant way.

151 Barnes, p. 85; EEBO 15204:49.

152 Perkins, *Discourse*, p. 82; EEBO image 10898:45. He allows only a few exceptions, such as the incompetence or the nonage of the promisor.

153 Ibid., p. 83; EEBO image 10898:45.

154 Again, it is possible that Perkins is at least partly concerned not so much with the substance of the obligation as with *evidence* of the obligation.

Conclusion

In the foregoing, I have essayed to outline elements of the 'Protestant' account of conscience, as it stood in the early decades of the seventeenth century[155] and to identify aspects of that account that could be relevant to an understanding of conscience in equity. The writers I have relied on as probably representative[156] are not addressing the question of Chancery conscience, so my application of their account to it can only be inferential. I am inferring from the fact that it was mainly religious writers who discoursed about conscience at this time that their account would reasonably reflect how the concept was generally understood. Many of the works I cite are sermons, and most could be described as 'popular theology', so that these views probably reached at least the educated public and not just specialists.[157] Although these writers themselves, while sometimes alluding to Chancery, do not develop the connection with it, I am inferring that certain aspects of their accounts would have been particularly germane to an appreciation of conscience as a juristic principle.

In this regard, I have focused on two broad points: how the Protestant account might have impacted on conscience as an objective concept, and how classifications of the objects of conscience given by that account might suggest guidelines for defining the scope of juristic conscience.

As for the first of these, it is evident that these Protestant writers did not break sharply with their Catholic predecessors in all respects. Conscience was, in their estimation, necessarily tied to an external law, essentially, the law of God. It was a matter of knowledge, not (or not just) of will or desire, and so it was subject to

[155] While I have emphasized explicitly religious writers in this chapter, analogous accounts of conscience are to be found elsewhere. For example, Lord Herbert of Cherbury, whose posture is aptly described as philosophical, in *De la vérité en tant quelle est distincte de la Révélation* (3rd edn, Paris, 1639) defines conscience as '*le sens commun des sentiments interieurs*' by which we examine '*ce qui est bon ou mauvais*' '*par le moyen des notions communes lesquelles y president avec vne souueraine authorité*' (pp. 137–8; EEBO images 14:73–4). These 'common notions '*sont grauees & emprainte*s' in all of us '*par le dictamen de la nature*' (p. 39; EEBO image 14:24); they are 'les principes, contre lesquels il n'est pas permis de disputer (p. 56; EEBO image 14:33). In his *The Ancient Religion of the Gentiles* (written 1643; London, 1711), he makes the connection of the common notions or principles with *synderesis* explicit (p. 331; ECCO image CW123338156:347).

[156] Obviously, one must be wary of assuming a unitary view in all these polemicists. I have tried to identify points of fairly general agreement.

[157] So, for example, Hughes, in defining conscience, says: 'I decline the Casuists and Schoolemen of purpose, that I may speake to the people, and to their consciences', and he uses 'plainenesse of speech' (p. 4; EEBO image 4483:5), and Dyke apologizes that his definition is not 'formall to the rules of Art', arguing that '[a] plaine familiar description agrees well enough' with 'that Auditory for whose sake it was first intended' (pp. 9, 10; EEBO image 17557:10–11).

the test of correctness. And its application involved logical processes leading to inevitable conclusions.

Where it differed perhaps most significantly from the Catholic account (or Catholic *practice*) was in its rejection or downgrading of the role of 'third parties'—human authorities and human interveners. The normative knowledge that conscience entailed was either right or wrong, but much of the factual knowledge in relation to which the norms had to be nuanced was exclusive to God and the person involved. The logic of conscience was ineluctable, but the minor, factual, premise was ultimately unfathomable to anyone else but God. So, in Ames's words, 'it is not enough for a good conscience to adhere to the authority of men, though they be learned and godly; because *the conscience is not by it selfe to be subjected to the judgement of man*'.[158]

The implications of this radical autonomy for conscience as a juristic principle are evident. Other persons can be neither authorities for the exercise of one's conscience, nor judges of that conscience. If the Chancellor, however learned and godly, cannot be an authority respecting another person's conscience, or really assess it, then his court can be a 'court of conscience' only in some diluted sense. So, although preoccupation with conscience was intense in the seventeenth century, it was a preoccupation that at least implicitly rendered the idea of a literal court of conscience less tenable, or untenable.

Regarding the other point—the possible scope of the objects of judicial conscience—these writers' classifications tend to illustrate how awkward it is to articulate *general* criteria for justiciable, as opposed to non-justiciable, conscience. For one thing, however we define its boundaries, justiciable conscience is only a small portion of what conscience at large relates to. This alone might call into doubt the aptness of calling any human tribunal a court of conscience. The jurisdiction of such a court, as regards conscience, is likely to be vastly more congruent with the jurisdiction of ordinary courts of positive law than it will be with the scope of conscience *per se*. Apart from this difficulty, however, there remains the problem of actually defining what things judicial conscience will concern itself with.

Broadly, an account like Perkins's might lead us to say that a court of conscience will hesitate to intrude where what is at issue affects only a person him or herself, or only involves that person's direct relation to God. Another way of putting this would be to say that, while conscience *per se* is very much—perhaps even characteristically—involved in matters internal and spiritual, these are generally beyond the pale of judicial conscience. Generally, we might say, the proper sphere of operation of that conscience is external matters involving a person's relationships as a member of society. But even here, some further, quite radically restrictive criteria, appear necessary. Notably, judicial conscience appears not to enforce generosity, even though in terms of certain basic Christian

---

158 Ames, p. 86; EEBO image 15139:81 (my emphasis). See also Charles H. George and Katherine George, *The Protestant Mind of the English Reformation 1570–1640* (Princeton, 1961), pp. 235–8.

imperatives this may be the most compellingly conscientious aspect of our social obligations. Rather, the conscience of equity requires only some kind of justice, understood in terms of *quid pro quo*, or at least induced reliance. But again, apart from distinguishing 'duties of charity' from 'duties of justice', one has difficulty discerning reliable criteria for justiciable conscience—perhaps because of the question-begging nature of the epithet 'justice'.

In the end, while this exploration of Protestant conscience offers structures of analysis that might assist us in thinking about the conscience of equity, it at the same time reminds us that the latter was much more circumscribed than the former.

Chapter 6

The Conscience of Early Seventeenth-Century Equity

Introduction

I would begin this chapter by reiterating my previous caveat regarding the chronological organization of this study. By moving from a chapter on the later sixteenth century to one on the early seventeenth, I do not mean necessarily to imply a discontinuity—and certainly not a sharp discontinuity. Indeed, it might be premature even to imply significant development. One need only reflect that two of the Jacobean chancellors—Ellesmere and Bacon—were also distinctly Elizabethan, the former having in fact been Elizabeth's last Lord Keeper before becoming James's Lord Chancellor. The fact is, as we shall see, that during the period I am about to consider the same themes are repeated, and the same authors—St. German especially, but also, say, William West—are cited for the same propositions, often without any discernible questioning or qualification.

At the same time, the early decades of the seventeenth century did witness significant developments relating to the *context* of Chancery as a court of conscience. Perhaps most obviously, in the Coke-Ellesmere confrontation over the role of Chancery there was a formal challenge to that court's jurisdiction, which called forth some reflection, or at least some defensiveness, on the part of its partisans. More broadly—and this is not an unrelated point—the Stuart theory of monarchy added fuel to the fire being stirred by those who did not like prerogative courts, especially such courts governed by what might appear to be a subjective and arbitrary quasi-juristic notion like 'conscience'. Moreover, this period witnessed the controversial tenure of the last ecclesiastical Lord Keeper, Bishop John Williams (1621–25), raising even more questions about the relationship of the sacred and the secular and perhaps calling for more explicit limitation of religious incursions into the civil sphere. Part of this concern was focused on the localization of 'conscience' in state authority.

So, partly because it is chronologically convenient, but partly because there were both explicit and inexplicit pressures on Chancery at this time, I propose in this chapter to address the conscience of equity roughly from James's accession in 1603 to about 1640, when the civil order was coming adrift. My focus in this chapter, unlike the last, will be on legal commentators on equity and conscience who, unfortunately, do not subject the latter to anything like the scrutiny of their religious counterparts—a fact that may itself be significant. But, again, I am assuming that, in a period of official religious conformity, what jurists meant when they used the word 'conscience' would have been informed by what the ecclesiastical commentators kept telling everybody it was.

One point worth making at this stage is that a sharp distinction between religious and legal commentary on this subject is hard to sustain. Sometimes, legal writers—or even chancellors, like Lord Ellesmere—discourse rather like divines, while on the other hand religious writers comment on law and justice, specifically in relation to conscience and/or equity.[1]

Perkins and Ames on Conscience and Law

William Perkins

An example of the latter is William Perkins, whom we have already encountered. Besides his *Discourse of Conscience* and his *Whole Treatise of the Cases of Conscience*, which are mainly concerned with the spiritual condition of the soul, he wrote *Epieikeia, or a Treatise of Christian Equity and Moderation*,[2] which is rather more secular in emphasis. As the title suggests, this book too is concerned with persons' moral dispositions, but what Perkins says does have implications for the law. Notably, he asserts that while the proper province of lawyers is the 'extremity and the letter of the law', they should take the advice of divines 'touching the equity which is the intent of the law', and about which the latter are particularly knowledgeable because their law—the word of God—is 'the fountain of equity' (p. 491).

Much of what Perkins says about judicial equity is fairly standard: like everybody else, he cites the proverb *summum jus, summa injuria* and says that in some circumstances there must be 'moderation, relaxation or mitigation' of the law's 'extremity'; and the reason for the law's intractability is that 'no lawmakers, being men, can foresee or set down all cases that may fall out' (pp. 485–6).

Potentially more tellingly for our purposes—because, at least superficially, it should remind us of the public conscience *versus* private conscience dubiety which is a central conundrum in this study—he distinguishes between public and private equity. The former, exercised in 'public meetings and assemblies … as in courts of justice', involves 'the right and convenient, and the moderate and discreet execution of the laws of men' (pp. 483–4). Private equity, by contrast, 'is

---

1 Thus, for example, Thomas Wood, *English Casuistical Divinity During the Seventeenth Century* (London, 1952) points out that the Protestant casuists aimed not only at inculcating 'personal holiness' but also at 'educat[ing] society in the way of justice' (p. xiii).

2 William Perkins, *Epieikeia, or a Treatise of Christian Equity and Moderation* (1604) in *The Works of William Perkins*, ed. Ian Breward (Abingdon, Berkshire, 1970), pp. 477–510. Since Perkins died in 1602, this work was written prior to the period I am considering.

a moderate, even and equal carriage of a man's self, in all his private words and deeds, towards all other men ...' (p. 492).

Perkins identifies two related aspects of public equity. One is the moderation of the law directly; the other respects 'all the public actions of a man's life' (p. 489). The first involves the conduct of magistracy itself; the second, persons comporting themselves in certain ways in the context of at least some social interactions.

Regarding the first, because applying the extremity of the law may sometimes be appropriate, there must be limits on when equitable mitigation is to be exercised. Perkins identifies three, and only three, circumstances when mitigation is appropriate: when it 'stands with the law of nature'; 'when it agreeth with the moral law'; and 'when an inferior law is over-ruled or countermanded by a higher law' (p. 486). These raise many questions and require explanation. Suffice it to say, however, that they all involve identifying a countervailing *law*: that is, the positive law may be moderated only on the basis that some more compelling *law* demands it. We have seen this before: the concern is that the interference with the positive law not be simply discretionary or arbitrary. At this stage, Perkins says nothing about conscience.

Regarding the second aspect—a person's public actions generally—Perkins does link equity to conscience. The issue, he says, is 'how men may with good conscience carry themselves in suretyships, in taking of fines, in letting leases and in all manner of mutual bargains betwixt man and man' (p. 490)—in short, the very kinds of transactions that might have come before the Court of Chancery. '[A] man that hath any conscience', and responsive to the 'law of God', will know when and when not to insist upon the extremity of the 'laws of men' (p. 490), If people do not, of their own accord, so conduct themselves, but 'stand strictly upon forfeitures and other extremities, then must the godly magistrate exercise his power, and .. cause them to mitigate their extremity and to put into practice that equity which becometh Christians' (p. 491). In other words, the conscience that the magistrate enforces is congruent with the private conscience of the individual, and is enforced in default of its operating. Again, the issue becomes, 'Which dictates of conscience?' Perkins speaks of 'that equity which becometh Christians', which sounds very comprehensive indeed.

However, in distinguishing 'private equity', he offers some indications of the boundaries of magistrates' jurisdiction respecting conscience. The social dimension cannot be the distinction, because private equity itself involves 'a moderate carriage' of oneself *vis-à-vis* 'all other men' (p. 492). Perkins suggests that this kind of equity has four 'principal duties': '[f]irst, to bear with natural infirmities. Secondly, to interpret doubtful things in the better part. Thirdly, to depart from our own right sometimes. Fourthly, to forgive private and personal wrongs' (pp. 492–3). I shall not examine these in detail, but merely observe that they all involve obligations corresponding roughly to what I have elsewhere referred to as generosity. Respecting the first, Perkins identifies it with 'true love' (p. 493); the second he associates with judging others' conduct 'mildly and mercifully' (p. 495); the third involves giving up what might rightfully be one's own; and the fourth is in its own terms a matter of forgiveness. All of these things are dictated by conscience (pp. 493, 497, 498). But what distinguishes them from those matters of conscience which, on our failure to act of our own accord, the magistrate will impose upon us is their gratuity.

William Ames

Another religious casuist who, in addition to discoursing at large about conscience, has something to say specifically about law is William Ames—again, an old friend. In the fifth book of his study of conscience,[3] entitled 'The Duties of Man Towards his Neighbour', he explores how conscience might impact upon a number of legal issues.

Unsurprisingly, he begins with a discussion 'Of Right', making the point that 'Right' is either divine—that is, authored by God, or human—that is, contrived by men.[4] Divine right is, in turn, either '*Right Naturall*' or '*Right Positive*', the former being 'that which is apprehended to be fit to be done or avoided, out of the naturall instinct of Naturall Light; or that which is … deduced from Naturall Light by evident Consequence'[5] and the latter being actual divine decrees. Human law includes the general law of nations as well as 'Civill Law', the law which 'every City or Society of men enacts currant for it selfe'.[6] This is somewhat reminiscent of, say, St. German's identification of three laws (of God, of reason, and of man) in his discussion of equity and conscience, and is quite commonplace. Moreover, like St. German and others, Ames makes the 'Law of Nature' criterial for 'Civill Law', so that 'that is not Law which is not just and right, and that in morality is called Right, which accords with right practicall reason …'.[7]

Because human reason 'can onely imperfectly judge', the civil law is often wanting—for example, in so far as it does not comprehensively reflect the law of nature, in so far as it can only aim to make 'good Subjects or Citizens' and not 'good men', and in so far as it often admits 'addition, detraction, or correction'.[8] Ames does not specifically mention equity in this context, but these defects are reminiscent of the standard rationales given for equitable relief, although whether judicial equity is concerned with making 'good men' is, to say the least, controversial. Not long after, discussing 'Iustice', Ames does consider equity, which he says civilians call *epieikeia* and which he describes conventionally as '*a Moderation of the strickt*

---

3 William Ames, *Conscience with the Power and Cases Thereof* (Leyden and London, 1639).

4 Ibid., p. 100; EEBO image 15139:140. Re-numbering of pages from '1' begins at Book Four.

5 Ibid.

6 Ibid., p. 105; EEBO image 15139:142.

7 Ibid.

8 Ibid., p. 106; EEBO image 15139:143.

Law'.[9] He appears to regard equity, at least at this point, mainly as an interpretive principle, involving getting at the true intent of law, explaining that '[a]ll Law ... hath alwaies a double end', namely, 'one Intrinsecall and Immediate, which the Lawgiver doth immediately looke upon: the other Extrinsecall and mediate'.[10] Strict law regards the immediate end, while equity 'respects the more remote End'.[11] So while '[l]egall Iustice taken strictly, considereth the words just as they are written', 'Equity considereth the End, scope and intent of the Law'.[12] Ames does not expressly relate conscience to this discussion, although conscience may be implicit in so far as it is the general subject of his book. But it is also consistent with other writers such as St. German and Edward Hake, who speak of the equity which is implicit in all law as distinguishable from Chancery equity, the particular domain of conscience.

Ames does go on to consider several explicitly legal topics, in terms of what the 'Court of Conscience', by which he, like others, means personal conscience or the tribunal in a person's breast, might say about them. He does not directly address the conscience of equity or Chancery, so his treatment seems to be very much in terms of the dichotomy law *versus* (private) conscience, but some of what he says is instructive for our inquiry.

As a preliminary he makes the point, which we have considered in Chapter 5, that human law and human tribunals cannot *directly* bind the conscience, for the reasons we have already noticed, namely, that 'the Conscience or Soule of man, is not properly subject to any, but God alone', that 'the onely rule of our conscience, is the Law of God written in our hearts', that 'man cannot indeed judge of the conscience' of another person, and that 'they cannot inflict any spirituall punishment upon the conscience'.[13] As we have previously noted, this complex of incapacities makes it difficult to sustain the literal idea of an external court of conscience. Ames, typically, does say that we are bound in conscience to obey the civil law, because (among other reasons) God has commanded us to. In view, however, of the intractability of the conscience to human tribunals, it makes sense for Ames to speak of the court of conscience as an essentially internal forum.

He discusses property under the rubric 'Of the Dominion of external things'. Again, he considers whether the 'division of things' has its warrant only in human law, or also in 'naturall and divine right', concluding that it is also mandated by the latter.[14] At this point it might be worth distinguishing the matter of division

9 Ibid., p. 111; EEBO image 15139:145.

10 Ibid.

11 Ibid. He gives the familiar example (which we have seen in Aquinas and St. German) of a law forbidding the opening of city gates during a war—the immediate end of which is to keep the enemy out, but the more ultimate end of which is to safeguard the citizenry.

12 Ibid.

13 Ibid., pp. 166–7; EEBO image 15139:174.

14 Ibid., p. 222; EEBO image 15139:202.

per se from the particular rules of attribution of things. That is, while, say, natural law might require that things be attributed, in some manner, to particular persons, it might theoretically remain indifferent as between different human schemes for determining the manner of the distribution. Moreover, once the attribution is made—even though its specific form is not dictated by divine or natural law—it might still be a matter of such law that the attribution not be improperly disrupted. So, ostensibly, divine or natural law might dictate that things be divided (that is, that there should be 'property'), but not who gets what or how much; once the division occurs, divine or natural law might then re-emerge and say, 'Thou shalt not steal'. I do not pretend to say anything conclusive about this here, but only to make these distinctions as a possible way of reconciling property as in some ways mandated by divine or natural law with assertions we have seen (for example, in St. German) that property arrangements are simply a matter of human law or custom.

We will recall that St. German maintained that conscience must always be grounded in some law—of God, of reason, or of man—and that the last of these would suffice, as long as it was not inconsistent with the first or second. Ames asks the question whether the civil law alone suffices in the 'Court of Conscience', and concludes, 'No': 'Vnlesse ... the title of Dominion is manifest to be lawfull, and true by the law published by God either in nature, or in his word, it cannot stand in the Court of Conscience.'[15] This is again consistent with the position that human law cannot directly bind conscience.

Interestingly, Ames seems to envisage the possibility of a human law standing even though it apparently contradicts the law of nature or of God. So, he speaks of the acquisition of property by contract, in circumstances where the civil law prescribes some 'ceremony, or formality'.[16] Ames appears to say that, where only this formality is lacking, but the essential features of a contract are present, 'the title [given] is of force, either in the law of nature, or in the Divine law, it gives true Dominion according to the Court of Conscience, although it bee disannulled in the Civill law'.[17]

One might be tempted to say, 'since human law that contradicts divine or natural law is invalid, or a corruption of law, that requirement of human law should be void'. But that is not what Ames says. He says that the contract is valid in the *private* court of conscience, even though the civil law does not recognize it. What this means, presumably, is that the obligor, though not bound in law to perform, is bound as a matter of personal conscience. So, the court of (his own) conscience will tell him that he must transfer title, but, if he does so, this will be a voluntary or gratuitous act as far as the strict positive law is concerned.

Ames is operating in terms of a strict law *versus* private conscience dichotomy, so he understandably does not address the point at which an *external* court of

15 Ibid., p. 223; EEBO image 15139:202.

16 Ibid.

17 Ibid.

conscience like Chancery should intervene. We know that it does intervene in some such circumstances, notably in the case of the debt repaid without taking an acquittance. We have seen that that case can be analysed in terms of unjust enrichment, because by hypothesis the creditor is being paid twice. On that basis Ames's example of the contract to confer title may be distinguished, because property has not yet been conveyed, so there is no issue of restitution. One might argue, then, that the point at which issues of conscience should engage the external tribunal is where there is a withholding of what belongs to another. Where a contract is invalid for want of a formality, the property has not yet become another's. Of course, as we have also seen, if value has been given by the obligee, then, on the basis of the restitutionary principle, that value must be returned, since for the obligor to keep it would be to withhold something belonging to another.

Drawing the line at restitution is, however, problematic in terms of another of Ames's examples—that of a formally invalid will, a will being, like a contract, a mode of conferring property. In Ames's view, 'Dominion is transferred in the Court of Conscience' by such a will.[18] The mechanism of the binding of conscience is rather unclear here. If we analogize it to the contract situation, it would presumably be the testator's conscience that is bound. But here we do not have even the mutuality or reciprocity of agreement that might justify imposing on the transferor's conscience. We could say that the conscience of whoever takes in lieu of the intended beneficiary should be bound, on the basis that he holds what was intended for another. But this too is problematic, since one might want to say that that person takes the property subject to obligations affecting the owner-testator's conscience; however, we have already doubted these obligations here. Moreover, the default beneficiary is not holding something that is actually another's. Obviously, if the testator's failure to observe the formal requirements was induced by the default beneficiary, a factor affecting that beneficiary's conscience might be more palpably present.

Ames's analysis—and, again, he is not talking about conscience of which cognizance should necessarily be taken in an external forum—is that these formal requirements for contracts and wills are 'prescribed in the Civill lawes, to prevent deceit, and cousening'.[19] But, if there is no deceit—that is, on the part of the putative recipient, 'that reason ceaseth, as also the force of the Civill law doth cease'.[20] This assertion is pregnant with implication. For one thing, is Ames saying, literally, that the civil law rule ceases in these circumstances—or only that the rule continues to apply externally although the conscience of the obligor/testator is affected? Does what he says bear some relation to his account of equity—that is, that the strict law notices only the immediate import of the rule, but that the rule should be applied in terms of its ulterior intent? He goes on to say that the 'disannulling' of such a contract is based on a 'presumption of deceit: but that false presumption takes no

18 Ibid.

19 Ibid.

20 Ibid.

place in the Court of his Conscience, that knowes the contrary'.[21] Again, this raises questions. Does the annulment of the contract stand, only the private conscience of the obligor being affected by his knowledge that the contract alleged manifests the actual agreement? If the *judge* knows the contrary, is his conscience bound to resist the false presumption?

This takes us back, indirectly, to the question whether what typifies Chancery is its freedom from the procedural and evidentiary constraints of the common law. A common law court may take cognizance only of evidence in certain prescribed forms. The Chancellor, not so limited, may examine facts at large, informing his conscience of the real 'truth'; knowing that truth, he is bound in conscience to make the right (not just formally constrained) decision. Again, the argument is that both the common law and equity recognize the force of contracts 'made out of free will, upon deliberate Counsell',[22] but that the common law is more parsimonious about how these may be proven.[23]

Ames does not explicitly address these questions here, but elsewhere in Book 5 he does ask '*Whether the Judge ought alwayes to give sentence according to the things alleaged and proved*?'[24] We will recall the conventional position that whereas common law judgments are to proceed *secundum allegata et probata*, Chancery examines causes *omnibus viis et modis, ad informandum conscientiam judicis*. This suggests, again, that an ordinary court is limited by strict rules of proof. Ames takes the position that, generally, judges—and he is not referring to the Chancellor here—are to be limited to 'the things alleaged and proved'.[25] Specifically, though, he is contemplating the rather extreme case of a judge deciding on the basis of his own private knowledge. That is, he is not envisaging another court, in which what counts as *presented* evidence is different. His concern is that the judge decide 'according to *publique* knowledge which ariseth out of the things alleaged, and proved …'.[26] But this presumably would not foreclose the 'public' modes of accessing the truth applicable in the Court of Chancery.

The only situation in which Ames says a judge must act on his private knowledge is in refraining to condemn to death a person he knows is innocent. The reasons he gives seem not, however, in principle limited to that situation. One is that what is alleged and proved is only a means of getting at the truth; if the truth is more absolutely available, these means must yield to it. Moreover, 'a

---

21 Ibid.

22 Ibid., p. 224; EEBO image 15139:203.

23 Of course, free will and 'deliberate Counsell' are not enough to make a binding contract in law or in equity—although they (with the promise flowing from them) may suffice in the private court of conscience. So, notably, equity—consistent with its emphasis on substantial mutuality—will require real consideration, although law may allow a formality (say, a seal) to stand in lieu of consideration.

24 Ibid., p. 281; EEBO image 15139:231.

25 Ibid.

26 Ibid., pp. 281–2; EEBO images 15139:231–2 (my emphasis).

Iudge which pronounceth that to bee true which certainly hee knoweth to bee false, would be a lyer, and sinne against his owne conscience'.[27] Both these rationales would seem to be generally applicable: truth always trumps the inadequate means prescribed to reach it, and a judicial determination against what the judge knows to be true violates conscience. Ames explicitly rejects the argument based on 'that distinction, betweene the publique and private conscience of a Iudge', for the 'private conscience ought not to be violated at any time'.[28] That Ames limits this exception to the case of condemning an innocent person to death seems, in the end, to arise from the enormity of the consequences—but, if 'conscience' is to be in play at all, the exception does not seem to be dictated by a compellingly principled distinction.

Unlike St. German, whose project was to show how the common law was largely consonant with conscience, Ames tends to emphasize the dissonance of legal rules and the dictates of conscience. But he does not say that therefore the legal rules are invalid. He does say that 'the Civill law cannot abrogate the law of nature',[29] but neither does he say that the law of nature abrogates the civil law. Rather, he tends to assign these to separate spheres. A civil law that does not accord with conscience may be allowed to persist, on the basis of expediency or convenience. Thus, the annulling of formally defective contracts 'is onely not to helpe them in the externall Court … because of the Common good'.[30] Ames criticizes the doctrine of prescriptive acquisition on the basis that detention of another's property is always, or almost always, against conscience. 'No just cause can bee brought', he says, 'why prescription *bonæ fidei* should transferre Dominion'.[31] Two of the standard rationales—that property should not be uncertain, and that 'contention should not bee infinite'—are not matters of conscience, but of expediency. A third reason, that 'the negligence and sloath of men in regaining their goods might bee punished', involves a disproportion between the fault and the consequence.[32] Nevertheless, as in the case of formal requirements for contracts, Ames does admit prescription in the external forum on the basis of overall utility: 'the course of particular Right is stopt, for the sake of publike right and good, that so an infinite number of suites might bee prevented'.[33]

What is perhaps most noteworthy about Ames's treatment of these distinctly legal questions is his 'privatization' of the issues of conscience surrounding them. The civil law is not necessarily congruent with conscience, although people are bound to obey it for conscience's sake. To the extent that it departs from divine law or the law of nature—those laws which bind conscience directly—a person may

27 Ibid., p. 282; EEBO image 15139:232.

28 Ibid.

29 Ibid., p. 224; EEBO image 15139:203.

30 Ibid.

31 Ibid., p. 225; EEBO image 15139:203.

32 Ibid.

33 Ibid., p. 101; EEBO image 15139:140.

be privately bound in conscience not to pursue his *legal* rights. Thus, although the law permits the acquisition of property by prescription, a person should not in conscience rely on this legal rule to acquire property. Although the law, for its own reasons, might insist on the presence of certain formalities before it will enforce contracts, it may be personally unconscionable for an obligor under a contract valid according to natural law to invoke these legal strictures.

Again, Ames (unlike Perkins, who depicts a kind of public equity justifying judicial intervention, as opposed to private equity) does not address one of the main questions that concerns us—namely, how to delimit when an external tribunal should intervene, on the basis of conscience, where the civil law and conscience are not congruent. But his position may be indicative of a growing hiatus between the public sphere of law and the private sphere of conscience.

Secular Commentary on Conscience and Equity

Unfortunately, what the secular commentators have to say—at least concerning conscience—tends to be much less rich and suggestive than what the religious writers offer. We have no equivalent of St. German or even of West or Hake. Thus, for example, Thomas Ashe, in a work devoted to equity,[34] does not even mention, much less analyse, conscience. To be sure, his focus is on equity as a principle of statutory interpretation, which was, as we know, conventionally distinguished from Chancery equity. However, in his preface 'To the courteous *Reader*' he does purport to say 'something concerning Equitie in generall'. This treatment tends to consist of quotations from a wide range of other writers, including St. German and West. So, for example, he quotes the observation of the former that equity involves 'an exception of the law of God, or the law of Reason, from the generall rules of the law of man',[35] but he makes no explicit connection with conscience. Again, we may remember that Hake divides his treatise into three parts: equity in general, the equity of the common law, and Chancery equity. If the 'Equitie in generall' that Ashe is considering corresponds to Hake's, then he would have no particular reason to mention Chancery equity, which, recall, Hake associates specifically with conscience.

That legal considerations of the conscience of equity tend to be rather thin may itself be telling. It may, for example, suggest that conscience is so well understood as not to require elaboration. Or, it could indicate that, although Chancery continues to be referred to as a court 'of conscience', conscience is not regarded as substantively important. Or it could suggest an awareness of the shortcomings of conscience as a juristic principle, and a reticence about facing them. 'Conscience' in this context may remain rhetorically appealing, but be resistant to analysis.

---

34 Thomas Ashe, *Epieikeia* (London, 1609).

35 Ibid., sig. A1r; EEBO image 382:8.

Certain commentators do, however, take some account of conscience as a criterion of judgment, or at least discuss equity (and, indeed, law itself) in terms that parallel discussions of conscience that we have seen elsewhere.

Sir John Doderidge

One of these is Sir John Doderidge's (1555–1628) *The English Lawyer.*[36] He observes that 'the minde of man is beautified with two faculties or powers', namely, '*Capacitie*' and '*Discourse*'.[37] The first allows us to 'apprehend, as with the inward eye, the naturall light and resplendencie of many *Primary Propositions*'.[38] These primary propositions, or 'Primarie Conclusions of Reason', 'are imprinted in the minde of euery Man, and discerned by the light of very Nature it selfe'.[39] This description is reminiscent of the typical descriptions of *synderesis*, that faculty which allows us to apprehend basic moral principles directly. Doderidge does not, however, mention *synderesis* here—understandably, since he is not discussing conscience (as an aspect of which *synderesis* is conventionally treated) at this point, or for that matter even equity, but the basis of law generally.

He in fact considers equity, and subsidiarily, the conscience of Chancery, in connection with secondary principles of reason. Secondary principles, unlike primary principles, are not directly given to us by the light of nature, but are derived or inferred. Some are empirical—'deduced and drawne from the vsuall and ordinary disposition of things … and by the obseruation of humane nature'.[40] Others 'rest vpon discourse of Reason deducted in Argument'.[41] I shall return to this second kind, which require somewhat detailed treatment, anon, but before doing so I want to make a point about the first. As Doderidge treats them, these secondary principles based upon experience and observation are essentially presumptions—either conclusive or rebuttable. With respect to the first sort, Doderidge says that a decision-maker (in his example, a juror) does not act contrary to conscience in applying the presumption, even if he personally knows that it is not true in the particular case.[42] We will recall that Ames considers a similar situation, in which a judge personally knows a fact that is contrary to what is alleged and proved. Generally for Ames, as for Doderidge in this instance, the public function of the court absolves the conscience of the person exercising that function from

36 Sir John Doderidge, *The English Lawyer, Describing a Method for the Managing of the Lawes of this Land* (London, 1631). This book went through several editions, and was even pirated: see *The Lawyers Light* (London, 1629). 'Doderidge' is the spelling on the title page; alternatives are 'Doddridge' and 'Dodderidge'.

37 *English Lawyer*, p. 208; EEBO image 10306:109.

38 Ibid.

39 Doderidge, *The Lawyers Light*, p. 42; EEBO image 10308:29.

40 Ibid., p. 47; EEBO image 10308:31.

41 Ibid.

42 Ibid., p. 53; EEBO image 10308:34.

the contumely of perjury. That is, public conscience, based on convenience or the need for legal certainty, may overbear private conscience. The issue, though, is again whether the actual substantive truth is the ultimate test of conscience where it comes up against fixed and partial rules setting out procedures meant to determine the truth.

But to return to *The English Lawyer* and to the second kind of secondary principles—those which 'we doe Collect, Reason, Argue, and inferre' from primary principles, 'descended and derived from the first, as branches from the Roote, or Rivers from the Fountaine ...'.[43] Unlike the primary principles, which are absolute, these principles may be incomplete or deficient:

> sith that every Science is not of like certainty, by reason of the variable condition of the subject whereupon it is imployed; so that rightly of Morall Philosophy (consisting wholy of mans changeable and inconstant conversation, and frõ whence indeed, the knowledge of all Lawes are [*sic*] in a generality derived …). It followeth of necessitie, that it is scarcely possible to make any secondary Rule of Law, but that it shall faile in some particular case ….[44]

Since, therefore, it is not possible 'by any positive Law to make provision' for 'every particular circumstance'—a point that we have regularly met—it is necessary to develop mechanisms whereby those rules arising from the 'discourse & disputation of reason' might be 'restrained by exceptions'.[45] One of these mechanisms involves competing rules of law; the other, which is our concern here, is equity.

Doderidge then quotes the very familiar passage from St. German in which equity is described as an exception, based on the law of God or of reason, from general human laws. He cautions that equity so described is not limited to the equity 'which either enlargeth or restraineth Statute Lawes', but that equity has a triple use in English law, namely, '1… it keepeth the common Law in conformity [by considering the reason of like or unlike cases]. 2 Or it expoundeth the Statute Law. 3 Or thirdly giveth remedy in the Court of Conscience in cases of extremity, which otherwise by the Lawes are left unredressed'.[46] This last is obviously of greatest interest in the present context.

---

43 Doderidge, *English Lawyer*, p. 208; EEBO image 10306:109.

44 Ibid., p. 209; EEBO image 10306:109. Compare John Davies, 'A Preface Dedicatory' to Lord Ellesmere, in *Le Primer Report des Cases & Matters en Ley resolues & adiudges en les Cours del Roy en Ireland* (Dublin, 1615): '*lawe* is nothing but a rule of reason, & humane reason is *Lesbia regula*, pliable euery way … so as not onely the knowledge of the *lawe*, but all other *rationall* sciences that are subject to *Argument & discourse*, must needes bee subiect to *vncertainty* & to *error* ...' (sig. A4r; EEBO image 7771:5).

45 Doderidge, *English Lawyer*, p. 209; EEBO image 10306:109.

46 Ibid., pp. 210, 211; EEBO image 10306:110.

Respecting the qualification of law by conscience, Doderidge issues a caveat. Law must

> stand upon permanent Rules, as of Iron not to be bent or broken upon this or that occasion, or to be infringed upon this or that occurrence (for else there need no Court of Law, but all should be one with the Court of Conscience, and have their proceedings framed according to the Arbitrary conceipt of the Iudge).[47]

His characterization of the court of conscience here is telling: it involves a kind of arbitrariness. At this point, at least, Doderidge appears not to acknowledge the objectivity of conscience as a juristic principle. Nevertheless, equity does have a role to play, for circumstances 'of time, person, place, and the manner of doing' will sometimes render *summum jus summa injuria*.[48] Therefore a balance, which Doderidge does not describe with any precision, must be struck.

Each of the kinds of equity Doderidge identifies can have one of two effects in a particular case—either it extends the scope of an overly narrow law or it limits the scope of an overly broad one. For the kind of equity which is our main concern here 'equity extendeth forth her hand in the Court of Conscience to helpe .. the .. defect of the Lawes' or '[i]n the Court of Conscience it giveth … comfort, considereth all the circumstances of the fact, and is as it were tempered with the sweetnesse of mercy, and mitigateth the rigour of the common Law; and leaving the inflexible stiffe Iron rule, taketh in hand the Leaden Lesbian one ...'.[49] All this is very general, not to say platitudinous; it does not even really discriminate between enlarging and narrowing the letter of the law. The only help that Doderidge offers respecting when conscience is to be resorted to is that it should be 'in such cases only as are of extremity'.[50] Criteria for what constitutes extremity are not offered—although a quote from Cicero suggests that this is to be left to the discernment of the wise Chancellor.[51]

Doderidge concludes that the effect of equity (in all its forms) is to make the positive law based on secondary principles arrived at by discourse more conformable to the 'originall fountaine'—that is, the primary principles themselves. Indeed, the equitable exceptions spring from this fountain.[52] As regards the third kind of equity, then, the Chancellor, presumably, presiding in the court of conscience, is able to assess and apply those primary principles. This reminds us, conceptually, of the operation of conscience that is outlined by others. But Doderidge does not analyse this process further.

---

47 Ibid., pp. 211–12; EEBO images 10306:110–11.

48 Ibid., p. 212; EEBO image 10306:111.

49 Ibid., p. 214, EEBO image 10306:112.

50 Ibid.

51 Ibid., p. 215; EEBO image 10306:112.

52 Ibid.

Sir Henry Finch

Like Doderidge (and many others) Sir Henry Finch (d. 1625) distinguishes reason, the essence of what he calls 'Native Laws', into two parts: one is 'that faculty of the soul that offereth vnto vs things clear & lightsome of themselues, without any further reasoning or discourse', and the other, 'that faculty of the soul, that by discourse of reason doth deduce and draw one thing from another'. Laws given by the first are 'Primitiue', or 'the law of Nature'; those given by the second are 'secundarie rules of reason' or 'the law of Reason'.[53] For him, the law of nature is 'that soueraigne reason fixed in mans nature, which ministreth common principles of good and euill'.[54] This again sounds very much like *synderesis*, and, indeed, the principles that Finch gives as instances (for example, '[t]hat we are not to do unto another that which we would not have done unto us'[55]) are essentially those commonly said to be given by *synderesis*. But Finch does not use that term, nor does he at this point say anything about conscience. He does, however, 'christianize' these classical concepts by remarking (much as particularly a Protestant theologian might) that 'through *Adams* fall … that excellent image of Reason is now so wonderfully defaced', although it still shines 'so that from it all the other Lawes receiue their Light'.[56] The rules given by this faculty are such that 'the very maximes and principles of the positiue law will yeeld [to them], as to a higher and more perfect Law'.[57] Again, although Finch does not frame this discussion in terms of conscience, we will recognize the argument: positive law derives ultimately from a more perfect law and is subject to that law.

What Finch says about equity specifically is not directly related to this discussion, and tends once more to be pretty conventional. He recognizes the three kinds of equity identified by Doderidge, but not as clearly. Thus, he refers to a kind of equity identified by Bracton—'*Æquitas est rerum conuenientia, quæ paribus in causis paria jura desiderat*'[58] and equity as a kind of moderate construction of the law.[59] He then suggests that these two kinds of equity 'haue a further & more shining vse in the exposition of Common Law it selfe ...'.[60] Whether he is thinking in terms of exactly the categories that Doderidge treats is debatable. Broadly, he regards equity as '[a]bridging, diminishing, and taking away the

53 Henry Finch, *Law or a Discourse thereof, in Four Books* (London, 1627), p. 3; EEBO image 22891:8.

54 Ibid., pp. 3–4; EEBO images 22891:8–9.

55 Ibid., p. 4; EEBO image 22891:9.

56 Ibid., p. 5; EEBO image 22891:9.

57 Ibid., pp. 5–6; EEBO images 22891:9–10. Indeed, positive laws 'which are directly contrarie to' the laws of nature 'are no lawes at all' (p. 75; EEBO image 22891:46).

58 Ibid., p. 20; EEBO image 22891:17. Broadly, this is the principle that equity requires that like cases should be decided in the same way.

59 Ibid., p. 55; EEBO image 22891:35.

60 Ibid., p. 57; EEBO image 22891:36.

seueritie of [the law], and mollifying the hardnesse thereof',[61] which is pretty old hat. As for conscience itself, the only reference I find to it is his observation that Chancery 'dealeth with matters of Conscience, and moderating the strictness of the Common Law by an absolute power'.[62] Presumably, although he does not make the connection explicitly, this involves that 'more shining use' of equity to which he referred earlier.

Barnabe Barnes

Another writer who, though hardly an eminent lawyer like Doderidge or Finch, has something, though not a whole lot, to say about equity and conscience is Barnabe Barnes (c. 1571–1609). Like almost everyone else we have noticed, he begins with a lofty conception of law and the knowledge of law. '*Iuris prudentia*', is '*the knowledge how to discerne of any cause aright*'; it is 'a science which maketh a true difference betweene right and wrong' and comprehends 'Sapience', the 'science of diuine and humane matters'.[63] It is a science, a matter of knowledge, not opinion, and has its eye on the sacred as well as the profane, indeed, understands the profane in the light of the sacred. As for justice, it is 'compounded … of three principall elements of the minde', namely, honesty, innocency and equity.[64] Our primary interest is in this last quality.

Equity, which Barnes says 'is as the heart of iustice',[65] is 'a vertue by which the law (failing, or wanting in many principall, vehement, and vrgent points) is corrected and moderated'.[66] There is not much new about this, although Barnes goes on to say that this 'lawe which ruleth in his Maiesties Courtes [*sic*] of Chauncerie' involves 'the mercifull interpretation' of statutes[67]—which others see as a kind of equity distinct from that administered in Chancery and which they do not necessarily associate with 'mercy'. He does, however, refer to the Chancellor's merciful *discretion* as well, and later observes that 'the conscience of the Iudge with the causes of equitie, should make the true ballance of right'.[68]

He goes on to describe the operation of the Court of Chancery in terms that are familiar to us. This 'seate of equitie' 'should seeme to distribute and execute the Lawe of nature and conscience, being corrected by reason, but confirmed by Religion'.[69] He then refers to *synderesis* 'that naturall facultie [which] perswadeth

[61] Ibid., p. 56; EEBO image 22891:36.

[62] Ibid., p. 238; EEBO image 22891:129.

[63] Barnabe Barnes, *Foure Bookes of Offices* (London, 1606), p. 128; EEBO image 7337:72.

[64] Ibid.

[65] Ibid., p. 129; EEBO image 7337:72.

[66] Ibid., p. 128; EEBO image 7337:72.

[67] Ibid.

[68] Ibid., p. 143; EEBO image 7337:79.

[69] Ibid., p. 135; EEBO image 7337:75.

the good, and diswadeth that which is euill'.[70] So, albeit in cursory form, it is all here—law of nature, conscience, reason, religion, *synderesis*. Presumably, this suggests that Barnes's view of the jurisdiction of the court of conscience was more or less conventional for his time. But he proffers no very useful explanation, perhaps (like others) resorting to rather striking but not hugely informative metaphor instead: '[e]quitie should seeme to bee that Balme, which modefieth and molefieth the rigorous Letter and rugged forehead of Law, graciously smoothing the same with a blessed serenitie'.[71]

Barnes does make a number of other references, more or less relevant, to conscience. One occurs in a sentence whose syntax is rather opaque, but he appears to be calling into question certain judicial strategies in softening the extremity of the law. He refers to 'some prudent sentences, also deliuered in such misticall Oracles, as might be wrested, mollified, or hardened, as should be thought most fit in the Iudge his discretion by conscience and equitie; onely to terrifie men from hainous sinnes'.[72] This suggests to me that the operations of judges' consciences are sometimes rather mysterious ('misticall Oracles'), and that the judge might be exercising his discretion rather numinously—but my reaction may reflect a modern secular rationality suspicious of the oracular, or of what have been dismissively called 'delphic vaticinations'.[73] Moreover, what this judge is doing is dissuading people from *sin*—again, a notion traditionally associated with Chancery. Elsewhere, Barnes notes that the law itself, while it can discourage outward actions, or perhaps the outward manifestations of sin, cannot really act upon or correct the conscience: 'the lawes may punish offences, but haue no power to corroborate or munite [fortify] the Conscience'.[74] This would be consistent with what we have seen to be the Protestant commentators' insistence that courts can neither judge nor directly operate on a person's conscience.

Neither Doderidge nor Finch nor Barnes tells us what we want to know—what, precisely, the conscience of equity was conceived to be. But in their clear locating of human law under the law of God, or the law of nature, they evince a context of understanding that displays a conviction (however awkwardly articulated or even misguided) that the criteria for conscientious judgment are pre-established and objective. Moreover, such inklings as they proffer suggest that they essentially shared the views of the religious expositors.

---

70 Ibid.

71 Ibid.

72 Ibid., p. 130; EEBO image 7337:73.

73 Review of John Stores Smith, *Social Aspects*, *Eclectic Review* (N.S.), 1 (1851), p. 162.

74 Barnes, p. 131; EEBO image 7337:73.

The Early Stuart Chancellors and Conscience

One might expect the most obvious source of information about the conscience of equity to be the Chancellors or Keepers themselves: Ellesmere (to 1617), Francis Bacon (1617–21), Bishop John Williams (1621–25), and Sir Thomas Coventry (1625–40). All of them characterize Chancery as a court of conscience, but what they understand by conscience remains sketchy. None—as far as I have been able to ascertain—has left a tract entitled anything like 'The Meaning and Limits of Conscience as a Juristic Principle'. So, again, we have to rely upon rather fragmentary evidence to get an idea of what they had in mind.

Lord Ellesmere

Sir Thomas Egerton, Lord Ellesmere, is likely best remembered for his well-documented[75] confrontation with Sir Edward Coke over the jurisdiction of the Court of Chancery. The focus of the conflict was, broadly, whether the Chancery might 'interfere' with judgments of the common law courts, and, correspondingly, the extent of the power of the prerogative courts, the most important of which was arguably the Chancery. As Baker points out, the controversy was 'in some ways' 'the first phase of the seventeenth century constitutional revolution'.[76] The *fact* of 'review' by the Chancery, and not so much the criteria of judgment it applied, was at the forefront of the dispute, so the controversy did not comprehend an analysis of judicial conscience. However, conscience was relevant to the issue. For one thing—and this does relate to the nature of conscience in this setting—conscience was associated with discretion, and this was one of the concerns the common lawyers had with the prerogative courts. For another (as we have already seen, and will see again), a conventional response to the charge that Chancery was overturning judgments of the common law courts was that it was not questioning the judgments themselves, but merely correcting the 'corrupt conscience' of a litigant. So conscience is in some ways both peripheral to and central to the dispute, but the *quality* of conscience *per se* was not a subject of much elaboration.

Ellesmere apparently regarded the Chancery very much as a court of conscience. In Chapter 4, we noticed a number of aspects of the Elizabethan Lord Keeper Egerton's invocation of this notion regarding his jurisdiction. In a defence of the Court against the claim that the exercise of its jurisdiction violated *Magna*

---

[75] See, for example, J.H. Baker, 'The Common Lawyers and the Chancery: 1616', in *The Legal Profession and the Common Law: Historical Essays* (London, 1986), pp. 205–29, and Charles M. Gray, 'The Boundaries of the Equitable Function', *American Journal of Legal History*, 20/3 (1976): pp. 192–226, and, more recently, Mark Fortier, *The Culture of Equity in Early Modern England* (Aldershot, 2005), pp. 76ff. W.J. Jones, *The Elizabethan Court of Chancery* (Oxford, 1967) cautions against exaggerating the general opposition between the common law courts and Chancery (see, for example, pp. 490–91).

[76] Baker, 'Common Lawyers and the Chancery', p. 205.

Carta and other statutes, he insistently speaks of it as a court 'of Equitie and Conscience'.[77] So, for example, he says,

> [i]t is *lex terrae* [the words of *Magna Carta*], that is, the Iudges of the Common Law shall determine questions in Law, and *Pares & Iurors* to try matters in fact, so the *Chancery* is to order and decree matters of Conscience and Equitie, which cannot be remedied by the strict rules of the common Law.[78]

What Chancery does *is* part of the law of the land; it addresses matters of law and fact that the ordinary law does not contemplate. Later on, he makes the point that *sententia Iudicis ... conscientiam non purgat*"[79]: the judgment at law does not clear the conscience. Something else is required for that, and this is the special purview of Chancery. Again, in *The Earl of Oxford's Case* he repeatedly refers to conscience as essential to his jurisdiction: 'the Chancellors have always corrected … corrupt Consciences'; 'Conscience and Equity is always ready to render to every one their Due'; '[t]he Office of the Chancellor is to correct Mens Consciences for Frauds, Breach of Trusts, Wrongs and Oppressions, of what Nature soever they be'.[80]

An important aspect of his insistence that Chancery is a court of conscience is his concern to make the point that it does not really interfere with the common law, but operates in a different sphere. We have already noticed, in Chapter 4, his making this point in cases from 1596 and 1598.[81] He continues to press it, observing that the 'ordinary iudiciall proceedings by the *Chancery*, according to conscience and equity, is not any disturbance, or delay of Common right',[82] that the Chancellor 'intermedleth only with matters of Conscience',[83] and that 'when a Judgment is obtained by Oppression, Wrong and a hard Conscience, the Chancellor will frustrate and set it aside, not for any error or Defect in the Judgment, but for

[77] Thomas Egerton (Lord Ellesmere), *The Priviledges and Prerogatives of the High Court of Chancery* (London, 1641), sig. A3r (three times), sig. A3v (three times), sig. A4r (three times), sig. A4v (once), sig. B1r (twice), sig. B1v (three times), sig. B2r (twice), sig. B2v (twice), sig. B4v (once), sig. C1r (twice) and sig. C1v (once) (EEBO images 93844:3, 4, 4, 5, 5, 6, 6, 7, 9, 9, and 10, respectively).

[78] Ibid., sig. A3r; EEBO image 93844:3.

[79] Ibid., sig. B1v; EEBO image 93844:6.

[80] *The Earl of Oxford's Case* (1615) 1 Chancery Reports 1, 21 ER 485, p. 486.

[81] See *Ward* v. *Fulwood* (1597), in *Cases Concerning Equity and the Courts of Equity 1550–1660*, W.H. Bryson (ed.) (2 vols, London, 2001), item 118 ('Cases and Notes [Ch. C. 1580–1600]'), case 201, vol. 1, p. 258, and *Sheffield* v. *Lopton* (1598), ibid. For an argument that the jurisdiction of Chancery was not merely 'suppletory' but corrective of the common law, see George Spence, *The Equitable Jurisdiction of the Court of Chancery* (Philadelphia, 1846), pp. 408–9.

[82] Egerton, *Priviledges*, sig. A3v; EEBO image 93844:4.

[83] Thomas Egerton (Lord Ellesmere), *Certaine Observations Concerning the Office of the Lord Chancellor* (London, 1651), pp. 45–6; EEBO images 51548:27–8.

the hard Conscience of the Party ...'.[84] If the insistence on conscience is in aid mainly of maintaining the legitimacy of the jurisdiction, it may make sense that his asserting this, and not giving content to the notion of conscience, tends to be what strikes us.

What conscience as a juristic principle means for Ellesmere is again something that we have to gather from contexts and suggestions, rather than from a developed analysis. In considering this matter, we should be mindful of two of W.J. Jones's observations: first, that Ellesmere 'made little attempt to record and publicize his decisions and arguments', and, second, that '[h]e was a technocrat rather than a theorist'.[85] The first points to a paucity of information; the second suggests that even if there were more information it might be concerned more with procedure than with a substantive concept of conscience. Nevertheless, such information as we do have points to what we might by now describe as an 'orthodox' view of conscience.

Certainly, and not surprisingly, Ellesmere sees conscience as rooted in some higher law. Two of the grounds he advances in *Oxford* are that '[t]he Law of God speaks for the Plaintiff' and that 'Equity and good Conscience speak wholly for him'.[86] But, he adds, 'Equity speaks as the Law of God speaks' (p. 486). Further, the 'Law' appears to include 'the Law of God, the Law of Reason, and the Law of the Land', and apparently that basic rule of equity (or conscience), 'To do as one would be done unto', is grounded upon 'both the Laws of God and Reason' (p. 487).[87] Similarly, in his speech in the Exchequer in *Calvin's Case*—although he is not talking about either equity or conscience—he says that '[t]he common Law of *England* is grounded vpon the Law of God, and extendes it selfe to the originall Lawe of Nature ...'.[88] These are all indicia of a religious intellectual framework which we can surmise corresponded to that of the Protestant commentators we considered in Chapter 5, and of which we have previously seen intimations in Ellesmere.[89]

There are other indications of a religious perspective in Ellesmere's judicial outlook. Not surprisingly, given the prominence he accords to 'God's law', he cites scripture, apparently as legal authority. Thus, his first argument in *Oxford*,

---

84 *Earl of Oxford's Case*, p. 487.

85 Jones, p. 98.

86 *Earl of Oxford's Case*, p. 486.

87 Ellesmere is explicitly referring to St. German here.

88 Thomas Egerton (Lord Ellesmere), *The Speech of the Lord Chancellor of England, in the Eschequer Chamber, touching the Post-nati* (London, 1609), p. 32; EEBO image 366:22.

89 In his dedication of *Le Primer Report* to Ellesmere, Davies names 'Diuinity' as the first kind of learning the Chancellor must have (fol. 10v; EEBO image 7771:12). John Hacket (1592–1670) says that Ellesmere was 'a great Patron to Divines', among whom were a number of eminent churchmen (*Scrinia Reserata: A Memorial Offer'd to the Great Deservings of John Williams, D.D.* (London, 1693), p. 19; EEBO image 49492:11.

as we have seen, is that the law of God supports the plaintiff's position, and he quotes Deuteronomy 28:30 for the proposition—obliquely on point in the case—that '[h]e that builds a House ought to dwell in it' (p. 486). In the case of the *Post-nati*, he again cites the Bible—this time Ecclesiastes 8:2 and 4—as authority for the proposition that temporal rulers have their power from 'God almighty'.[90] Incidentally, he also cites St. Augustine and Aquinas for the same principle, and, while acknowledging that Plato and Aristotle were 'men of singuler learning and wisedome', he says that they 'lacked the true learning of the knowledge of God'.[91] And perpetuities are not to be countenanced in Chancery because 'they fight against God'.[92]

Moreover, he evinces something of the chancellor's traditional concern with the *soul*. We may recall the case cited in Chapter 4 where he comments that a corporation cannot be relied on to carry out a trust, because a 'body politic [has] no soul to lose but private men [have]'.[93] The implicit reasoning here seems to be: a trust is a creature of equity; equity acts on the soul or conscience of the trustee; a person upon whom equity cannot act cannot be a trustee. He repeats a similar point in another case: corporations 'will not be sworn because they do not have a soul'.[94] This kind of thinking is reminiscent of the medieval chancellors. Similarly, in a rather different context, he says in his speech on the *Post-nati* that a subject's bond of allegiance 'is *Vinculum fidei*; it bindeth the soule and conscience … and as a Soule or Conscience cannot bee framed by Policie [that is, the political state]; so Faith and Allegeance cannot bee … put into a politike bodie'.[95] Certain kinds of juridical acts require a soul and a conscience.

At the same time, Ellesmere does apparently distinguish justiciable from non-justiciable conscience. In his book about the Lord Chancellor's office, he recounts the Fineux-Morton exchange, in which the former argues that some matters are to be relieved by the common law, others in Chancery, and still others 'are in conscience between a man and his Confessor'.[96] Morton's view was the more comprehensive one that 'every Law is or ought to be according to Gods Laws' and

[90] Egerton, *Post-nati*, p. 106; EEBO image 366:60.

[91] Ibid., p. 105; EEBO image 366:59.

[92] Anon., *The Practice of the High Court of Chancery Unfolded* (London, 1672), p. 49; EEBO image 33548:29. See also an anonymous case (1599) Cary 9, 21 ER 5 where Egerton pronounced that 'perpetuities … be fights against God' (p. 5). Compare Doderidge J.'s observation in *Pells v. Brown* (1620): 'si homes poient faire continuance de terre in lour families for ever, ceo fuit a preventer le providence de Dieu' (Henry Rolle, *Un Continuation des Reports de Henry Rolle* (London, 1676), p. 221; EEBO image 53314:112).

[93] *Cases Concerning Equity*, item 119 ('Cases in Tempore Egerton [Ch. C. 1598–c. 1602]'), case 123, vol. 1, p. 290.

[94] Ibid., item 167 ('Notes and Cases [c. 1608–c. 1620]'), case 576, vol. 1, pp. 380–81. That is, presumably, they cannot take the oath so integral to Chancery procedure.

[95] Egerton, *Post-nati*, p. 101; EEBO image 366:57.

[96] Egerton, *Certaine Observations*, pp. 48, 105; EEBO images 51543:29, 56.

that the defaulting executor in the case would be 'damned in Hell' if he did not make restitution to the estate.[97] At this point, Ellesmere does not indicate which view he prefers. But he does go on to cite St. German for the proposition, which we have seen before, that 'many times it must be left to the Conscience of the party'.[98]

Ellesmere makes his position more explicit when (referring to the preceding 'authorities') he says that

> there are two sorts of *leges conscientiæ*, the one is *lex conscientiæ politicæ*, by which the Chancellor ordereth matters; In which Law of Conscience, there is respect had unto the Lawes, Customes, and State of this Commonwealth, and the other is *lex conscientiæ Divinæ*, by which there is no compulsive relief in this world, but the offendor standeth at the judgment of God only, and this in times past was said to be examinable between the Offendor and the Confessor.[99] (p. 48)

Several things are worth remarking here, besides the obvious point that Ellesmere distinguishes two laws of conscience in a way that broadly anticipates Lord Nottingham's distinction. For one thing, the notion of a political law of conscience appears inconsistent with his apparently radical separation of conscience and 'policy' elsewhere. The apparent contradiction is reinforced by his observing that the *lex conscientiæ politicæ* is in some sense constrained by the laws and customs of the commonwealth. Although 'policy' may not be able to create conscience, it can in some way bind it. Unlike the religious writers, Ellesmere does not really explain this point. Conversely, *lex conscientiæ Divinæ* involves situations in which there is no temporal relief. But this rather begs the question, since the absence of temporal sanctions is presumably the result of a decision by the legislature or courts not to provide them. Again, this does not offer a criterion on the basis of which we can distinguish justiciable from non-justiciable conscience: it merely asserts that this distinction is an outcome. Further, he refers to the fact that, formerly, matters of the spiritual law of conscience were determinable between the offender and the confessor. This does not necessarily imply that they were also determinable in Chancery, but to the extent that, say, the medieval Chancellor was a confessor, this might be a defensible inference. Whatever the case formerly, however, Ellesmere seems to insist that now the Chancery's powers do not reach the *lex conscientiæ Divinæ*. The maxim *nullus recedat a cancellariæ sine remedio*, although it includes the issuing of writs for common law actions and matters of conscience examinable in Chancery, does not 'any way extend to the Law of Conscience divine'.[100] (p. 49)'.

97 Ibid.

98 Ibid., p. 48; EEBO image 51543:29. Compare George Cary, *Reports or Causes in Chancery* (London, 1665), p. 16; EEBO image 105479:17.

99 Egerton, *Certaine Observations*, p. 48; EEBO image 51543:29.

100 Ibid., p. 29; EEBO image 51543:29.

Related to, but not necessarily congruent with, this distinction between political and 'divine' conscience is the distinction between public and private conscience. That Ellesmere is at least sometimes thinking in terms of the former, public form of conscience, is suggested by his stating, on more than one occasion, the standard proposition that it is the King's conscience, not his own, that he is administering.[101] Thus, he cites the observation '[*e*]*quitas est publici iuris moderatio a pectore Regio, velut ab Oraculo petenda*'.[102]

But this cuts both ways: equity comes from the bosom of the *king*, but it is the king's *bosom*. Moreover, there is something oracular—emanating from perhaps incommunicable insight—about it. And when the Chancellor administers equity, it may be rather a fiction to say that it is the King's conscience he is administering. Indeed, in the *Post-nati* case, in his 'Preface to the Reader', Ellesmere says that he is to judge the case in Chancery 'following the rule of mine owne Conscience, and the measure of mine owne vnderstanding'.[103] Moreover, in terms rather reminiscent of some of the religious writers, he asserts that 'hauing the warrant of a sincere conscience, which is truly said to be, *veluti Comes, & Testis, & Iudex actionum*', he has decreed for Calvin in the Chancery.[104] So, both the authority and the measure of his judgment in Chancery appear to be his own conscience. Elsewhere, he tells us that the 'names or generall notions the Lord Chancellor doth assigne unto himselfe for limitation of equity and direction of his Conscience that lyeth hidden and concealed in his owne breast …'.[105] Significantly, he offers as support for this proposition the explanation of the influential medieval canonist, William Lyndwood (1375?–1446): '*Conscientia est Cognitione sui ipsuis* [*sic*] *Cordis & Conscientiæ alicujus quando quid relinquitur ipsemet erit judex*',[106] involving

---

101 See, for example, an anonymous case of 1612, where he observes that 'the lord chancellor judges as by the king's own conscience' (*Cases Concerning Equity*, case 189, vol. 2, p. 398) and *Martin* v. *Marhsall* [*sic*] (Common Pleas, 1615), where the plaintiff's counsel says that he has heard the Lord Chancellor say that 'he is the king's deputy and speaks the king's conscience' (ibid., case 231, vol. 2, p. 444).

102 Egerton, *Priviledges*, sig. B1v; EEBO image 93844:6.

103 Egerton, *Post-nati*, sig. A4v; EEBO image 366:4. Addressing Ellesmere, Davies similarly says that the Chancellor decides cases 'by the rules of his owne conscience' (*Primer Report*, fol. 10v; EEBO image 7771:12.

104 Egerton, *Post-nati*, sig. A5v; EEBO image 366:5. Although the first term of the triad—*comes*—is somewhat anomalous, we have seen conscience conventionally characterized as witness and judge.

105 Egerton, *Certaine Observations*, p. 7; EEBO image 51543:8.

106 Ibid. Egerton cites Lyndwood's *Provinciale seu Constitutiones Angliae*, of which there are several editions. The 'conscientia' definition seems to be taken from the alphabetical 'Tabula' prefixed to the work; a variant occurs in the annotation at fol. 15r of the 1506 (Paris) edition and p. 27 of the 1679 (Oxford) edition (EEBO images 23177:33 and 95644:46, respectively). The 'conscientiæ' (or 'cõscientias') annotation appears at fol. 67r of the 1506 edition and p. 213 of the 1679 edition (EEBO images 23177:84 and 95644:139, respectively).

the knowledge of one's own heart that we have encountered elsewhere. Contrary to what is implied in allusions to the 'King's conscience', the very criteria for limiting equity and directing the Chancellor's conscience are not 'public', but are cached in his own heart. Ellesmere acknowledges that a problem with this is that it makes the law uncertain—although this defect is at least partially remedied by there being 'a competent store of cases whereupon reasonable conjecture may be grounded what is like to fall out in matters of many natures'.[107]

Perhaps an indication of the kind of reckoning that this can lead to appears in *Allen's Case*, where Allen 'dealt so mercilessly' with others, where his dealings were 'unchristian and barbarous', so that '[t]he pitiful cries of the father and mother dying … and of the poor orphans do call to God for relief, and moved the heart of the chancellor to take compassion upon them …'.[108] What even so austere a chancellor as Ellesmere dispenses seems to involve emotion and religion, as well as reason. However objective and public the Chancellor's conscience purports to be, it still appears to be a site of subjectivity and variation.[109]

As for so many others, for Ellesmere 'conscience' appears to have involved a significant dimension of factual inquiry. We have already noticed, in Chapter 4, several indications of this in the Elizabethan Egerton. We have also seen Ellesmere's observation in *Priviledges and Prerogatives* that just as, at law, the judge and jury are to determine matters of law and fact, respectively, so in Chancery the Chancellor is to determine both law and fact by 'Conscience and Equity'. For Ellesmere, much of what a court of conscience is about is getting at the truth. For example, he cites the observation '*sententia Iudicis non præiudicat veritati*'.[110] What this seems to imply is that more complete truth than that upon which legal judgment is based may be accessible by other means.

This focus on the Chancellor's superior truth-ascertaining capacity occurs in a number of forms. Probably most commonly, it appears as remarks upon the limits of the common law. In a slight variant of an observation that we have encountered more than once already, Ellesmere writes that in Chancery, 'a man shall not bee prejudiced for his mispleading, or for default of forme, but according to the truth of the matter … according unto conscience, and not *Ex rigore Juris*'.[111] But it may also relate to the competence of the respective fact-finders: in *Clench v. Tomley*,

[107] Egerton, *Certaine Observations*, p. 7; EEBO image 51543:8.

[108] *Allen's Case* (1610), in *Cases Concerning Equity*, case 174, vol. 1, p. 390.

[109] Chancery is portrayed as being too lenient on 'foul and notorious … fraud and cosinage' and whether it is really giving effect to 'equity and conscience' is vigorously questioned in *Glanville's Case* (1615), ibid., case 230, vol. 2, p. 441. *Allen* and *Glanville* are contextualized and discussed by Baker, 'Common Lawyers and the Chancery', pp. 213 and 211–12, respectively, and pp. 216–18.

[110] Egerton, *Priviledges*, sig. B1v; EEBO image 93844:6.

[111] Egerton, *Certaine Observations*, p. 30. See also p. 47. (EEBO images 51543:20 and 28, respectively.)

Ellesmere opines that his court is better able to assess complex evidence—'books and deeds'—'then a jury of plough-men'.[112]

Again, he expresses this concern with comprehensive fact-determination in terms of a familiar formula. 'The Chancellor', he says, 'must judge *secundum conscientiam, & non secundum allegatum.*'[113] This inquiry *secundum conscientiam* ostensibly involves very sweeping powers of information-gathering indeed: the *potentia absoluta* of the Chancellor 'useth all meanes to know the verity'.[114] This is not the only thing that the 'absolute power' entails—it also presumably entails a power to discern and enunciate the norms to be applied and freedom from most kinds of external control[115]—but it is certainly something that the writers, including Ellesmere, emphasize. His position is perhaps summarized when he says, 'A man will not be prejudiced in Chancery by mispleader nor by the default of form. But if he can prove his matter that serves for him in conscience *viis et modis*, this is sufficient, because the chancellor has *potestatem absolutam*'.[116] The Chancellor is not limited by the rules of pleading.

This wide-ranging approach to discerning the truth may also involve the Chancellor's personal knowledge and conscience. So, even if a defendant fails to answer a plaintiff's allegation of wrongdoing, 'if the Chancellor hath knowledge that he hath done no wrong … the Complaintiffe shall not recover at all'.[117] A slightly different point, but one again involving the Chancellor's private conscience appears in *Mynn* v. *Cobb.* There, although a 'trust was not so fully proved as the Lord Chancellor would make a full decree thereupon', yet 'it satisfied him as a private man', and therefore he determined to write to the defendant encouraging him 'to conform himself to reason'.[118] Here the issue is apparently one of proof, and there is a disparity between what should satisfy the public *persona* of the Chancellor and what might persuade his private conscience. At the same time, what persuades his private conscience is enough to move him to act in his role of Chancellor, if only informally.

From the rather sketchy intimations available, one can at best tease out Ellesmere's conception of conscience as a juristic principle. Certainly, conscience

---

112 *Clench* v. *Tomley* (1603), Cary 23, 21 ER 13 at 13.

113 Egerton, *Certaine Observations*, p. 46. Compare p. 69. (EEBO images 51543:28 and 38, respectively.) Curiously, in *The Earl of Oxford's Case*, he appears to say that the Chancellor 'is to judge according to that which is alledged and proved', but he contrasts this with the 'strict and ordinary (or limited) Power' by which common law judges are to proceed (p. 488).

114 Egerton, *Certaine Observations*, p. 44; EEBO image 51543:27.

115 Ibid., p. 41; EEBO image 51543:25.

116 *Mainwaringe* v. *Lovelace* (1612), *Cases Concerning Equity*, item 167, case 254, vol. 1, p. 376.

117 Egerton, *Certaine Observations*, p. 46; EEBO 51543:28. Ellesmere is in fact citing earlier materials here, but he expresses no objection to this point.

118 *Mynn* v. *Cobb* (1604) Cary 25, 21 ER 14 at 14.

was important to him, perhaps even taken for granted, and what indications we have appear to be pieces of the conventional picture. But the boundaries of conscience as a criterion for judgment in Chancery are not perspicuous. No doubt he thought that there were such boundaries, as his distinction between *conscientia politica* and *conscientia divina* makes clear. But, at the same time, where the line is to be drawn remains blurred, or at least unexplained. The close relationship between the two, indeed, their interconnectedness, is perhaps well-illustrated in his response to the objection that judges' opinions expressed in Parliament should not be taken as seriously as their pronouncements in court, where they are bound by their judicial oath: 'if men of so great and eminent places feare not God and his iudgements, euen out of a religious conscience, which is *Frœnum ante peccatum, & flagrum post peccatum*, it may be doubted that the externall ceremony of adding a Booke will little auaile'.[119] A person who expresses such a sentiment is unlikely, I think, consistently to insist upon the dodge of a separate political conscience where he thinks that what religious conscience directs is seriously at stake.

Sir Francis Bacon

As for Ellesmere, for Bacon too the evidence for how he understood the conscience of equity is rather inchoate. Notwithstanding John Ritchie's collection of Bacon's Chancery cases,[120] Daniel Coquillette remarks that 'we are left with very poor resources to describe Bacon's four years as [Chancellor]', since the 'official Chancery record' contains 'only a pale reflection of Bacon's words and rationales'.[121] So, for example, conscience is mentioned only a few times.[122]

Again, as for Ellesmere, for Bacon the Elizabethan materials are in some ways as illuminating as the Jacobean. Probably the main text in this regard is his *Reading on the Statute of Uses*,[123] to which I have referred previously and which contains a number of references to equity as involving conscience. We have noted, for example, his recognition of a distinction between 'private conscience' and 'the general conscience of the realm, which is Chancery' (p. 401). He is not making this observation, however, to draw a line between the two, but rather to

---

119 Egerton, *Post-nati*, pp. 16–17; EEBO image 366:14.

120 *Reports of Cases Decided by Francis Bacon ... in the High Court of Chancery (1617–1621)*, ed. John Ritchie (London, 1932).

121 Daniel Coquillette, *Francis Bacon* (Stanford, 1992), pp. at 201, 206.

122 In *Helme* v. *Conham* (1617), the defendant resists the bill for an injunction by saying that it would be 'against equity and conscience' (*Reports of Cases Decided by Francis Bacon*, p. 23); in *Carter* v. *Scoble* (1618, 1619) an order was made permitting the plaintiff to examine witnesses *ad informandum conscientiam judicis* (ibid., p.140); and in *Parke* v. *Wannell* (1619) a transaction was described as 'unconscionable usury' (ibid., p. 144).

123 Francis Bacon, *Reading on the Statute of Uses*, in J. Spedding, R.L. Ellis and D.D. Heath (eds), *The Works of Francis Bacon* (14 vols, London, 1857–74), vol. 7, pp. 395ff.

acknowledge them as alternative or concurrent bases for enforcing trusts. Thus, he notes, at first Chancery gave no remedy, but left it to 'the particular conscience of the feofee' (p. 410).

He does say some, occasionally tantalizing, things about the general nature of conscience in this context. For example, he notes that the scope of law and conscience are different, so that although a use 'be nothing in law' so as to evoke a legal remedy, 'yet it is somewhat in reputation of law and in conscience'; conversely, 'that may be something in law which is nothing in conscience' (p. 400). This is unremarkable. But earlier he had considered the point, asking rhetorically whether a use had 'any being in nature or in conscience' (p. 399). What this seems to suggest is that conscience and 'nature' are nearly allied, and that equity looks to the real nature of the thing. By contrast, law appears to be more artificial. Bacon goes on to say that an equitable owner meets the property requirements to be "sworn of an inquest, for that is ruled *secundum dominium naturale*, and not *secundum dominium legitimum; nam natura dominus est, qui fructum ex re percipit*' (p. 399). Nature is the lord that extracts the fruit of the matter. So conscience, related to nature, identifies the essentials of things. Later, he makes a rather perplexing connection between common law and conscience. First, he says that a use involves trusting 'the conscience of another better than his own estate and possession'. Because this is 'an accident or event of human society' universally, it must have been at common law, 'which is common reason' (p. 415). Then, citing Fitzherbert, he says 'common reason is common law, and not conscience'. This I do not fully understand, unless the distinction he is making is that common reason is a matter of convention—what is generally accepted—while conscience is a matter of apprehending something like 'natural law'.[124] He proceeds to assert that 'common reason doth define that uses should be remedied in conscience and not in courts of law, and ordered by rules in conscience and not by strait cases of law' (p. 415). Uses are a matter of common reason, which somehow equates to common law, but which nevertheless determines that uses are to be ruled and remedied in conscience. By this chain of rather opaque reasoning, he is able to conclude 'that the force and strength that an use had or hath in conscience is by common law' (p. 415). Whether this is an attempt somehow to give pre-eminence to the common law, even when it comes to uses, I cannot tell. And, of course, it gives little indication as to the content of conscience.

Some fragmentary indications of the content, or perhaps quality, of conscience appear in particular cases that Bacon mentions. We have seen before his observation that a purchaser, even for valuable consideration, of land subject to a use will 'stand seised to the ancient use' if he has notice of it—the reason being that 'the chancery looketh farther than the common law, namely, to the corrupt conscience' of the purchaser (p. 405). So, equity goes further than the law by considering matters engaging conscience, which in this case involves issues of awareness. Elsewhere,

---

[124] His use of the word 'accident' probably reinforces this. If he is using it in the technical, Aristotelian, sense it should be contrasted with 'essence'.

Bacon observes that 'no court of conscience will inforce *donum gratuitum*, though the intent appear never so clearly …' (p. 404). Conscience in equity does not extend to enforcing mere inchoate generosity; it requires a *quid pro quo*, mutuality.[125] Elsewhere again he says that the law of collateral warranty is a hard law, and not to be considered in a court of conscience.[126] The court of conscience considers the 'hardness' of—apparently substantive—legal rules, but Bacon offers no general principle which tells us where equity draws the line between hard law that it will and hard law that it will not countenance. Interestingly, Bacon notes that a corporation cannot be a feoffee to uses, but, unlike Ellesmere, he does not attribute this to a body politic's want of a soul, but to more mundane reasons. This may be a small indication of Bacon's more pragmatic and secular approach to the law in general and Chancery in particular.

Some insight into Bacon's position may be garnered from materials relating to the crisis of 1616 and its immediate sequelæ. Bacon was one of James's 'law officers' asked to respond to the question about Chancery's power to hear cases after a judgment at law. This question was formulated in rather tendentious terms: is there any statute which so restrains Chancery that 'Conscience and Equity [are] excluded, banished and damn'd'?[127] Not surprisingly, Bacon (who was of the 'anti-Coke' faction) and the others answered 'No'. Part of their rationale was the standard point that Chancery never reverses the judgment itself, but 'leaves [it] in peace, and only medleth with the corrupt Conscience of the Party'.[128] Just previously they had explained that, just 'as the point in Equity was never in question in the Common Law Courts, so the point of Law or Fact, that concerns the Law is never in question in the Chancery'.[129] Chancery is not questioning the judgment, because it is addressing itself to different issues, both normative and factual. That different inquiry is defined in terms of 'conscience', but no effort is made to explain the extent or defining qualities of this jurisdiction. In response to this report, James issued his well-known decree upholding the jurisdiction of the Chancery, so that his subjects 'should not be abandoned and exposed to perish under the Rigor and Extremity of our Laws …'.[130]

James revisited this issue in his speech in the Star Chamber in 1616. In this discourse, in which the King repeatedly invokes his own (ostensibly personal)

---

125 Although, apparently, legacies for charity are to be preferred before legacies to persons—perhaps reflecting concern (as in the case of payment of the testator's debts) for the soul of the deceased (*Rolt* v. *Smith* (1617), *Reports of Cases Decided by Francis Bacon*, pp. 53–4).

126 Bacon, *Reading on the Statute of Uses*, p. 403.

127 These materials are reproduced, for example, in 'The Jurisdiction of the Court of Chancery Vindicated', in *Reports of Cases Taken and adjudged in the Court of Chancery* (London, 1693); see p. 24; EEBO image 29452:184.

128 Ibid., p. 47; EEBO image 29452:196.

129 Ibid.

130 Ibid., p. 49; EEBO image 29452:197.

conscience,[131] he acknowledges the supremacy of God's law,[132] describes Chancery as 'the dispenser of the Kings [ostensibly public] Conscience',[133] and observes that it 'mixeth Mercie with Iustice'.[134] He emphasizes the importance of the certainty of law and the bounded jurisdiction of all courts. So, famously, he tells the judges that their office is '*Ius dicere* and not *Ius dare*'.[135] Moreover, with reference to Chancery, he protests that he never gave Ellesmere 'other warrant, then to goe on in his Court acording to Presidents, warranted by Law in the time of the best gouerning Kings, and most learned Chancellors; These were the limits I gaue vnto him …'.[136] This is palpably a response to concerns that the jurisdiction of that court was too arbitrary and irregular. James claims that Ellesmere promised never to exceed these limits. As for the relative powers of the courts, James cautions judges 'hereafter' to 'keepe within your limits and Iurisdictions' so that there might be 'a concordance, and musicall accord' among them.[137]

This is the immediate context of Bacon's accession to the Keepership in 1617. The concern was to make Chancery appear more ruled, and to address the perception that the potentially unbounded arbitrariness of the Chancellor should not override the regular law. Thus, in his charge to Bacon on tendering the Great Seal to him, James ordered him to 'contain the jurisdiction of [Chancery] within the true and due limits, without swelling or excess'.[138] Bacon's response, in which he promises to deal with 'the excess or tumour of this court of Chancery',[139] says

[131] James I, *His Maiesties Speech in the Starre-Chamber the XX of June Anno 1616* (London, 1616), fols 6r, 8v, 9v, 13v; EEBO images 26198:7, 10, 11 and 15, respectively. Something of James's understanding of conscience is evident from his *Basilikon Doron* (Edinburgh, 1599): it is, he says, 'nothing else but the light of knowledge that God hath planted in man' (p. 17; EEBO image 1192:13); if it is not 'grounded vpon sure knowledge', that is, Scripture, it 'is either an ignorante fantasie, or an arrogante glaikerie' (p. 23; 1192:16). These comments reflect, in unelaborated form, what we have seen to be the conventional account.

[132] *His Maiesties Speech*, fols 8r, 9r; EEBO images 26198:9 and 10, respectively.

[133] Ibid., fol. 13r; EEBO image 26198:14.

[134] Ibid., fol. 13v; EEBO image 26198:15.

[135] Ibid., fol. 10r; EEBO image 26198:11.

[136] Ibid., fol. 14r; EEBO image 26198:15. Arguably, the 'Presidents' he is referring to are mainly procedural.

[137] Ibid., fol. 15r; EEBO image 26198:16.

[138] 'The Effect of that which was spoken by the Lord Keeper of the Great Seal of England, at the taking of his Place in Chancery', in *Works of Francis Bacon*, vol. 13, p. 184.

[139] Ibid. His restraint is perhaps exemplified in *Roswell* v. *Everie* (1619?), which stands for the proposition that 'Le Chancerie ne relieuera un home encontre un Maxime del ley sur un matter de equitie … car ceo est a faire un novelle ley' (Henry Rolle, *Un Abridgment des Plusieurs Cases et Resolutions del Common Ley* [London, 1668], pp. 375–6; EEBO images 103278:194–5). For a discussion of the supposed inviolability of the 'maxims' of the common law by equity, see Gray, 'Boundaries of the Equitable Function', pp. 203ff.

nothing about conscience *per se,* perhaps because it is a concept that might appear inconsistent with his declared aspiration to follow the rules.

As Chancellor, Bacon does display frequent deference to the 'course of the Court',[140] precedent,[141] and so on, and refuses to cross a 'ground and rule of the common law' even though he 'mislikes' the outcome.[142] At the same time, there are intimations of a readiness to respond to more general or even 'affective' considerations: in *Freeman* v. *Blagrave* (1617), he 'utterly dislik[es] the nature of the suit', because it tends to make knighthood 'venal and mercenary';[143] in *Simeon* v. *Dean and Cannons of Windsor* (1617) he finds a 'weighty, difficult and new' cause to be 'full of equity on the complainant's part';[144] in *Moreton* v. *Briggs* (1618), he resists a particular decision on the basis that it would be 'a hard case and evil example';[145] and in *Hoskett* v. *Hellier* (1619) he again 'much mislik[es]' the conduct of certain of the defendants, and shapes a decree accordingly.[146] While trying to adhere to rules and regularity, Bacon does appear to be affected by what might be seen as matters of conscience more generally.

More suggestive is the case of *Earl of Northumberland* v. *Bowes* (1621),[147] the report of which contains more substance than many. The question is the familiar one of extent to which a human law respecting things otherwise indifferent binds the conscience. The particular point addressed here is how the conscience is to be purged in such a case. The Chancellor opines that, where an action that is not intrinsically a crime is made a crime by statute,

> this binds the conscience with this difference, if this thing prohibited was bad in itself, scil. *malum in se* … there such an act binds the conscience, and it is not sufficient to submit oneself to the penalty. But if the thing was not bad before, but now is prohibited by the said act and a penalty is annexed, this binds the conscience only to the suffering in submission to the penalty and not to refrain [from] the thing (p. 490).[148]

Bacon here is apparently thinking within a framework reminiscent of contemporary religious writers. This issue, which was not uncontroversial, was addressed by several Protestant casuists. Notably, Perkins expressed a similar view respecting

---

140 *Dodson* v. *Lutterford* (1617), *Reports of Cases Decided by Francis Bacon*, p. 63.

141 *Hunt* v. *Bancroft* (1617–19), ibid., p. 67; *Chapman* v. *Emery and Porter* (1617, 1618), ibid., p. 80; *Goodfellowe* v. *Morris* (1618), ibid., p. 133.

142 *Eldred* v. *Rawleigh* (1618), ibid., p. 83.

143 *Freeman* v. *Blagrave* (1616, 1617), ibid., p. 13.

144 *Simeon* v. *Dean and Cannons of Windsor* (1617), ibid., p. 51.

145 *Moreton* v. *Briggs* (1618), ibid., p. 136.

146 *Hoskett* v. *Hellier* (1619), ibid., p. 199.

147 *Earl of Northumberland* v. *Bowes* (1621), *Cases Concerning Equity*, case 261, vol. 2, pp. 489–91.

148 Brackets present in text.

laws '*meerely penall*', having the form '[i]f any person doe this or that, then he shall forfeit thus or thus': '[t]his kind of law binds especially to the punishment, & that in the very intent of the lawgiuer, and he that is readie in omitting the law to pay the fine or punishmēt, is not to be charged with sinne before God …'.[149] My point here is not to draw an exact parallel or to analyse this position critically, but merely to suggest that, in some respects at least, Bacon reflected the attitudes of his theological contemporaries.

Perhaps the most comprehensive insight into Bacon's considered views on these matters is afforded by his 'Example of a Treatise on Universal Justice or the fountains of Equity, by Aphorisms',[150] which Coquillette (rather too encomiastically) calls a 'brilliant articulation of a theory of equity'.[151] Bacon begins 'Title I' with the observation that the 'Primary Dignity of Laws' is 'that they be certain': '[c]ertainty is so essential to law, that law cannot even be just without it' (p. 90).[152] At the same time he recognizes (with so many others) that '[t]he narrow compass of human wisdom' cannot anticipate every situation that might arise, and that some remedy is required for the shortcomings of the prescribed law. He mentions three remedies; the one which concerns us is the provision of 'jurisdictions empowered to decide according to the arbitration of a good man and sound discretion' (p. 90). He divides these jurisdictions into Censorian (for criminal matters) and Praetorian (for civil matters), the latter of which relates most directly to the Chancery.

Bacon does not say much here about conscience, but he does use the word in connection with Praetorian courts: their jurisdiction involves 'the judgment and discretion of a conscientious man' (p. 94); the court of 'equity and conscience' should be kept separate from courts administering 'strict justice' (p. 96). In this admittedly tentative work, where one might expect to find some analysis of conscience, there is none. Rather, Bacon repeats some clichés about courts of equity—that they are there to 'abate the rigor of the law and to supply its defects' (p. 95). Consistently with the concern we have seen with 'excess', he does say that Praetorian courts should 'entirely confine themselves to monstrous and extraordinary cases' (p. 95)—suggesting, perhaps, that the test is the *degree* to which conscience is offended. One reason for so confining themselves is that 'the power of supplying, extending, and moderating laws, differs little from that of making them' (p. 95). This may remind us of James's caution that the function of courts is to speak the law, not to make it. Bacon acknowledges an ultimate freedom

[149] William Perkins, *A Discourse of Conscience* (Cambridge, 1596), p. 69; EEBO image 10898:38.

[150] Francis Bacon, 'Example of a Treatise on Universal Justice or the Fountains of Equity, by Aphorisms' appended to Book 8 of *De Augmentis* (1623), *Works of Francis Bacon*, vol. 5, pp. 88–110.

[151] Coquillette, p. 211.

[152] In support of this proposition, he cites both sacred (I Corinthians 14:8) and profane (Aristotle, *Rhetoric*, i.1) authority.

in these courts, but suggests as another way of limiting them the publication of their reasons for judgment—'so that what is free in point of power may yet be restrained by regard to character and reputation' (p. 95). The reason he offers for keeping the Praetorian courts separate is that this is a way of containing discretion: if the Praetorian function were assimilated to the ordinary courts 'the distinction of cases will not be retained, but discretion will in the end supersede the law' (p. 96).

In short, Bacon appears concerned 'that Praetorian Courts be not allowed to swell and overflow' (p. 96). But addressing this concern does not, for him, necessarily involve advancing a narrow definition of conscience. Rather, it emphasizes institutional arrangements—keep the court of discretion separate, publish reasons for the exercise of discretion—that will make it subject to open scrutiny. It does, of course, involve counselling restraint: interfere only in the most egregious cases. But he offers no general touchstone for determining what is sufficiently 'monstrous'. Indeed, one wonders whether this criterion might not be setting the bar a little high.

Further light is cast on Bacon's attitude to conscience by his observations on 'the light and law of nature'[153] in Book 9 of *De Augmentis*:

> For we must observe that the light of nature is used in two several senses; the one, as far as it springs from sense, induction, reason, argument, according to the laws of heaven and earth; the other, as far as it flashes upon the spirit of man by an inward instinct, according to the law of conscience; which is a spark and relic of his primitive and original purity. And in this latter sense chiefly does the soul partake of some light to behold and discern the perfection of the moral law; a light however not altogether clear ....[154]

His reference to 'sense, induction, reason, argument' accords with a 'scientific' method that we have come to associate particularly with Bacon's intellectual outlook. Thus, for example, Coquillette observes that Bacon's approach to law-making, as to other areas of inquiry, was 'empirical' and 'inductive'.[155] But we should not under-rate the other sense of 'the light of nature' which he acknowledges. It 'flashes upon his spirit ... by an inward instinct, according to the law of conscience'; that law is a 'spark' of an original purity, allowing the soul 'to behold and discern the perfection of the moral law', albeit somewhat darkly as a result of the Fall. As Greene says of a similar passage in the *Advancement of*

---

[153] In his argument in the case of the *Post-nati* in the Exchequer Chamber, he had affirmed that '*our Law is grounded upon the Law of Nature*' (*Three Speeches of the Right Honorable, Sir Francis Bacon* ... [London, 1641], p. 35 [mistakenly numbered '25']; EEBO image 51155:19).

[154] Bacon, Book 9 of *De Augmentis*, in *Works of Francis Bacon*, vol. 5, p. 113.

[155] Coquillette, p. 3.

Learning,[156] this description could amount to 'an uncannily accurate restatement in English of [the] medieval doctrine [of *synderesis*] in the absence of the term itself'.[157] In other words, Bacon's understanding of conscience appears not to be far removed from the orthodox account that we have described. Thus, we should probably not assume that, when, early in his career, he wrote that his age was one 'wherein if science bee increased, conscience is rather decayed'[158] he was being disingenuous, or that he might not still have felt that sentiment later in life, however he might have experienced some frustration at the resistance of the directives of conscience to demonstration.

Bishop John Williams

As might be expected, the writings of Williams—whom Jones describes paradoxically as 'ungodly but legally percipient'[159]—do evince a preoccupation with conscience. He often proclaims that his personal conscience is the director of his actions. When Ellesmere sought to engage him, he requested a year's deferral so that he could remain at Cambridge where he had undertaken to be university proctor, a position that he could not delegate because 'I dare not trust my Oath with another Man's Conscience'.[160] Similarly, he scrupled to be consecrated by

---

[156] Francis Bacon, *Advancement of Learning*, *Works of Francis Bacon*, vol. 3, p. 479. In this passage he says specifically that the light of nature is 'imprinted on the spirit of man by an inward instinct'—language specifically reminiscent of Lord Herbert of Cherbury's account.

[157] Robert A. Greene, 'Synderesis, the Spark of Conscience, in the English Renaissance', *Journal of the History of Ideas*, 52/2 (1991): 195–219, p. 214. Greene goes on to say that, because Bacon 'emphasize[s] the dimness of the sparkle and … restrict[s] its capacities, his view was essentially Calvinist' (p. 215).

[158] Francis Bacon, 'Epistle Dedicatorie' to Queen Elizabeth in his 'Maxims of the Common Law' (1597), published in *The Elements of the Common Lawes of England* (London, 1630), sig. A3v; EEBO image 447:5. Bewailing the waning of conscience was something of a rhetorical convention during the period. For example, Immanuel Bourne complains that conscience '*is fled already from* Earth *to* Heauen' ('Epistle Dedicatory', *The Anatomie of Conscience* [London, 1623], sig. A2r; EEBO image 7186:2) and John Hughes says that it has recently '*lyne bed-rid & speechlesse*' ('The Epistle', *St. Pavls Exercise, or, a Sermon of Conscience* [London, 1622], sig. A2v; EEBO image 4483:3), and, like Bacon, that he wishes 'that many had lesse Science, vpon condition they had more conscience' (p. 9; 4483:7). On the title page of *The Christians Iewell, or, the Treasure of a Good Conscience* (London, 1617), William Worship quotes the Latin maxim '*multi querunt scientiam, pauci conscientiam*', as does Nathanael Vincent on the title page of *A Heaven of Hell upon Earth, or, a Discourse Concerning Conscience* (London, 1676).

[159] Jones, p. 31.

[160] Ambrose Philips, *The Life of John Williams* (Cambridge, 1700), p. 25; EEBO image 98394:17. Philips says that this shows that Williams 'was too Honest to act short of his Conscience' (ibid.).

Archbishop George Abbot, who had accidentally killed a man, because of the wounding of his conscience that this might entail.[161] He admonished the newly called serjeants-at-law in 1623 that they were 'in your highest Title the Servants of God. Therefore keep a good Conscience in all things'.[162] For him, the rule of personal action, at least in outward profession, seems to have been conscience.

At the same time, he appears aware of the rhetorical force of invocations of conscience, and of their frequent disingenuousness. Although 'Conscience is offered, and set out as it were for a Lanthorn upon the Pharos of this Motion [that is, the appeal of Catholics in England for priests]', it is well known that 'the greatest Cheats that are put upon the World, are in the good Names of Love and Conscience'.[163]

We can probably say even more confidently of Williams than of Bacon or even of Ellesmere that his concept of conscience was the 'standard' Protestant one. Schooled in divinity, he would have undoubtedly encountered the usual accounts and, indeed, he was a disciple of William Perkins at Cambridge.[164] As we have previously seen, at least two Jacobean tracts on conscience[165] were dedicated to him as Lord Keeper—a plausible assumption being that he would have shared the interest they evince and would likely have endorsed their contents.

Some indication of Williams's general attitude towards conscience in Chancery may be gleaned from his reflections on his appointment as Lord Keeper. This appointment was, of course, controversial, Williams being an ecclesiastic and not—his tutelage by Ellesmere notwithstanding[166]—a lawyer. Moreover, apart from his lacking the obvious qualifications, his appointment was highly political, in that it further evidenced James's linking of his own prerogative and divine law.[167] So, for example, in his speech on his accession to his new post, Williams offers an *apologia* which tells us something about his view of the Chancellor's function.

Particularly, he suggests that being learned in the law alone might not suffice for the office. Indeed, 'it may be the continued Practise of the strict Law, without a special mixture of other knowledge, makes a Man unapt, and undisposed for a Court of Equity'.[168] What is really required is to be "Richly enabled in all Moral

---

161 Hacket, p. 68; EEBO image 49492:36.

162 Ibid., p. 113; EEBO image 49492:58.

163 Ibid., p. 216; EEBO image 49492:112.

164 Ibid., p. 9; EEBO image 49492:6.

165 Those of Bourne and Hughes.

166 Hacket relates that the Lord Chancellor, during his time of leisure, would discuss Chancery and Star Chamber cases with his chaplain (p. 28; EEBO image 49492:16). Would that we had transcripts of those conversations.

167 See, for example, G.W. Thomas, 'James I, Equity and Lord Keeper John Williams' *English Historical Review*, 91/360 (1976): 506–28, pp. 517–18.

168 Hacket, p. 72; EEBO image 49492:38.

and Intellectual Endowments'.[169] Williams is careful to note that there are 'many Scores' of those 'which profess our Laws', who have those endowments.[170] But, for him, they appear to be the *sine qua non*; they may even suffice. This brings into sharp focus a central issue: is it enough that the Chancellor be a person of fine moral discernment, or must he actually know the law?

Hacket offers a fuller elaboration—admittedly many years later and as likely to reflect his own views as Williams's. Responding to those who claim that an ecclesiastic should not sully his hands with temporal offices, he maintains that the Lord Keepership is not 'an Employment merely Secular', but that '[t]o mitigate the strict Cases of the Law with the Conscience of the King … is it not as fully Ecclesiastical, as a Consistory of teaching and ruling Elders?'[171] For him, it is 'in effect … the merciful Voice of God' which, in the guise of equity, 'mollifie[s] the Strictness and Inconveniencies of the Voice of Man'.[172] If Thomas is right, this would appear to to be something like James's, and probably Williams's as well, view of the office of the Chancellor.

At the same time, Williams expresses diffidence about his own qualifications, noting that '*a Sincere, Upright, and well-meaning Heart*' might not suffice to '*cover Thousands of other Imperfections*'.[173] In other words, he makes it clear that affective conscience—an inclination or desire to do the right thing—is not enough for the Chancellor. He does not say much more about his positive qualifications, preferring to ask, in effect, 'If God and the King have decided that I should be in this place, who am I to gainsay them?'[174]

Again, Hacket has more to say on this subject—and, again, this may be more his view than Williams's. He cautions that being 'the chief Arbiter in a Court of Equity' requires more than 'Reason and Conscience … the good stock of Nature', for 'there is no strein of Wisdom more sublime, then upon all Complaints to measure the just distance between Law and Equity'.[175] This just measurement cannot be achieved by 'Equity at Lust and Pleasure … but Equity according to Decrees and Precedents foregoing, as the Dew-beaters have trod the way for those that come after them'.[176] The conscience of the Chancellor is not a personal and subjective faculty, but has to be regular and consistent. Stable rules are necessary 'to keep the Keeper from Extravagancies of his own Fancies and Affections, and to hold him really to Conscience'; conscience 'is ever the same'.[177]

---

169 Ibid.

170 Ibid.

171 Ibid., p. 56; EEBO image 49492:30.

172 Ibid.

173 Hacket, p. 72; EEBO image 49492:38.

174 Ibid., p. 73; EEBO image 49492:38.

175 Ibid., p. 57; EEBO image 49492:30.

176 Ibid.

177 Ibid.

There is, of course, some ambiguity in this position. On the one hand, conscience can be 'ever the same' just by virtue of following precedent. This seems to be what Hacket is talking about. At the same time, conscience might be 'ever the same' because, to the correctly knowledgeable, it always provides the same answer. Hacket seems to suggest something like this when he responds, elsewhere in his book, to the charge that many of Williams's decrees had to be reversed by his successor, Coventry. Hacket denies the allegation, and then counsels Williams's detractors not to 'traduc[e] the Gifts of them, that are excellently seen in Theological Cases of Conscience ...'.[178] This seems to imply that what is important is knowing the *method* of conscientious inquiry, and that theological casuistry may be transferable to the enforcement of conscience in Chancery.

In any event, Williams proclaims his commitment to ruledness and regularity, comforting himself with being able to '*see in this Court the Footsteps of Wise Men, many Excellent Rules and Orders for managing the same*' and dedicating himself to following them '*without the least deflexion at all*'.[179] Among the rules that he lays down for himself are that he will never '*Cross the Grounds of the Common or Statute Laws*', and that he will not, '*without special Motives*' overturn his predecessors' decisions.[180] As Hacket observes, 'the New Lord Keeper walk'd so Circumspectly; [h]e kept constant to Justice in its Flat Square'.[181] Thomas suggests that the triumph of equity over common law occurred not in 1616, but in 1621, with Williams's appointment as Lord Keeper.[182] But the implications of his appointment are double-edged: if the appointment of an ecclesiastical Chancellor comported with James's view of prerogative courts, it also appears to have created a target for criticism that intensified the sense that the Chancery must at least be seen to be a 'regular' court.

Williams, like others, recognized some kind of distinction between public conscience and private conscience. One instance of his invoking the distinction occurs in the report of his exchange with the French Ambassador Villoclare regarding the position of Catholics in England. 'Surely', he says, 'a publick Conscience ought to be more scrupulous than a private.'[183] The notion of public conscience he relates to 'external compliance'. This is not the same as Bacon's distinction between private conscience and the conscience of the realm, which provide two separate sanctions for uses. Nor is it congruent with Perkins's distinction between public and private equity. What Williams seems to be saying is that public conscience involves outward acts and demeanour, especially of

---

178 Ibid., p. 200; EEBO image 49492:103.

179 Ibid., p. 73; EEBO image 49492:38. He is probably referring mainly to procedural rules here, but, as we shall see, he appears as well to have committed himself to following substantive precedent as well.

180 Ibid.

181 Ibid., p. 71; EEBO image 49492:37.

182 Thomas,'James 1, Equity and Lord Keeper John Williams', pp. 507–8.

183 Hacket, p. 216; EEBO image 49492:112.

those in a position to lead or set a standard. He is, of course, not talking about the conscience of equity here. But it does suggest that private conscience might be kept intact while one adopts an appropriate public posture as an acknowledgment of the imperatives of social order.

Another, notorious instance, long after he was no longer Lord Keeper, was his evidently politically-motivated advice to Charles I in the matter of the attainder of the Earl of Strafford. The King had taken the position that assenting to the bill of attainder was 'directly contrary to his Conscience'. In response, Williams argued that there was 'a Private and a Publick Conscience; that his Publick Conscience as King, might not only dispense with, but oblige him, to do that which was against his Private Conscience as a Man …'.[184] The idea that a person acting in a public capacity must keep separate the considerations (notably, reasons of state) that should inform his conscience in that capacity from those affecting his private 'Understanding, Judgement, and Conscience' was something of a commonplace. This does not mean that it was universally approved. We will recall, for example, Ames's treatment of the issue. And Lord Clarendon (1609–74)—himself Chancellor from 1658–67, calling Williams 'that unhappy Casuist', describes his arguments as 'Unprelatical' and 'Ignominious'.[185] Jeremy Taylor, discussing the issue in a different context, questions whether the postulation of two capacities can absolve a public official from following the dictates of private conscience.[186] To the extent that Williams's position is tenable, it illustrates that the way in which conscience operates might be affected by the consequences its exercise has for the public order.

Another aspect of the public nature of the Lord Keeper's conscience was, again, the precept that it was the King's conscience, not his own, that he was administering. Sir Francis Moore (1558–1621) wrote to Williams in 1621 to remind him that the conscience according to which he was to judge 'is the King's committed to the Chancellor and if the Chancellor shall in his own private conscience be of another opinion than he is persuaded the King his master would be, he is to judge according to the King's conscience and not his own …'.[187] Presumably the King's conscience here is his political or public conscience, and

---

184 Edward Hyde (Earl of Clarendon), *The History of the Rebellion and Civil Wars in England* (3 vols, London, 1704), vol. 1, p. 202; see also pp. 274–5 (ECCO images CW3302711078:224 and 294–5, respectively).

185 Ibid., pp. 275, 202. Clarendon appears here to be using the word 'casuist' in a pejorative sense, implying someone who splits hairs to justify morally-questionable positions.

186 Jeremy Taylor, *Ductor Dubitantium* in *The Whole Works of the Right Reverend Jeremy Taylor, D.D.*, ed. A. Taylor (10 vols, London, 1883), vol. 9, pp. 107–16. At one point the editor suggests that Taylor might have had in mind Williams's advice to the King (p. 114n).

187 Francis Moore, *Letter to Bishop John Williams*, 1621, Cambridge University Library MS. Gg 2.31, f. 298, reproduced in *Lord Nottingham's 'Manual of Chancery*

not his private conscience. Williams himself, predictably, acknowledges more than once that it is the King's conscience, and not his own, that he is applying. One reason he gives for his promise not to cross any ground of the common law is that he holds by his place '*the Custody not of mine own, but of the King's Conscience; and it were most absurd to let the King's Conscience be at Enmity and Opposition with his Laws*'.[188] Public conscience and the law must be in accord.

An interesting wrinkle in the case of Williams is that, in addition to his seeing himself as distributing the King's (public) conscience in Chancery, he also appears to have regarded himself as the keeper of the King's conscience in the older, ecclesiastical sense. At times, he appears to have adopted a confessional role *vis-à-vis* James.[189] On one occasion when the King, concerned 'to set his House within himself in good Order' in preparation for receiving communion, sent for Williams as his chaplain, Williams 'took Opportunity, when the King's Conscience was most tender and humble, to shew him the way of a good King, as well as of a good Christian' in a number of matters of state.[190] A rather curious example of exploiting the private conscience so as to direct the public one! Williams relates another instance in which James 'made him for this time his Counsellor and Confessor' and Williams gave him advice explicitly in relation to '*a Conclusion of Conscience*', regarding a political issue, to which the king had provisionally come.[191] This may stand as a reminder of the point made earlier: for many, perhaps most, at this time, the line between divinity and law was at best blurred.

Sir Thomas Coventry

Williams—to the relief of many—was succeeded in 1625 by Lord Keeper Coventry, by most accounts an able and honourable lawyer who, Baker notes, 'made efforts to continue the reforms of the Chancery' initiated by his predecessors.[192] As for conscience, there is not much in the records we have to suggest a developed general analysis. What we see is essentially a jurist applying the law.

Practice' and 'Prolegomena of Chancery and Equity', ed. D.E.C. Yale (Cambridge, 1965; reprinted Holmes Beach, Fla., 1986), p. 78.

188 Hackett, p. 73; EEBO image 49492:38.

189 Williams certainly adhered to the Protestant doctrine that one's conscience was one's own responsibility (see Hacket, p. 131; EEBO image 49492:67) and he rejected the Catholic doctrine of confession: '[i]s [the sinner] bound, as soon as he hath committed a mortal Sin, with all competent Celerity, to confess, that he may be absolv'd? *Not so*, says the Chancery of Divinity' (ibid., p. 219; EEBO image 49492:114). Interestingly, he pretends to test the Catholic 'Law' of auricular confession in 'a Court of Equity' (ibid.), considering all the variable circumstances to suggest that the true rule is that a person '*may quiet his Conscience, when he confesses to none but GOD*' (p. 220; 49492:115).

190 Ibid., p. 85; EEBO image 49492:44.

191 Ibid., p. 142; EEBO image 49492:73.

192 Baker, 'Common Lawyers and the Chancery', p. 227.

There are in his cases very few references to conscience, and most of these are unremarkable. In a case involving the liability of a surety, he says that 'in conscience, [the creditor] should not have more upon the bond than that which he is endamnified'.[193] In *Carpenter* v. *Tucker*, we learn that a bond which had long since been satisfied 'ought not either in Equity or good Conscience, after so long a time, to be put in Suit against the Plaintiff …'.[194] And, in the role of Lord Steward, invoking a cliché, he exhorted the Earl of Castlehaven to confess to the charges against him, saying 'if truth touch you at the heart, and your conscience is a thousand witnesses, and God is greater than both, stand not against it'.[195] Others might have regarded him as very much a 'IVDGE of the Court of Conscience',[196] but it seems not to have been a point that he made much of himself.

To be sure, his cases reflect concern with the usual conscientious preoccupations of Chancery: 'Circumvention, Fraud and Practice';[197] 'fraud or surprise';[198] questionable contracts, notably those involving 'simoniacal' bargains[199] and agreements where the consideration is a promise to effect a marriage;[200] attempts to take a benefit while avoiding a burden attached to it;[201] laches;[202] and so on. However, these matters tend not to be described explicitly in terms of conscience, although there are hints of where Coventry would draw the line. So, for example, in *Ramsay* mere disproportion in mutuality (that is, an excessive price) is not enough to engage the conscience of equity, without the presence of an additional factor—fraud or surprise.

Occasionally, Coventry does appear to go beyond established doctrine, responding *ad hoc* to the particular features of a case. In *Havers* v. *Burton*, in which the Custom of London precluded a young widow from benefiting under her minor husband's will, the court determined that it was 'an hard Case' against her, especially since she had brought into the marriage a 'good Portion', and

---

193 *Giles* v. *Gesling* (1631), in *Cases Concerning Equity*, case 351, vol. 2, p. 619.

194 *Carpenter* v. *Tucker*, 10 Car. I, *Reports of Cases Taken and adjudged in the Court of Chancery*, pp. 78–9; EEBO image 29452:64.

195 *The Arraignment and Conviction of Mervin Lord Audley, Earl of Castlehaven* (London, 1642), p. 3; EEBO image 54386:3. As we have previously noticed, the portrayal of conscience as 'a thousand witnesses' was commonplace among religious writers.

196 Henry Mason, 'Epistle Dedicatorie', *The Tribvnall of the Conscience: or, a Treatise of Examination* (London, 1626), sig. A3v; EEBO image 12751:4.

197 *Herbert* v. *Lowns*, 3 Car. I, *Reports of Cases Taken and adjudged in the Court of Chancery*, p. 23; EEBO image 29452:36.

198 *Ramsay* v. *Goslin* (1631), *Cases Concerning Equity*, case 349, vol. 2, p. 617.

199 Anon., ibid., case 363, vol. 2, p. 628.

200 *Arrundel* v. *Trevillian*, 10 Car. I, *Reports of Cases Taken and adjudged in the Court of Chancery*, p. 87; EEBO image 29452:68. The court 'utterly dislik[es]' them.

201 *Pool* v. *Pool*, 1 Car. I, ibid., p. 18; EEBO image 29452:34.

202 *Winchcomb* v. *Hall*, 5 Car. I, ibid., p. 40; EEBO image 29452:45.

she was granted at least partial relief.[203] Some sense of unjust enrichment seems to be operating here: she got nothing in return for what she gave. Similarly, in *Isham* v. *Cole*, although the Court decided it would be 'a dangerous President to relieve Mortgages after so long an elapse of Time', it nevertheless found 'Badges of Equity' on the part of the plaintiff, leading it to 'propose' to the defendant that he 'do something for the Plaintiff'.[204] Such cases suggest attempts to make a finer calibration, based on conscience, than applying even an equitable rule would permit. In the latter case, apparently, the court is not *ordering* the defendant to act, but rather suggesting that he do something like Perkins's 'private equity'.

When Coventry does invoke general equitable notions, more often than not they are something besides conscience. Sometimes we find just 'equity', alone;[205] sometimes 'Justice and Equity';[206] sometimes just 'Justice';[207] and sometimes 'Right and Equity'.[208] One has the sense that these concepts are invoked as rough equivalents, but that they are not given much definitional content—that is, apart from what is suggested by the particular cases they refer to.

Perhaps more striking in many of these cases are the indications that Chancery will be governed by rules—not just procedural, but substantive as well. So, in many cases, precedents are searched for and followed.[209] An example is *Atkins* v. *Temple*, in which an injunction was sought to restrain the ploughing of meadow and pasture lands. The court, 'in respect of the generality of the Case, directed Presidents to be produced'; the precedents, from the time of Lord Ellesmere and later, showed that the Chancery did restrain 'the plowing of ancient Pasture'.[210] It

203 *Havers* v. *Burton*, 4 Car. I, ibid., pp. 26–7, EEBO image 29452:38.

204 *Isham* v. *Cole*, 15 Car. I, ibid., p. 128; EEBO image 29452:89.

205 Ibid. and *Petty* v. *Styward*, 7 Car I, ibid., p. 58; EEBO image 29452:54.

206 *Levington* v. *Wooton*, 7 Car. I, ibid., p.55; EEBO image 29452:52, and *Scott* v. *Wray*, 10 Car. I, ibid., p. 86; EEBO image 29452:68.

207 *Kennedy* v. *Vanlore*, 9 Car. I, ibid., p. 76; EEBO image 29452:63.

208 *Revet* v. *Rowe*, 10 Car. I, ibid., p. 83; EEBO image 29452:66.

209 Thomas questions the role of precedent in Chancery at this time, and, indeed, cites Coventry on the point; 'Examples bind not, they encline some tymes to error, as well as to truthe' ('James I, Equity and Lord Keeper John Williams', p. 513, citing B.M. Harleian MS 1576 fol. 144v). There is, however, a difference between an 'example' and a precedent, as Bacon makes clear in the *De Augmentis*. There are, he says, three ways to remedy the inability of human wisdom to anticipate all cases. One of these—the creation of Praetorian courts—we have considered. The other two are 'reference to similar cases' and 'employment of examples which have not yet grown into law' (p. 90). It appears that an example is not a previous legal ruling, but what we would probably call a 'hypothetical'.

210 *Atkins* v. *Temple*, 1 Car. I, *Reports of Cases Taken and adjudged in the Court of Chancery*, p. 14; EEBO image 29452:32. For other examples of cases in which precedent is deferred to, see *Midleton* v. *Jackson*, 5 Car. I, ibid., p. 33; *Tuphorne* v. *Gilbie*, 5 Car. I, ibid., p. 40; *Lake* v. *Phillips*, 9 Car. I, ibid., p. 69; and *Arrundel* v. *Trevillian*, ibid., p. 87 (EEBO images 29452:41,45, 59 and 68, respectively). In *Vendal* v. *Harvey* (1633) we are told that Coventry invoked 'a multitude of precedents upon great deliberation' from Sir Nicholas

is worth highlighting the words 'in respect of the generality of the Case': this case did not involve simply an assessment of unique facts, but was 'typical', calling for the application of a relevant rule. In *Mayor of London* v. *Bennet*, in spite of the fact that the 'Defendant offered divers Reasons against the Injunction', the Court determined on the basis that there was 'a President where in the like Case an Injunction was granted'.[211] In a somewhat analogous case, the court preferred a strict rule to 'reasons', saying that it 'would not reverse [a] Decree notwithstanding any thing urged against it'.[212] This reliance on what has already been done—whatever substantive arguments might be advanced against it—indicates that certainly by this time the Lord Keeper was not assessing cases purely on the basis of their merits in respect of 'conscience' at large. We might recall West's observation about ordinary people calling Chancery the court of conscience: the 'conscience' defined by the cases was becoming a complex of specific doctrines, accessible to experts.

Conclusion

The foregoing perhaps does not yield any very clear conclusions. One thing we can say is that, even in relation to law, religious writers' analyses of conscience tended to be much more searching than those of legal writers. One might argue that this is because those religious writers were specifically and directly concerned with conscience. But writers on equity and Chancery judges themselves were ostensibly—indeed, explicitly—deploying a jurisdiction which was defined in terms of conscience, and conscience continued not only to be referred to but to be *argued* in courts exercising equity,[213] so why no similar depth of self-reflection? One might argue here that every case decided in Chancery was a development of its concept of conscience and that, at the end of the day, the 'meaning' of conscience in equity is the sum of all those decisions, a sum that cannot be reduced to more general propositions. But this would mean that the law is just a collection of individual instances—which, as Doderidge contends, cannot be the substance of any 'Art, Science, Method, or certaine knowledge'.[214] Sir Henry Finch, who

---

Bacon, Sir Thomas Bromley, Ellesmere and others (*Cases Concerning Equity*, case 377, vol. 2, p. 640).

211 *Mayor of London* v. *Bennet*, 6 Car. I, *Reports of Cases Taken and adjudged in the Court of Chancery*, p. 45; EEBO image 29452:47.

212 *Yate* v. *Southby*, 3 Car. I, ibid., p. 25; EEBO image 29452:37.

213 See, for example, *Arden* v. *Darcy* (Exchequer, 1610–14) (*Cases Concerning Equity*, case 218, vol. 2, 431–3): '[it is] more unconscionable to foreclose one from his inheritance ..." (p. 432 [brackets in source]) and *Attorney-General* v. *Abington* (Exchequer, 1619) (ibid., case 210, vol. 2, p. 411): 'although ... we are in a court of conscience, yet equity should have some ground ...'.

214 Doderidge, *The English Lawyer*, p. 240; EEBO image 10306:125.

says that law is 'not only … *scientia*, but … *Scientificissima*',[215] argues that a person who

> will take the whole body of the law before him, and go really and iudicially to worke, must not lay the foundation of his building in Estates, Tenures, the gift of Writs, and such like, but at those currant and sound principles which our bookes [in many disciplines] are full of. [216]

And Bacon's *Elements* consists of a number of maxims, illustrated by more specific cases. So the impulse to generalize and explain was hardly absent from the early seventeenth-century legal mind—including, presumably, the mind of equity.

Thomas likens 'the importance of conscience' in early seventeenth-century equity to 'that of the doctrine of the sovereignty of Parliament', explaining that 'the fact that its scope is … not accurately defined, or that it is seldom referred to in the conduct of business' does not mean that it is not 'a basic and accepted tenet'.[217] What this seems to imply is that conscience is fundamental, albeit not self-consciously elaborated by the Chancery in the course of its business. In other words, 'we don't have to explain it—or maybe we can't explain it—but it's implicit in everything we do'. Perhaps, then, it is rather perverse to attempt, as I have been doing, to explain what the conscience of equity was. Perhaps it was just *there*. But what is unarticulated comes from somewhere. What is commonly accepted as so fundamental as to require no explanation has a provenance of some kind. It may be that, for jurists of this period—as for theologians—conscience was understood as innate, essential, a part of every person's very nature, and therefore known immediately. But the theologians seem to have been at great pains to explain it, even if only to make this point. Plausibly, what they had to say about conscience was what 'everyone else'—including the Chancellors—implicitly knew it to be. Indeed, the rather fragmentary evidence we have from the Chancellors and others seem to be bits of the concept that the theologians elaborate more comprehensively. Arguably the mention of these fragments suggests implicit acceptance of the whole picture of which they are parts.

At the same time, we can discern during this period an emphasis—not entirely new—on the need for Chancery equity to be more ruled. This is evident not only in, say, Bacon's and Williams's proclamations that that they will adhere to procedural regularities, but in a stated deference to substantive consistency. As we have seen, Bacon regarded certainty as absolutely fundamental to law, as law, and wanted to confine the Praetorian function to really extraordinary cases. But once a case of a particular type has been decided, the next case like it is no longer

215 Finch, p. 2; EEBO image 22891:8.

216 Ibid., p. 6; EEBO image 22891:11.

217 Thomas,'James I, Equity and Lord Keeper John Williams', p. 513n.

so extraordinary: there is a precedent for it.[218] Thus, as we have seen, Coventry appears to have been prepared, at least some of the time, to follow precedents, whatever the 'reason' of the case. I do not mean to suggest that this is a complete explanation of Chancery equity: the issue of the Chancellor's conscience—or some abstract conscience not having a local habitation—continued to be a live one. But, apart from deliberate efforts to make equity more law-abiding (for example, by making its procedures more regular and by its exercising restraint), it was evolving in that direction by virtue of its having an increasingly recorded history. If, as Ellesmere says, the 'generall notions' the Chancellor uses to limit his jurisdiction and direct his conscience ultimately lie 'hidden and concealed in his own breast', it is also true that there is an ever-increasing 'competent store of cases' to give definition to those notions. Conscience may not be much elaborated by the Chancellors because everybody already knows what it is. Just as likely, however, it (as a general concept) may be perceived not to require elaboration because many of its specific rules have already been identified.

[218] J.J. Park makes this point, specifically in relation to Bacon's view of the Chancery as 'Praetorian', in his *What Are Courts of Equity*? (London, 1832): 'The very existence … of a tribunal for the assumed purpose of supplying the deficiencies of the law by a species of arbitrium, must ultimately result in that extension of the science and rules of jurisprudence … which puts an end to its discretional functions' (p. 21).

Chapter 7
Protestant Conscience Two: The Later Seventeenth Century

Introduction

As I have previously intimated, it is not only the volume of material and chronological convenience that have dictated my treating 'Protestant conscience' in two separate chapters. There were important substantive developments that contributed to re-casting the concept of conscience as well. These developments were not discrete revolutions but gradual processes akin to erosion and accretion, involving tendencies that gained force over time. Moreover, for long periods, quite radically disparate views, if not of conscience directly, at least of the contexts in which conscience was understood, continued to co-exist. Thus, for example, Thomas Hobbes's *The Elements of Law Natural and Politic*,[1] which anticipates the *Leviathan* and manifests some of these revisionist tendencies, first appeared in 1640, while Ralph Cudworth's (1617–88) *A Treatise Concerning Eternal and Immutable Morality*,[2] in large part a rejoinder to Hobbes and the tendencies he represented and an embodiment of the kind of view that was supposedly superseded, was written decades later and not published until more than forty years after Cudworth's death.

Indeed, as we shall see, many of the writers who addressed conscience centrally—Joseph Hall (1574–1656), Robert Sanderson, Richard Baxter (1615–91), Jeremy Taylor—conceived it in ways that are continuous with what we have already seen. Moreover, we can plausibly assume that, apart from the period of the Interregnum, the Chancellors, as officers of the establishment, would have been partisans of this more mainstream, conservative view. To take just a couple of examples: Lord Clarendon was notable for, among other things, his aggressive defence of the Anglican Church and for writing a refutation of Hobbes's views,[3]

---

1 Thomas Hobbes, *The Elements of Law Natural and Politic*, ed. J.C.A. Gaskin (Oxford, 1999).

2 Ralph Cudworth, *A Treatise Concerning Eternal and Immutable Morality* (London, 1731).

3 Edward Hyde, Earl of Clarendon, *A Brief View and Survey of the Dangerous and Pernicious Errors to Church and State, in Mr. Hobbes's Book, entitled Leviathan* (Oxford, 1676).

and Cudworth dedicated his *The True Intellectual System of the Universe*[4] to Lord Nottingham, 'a worthy Patron' of the Church of England,[5] who presumably would have been sympathetic to its general purport, the defence of religion, whatever he might have made of its labyrinthine arguments.[6] While, therefore, there were destabilizing influences at work on the concept of conscience in the seventeenth century, they had not wholly displaced the traditional account, perhaps especially in so far as the judges in the Court of Chancery were concerned.[7]

Probability

One broad development during this period deserving of mention at the outset is the ostensible change in emphasis from certainty to probability in epistemology. Barbara Shapiro, who has documented this development in a range of disciplines, observes that, '[b]y the end of the seventeenth century, most English thinkers found considerable satisfaction in a highly probabilistic knowledge',[8] an observation re-iterated by others.[9] The paradigmatic locus of this change was in the physical sciences, both Shapiro and Van Leeuwen stating, for example, that while even

---

4 Ralph Cudworth, *The True Intellectual System of the Universe* (London, 1678; reprinted Stuttgart, 1964).

5 Bishop Gilbert Burnet (1643–1715), in the preface to his *History of the Reformation of the Church of England, the Second Part* (London, 1681), says that Nottingham was 'in nothing more eminent than in his zeal for, and care of this Church' and thanks him for having read the manuscript and made corrections to it (sig. A2r; EEBO image 65548:411).

6 In a letter to Nottingham's grand-daughter, Bishop Warburton (1698–1779) says that Nottingham gave his 'protection' (that is, patronage) to Cudworth, among others (Lord Campbell, *Lives of the Lord Chancellors and Keepers of the Great Seal of England*, 3rd edn (8 vols, London, 1848), vol. 3, p. 332.

7 In this connection, it is worth remarking that religious writers on conscience continued to invoke the 'Chancery metaphor': John Tillotson (1630–94) refers to conscience as 'the Equity and Chancery of our own Breasts' ('Wherein lies that exact Righteousness, which is required between Man and Man?' in *The Morning-Exercise at Cripplegate: or, Several Cases of Conscience, Practically Resolved, by sundry Ministers*, ed. Samuel Annesley [London, 1664], p. 235; EEBO image 105033:122), and John Goodman (1625/6–90) speaks of the '*Chancery* and Court of Equity' that resides 'in our own Bosoms' (*The Golden Rule, or, the Royal Law of Equity Explained* [London, 1688], p. 11; EEBO image 60390:8).

8 Barbara J. Shapiro, *Probability and Certainty in Seventeenth-Century England* (Princeton, 1983), p. 5. See also, generally, Henry G. Van Leeuwen, *The Problem of Certainty in English Thought 1630–1690* (The Hague, 1963). For a somewhat different account of the position of certainty, at least in the law, after the mid-seventeenth century, see Stephen A. Siegel, 'The Aristotelian Basis of English Law 1450–1800', *New York University Law Review*, 56/1 (1981): 18–59, esp. pp. 45ff.

9 See, for example, James Tully, 'Governing Conduct', in Edmund Leites (ed.), *Conscience and Casuistry in Early Modern Europe* (Cambridge, 1988), pp. 12–71, p. 27.

Francis Bacon still postulated certainty of scientific knowledge, his successors were more likely to aspire only to probable knowledge.[10]

More directly relevant to my project are parallel developments in theology. Indeed, Shapiro notes the influence of such 'natural theologians' as William Chillingworth (1602–44), John Wilkins (1614–72) and John Tillotson[11] in this regard, as does Van Leeuwen that of essentially the same *dramatis personæ*, whom he describes as 'liberal Anglican theologians'.[12] Wilkins, fairly typically, postulates a continuum of modes of degrees of 'assent', his basic distinction being between 'knowledge' and 'opinion'. Within the category of knowledge he includes absolutely infallible certainty (which is the prerogative of God), conditionally infallible certainty, including mathematical propositions and the kind of certainty afforded by direct observation by the senses, and, finally, 'moral certainty'—the kind of certainty, short of physical or mathematical certainty, that is nevertheless so probable that it does not admit of reasonable doubt.[13] This last kind of certainty, he maintains, should suffice to satisfy reasonable persons with respect to many matters—including, significantly, the principles of religion.[14] Similarly, Tillotson, writing in part to refute those sceptics who insist on 'mathematical demonstration' of the truths of religion, cites Aristotle for the observation 'that things of a moral and civil nature ... are incapable of Demonstration; and that it is madness to expect it for things of this Nature'.[15] He goes on to say, again, that reasonable persons ought to be satisfied with the kind of evidence, and hence certainty, of which the subject-matter in question is capable.[16]

If moral propositions can be only very probably but not absolutely certainly known then this might be expected at least to qualify, if not to compromise, conscience as a principle of objective judgment. Indeed, Tillotson's project in *The Rule of Faith* was to refute a Roman Catholic writer who argued that the only way to impart certainty to matters of religion was by way of the authority of the Church. So, to re-iterate what I have said previously, it may make more sense to invoke conscience as the basis of legal judgment if there is an 'official' position with respect to what it dictates. If moral certainty is all we can have, this might even cast doubt on the idea of *synderesis*, which, as we have seen, was traditionally portrayed as entailing nothing less than knowledge *per se*.

Although this development from certainty to probability is doubtless significant, its effect should not be overstated. For one thing, we must recall the distinction between moral rectitude and our apprehension of it: right and wrong may still

---

[10] Shapiro, p. 67; Van Leeuwen, p. 1.

[11] Shapiro, pp. 80–88.

[12] Van Leeuwen, p. 1, and see, generally, his Chapter 2.

[13] John Wilkins, *Of the Principles and Duties of Natural Religion: Two Books* (London, 1675), pp. 5–11; EEBO images 62179:13–16.

[14] Shapiro, p. 86.

[15] John Tillotson, *The Rule of Faith* (London, 1688), p. 96; EEBO image 107809:51.

[16] Ibid., p. 98; EEBO image 107809:52.

persist, even though we cannot have certain knowledge of them. Moreover, 'moral certainty' was, for the writers to whom we have referred, a very strong, though not absolute, certainty. It was, for them, the degree of certainty that admitted of no reasonable doubt; it was sufficient to secure the assent of all reasonable persons. Thus, in postulating something less than infallible certainty, these commentators were hardly postulating a wildly idiosyncratic moral dispensation. Further, both Wilkins and Tillotson, for example, seem to accept an account of conscience that suggests our ability to apprehend moral truths directly and presumably unambiguously. Introducing Wilkins's *Natural Religion*, which he saw through publication after the author's death, Tillotson writes that 'all the great *Duties* of *Piety* and *Justice* are written upon our hearts, and every man feels a secret obligation to them in his own Conscience'.[17] We have innate knowledge not only of the great religious ('piety') principles but also of moral or civic ('justice') ones. Wilkins, speaking of '*Natural Conscience*', calls it 'Gods Deputy' which 'doth *internally* witness for him'.[18] We have, he says, 'natural notions … concerning *Good* and *Evil*'; the bounds of these 'are fixed in the nature of things, and do not depend either upon *Custom* or *Positive Law*'.[19]

Shapiro does not say much about conscience specifically in this context and her discussion of probability and law focuses mainly on issues involving evidence of matters of fact as opposed to deriving norms. However, Tully for example does include casuistry among the disciplines in which probabilistic reasoning came to predominate in the late seventeenth century, observing, as we have previously noticed, 'the remarkably sceptical and unsure' tenor of Taylor's *Ductor Dubitantium*.[20]

To be sure, the main schools of casuistry—even before the seventeenth century—acknowledged that moral choice often involved deciding among merely plausible alternatives. Thus, probabilism countenanced choice of an alternative that, on the basis of learned authority, had some probability, and probabiliorism, while insisting on selection of the *most* probable alternative, still acknowledged the relativity of moral reasoning. Even tutiorism, the doctrine that insisted on making the safest choice, or, in the words of Sir Matthew Hale (1609–76), forbearing 'what might be probably lawful' rather than doing 'that which might be possibly unlawful',[21] recognized that there might be degrees of conviction in

---

[17] John Tillotson, 'The Preface', Wilkins, sigs A2v–A3r; EEBO image 62179:5.

[18] Wilkins, p. 90; EEBO image 62179:56.

[19] Ibid.

[20] Tully, 'Governing Conduct', p. 28.

[21] Matthew Hale, *Contemplations Moral and Divine* (London, 1705; first published 1676), p. 231; ECCO image CW3319804244:242. Hale is best known to us as a jurist, of course, but his bibliography includes many works on religious and moral topics. He is almost certainly not atypical of jurists of the period in accepting a certain *mixité* of religion and law.

such matters.[22] But, as I hope to show in more detail, we cannot affirm, *tout court*, that Protestant casuistry was simply a matter of probabilities. At least much of its *rhetoric* suggests a continuing attachment to some notion of certainty. Even if we can only probably know what the right answer is, that does not mean that there is no right answer.

So, for example, I think that Tully's identifying Taylor's work with this trend may need to be qualified. Some diffidence is consistent with the Protestant view of the casuist as guide or advisor rather than authoritative director of conscience: witness Joseph Hall's '[i]t is farre from my thoughts to obtrude these my Resolutions as peremptory, and magisteriall upon my Readers, I onely tender them submissely, as probable advises …',[23] and Taylor's own 'although I have not given answers to every doubt …'.[24] Moreover, Taylor does acknowledge that moral theology involves 'some things [that] are demonstrable and many [that] are probable, and other things … better than their contraries …' (p. xiv) and that conscience might be informed by resort to 'any faculty or science … because whatever can guide the actions or discourses … does belong to conscience and its measures' (p. xv). Both these attitudes—modesty about offering definitive answers to every question, and willingness to seek wisdom where one can find it—ostensibly involve a less dogmatic stance *vis-à-vis* questions of conscience.

At the same time, I do not detect in Taylor's approach any very obvious 'unsureness'. While he does not claim to resolve every doubt, he does claim to be able to say 'what we are to do when any doubt arises', and to 'have conducted the doubting conscience by such rules which in all doubts will declare her duty' (p. xx). Indeed, he complains that it was Catholic casuistry, especially in the form of probabilism, that had made cases of conscience as 'unstable as the face of the waters and unmeasurable as the dimensions of the moon' (p. x);[25] his announced project is to make at least a start 'to describe the right and plain measures of simplicity' in approaching moral questions (p. xiv). To be sure, he does take account of opposing views, and his arguments are often quite intricate, but he strikes me as addressing the issues with considerable assurance and as generally

---

22 The Protestant casuists, deploring what they regarded as the jesuitical sophistry of probabilism, were generally tutiorists or probabiliorists (see, for example, Thomas Wood, *English Casuistical Divinity During the Seventeenth Century* (London, 1952), p. 77.

23 Joseph Hall, 'To the Reader', in *Cases of Conscience Practically Resolved* (3rd edn, London, 1654), sig. A4v; EEBO image 47749:4. Compare Robert Sanderson, *Ten Lectures on the Obligation of Humane Conscience* (1647) (London, 1660), p. (first of two numbered) 175; EEBO image 154344:100, where he says respecting one issue he explores: 'I have given my opinion concerning this most difficult … question, determining *possitively* of nothing, but being ready, if any man shall render more certain reasons, to correct what hath been spoken …'.

24 Jeremy Taylor, *Ductor Dubitantium*, ed. A. Taylor, in *The Whole Works of the Right Rev. Jeremy Taylor D.D.* (10 vols, London, 1883), vol. 9, p. xx.

25 And see Wood, p. 46.

coming to positive conclusions. My point here is that, as we shall see in more detail presently, Taylor in many ways participated in the more traditional Protestant view. But, as I have already intimated, even that view carried with it the seeds of destabilization.[26]

Thus, 'conventional' Protestant casuistry, although perhaps afflicted with some internal awkwardness and fighting something of a rearguard action, was still very much in evidence for a large part of the century, defended by a number of eminent proponents and perhaps still defining an important—though diminishing—mainstream position. I wish to begin with this mainstream, showing how it was a continuation of positions that we have already seen, while taking account of certain difficulties or inconsistencies that were appearing and that were more or less candidly acknowledged.

Protestant 'Orthodoxy'

As I have noted before, that mainstream, or orthodoxy, adhered to the concept of objective conscience, 'an act of deliberate judgement, which could be mistaken'.[27] So, for example, Samuel Annesley (1620–96) can say that the 'design' he is driving at is 'an universal and exact conscientiousness'.[28] This objectivity involved at least two aspects: the law which governed conscience, and the process by which conscience operated. For much of the seventeenth century, that position was widely accepted, or at least purveyed. It is the position of John Norman (1622–69), who while depicting himself not as 'a Polemical School-querist' but rather as 'a sober practical Casuist', nevertheless says that the *synteresis–syneidesis–krisis* account of conscience is within its 'large and usual acceptation'.[29] Similarly, Henry Hammond (1605–60) presents a version of objective conscience which he claims accords with 'its naturall primitive simplicity'.[30]

---

[26] See, for example, Keith Thomas, 'Cases of Conscience in Seventeenth-Century England', in J. Morrill, P. Slack and D. Woolf (eds), *Public Duty and Private Conscience* (Oxford, 1993), pp. 29–56, p. 53, suggesting that the subjectivization and relativization of conscience tended to involve pushing the Protestant notion of 'the priesthood of all believers' 'to its logical conclusion'.

[27] Ibid., p. 30.

[28] Samuel Annesley, 'How we may be universally and exactly conscientious', in *The Morning-Exercise at Cripplegate*, p. 3; EEBO image 105033:6.

[29] John Norman, *Cases of Conscience Practically Resolved* (London, 1673), pp. 16 and 21–2; EEBO images 46170:13 and 15–16.

[30] Henry Hammond, *Of Conscience* (Oxford, 1645), p. 1; EEBO image 123411:2.

The Rule of Conscience and its Difficulties

That conscience is governed by an objective law remains a commonplace among these writers. Late in the century, Robert Eyre (1666–1735) insisted that conscience 'hath a fixt and standing Rule given it, by which it self ought to be directed'.[31] He explicitly rejects subjective conscience—in the sense of conscience guided by 'Principles of [one's] own forming' or one's 'own particular Scheme of Justice and Honesty'.[32] This point about the objective ruledness of conscience recurs frequently. Sanderson points out that 'the *Rectitude* of every thing consisteth in its conformity to its *next and immediate Rule*, and so gradually ascendeth to its *first* and most *chief Rule*';[33] 'it is necessary that there should be a certain *Rule* according to which [conscience] should be examined'.[34] In Taylor's view, '[a]ll consciences are to walk by the same rule, and that which is just to one, is so to all, in the like circumstances'.[35] For Hammond, 'he that draweth a line of direction for another, must have a rule to draw it by, and that a strait exact one …',[36] and John Nalson (1637–86) insists that 'to make up Conscience, there must be first, a true and exact Rule for all our Actions …'.[37] Sir Matthew Hale is one jurist who explicitly adopts this position: the conscience 'doth of necessity presuppose a Rule or Principle given unto Man'.[38] Again, a corollary of this is that personal conscience is not the ultimate criterion or justification; it may be erroneous. So, for example, Benjamin Calamy (1646–85/6) reminds us that 'that which is our Duty remaineth so … notwithstanding we in our Consciences think it unlawful to be done; and what is really Evil continueth such, and is Sin in us however our Consciences tell us it is our duty to do it'.[39]

For most of these writers, what Sanderson describes as the '*first* and most *chief Rule*' of conscience is the law of God. So, for Thomas Pierce (1621/2–91),

---

31 Robert Eyre, *A Discourse Concerning the Nature and Satisfaction of a Good and Inoffensive Conscience* (London, 1693), p. 5; EEBO image 62636:6.

32 Ibid., p. 19; EEBO image 62636:13.

33 Sanderson, p. 38; EEBO image 154344:31.

34 Ibid., p. 107; EEBO image 154344:65. Here, 'rule' is rather ambiguous: it could refer to the standard against which actions are to be judged by conscience, or it could refer to the set process by which conscience operates.

35 Taylor, vol. 9, p. 43.

36 Hammond, p. 8; EEBO image 123411:6.

37 John Nalson, *The True Liberty and Dominion of Conscience* (2nd edn, London, 1678), p. 28; EEBO image 56946:18.

38 Matthew Hale, *A Discourse of the Knowledge of God, and of our Selves* (London, 1688), p. 52; EEBO image 94495:47.

39 Benjamin Calamy, *A Discourse About a Scrupulous Conscience* (2nd edn, London, 1683), p. 5; EEBO image 54114:6.

'the known *Law* of *God* is the *Rule* of *Conscience*';[40] for Calamy '[t]he Divine Law … is the rule of Conscience …';[41] for Nalson, 'we are bound to follow the directions of the *Supreme Being*, so far as he has been pleased to manifest his Will and Pleasure to us'.[42] This means, generally, that at least for Christians the rule of conscience is to be found in scripture, as Nalson, fairly typically, says: 'the *Canon* of the *Holy Scripture* has always been taken for this *Rule* of *Direction*, as being the *Divine Revelation of the Will of God*'.[43]

To say that conscience is subject to an external law, that that law is given by God, and that it is expressed in holy writ does not, however, obviate all difficulties respecting 'objective conscience'. For one thing, it does not address the predicament of the non-Christian. Sanderson states the dilemma in this way: 'it is necessary that there should be another Rule of Conscience besides the holy Scripture, for otherwise the Gentiles who have not the Scripture should have no Rule for their Conscience'.[44] Since all humans have consciences, and since conscience must be under a law, it follows that those who do not have the scripturally-revealed law must have another law, or the law in another form.[45] Thus, '[t]he Scripture … is not the sole and Adæquate Rule of Conscience'.[46] This does not mean that the rule of conscience is not always the will of God, but it does mean that God's will is revealed in different ways.[47]

One implication of this, according to Sanderson, is that even if these laws are consistent with each other, they bind in different degrees. No man, he says, is 'bound to that which is impossible'.[48] The Gentiles, to whom the Gospel was not preached, are not obliged in conscience to believe in Christ or the Gospel, because

---

40 Thomas Pierce, *A Decad of Caveats to the People of England* (London, 1679), p. 108; EEBO image 65411:71.

41 Calamy, p. 4; EEBO image 54114:6.

42 Nalson, pp. 25–6; EEBO image 56946:16–17.

43 Ibid., p. 26; EEBO image 56946:17.

44 Sanderson, p. 119; EEBO image 154344:71.

45 Robert Wilde (1609–79), *The Arraignment of a Sinner at the Bar of Divine Justice* (London, 1656), p. 5; EEBO image 54555:7, in a sermon to the judges of assize at Oxford, speaks of 'the *Synderesis* and *Syneidesis* in naturall conscience' and Henry Carpenter (1605/6–62), *The Deputy Divinity, or, Interior Deity and Subordinate God in the World, Conscience* (London, 1657), p. 11; EEBO image 170295:12, observes that 'there [are] no People so barbarous, but that part of *Conscience* which is called *synteresis*, keepeth in them some sparks of the knowledge of good and evil'. Nathaniel Culverwell (1619–51), who was not a 'Protestant casuist', puts it this way: the 'Law of *Nature* … does binde *in foro Conscientiae* … Natural Conscience 'tis *Centrum Notitiarum Communium* [the centre of general knowledge] …' (*An Elegant and Learned Discourse of the Light of Nature*, eds R.A. Greene and H. MacCallum (Toronto, 1971), p. 56.

46 Sanderson, p. 120; EEBO image 154344:72.

47 Ibid., p. 126; EEBO image 154344:75.

48 Ibid., p. (second of two numbered) 127; EEBO image 154344:76.

'the light of Reason cannot ascend so high'.[49] Even this relativity of the law of conscience entails problems for conscience as a juristic principle. Can it be said that the believer is bound, civilly, to a higher standard than the non-believer? Or, civilly, should the rule of conscience be only the lowest common denominator—that is, the law of conscience as it binds the natural person?

Moreover, apart from the fact that divine law may bind more intensely or more comprehensively in one form than in another, there may be ostensible incompatibilities between the dictates of the two forms. This may be illustrated by Sanderson's reference to the Abraham-Isaac story, involving a direct command from God to the patriarch to sacrifice his son. Presumably, 'natural' law (not to mention divine law itself) binds the conscience not to kill, especially not to kill one's innocent child. So the divine will appears to conflict with a precept of natural law. Obviously, God does not 'really' intend Abraham to kill Isaac, but Abraham is not privy to this hidden intent. Nevertheless, Abraham is bound in conscience to do God's bidding. As Sanderson explains,

> Although God in the *will of his good pleasure* would not have had that done which at the same time he commanded to be done … yet *Abraham* was bound to will the very same thing, because God by *commanding* it, did signifie that *it was his will that* Abraham *should have a will unto it*.[50]

In reaching this conclusion, Sanderson invokes the scholastic distinction between *Voluntatem bene placiti*—the will of God's good pleasure, and *Voluntatem signi*—the will of the sign, or as manifested in the sign. What God wills of his good pleasure we do not necessarily know; all we can know of his will is what He signifies to us in a law. Only this, the will of the sign, can be 'the rule of our Consciences'.[51] Not only may the signified will differ from the real will, but, as this example illustrates, the signified will may appear to conflict with a dictate of natural law. To be sure, the will of God supervenes, but such an instance reveals that there might be dissonance between two rules of conscience. This phenomenon is almost certain to be destabilizing—particularly as regards conscience as a juristic criterion, which in some sense must depend upon 'reason', the concomitant of natural, as opposed to supernaturally revealed, law.

Another implication of this, or another way of putting its implications, is that, while certainly the manifested will of God provides an objective rule, this might not accord with reason. To hold, as Sanderson apparently does, that '*we are always bound to will that which God willeth, that we should will*'[52] creates the possibility of a disparity between the dictates of reason and the posited (divine) law, which tends to bifurcate conscience, to create the potential for conflict. Again,

49 Ibid.

50 Ibid., pp. (both numbered) 127–7; EEBO image 154344:75–6.

51 Ibid., pp. 126–7; EEBO image 154344:75.

52 Ibid.

although these writers would scarcely have admitted this as a radical problem, it suggests how the notion of a uniform objective rule of conscience might have been incipiently problematic.

Furthermore, even the revealed will of God itself betrays an element of relativity. One of the reasons Sanderson gives for saying that scripture is not the *adequate* rule of conscience is that it contains

> very many precepts, but not all of one kind, some of them pertayning to *Manners*, some to *Rites*, and some indifferently common unto all, and some peculiar only to some Nation, and some again to some one *order* or *person*; Some of them induring only for a *time*, and others of *a perpetual obligation*, some by way of Counsel, of things expedient according as the exigence of the affairs requireth, and some again in the way of *mandate* or command, of things simply or absolutely necessary in themselves ….[53]

Not only might the meanings of biblical precepts be controversial, but so might their very status as counsel or command, universal or particular, temporary or enduring. Because of this variability there must be 'some other rule, besides the Scriptures, for the discerning of *moral* from *ritual precepts*, and of things *temporary* from *perpetual* and of things *peculiar* from *common*'.[54] Without such a rule, 'the Conscience would oftentimes labour in a Labyrinth of doubts, and know not which way to turn'.[55] This rule, the principle for distinguishing the incidental from the essential, appears to be 'the judgment of *reason* and *prudence*'.[56] This is paradoxical: although scriptural rules take precedence over rules discerned by reason, reason is the faculty which sorts and selects scriptural rules.

The paradox is intensified when we read observations such as Taylor's regarding reason as a measure of law: 'reason is such a box of quicksilver that it abides no where; it dwells in no settled mansion; … it looks to me otherwise than to you who do not stand in the same light that I do'.[57] Both Scripture and reason are unstable. Writers like Sanderson and Taylor scarcely emphasize such implications, which nevertheless expose the tenuousness of the postulation of objective law—or, at least, of objectively-accessible law. Taylor can maintain that 'christianity is a perfect system of all the laws of nature, and of all the will of God',[58] but, unfortunately, just what Christianity was was precisely the site of vehement, and often bloody, contention. The assertion of the existence of an objective, cohesive law governing conscience did not mean that the substance of that law was a matter of consensus, or even that the source of that law was agreed.

53 Ibid., p. 121; EEBO image 154344:72.

54 Ibid., pp. 121–2; EEBO image 154344:72–3.

55 Ibid., p. 122; EEBO image 154344:73.

56 Ibid., p. 123; EEBO image 154344:73.

57 Taylor, vol. 9, p. 293.

58 Ibid., p. 307.

Perhaps the most radical aspect of this issue is suggested, albeit obliquely, by a comment by Thomas Hobbes about the dilemma of 'liberty of conscience'. The problem, he says, can be particularly related to the rise of Protestantism: '[t]his difficulty … troubleth those Christians only, to whom it is allowed to take for the sense of the Scripture that which they make thereof …'.[59] As Hobbes's observation suggests, the Reformation introduced a radical theory of the reading of the text of the law. Protestantism insisted upon the diversity of readership of scripture, albeit theoretically not upon the diversity of readings. The relevance for conscience is self-evident. If the rule of conscience is the law of God, and that law is essentially embodied in a sacred text, that text is where one ultimately must discover the rule of conscience. Where there are authoritative readers of the text—and perhaps where the text is in a language accessible only to such readers—it may be possible to maintain the fiction of an invariable rule. But, where there is no authority, or where such authority is provisional, or where each reader is authoritative, the notion of a uniform rule becomes much less tenable. This may be especially true if, as Sharp says, '[w]e are not only to look upon the letter of the Law, but to attend further to what that Law may be supposed by a Rational Man to contain in it'.[60] Sir Peter Pett (1630–99), significantly invoking the image of Chancery judgment, observes that, in the Protestant view, 'synods or conventions of Divines', or authorities, have to be cautious in purporting to settle matters of faith, since every such pronouncement is subject to review by 'more than ten thousand Chancellors, as many being Judges of the cause as there are rational men'.[61] Not only is there diversity of readers of the text, but the meaning of the text is to be measured in terms of some kind of implicit rationality. We have already noted for example Taylor's indictment of reason in this regard. There may be only one rule of conscience, but that rule may potentially be as protean as are readers of the text. Every person, Pett's observation implies, is his or her own chancellor.

Accessing the Rule

Just as the Protestant writers proclaimed that conscience was governed by 'a fixt and standing Rule', so they maintained that that rule could be apprehended and applied objectively, by measured processes. Most associated conscience particularly with understanding or knowledge, attributed to human beings a faculty (or habit or power) of *synteresis*, and portrayed the operation of conscience as involving logical processes. A striking example is Henry Carpenter's assertion that

[59] Hobbes, *Elements*, p. 142.

[60] John Sharp, *A Discourse Concerning Conscience* (London 1687), p. 9; EEBO image 37553:7.

[61] *A Discourse Concerning Liberty of Conscience* (London, 1666), p. 43; EEBO image 109702:23.

'Conscience is very rational and logical; it can hold and urge an argument well in right mood and figure … Conscience inlightened is a good natural Logitian'.[62]

Conscience and Understanding; Conscience and Faith

That conscience is a matter of knowledge (and not, say, opinion) is a point that was often made. Nalson is typical in this respect. We will recall his identifying as the first requisite of conscience 'a true and exact Rule'. The second is that '[t]here must be a true knowledge of this Rule, *Scientia* before *Conscientia*'.[63] He goes on to say that 'the very Essence of Conscience is Knowledge'.[64]

Nalson explains the implications of identifying conscience with knowledge: '*Scientia est de certis & indubitatis*, all knowledge is of certain and undoubted things …'.[65] That is, what we *know* must be so; if we merely *think* that we know something, and do not, we are wrong. The essence of conscience, knowledge, is objective. As Nalson summarizes, 'knowledge being of the Essence of Conscience, and certainty being of the Essence of knowledge, it follows, that Conscience properly so called, cannot be exercised, but about such things as are certainly known …'.[66] A corollary of this is that conscience is not a matter merely of personal conviction, as Nalson explicitly argues when he says that the differences among his countrymen regarding conscience arise from '*the mistake of Opinion, and private persuasion for Conscience*'.[67] Similarly, Pierce observes that '*Conscience* is not a *Perswasion*, but *Knowledge* rather; … but *knowledge compared with a Rule*';[68] 'it is not a being so fully perswaded in our minds, as not to have any *regret* or *scruple* …'.[69] Mere sincerity of conviction is not enough; we must (and we can) know aright.

---

62 Carpenter, p. 21; EEBO image 170295:17.

63 Nalson, p. 29; EEBO image 56946:18. The point that, etymologically and actually, conscience is a kind of 'science' occurs elsewhere: see, for example, John Sheffeild (d. 1680?), 'To the Conscientious Reader' in *A Good Conscience the Strongest Hold* (London, 1650), sig. A7v; EEBO image 169477:8: '*Conscience is the* Art of Arts, *and* Science of Sciences'—a science in which we are all '*bound to be skilled and exercised*'.

64 Nalson, p. 31; EEBO image 56946:19. Compare Sanderson, p. 26; EEBO image 154344:25 ('*Conscience* is a kind of *Science*, and all *Science* is in the *Understanding*'), Sheffeild, p. 15; EEBO image 169477:24 ('*Ego Conscientia cum scientia*, I Conscience dwell with knowledge'), Nathanael Vincent (1639?–92), *A Heaven or Hell upon Earth, or, a Discourse Concerning Conscience* (London, 1676), p. 32; EEBO image 44406:25 ('Knowledge is the Light which Conscience is directed by'), and Hammond, p. 2; EEBO image 123411:3 ('the word [syneidesis], *Conscience*, is no more then Science or knowledge').

65 Nalson., p. 32; EEBO image 56946:20.

66 Ibid., p. 34; EEBO image 56946:21.

67 Ibid., p. 40; EEBO image 56946:24.

68 Pierce, p. 105; 65411:69.

69 Ibid., p. 106; EEBO image 65411:70. See also Hammond, who observes that conscience is not 'humour', 'phansy', 'passion', 'diabolicall suggestion', etc. (p. 9; EEBO

Again, conscience so depicted would accord with what might conventionally be expected of a juristic principle. It appears to be measured, certain, objective. The depiction is, of course, subject to qualifications that we have previously elaborated—for example, it may still involve knowledge that is confined to the knower and to God.

Moreover, the depiction may conceal contrary tendencies. Thus, for example, Nalson's position is polemical. He is trying to counter the argument for liberty of conscience, based on the variety of religio-moral outlooks besetting seventeenth-century England. Although he complains that 'conscience', that is 'only the Name', is regularly exploited for its rhetorical effect,[70] so that controversialists make 'incredible advantages … of that single Word',[71] arguably he is himself invoking rhetorically the notion of the unity and objectivity of conscience, and the mere fact that he feels impelled to do so suggests that his position was contested, perhaps even becoming untenable. Thus, he maintains that, because conscience involves certain knowledge and that, therefore, 'rightly understood', it 'does universally and absolutely oblige all men',[72] it is essentially different from 'opinion' and 'persuasion', which involve matters 'not clearly and certainly known …'.[73] But the very matters which he assigns to 'opinion' are what those whom he criticizes consider to be matters of conscience. That he regards such matters as involving 'private judgment' only does not detract from the fact that others find those very matters morally compelling.

Further, although so many commentators insisted on linking conscience with knowledge or understanding, there was the ever-present awareness that something other than human rational processes might be the ultimate criterion of moral and/or spiritual insight. Thus, for example, Pierce reflects on the distinction between the things we *know* and the things we *believe*, suggesting that the latter might in fact involve a higher order of assent. So, he says, 'though 'tis the *office* of the *Intellect*, in the Intellect's own *Court*, to pass a verdict upon Things within its *Cognizance*; yet in such *Transcendentals* as are very much *without* and *above* its *verge* … a good understanding will confess, It must not *determine*, but *obey*'.[74] This implies that there are aspects of truth which are beyond knowledge. Moreover, those aspects of truth not accessible to understanding may be the most important ones: 'to *know* things exactly does onely denominate us *Learned*, but not *Religious*: good *Philosophers* indeed, but not good *Men*'.[75] To be sure, Pierce is here talking about 'transcendentals', spiritual truths, but it is significant that he distinguishes

image 123411:6).

[70] Nalson, p. 8; EEBO image 56946:8. Thus, he says, 'Conscience is a keen and two-edged Sword; a Weapon both offensive and defensive …' (p. 7; 56946:7).

[71] Ibid., p. 7.

[72] Ibid., p. 40; EEBO image 56946:24.

[73] Ibid., p. 50; EEBO image 56946:29.

[74] Pierce, p. 423; EEBO 65411:230.

[75] Ibid.

knowledge from belief and privileges the latter. If we *know* something, we have no choice but to assent to it; if we do not know it, we have '*Flexibility* of the *Will*', and choosing to obey in spite of not knowing is a higher kind of assent.[76]

One consequence of such a position is a discontinuity between reason and faith as sources of moral insight. I have already alluded to some ambivalence to reason and its role in certain of Sanderson's and Taylor's pronouncements. This kind of ambivalence appears as well in such observations as Pierce's that 'Knowledge … does *dispose* to Virtues', but 'naked *Science* is a meer *Intellectual Habit*' and not 'an *Ethick* Virtue'.[77] Again, respecting conscience, since the object of knowledge is the law, this imparts to that knowledge a moral character. But the privileging of belief or faith ultimately depreciates the role of human ratiocination, and certainly circumscribes the sphere of its applicability. At the very least, the relative positions of reason and will, knowledge and faith, tend to become less certain.

The Logic of Conscience

Just as many of the Protestant commentators continue to identify conscience (perhaps now more problematically) with knowledge, so too do they invoke other related aspects of the objective account, notably humans' possession of a faculty giving them access to the law, and deductive processes involving conscience that are ostensibly logical.

Thus Taylor, conventionally enough, calls *synteresis* 'the first act of conscience' and observes that it is 'the general repository of moral principles or measures of good';[78] it is 'the keeper of the records of the laws'.[79] In his view, each person has the means of accessing the law, which, as we have seen, is said to be uniform and objective. Sanderson similarly accepts that *synteresis* is an essential component of conscience, describing it as 'the habit of the first principles, about *Good* and *Evill*, from whence conclusions are deduced, out of which proceedeth Conscience',[80] or 'the knowledge of that first universal principle known by the light of Nature, or Revelation …'.[81] Once again, because the law is one, presumably the knowledge given by *synteresis* will be the same for everyone.

---

76 Ibid., p. 426; EEBO 65411:232.

77 Ibid.

78 Taylor, vol. 9, p. 14.

79 Ibid., p. 16.

80 Sanderson, p. 15; EEBO image 154344:19.

81 Ibid. Even writers who do not use the term *synderesis* seemingly accept the idea as basic to the idea of conscience. See, for example, Hale, *Contemplations*, p. 226; ECCO image CW3319804239:237: he imagines God saying to humans: 'I have furnished that Conscience of yours with light and principles of truth and practice, conformable to my will.' Recall John Wilkins's 'natural Notions of our Minds concerning *Good* and *Evil*, the Bounds of which are fixed in the Nature of Things' (p. 90; EEBO 62179:56).

Many—or, according to Sanderson, 'all who do treat of the nature and the method of [conscience]'—treat it as involving 'a practical Syllogism'.[82] Sanderson himself says that conscience involves the '*discourse of reason*'[83] and is a 'knowledge syllogisticall'[84] that 'addeth *Science* unto *Science*, that is, the universal knowledge, or the knowledge of Law, and Right, to the particular knowledge, or the knowledge of the fact'.[85] In other words, conscience involves the application of normative knowledge to known facts. Similarly, for example, Norman observes that conscience proceeds 'by discourse in some practical Syllogism', involving '1… [*synderesis*], or conserved truths and laws of Conscience', which provides the first proposition, '2 … [*syneidesis*]… or the consentient Testimony of Conscience, which is still assumed in the second proposition. 3. And the [*krisis*], or conclusory judgment …'.[86] Sanderson (hardly uniquely) presents the process as involving two linked syllogisms—the first deriving a lower-order norm from a precept given by *synteresis*, and the second applying that derived lower-order norm, as a major premise, to the facts of the specific conduct in question. He offers the following example:

> *Every thing that is unjust is to be eschewed.*
> *Every Theft is unjust, therefore*
> *Every Theft is to be eschewed.*
>
> Let this be the first Syllogism, the first proposition whereof is known of it self by the light of Nature: *Reason* doth prove the *Minor*, and the Conscience doth bring in the conclusion; which conclusion it presently takes up to be the beginning of the following Syllogism, and applying it to some particular Fact …
>
> *All Theft is to be eschewed.*
> *This which is now propounded to me to be done is a Theft,*
> *therefore it is to be eschewed.*[87]

---

82 Sanderson, p. 13; EEBO image 154344:18.

83 Ibid., p. 3; EEBO image 154344:13.

84 Ibid., p. 13; EEBO image 154344:18. Carpenter, p. 19; EEBO 170295:16, in a *sermon*, observes that 'Divines do usually express [conscience] by a practicall syllogism'.

85 Sanderson, p. 7; EEBO image 154344:15. Carpenter, invoking the etymology of 'conscience' as implying a knowing together, says that '*Objectively*' this means 'the joynt knowledge of two things together; *A Rule and an Act at once*'. '*Subjectively*', it implies 'anothers [that is, God's] knowledge joyned with ours' (pp. 16–17; EEBO image 170295:15).

86 Norman, pp. 19, 21–2; EEBO images 46170:14, 15–16. Compare Samuel Annesley, p. 5; EEBO 105033:7; Vincent, pp. 25–6; EEBO images 44406:21–2; Carpenter, pp. 19–20; EEBO images 170295:16–17; and Edward Fowler, *Libertas Evangelica: or, a Discourse of Christian Liberty* (London, 1680), p. 224; EEBO image 100709:131.

87 Sanderson, p. 14; EEBO image 154344:19.

Taylor offers a similar account of the operation of conscience as involving two related syllogisms.[88] Clearly, questions might arise about the cogency of this example. How, exactly, does reason 'prove' that theft is unjust? Is there not at least one step missing in the derivation of the minor of the second syllogism? However, my concern here is not so much with the cogency of particular arguments,[89] but with the depiction of the operation of conscience as a logical process.

It is worth emphasizing that it is not just theologians who adopt this account of conscience. Although few jurists present developed analyses of the general nature of conscience, one who does—albeit in a religious context—is Sir Matthew Hale, who adopts essentially the standard picture. Thus, he says, conscience is a 'high act of the Understanding', whose operation involves '*three Propositions*', namely, (1) the apprehension of rules of 'Natural Principles of Conscience', (2) a 'Minor Proposition', which involves our awareness of our acts and omissions, and (3) 'the Conclusion of acquittal or condemnation'.[90]

As I have remarked elsewhere, this account of conscience bears close affinities to legal judgment, which similarly involves drawing conclusions from the application of normative propositions to factual propositions. So, for example, when Taylor, having outlined the operation of conscience in these terms, remarks that '[t]his is the full proceeding of this court',[91] he may be speaking figuratively, but the metaphor he invokes is a fairly exact analogy. To the extent that this depiction of conscience is accepted, the idea of a court in which conscience is the standard of judgment makes sense. Conscience thus conceived does not, at least at the theoretical level, offend our standard notion of how a juristic principle should operate. It does not involve evaluating perceived facts intuitively, but rather assessing those facts against an external normative *measure*.

This is not to say, of course, that it is unproblematic. The problem, even with this objective account *in its own terms*, is, as we have seen before, with the identification of the minor premise in the second of the linked syllogisms. That is, this account posits shared normative knowledge provided by *synteresis*. This means that there can—indeed, *must*—be agreement about the basic moral precepts. These are the same for everyone, and are objectively knowable. Since the deductions of reason which provide the minor premise of the first syllogism are products of reason, they may be controversial. But they are at least 'on the table', subject to scrutiny and verification by rational discourse.

88 Taylor, vol. 9, pp. 14–15.

89 Although if it could be shown that the derived premises are not matters of reason but of intuition or opinion only, this would compromise the objective nature of the process.

90 Hale, *Discourse*, pp. 51–5; EEBO images 94495:46–8.

91 Taylor, vol. 9, p. 15.

The Knowledge of the Heart

But the minor premise of the second syllogism, while capable of being certain, is certain only to a very restricted class of knowers. As we have seen previously, commentators typically (relying partly on the etymology of 'conscience', but also on its ultimate objects) observe that it is 'knowledge with another'. That other is God. Sanderson for example observes that 'man not only knows what things he hath committed, but he hath God who searcheth the heart and reins, to be a conscious witness and an inspector into all his works, nay, into his most secret thoughts'.[92] Even a writer like Nathanael Vincent, who, allowing that '[m]ore eyes than we imagine, behold us when we are committing the most concealed abominations', says that not only God but angels and devils 'look on',[93] observes that it is not in the power of other persons 'to look into our Hearts'.[94] So an ordinary, external tribunal lacks the competence to access the factual information (or much of it) that is relevant to determinations of conscience. If the inaccessibility of propositions constituting the minor premise of the second syllogism is an obstacle to the use of conscience as a juristic principle, doubt about the objectivity of the major premise of the second syllogism—or, more radically, about the major premise of the first syllogism—would be correspondingly more problematic.

The observation that our 'Consciences are lockt up from the knowledg of others, and are comprehensively and fully known only by God himself'[95] takes us again to the issue of inward dispositions *versus* outward actions as the special sphere of conscience. To be sure, conscience is concerned with both: it 'sees into and sits upon and sentenceth' all our actions, 'whether external or internal', whether inward, involving 'the root, spring, and sincerity of our actions' or outward, involving their 'fruits and circumstances'.[96]

Nevertheless, the activities of conscience tend to be particularly associated with the 'inward'. This point is often made in distinguishing human laws from the laws of God: 'Human laws', says Taylor, 'only consider the outward action, not the secret opinion',[97] and Sanderson observes that there are acts of virtue and vice that human law cannot reach: 'the movings of the affections, to love, to hate, to grieve, and other cogitations … of the heart, and mind'.[98] God, he says, 'hath only permitted to the Magistrate the Government of the *external man*, and

---

92 Sanderson, p. 6; EEBO image 154344:15. Compare Norman, p. 18; EEBO image 46170:14: ''tis a knowledg together with God'.

93 Vincent, pp. 28–9; EEBO image 44406:23.

94 Ibid., p. 17; EEBO image 44406:17.

95 Norman, p. 132; EEBO image 46170:71.

96 Ibid., pp. 24–5; EEBO image 46170:17.

97 Taylor, vol. 10, p. 28. In Culverwell's words, 'Humane Lawes … rest satisfi'd with a visible and external obedience; but Natures Law darts it self into the most intimate Essentials …' (p. 57).

98 Sanderson, p. 317; EEBO image 154344:176.

hath reserved to himself alone the knowledge and judgment of the *inward actions*, and the inspection into the hearts of men'.[99] Although conscience is concerned with both, such observations suggest a more particular identification of conscience with the inward, the secret, the private. Sanderson thus observes that since only God knows 'the internal motions of the Conscience, he alone hath the power of prescribing a Law unto them'.[100] This does not exclude 'external motions' from the purview of conscience, but it makes the special focus of conscience the internal. To the extent that this identification, or this focus, becomes prevalent, the tendency will be to create a dichotomy between the spheres of human law and conscience. While civic law is said to be limited to the outward and public, and conscience to comprehend the outward and public as well as the inward and private, the dichotomy that tends to develop is between that to which civic law is limited (the outward and public) and that which is *distinctive* about the sphere of operation of conscience (the inward and private). Crudely, there may be a tendency to think in terms of law *versus* conscience, or alternatively to subsume the public aspect of conscience within 'law'. Either way, the process of the internalization of conscience is fostered.

Another distinction sometimes invoked in this context is between will and understanding. Taylor observes that, while the laws of God 'bind the will and the understanding', 'human laws meddle not with the understanding[;] the will is the subject of human laws'.[101] This means that a person can conscientiously obey human laws without assenting to them intellectually. The same is not true of divine laws. Conscience requires us not only to submit our will to these, but to assent to them with our understanding as well. Whether we genuinely assent to human law or not the human magistrate cannot know, and he will not 'meddle' with this. What is important is outward obedience.

This position may appear paradoxical. For one thing, emphasizing will in relation to human law and understanding in relation to God's law may seem to contradict a tendency, which we have adumbrated and about which we will say more, to shift the emphasis of conscience from knowledge to will. This seems to be the implication of Sanderson's insistence that Abraham was bound not merely to do what God commanded (sacrifice Isaac), but to *will* to do it. But the answer to this paradox lies in the example itself. There is, so to speak, an obedient will and a 'willing' will. The first submits to do the thing commanded. The second actually and concurrently wills the thing commanded. Human law expects the first kind of will; it does not concern itself with the concordance of the will with the thing commanded; it merely requires the will to manifest obedience by outward acts. So the emphasis on obedient will in relation to human law is not inconsistent with a shift in emphasis of conscience from knowledge to the willing will. There may also appear to be a paradox in that what is said to make conscience common—the

[99] Ibid.

[100] Ibid., p. 114; EEBO image 154344:69.

[101] Taylor, vol. 10, p. 27.

intellectual component—is now associated particularly with what only God can know, that is, whether there is really assent of the understanding. The paradox can be explained by saying that there are objective rules that can be objectively tested, but that any person's genuine intellectual assent to these rules is something that cannot be communicated to another. Again, these processes of internalization of conscience, or of more insistent recognition of its inherently internal nature, tend to isolate conscience from what human tribunals, including 'courts of conscience', can address.

Other Destabilizing Developments

Apart from developments within Protestant casuistry itself tending to compromise the objective character of conscience, there were, of course, wider destabilizing influences at work. While not determinative positions, these can at least be regarded as sites of controversy that almost certainly would have eroded the absoluteness of conscience—or perhaps the confidence with which that absoluteness was held or presented.

As we have seen, the traditional accounts of conscience based its objectivity on, among other things, the existence of a moral law and means of knowledge of that law. Two tendencies of thought which gained (or re-gained) prominence in the seventeenth century made those objective elements problematic.

Intellectualism versus Voluntarism

One of these involved the contention between 'intellectualism' and 'voluntarism', which James Tully describes as 'the two major theological traditions of the early modern period'.[102] The former, associated particularly with Aquinas, emphasizes that divine law accords with reason; the latter, associated with William of Ockham, emphasizes that divine law is simply God's will, and that to impose upon it the requirement of its being 'rational' would be to imply a fetter on God's omnipotence.[103] Neither of these views is, of course, inconsistent with the notion of an objective or absolute morality: whether God's law is constrained by reason or whether it is simply His will, it constitutes an external imperative to which man must conform. But, arguably, intellectualism is more consonant with the notion of a stable and accessible objective law than is voluntarism. At least it is more consistent with the idea of a separate tribunal authorized to consider positive or willed law against a prior and independent rectitude.

Ralph Cudworth, an adherent of the intellectualist position, offers some insight into what may be at stake. Perhaps tendentiously, he characterizes the voluntarist stance in the following terms: 'divers Modern Theologers', he says, assert that

---

102 Tully, 'Governing Conduct', p. 34.

103 Ibid.

'*there is nothing Absolutely, Intrinsecally and Naturally Good and Evil, Just and Unjust, antecedently to any positive Command or Prohibition of God; but that the Arbitrary Will and Pleasure of God* (that is, an Omnipotent Being devoid of all Essential and Natural Justice) *by its Commands and Prohibitions, is the first and only Rule and Measure thereof*'.[104] There is a law, but that law is arbitrary, irrational, and unpredictable. Against this view, Cudworth insists that 'the *Wisdom* of God is as much God as the *Will* of God', and explains the implications of this for law:

> For *Wisdom* in it self hath the Nature of a *Rule* and *Measure*, it being a most Determinate and Inflexible thing; but *Will* being not only a Blind and Dark thing … but also Indefinite and Indeterminate, hath therefore the Nature of a thing *Regulable* and *Measurable*. Wherefore it is the Perfection of *Will*, as such, to be guided and determined by *Wisdom* and *Truth*; but to make *Wisdom, Knowledge* and *Truth* to be Arbitrarily determined by *Will*, and to be regulated by such a *Plumbean* and *Flexible Rule* as that is, is quite to destroy the Nature of it …. (p. 35)

What this implies, at least, is that while wisdom provides a stable and predictable measure, will ultimately does not, because will is inherently arbitrary. This has implications not only for the nature of the (objective) law, but also for how it is accessed. Law based upon wisdom and in itself rational is presumably accessible by reason and communicable among reasonable creatures; law based upon will is accessible only by virtue of its commands being made explicitly known by the lawgiver, perhaps only by a pouring of divine grace into selected souls.

Tully notes that the resurgence of voluntarism was associated with the Reformation, and he observes that such luminaries as Sanderson and Taylor were voluntarists.[105] Again, he says that for them, '[c]onscience is the judgment of our actions relative to a moral law',[106] so the standard is certainly objective, but that objectivity, as it is a function of an arbitrary external will, has the potential for instability. So, when we are considering these Protestant writers on conscience we should keep in mind that their account of divine law may have profoundly different implications from those of the intellectualist tradition. We have seen intimations of the kinds of implications in Sanderson's account of the Abraham and Isaac story and in some of Taylor's deprecating remarks about reason. At the same time, they do write as if reason is a basis at least for communicating about the law governing conscience; indeed, the whole premise of their writing at all

104 Cudworth, *Treatise*, p. 9.

105 Tully, 'Governing Conduct', p. 37. The editors of Culverwell's *Light of Nature* include among voluntarists not only Ockham, but also Jean Gerson, Calvin, Luther, the English Puritan Calvinists, Hobbes, Sanderson and Taylor; in the intellectualist camp with Aquinas are Richard Hooker and the Cambridge Platonists (for example, Cudworth) (pp. xxiv, xxix).

106 Tully, ibid., p. 38.

seems to suggest this—unless they think of themselves as merely manifesting the grace that has been imparted to them.

Knowledge of the Moral Law: Innate or Imparted?

Another major aspect of the putative objectivity of conscience involves how we know the moral law. I have already alluded to this in intimating that such knowledge arises by reason or by grace. But the issue was raised in another form by the seventeenth-century critique of 'innatism', most typically associated with John Locke. Tully describes innatism as the doctrine 'that there are either innate ideas (knowledge) or innate predispositions that predispose us to assent to the true or the good and dissent from the false or evil …'.[107] The relevance of this doctrine to the traditional view of conscience is evident: in that view, *synderesis* is a faculty, implanted in men by God, which allows them to apprehend basic moral precepts. If, on the contrary, the human mind is, as Locke would have it, a *tabula rasa*, then our moral notions come not from within, but from without, perhaps from cultural convention.[108] This appears to open the door to moral relativism, which would make conscience not an independent, absolute 'knowing together with God', but a function of particular social contexts, forms of education, and so on. Of course, Locke's position had hardly carried the day in his own time. For example, Cudworth—who was far from being alone—would write that 'the Soul is not a meer *Rasa Tabula*, a Naked and Passive Thing, which has no innate Furniture or Activity of its own …'.[109] And we will recall that even such 'liberal' theologians as Wilkins and Tillotson appear to have accepted the idea of moral truths written in the heart. But now the destabilizing question—'Do we have innate ideas or dispositions towards good?'—was quite insistently 'out there'.

Tully suggests that, at different times, Locke proposed two different solutions to the problem of 'reconstruct[ing] belief on the blank and indifferent *tabula rasa* that remains'[110] after innatist theories have been rejected. These two solutions relate broadly to two tendencies more generally respecting moral reasoning, and hence conscience, in the seventeenth century.

One thing Locke advocated was a suspension of judgment and examination of the evidence for different beliefs. Examination of the evidence would not necessarily yield conclusive outcomes, but would establish 'probabilities', on the basis of which a judgment could be made. As we have noticed, probability is associated with relativism, or at least with provisional or tentative answers, and would tend to compromise the certainty postulated or implied by traditional accounts of conscience.

107 Ibid., pp. 17–18.

108 Tully, 'Governing Conduct', p. 23.

109 Cudworth, *Treatise*, pp. 286–7. Tully notes that Cudworth's *Treatise* is perhaps the best representative of the innate disposition theory ('Governing Conduct', 18).

110 Ibid., p. 25.

Tully states that by 1677, Locke had 'abandoned the idea that assent would be automatically governed by the probabilities', and began instead to emphasize the need to inculcate a 'love of truth'.[111] Without wanting to oversimplify, I would say that this indicates a movement from the primacy of intellectual inquiry to the primacy of volitional disposition—albeit in Locke's case not an innate disposition, but an imparted disposition. This, it seems to me, corresponds to a growing tendency during the period to associate conscience more with will than with intellect, in spite of many conventional protestations to the contrary. Thus, Edmund Leites speaks of an increasing emphasis on the need for individuals to possess 'a truly moral will'.[112] To be sure, this will did not entail the supersession of reason; indeed, Leites says that rationality was 'a chief property of a truly moral will' (p. 12) But it does signal a change in focus from getting the right answer to coming to a sincerely-sought answer.

Negotiating Desires

While Hobbes's views can hardly be said to have gained uncontested acceptance in his own time, they represent—at least in some of their formulations—a fairly extreme version of a volitional, or even affective, account of moral discernment, and indicate the kinds of tendencies that were in the air. Thus, in the *Elements*, he writes:

> Every man, for his own part, calleth that which pleaseth, and is delightful to himself, GOOD; and that EVIL which displeseth him: insomuch that while every man differeth from other in constitution, they differ also one from another concerning the common distinction of good and evil. Nor is there any such thing as … simply good.[113]

Similar assertions occur in the *Leviathan*, for example, 'whatsoever is the object of any man's appetite or desire that is it which he for his part calleth *good*; and the object of his hate and aversion, *evil* …'.[114] So, for him, the process of 'moral' choice apparently involves the alternating demands of appetite and aversion: he defines 'deliberation' as 'the whole sum of desires, aversions, hopes and fears, continued till the thing [envisaged] be either done or thought impossible'.[115] Correspondingly, 'the last appetite or aversion immediately adhering to the action, or to the omission thereof, is that we call WILL, the act (not the faculty)

111 Ibid., p. 32.

112 'Casuistry and Character' in *Conscience and Casuistry in Early Modern Europe*, Edmund Leites (ed.) (Cambridge, 1988), pp. 119–33, p. 120.

113 Hobbes, *Elements*, p. 44.

114 Thomas Hobbes, *Leviathan* (1651), Edwin Curley, ed. (Indianapolis, 1994), p. 28. Compare. p. 100.

115 Ibid., p. 33. Compare Hobbes, *Elements*, p. 71.

of *willing*'.[116] This account would appear to make will a function of affects, not of reason.[117] It certainly appears subjectivist and relativistic, at least initially, as regards moral 'reasoning'.

To leave the account there would, of course, be to caricature Hobbes's view, which is elaborated in the *Leviathan*. Significantly, he says that 'private appetite is the measure of good and evil' 'so long as a man is in the condition of mere nature (which is a state of war)', and that 'all agree … that peace is good' (p. 100). Thus, 'the first and fundamental law of nature … is *to seek peace, and follow it*' (p. 80), from which other 'laws of nature', which are the 'means of peace', such as 'equity, justice, gratitude, and other moral virtues, derive' (pp. 100, 174). Moreover, he sometimes uses expressions which are reminiscent of more traditional approaches: for example, the moral virtues are 'qualities that dispose men to peace and obedience' (p. 174); '[t]he laws of nature are immutable and eternal …' (p. 99); the first quality of a judge should be '*a right understanding* of that principal law of nature called *equity*, which [depends] not on the reading of other men's writings but on the goodness of a man's own natural reason and meditation …' (p. 184). Reading statements like these, one might be pardoned for thinking that Hobbes postulated an immutable natural law, discernible by reason, and that humans have an innate disposition to seek it. But the primary natural law rises out of the desire for self-preservation,[118] and the 'moral virtues' are negotiated positions, involving a surrender of natural liberty in return for security, ultimately guaranteed by the fiat of the sovereign. It may not be too much to say that, in some sense, the basis of Hobbes's account is 'I desire', and that such a position would have a tendency to shift the fulcrum of the moral lever.

The Diverging Protestant Mainstream

A shift in emphasis is evident even in the Anglican mainstream, as our consideration of 'probability' and other materials from later in the century illustrates. I shall consider only a few further examples.

One is *A Discourse Concerning Conscience* by John Sharp, who, incidentally, early in his career was chaplain to Heneage Finch, later Lord Nottingham. This work contains many elements of the conventional account. Thus, for example, Sharp insists that 'Conscience must always have a *Rule*', and that that rule is 'the *Law of God*'.[119] The law or will of God is made known us 'either by *Nature*,

---

116 Hobbes, *Leviathan*, p. 33.

117 So, in his chart categorizing the sciences, ethics is subsumed with the class 'Consequences from the *passions* of men' (ibid., p. 48).

118 For Sanderson, by contrast, we are bound in conscience to seek peace 'because that God the Lord of Conscience hath commanded us to love and follow … publick peace' (p. 192; EEBO image 154344:10).

119 Sharp, *Discourse*, pp. 6, 7; EEBO image 37553:6.

or by *Revelation*'.[120] Although he does not use the term *synderesis*, he seems to have it in mind when he describes the '*Law of Nature*' as 'those Principles of Good and Evil, Just and Unjust, which God hath Stamp'd upon the Minds of all Men, in the very Constitution of their Natures'.[121] Moreover, conscience involves logical derivation of lower-order norms from those basic precepts, that is, 'all the necessary Deductions from those Heads'.[122]

At the same time, his approach is rather more liberal than many we have encountered. He eschews inquiring 'into the Signification of the word *Conscience*, or the several *Scholastical* Definitions of it'.[123] Rather, he prefers to consider 'what every Man doth really mean by that word when he has occasion to make use of it'.[124] His appeal is to the ordinary meaning. To be sure, the common sense of the word does produce the elements noted in the previous paragraph. But the shift is from learned authority to what each of us, perhaps instinctively, knows. Moreover, conscience is '*our judgment and Perswasion concerning what we ought to do*'[125] and doing what we are 'perswaded in [our] Judgment' is right or wrong.[126] He goes on to explain that acting according to 'the best of [one's] Judgment' is a measure of one's '*sincerity* or *Hypoc[r]ysie*'.[127] We have seen before that one may have an erroneous conscience and that, for example, invincible ignorance of salient facts may mitigate one's culpability. And Sharp emphasizes that honestly believing something to be right does not make it right. But there is a kind of acknowledgment here that a person may be good, even if he or she is wrong.

This point appears even more clearly in a sermon Sharp delivered on Hebrews 13:18.[128] Again defining conscience as 'a Man's Judgment or Persuasion concerning moral Good or Evil', Sharp says that this might be taken to imply 'that that should be a good Conscience, wherein a Man's Judgment was rightly and truly instructed as to these Matters'.[129] However, he goes on to distinguish a 'right Conscience'—'[w]hen a Man hath true Notions of … what is lawful or unlawful'[130]—from a *good* conscience, which involves, as his biblical text says, '*being in all Things willing*

---

120 Ibid., p. 7; EEBO image 37553:6.

121 Ibid.

122 Ibid., p. 9; EEBO image 37553:7.

123 Ibid., p. 3; EEBO image 37553:4.

124 Ibid.

125 Ibid., p. 5; EEBO image 37553:5.

126 Ibid., p. 4; EEBO image 37553:5.

127 Ibid., p. 19; EEBO image 37553:12.

128 John Sharp, *Sixteen Casuistical Sermons Preached on Several Occasions* (4th edn, 3 vols, London, 1748).

129 Ibid., vol. 3, p. 363; ECCO image CW3319329215:372. The very fact that he speaks of 'Judgment or Persuasion' perhaps suggests an ambiguity. Some writers, as we have seen, insist on a strict distinction of knowledge from opinion or persuasion.

130 Ibid., p. 364; ECCO image CW33193299215:373.

to live honestly', which in turn involves being 'very sincere in his Purposes, and Desires, and Endeavours'.[131]

Similarly, Robert Eyre, in a sermon delivered at the Winchester Assizes in 1693, invoking the notion of incorrigible ignorance, which, as we know, has a long history in casuistical writing, observes that 'a Mans Conscience may misguide him, and yet he nevertheless continue the Character of an honest and sincere (I may add too) conscientious Christian'.[132] Shortly after, he characterizes a person of a good and inoffensive conscience as one who has been 'diligent and industrious to know and understand his Duty; and according to his best Knowledge thereof, hath been afterwards sincere and hearty in the performance of it …'.[133]

While being mindful of Eyre's caution that this does not mean that a person is justified just by being true to 'Principles of his own forming' or 'his own particular Scheme of Justice and Honesty',[134] and while not wanting two or three examples to carry too heavy a burden, we can see how this tendency bears some affinity to modern subjectivist notions of conscience, where sincerity of persuasion, not objective correctness, is the criterion. We can also see how such a position is problematic for law in at least two ways. For one thing, if conscience is a matter of litigants' sincerity, rather than of objective rectitude, it will be harder for courts to fathom.[135] And if conscience is a matter of the judge's sincere endeavour to do right (no contemptible thing!), rather than a matter of determining what *is* right according to agreed and predictable criteria, then we can see how conscience, as a juristic principle, might be faulted for being protean.

The Privatization of Conscience

Another phenomenon affecting the characterization and status of conscience during the period was the 'liberty of conscience' controversy, alluded to previously. As we have seen, Hobbes (perhaps correctly) notes that this issue, in a fairly fully-

---

131 Ibid. pp. 365, 373; ECCO images CW3319329215:374, 382. Indeed, he makes this willingness to live honestly the 'Rule and Standard' and the 'Measure of a good Conscience' (pp. 365, 367; ECCO images CW3319329215:374, 376).

132 Eyre, p. 14; EEBO image 62636:11.

133 Ibid., p. 20; EBBO image 62636:14. Earlier in the century, Sanderson argued that at least a good intention cannot itself render an act morally good, even at the level of will: 'out of a *good Intention alone* it doth not follow that either the *Will* it self, which is the first principle of acting, or any externall Act flowing from it should be said to be *good*' (Sanderson, p. 40; EEBO image 154344:32).

134 Eyre, p. 19; 62636:13.

135 As Vincent observes, '[t]he Persons whom we converse with, and that take notice of our Actions, are not competent Judges of our sincerity… (pp. 16–17; EEBO image 44406:17).

articulated form, was relatively new at the time,[136] and was brought to the fore by the rise of Protestantism and especially the idea of the direct access of the individual reader to the authoritative texts. We should first recall that the liberty of conscience controversy was concerned primarily with what might be termed 'religious' conscience, and, indeed, with outward observances associated with that conscience. As we have noticed before, a distinction was often drawn between 'natural' conscience and 'enlightened' conscience, the former sometimes said to direct people 'by the light of *nature* to a Civill outward good end',[137] while the latter was concerned with more purely spiritual or 'heavenly' things. One might therefore expect that a controversy engaging matters of enlightened conscience would be of limited relevance to the jurisdiction of Chancery. Nevertheless, consideration of 'liberty of conscience' entailed reflection on the nature of conscience generally, which is, of course, relevant to my inquiry. With respect to the distinction, in relation to religious conscience, between what William Penn for example calls '*Liberty of the Mind*' and the expression of that belief 'in a visible way of worship',[138] one might wonder whether freedom of worship specifically has a very direct connection with conscience as a juristic principle. But, again, discussions of the relationship between conscience as an internal matter and its public or outward expression are germane to the growing subjectivization and privatization of conscience generally. While acknowledging the specific emphasis of the liberty of conscience debate, I do want to take account of some of its implications for conscience as a juristic principle.

In the first place, of course, the intensity of the debate would have contributed to the relativization of conscience and thus to its being compromised as a legal measure. As Tully remarks, a central problem of the Reformation era was the presence of 'contradictory beliefs held with confidence and resolution'.[139] Indeed, at least one proponent of liberty of conscience regarded the diversity of conscientious belief as a matter for celebration, referring to 'the wonderful variety there is in that inward divine revelation' 'by which [people's] judgment, and consciences are in several [that is, disparate] measures settled and determined'.[140] Different consciences dictate incommensurate things. Particularly to the extent that conscience becomes identified with will, rather than knowledge, this phenomenon raises the possibility that inconsistent beliefs may be equally conscientious. By now, too, the disagreement was not so exclusively between Protestants and

[136] But history is littered with persecutions of conscientious dissidents.

[137] Francis Rous (1579–1659), *The Ancient Bounds, or Liberty of Conscience* (London, 1645), p. 1; EEBO image 158553:5.

[138] William Penn, *The Great Case of Liberty of Conscience* (London, 1670), p. 11; EEBO image 98352:8.

[139] Tully, 'Governing Conduct', p. 23.

[140] Charles Wolseley (1630–1714), *Liberty of Conscience* (London, 1668), p. 10; EEBO image 95413:5.

Catholics, but among varieties of Protestants themselves, and therefore perhaps even harder to rationalize away.

Apart from the phenomenon of the diversity of belief, rooted in conscience, one can identify more specific developments related to the controversy. These involve what I would describe as the privatization of, initially, a certain kind of conscience and, ultimately, conscience in general.

The key issue in the liberty of conscience debate was, of course, the matter of outward constraint of individual persons' consciences. Advocates of liberty of conscience emphasized that the conscience was, conceptually, not subject to such constraint, at least by secular authority. The steps in the argument were, generally, the following: (1) 'the Lordship in and over conscience … is Gods alone only and proper right and privilege';[141] (2) concomitantly, conscience 'is such a thing, as can by no means come under any possibility of force or restraint, beyond its own bounds; and is as much out of the reach of all humane power, as the soul it selfe is';[142] and (3) God's authority in this regard 'was never delegated to any substitute upon earth'.[143] The last is undoubtedly a direct response to the Catholic doctrine that such authority, or some of it, has been delegated to 'substitutes'. To be sure, these controversialists qualify their position by referring it to matters of faith or religious belief. But its implications are broader: if God is the sole lord of conscience, then it is at least awkward to affirm that this applies to conscience only in some of its aspects. Thus, for example, when we are told that 'there is but one *Judge*, *Law-giver* and *King* in and over the Conscience',[144] this sounds rather comprehensive. If God is the only judge of conscience, and has not delegated His power, it appears difficult to argue that the Chancellor is a judge of conscience in any very far-reaching way. The king's authority extends only to keeping 'the outward man in good order by just Judgment in all cases between man and man'.[145]

Even for those who advocated conformity, this issue could lead to conceding—albeit grudgingly—that dissent could be conformable to conscience. Sharp, whose project in *A Discourse Concerning Conscience* is to examine the situation, in conscience, of nonconformists, exemplifies the process.

Beginning with a consideration of how human laws bind in conscience, he makes the familiar point that 'though the *Laws of God* be the great, and indeed the

141 Edward Burroughs (1634–62), *The Case of Free Liberty of Conscience in the Exercise of Faith and Religion* (London, 1661), p. 5; EEBO image 58212:3. Compare, for example, Thomas Whitfield, *A Discourse of Liberty of Conscience* (London, 1649), p. 1, EEBO image 115971:2; Wolseley, p. 10; EEBO image 95413:5.

142 Wolseley, p. 10; EEBO image 95413:5. Compare Penn, p. 13; EEBO image 98352:9 and John Crook *et al.*, *Liberty of Conscience Asserted* (London, 1661), p. 5; EEBO image 61615:3.

143 Wolseley, p. 10; EEBO image 95413:5. Compare Burroughs, p. 5; EEBO image 58212:3.

144 Crook *et al.*, p. 4; EEBO image 61615:3.

145 Burroughs, p. 6; EEBO image 58212:4.

only Rule of Conscience, yet the *Laws of Man* … do also bind the Conscience', but only in 'a *Secondary* Sense'.[146] That is, as we have previously noticed, they are not as such directly binding on conscience, but bind because Scripture tells us to obey our rulers. In the case of laws relating to religious conformity, however, they are reinforced by a law of God, namely, the law that ostensibly requires church unity: 'whoever breaks this *Unity* of the Church … is Guilty of that Sin of *Schism*'.[147] So nonconformists are objectively sinning. However, in so doing, they claim to be following their consciences. And Sharp, like others, insists that acting against your conscientious convictions (or 'persuasions') is also sinful. Sharp is obviously troubled by the implications of this: a person in this situation must sin, either by breaking the law or by going against conscience.[148] He appears to resolve the dilemma in favour of the persuaded conscience. 'No Man', he says, 'can be Obliged to do more then what is in his Power to do.'[149] That is, even though the things a person does are, objectively, 'Transgressions of Gods Law', sin will not be imputed to him if, for example, 'he hath done all that he could do in his Circumstances to understand his Duty'.[150] Sharp goes to some length to show that many who do not conform fail to meet the stringent standard that would make them 'inculpable'. But the point is that some do. This is important, because it acknowledges that a sincere and diligent conscience justifies, or perhaps excuses, the dissenter. Ultimately, what is required is that the plea of conscience be '*truly and justly made*'.[151] Obviously, Sharp does not go as far as an enthusiastic proponent of liberty of conscience like Pett, who argues that 'the Protestant religion doth indemnifie us in the Court of Conscience, for believing in matters of Religion according to the Dictates of our private Judgements'.[152]

Concomitantly, the dispute over mandatory religious conformity appears to have led to a sharpened distinction between the secular and the sacred, at least for some controversialists. The author of *The True Magistrate*[153] is illustrative. He insists upon the distinction between 'civils' and 'spirituals' and identifies conscience especially, if not exclusively, with the latter: '[b]y things meerly relating to conscience, we must understand, those inward workings of our spirits, that form a perswasion in us of what we receive to be according to the mind of God …'.[154] The magistrate, he maintains, has been given no power from God 'in things spiritual

---

146 Sharp, *Discourse*, p. 9; EEBO image 37553:7.

147 Ibid., pp. 13–14; EEBO images 37553:9–10.

148 See, for example, ibid. pp. 19, 27; EEBO images 37553:12, 16.

149 Ibid., p. 24; EEBO image 37553:15.

150 Ibid., p. 23; EEBO image 37553:14.

151 Ibid., p. 25; EEBO image 37553:15.

152 Pett, p. 41; EEBO image 22.

153 *The True Magistrate, or the Magistrates Duty, and Power in Matters of Religion, or, in Things Meerly Relating to Conscience* (London, 1659).

154 Ibid., p. 8; EEBO image 119150:5.

or meerly relating to conscience'.[155] I do not mean to say that conscience on this view has nothing to do with 'civils', but implicit in this approach is the hiving off of conscience into the sphere of the private and the personal. So, Edward Bagshaw (1629/30–71) says that 'Civil Government is properly and adequately concerned only in Civil things; but Religious matters belong only to him that is Inspector and Lord of the Conscience'.[156] The effect of the tendency that this represents would be to make conscience fit rather less comfortably with the magistrate's function—in the sense of providing a criterion for what the general law should be. No doubt the magistrate should conscientiously administer the law, but that is not the same as making his conscience a measure of the law or presuming to direct the consciences of others.

A slightly different take on this point is suggested by Nathaniel Culverwell's rather cryptic observation that 'there are no representatives in intellectuals and spirituals', which he explains: 'there is none can alwayes represent the minde and judgement of another in the vitals and inwards of Religion'.[157] This observation may involve two kinds of implications: first, that we cannot rely on the precedent authority of others for our exercise of conscience, and, second, that others cannot make judgments of conscience for us. Sanderson (who is likely not coming from the same place as Culverwell) makes both points: 'neither the example nor the judgment of any man ought to be of so great *authority* with us, that our *Consciences* may securely rest in either of them';[158] 'the word of God doth expressely forbid us to subject our Consciences to the judgment of any other, or to usurp a Dominion over the Consciences of any one'.[159] Such a position, taken literally, radically vitiates the possibility of juristic conscience in any but an attenuated sense. If prior judgment cannot determine subsequent cases, the consistency which we expect of law does not obtain. But even more radically, no other can 'represent' us in our quest for the insights of conscience.

This phenomenon—the separation of 'civils' from 'spirituals'—finds expression in other terms as well. Hammond, for example, writes that there are different laws of conscience for different spheres of human action. Thus, '[t]he *Christian law* is the rule of Conscience for Christian actions; the *law of reason*, or morall law, for morall, the *law nationall*, municipall, or locall, for civill …'.[160] At one point, Nalson observes that the 'Judge' of right and wrong 'in the Affairs

155 Ibid., p. 9; EEBO image 119150:5.

156 Edward Bagshaw, *The Second Part of the Great Question Concerning Things Indifferent in Religious Worship* (London, 1661), p. 12; EEBO image 54584:10.

157 Culverwell, p. 133. This may also resonate to the Roman Catholic doctrine that the priest may be 'a judge of Mens consciences and conditions' (see John Goodman, *A Discourse Concerning Auricular Confession* (London, 1684), p. 17 and *passim*).

158 Sanderson, p. 71; EEBO image 154344:47.

159 Ibid., p. 101; 154344:62.

160 Hammond, p. 11; EEBO image 123411:7.

of the World' is reason, while in 'the Concerns of Religion' it is conscience.[161] Clearly, there is a hierarchy here—the Christian law prevailing in cases of inconsistency[162]—but the clear implication is that there is a discontinuity between spiritual and civil conscience and that different considerations apply to each. It is, Hammond insists, both 'very irregular, and unreasonable to measure any action by a rule that belongs not to it'.[163]

The observation that the conscience has to do with inward things and that civil magistrature is concerned only with the 'outward man' can cut both ways. On the one hand, it suggests that the civil authority should not meddle with inward matters and therefore should not encroach on conscience. On the other hand, because it postulates an incapacity of the civil power to reach conscience, it can lead to the argument that a person may be made to conform outwardly, even in matters of religious observance, but nevertheless maintain an inward integrity. Again, the tendency would be deeply to internalize conscience. So, for example, Rous observes that, since conscience is not 'capable of outward restraint', but is subject only to 'morall or spirituall instruments', service to the state, which is '*outward*, civilly, bodily' can be exercised without engaging a person's conscience.[164] Similarly, Edward Fowler (1631/2–1714), sometime Bishop of Gloucester, asking rhetorically 'the Acts of Conscience [in exercising its typical offices] being all Internal, and within a mans Soul, how can its Liberty in exerting those Acts be infringed by any Humane Power? What Earthly Power can make me *Assent* to or believe what it pleaseth?' observes that what is claimed as 'Liberty of *Conscience*' is really 'Liberty of *Practice*'.[165] Tully relates this argument to the distinction between judgment and will: '[i]f practical judgment, and hence conscience, is separate from the will, then dissenters can be forced to conform to religious practice without compromising their religious beliefs, since conformity requires only an act of the will'.[166] As noted previously, such an observation may have to be made subject to the further distinction between a merely obedient will and a willing will.

There were, obviously, those who resisted this argument. For example, Edward Bagshaw specifically addresses and rejects the contention of 'many Learned men' that 'Christian Liberty consists not in *Freedom of Practice*, but in the *Freedom of* Judgment' and since matters of religious observance 'are merely enjoyned by the Magistrate, as thing of Outward order, so long we may freely do them, and

---

161 Nalson, p. 3; EEBO image 56946:5.

162 So, the approach Hammond advocates is that the "particular action" be "regulated by the rule, or rules which are proper to it, and have nothing contrary to any superiour transcendent rule" (p. 16; EEBO 123411:10).

163 Ibid., p. 11; EEBO image 123411:7.

164 Rous, p. 2; EEBO image 158553:6.

165 Fowler, pp. 224–5; EEBO image 100709:131.

166 Tully, 'Governing Conduct', p. 51.

still retain our Liberty of Conscience'.[167] As Tully notes, some dissenters 'broke with the long-standing Protestant separation of judgment and will',[168] and, like Bagshaw, refused to exercise their will in acts of conformity against their moral/religious judgment. Indeed, the tendency to associate conscience as much or more with will than with judgment would presumably have reinforced this resistance.

Ostensibly, the positions, both of those proposing this argument and of those opposing it, could have had the effect of relegating conscience to the private sphere. Proponents of the argument, by separating moral judgment from will, are saying, in effect: 'What you think in your own mind and/or heart is of no concern, as long as you *do* what the law commands.' In other words, conscience is purely private, between God and oneself, isolated from one's social persona. For opponents of the argument, moral judgment and will are united, but they acknowledge that respecting some things—'civils'—conscience is not really in play, or not in play in the same way. By identifying conscience more or less exclusively with 'spirituals' they implicitly bifurcate the world and accept the priority of 'law' in the secular realm. As Leites suggests, law or legal judgment, to the extent that is was merely secular, 'could modify intentions without having to modify judgments about what was morally right or wrong'.[169] In other words, obeying the law respecting 'civils' did not involve the kind of moral compromise that obeying it respecting 'spirituals' would have. Both positions—that of proponents and that of opponents—would tend to make conscience a separate, private, spiritual thing.

Again, Hobbes illustrates some of these tendencies and their implications in an accentuated—and therefore fairly clear or even stark—way.

We will recall that, in Hobbes's view, for humans in a state of nature, good and evil are matters of appetite and aversion. But since this condition is common to everyone, the individual person's position in the state of nature is precarious. The imperative of self-preservation leads people to desire peace; this disposition towards peace becomes a primary natural law. But, failing the means of security that will ensure peace, the realization of that natural law may remain only internal. So, in the *Leviathan*, he observes that '[t]he laws of nature oblige *in foro interno*, that is to say, they bind to a desire that they should take place; but *in foro externo*, that is, to the putting them in act, not always'.[170] That is because, until there is some guarantee that others will be tractable, will fulfil their promises, and so on, a person who, in the external forum, realizes the natural law will become 'a prey to others'. So, earlier, in the *Elements*, he had said that '[t]he force … of the law of nature is not *in foro externo*, till there be security for man to obey it; but is

167 Bagshaw, p. 13; EEBO 54584:10. See also, for example, Burroughs, p. 6; EEBO image 58212:4.

168 Tully, 'Governing Conduct', 51.

169 Leites, 'Casuistry and Character', p. 129.

170 Hobbes, *Leviathan*, p. 99.

always *in foro interno*, wherein the action of obedience being unsafe, the will and readiness to perform is taken for the performance'.[171]

These observations carry a number of implications. For one thing, they radically separate internal obedience to the law of nature from actual or outward obedience. Moreover, they tend to identify performance with the internal will to perform. Both these positions, I think, tend to make conscience—even with respect to acknowledging 'natural law'—a private matter.

This tendency is further reinforced by the mechanism by which natural law becomes operative in the external forum. Indeed, as we have noticed previously, Hobbes says that 'the laws of nature'—equity, justice, gratitude, and so on—are not properly laws 'in the condition of mere nature': they become 'actually laws' 'when a commonwealth is once settled', at which time they become 'commands of the commonwealth'.[172] We have noticed as well that, whereas in the state of nature the 'rule of good and evil' is taken 'from the person of the [individual] man', in a commonwealth it is taken 'from the person that representeth it'.[173] In other words, it is 'the reason of this our artificial man, the commonwealth, and his command that maketh law ...'.[174]

In a sense this is obvious: of course the sovereign makes law. But Hobbes's claim is more radical than this: the law of the sovereign is the measure of good and evil. An implication of this is that that law becomes in some sense the measure of the citizen's conscience, in a much more comprehensive way than it is, for example, for St. German.

Further insight as to where this leaves conscience may be gained from considering Hobbes's position on the 'liberty of conscience' issue. In the *Elements*, his strategy is to narrow what is absolutely essential to Christian belief to a single tenet: belief in Jesus as Saviour; everything else is 'SUPERSTRUCTION'.[175] On this view, the only circumstance in which a subject would be justified in asserting his conscience against the sovereign would be where there was a command which amounted to 'a denial of that faith which is necessary to our salvation'.[176] Since almost no professedly Christian sovereign would issue such a command, liberty of conscience would almost never justify disobedience. In the *Leviathan* Hobbes takes the argument even further. Even if a sovereign should forbid belief in Christ, '[t]o this I answer that such forbidding is of no effect, because belief and unbelief never follow men's commands'.[177] If people are commanded to deny Christ, they apparently should obey the command, because '[p]rofession with the tongue is but an external thing', not inconsistent with their holding in their hearts the faith of

171 Hobbes, *Elements*, p. 97.

172 Hobbes, *Leviathan*, p. 174.

173 Ibid., p. 29.

174 Ibid., p. 176.

175 Hobbes, *Elements*, p. 144.

176 Ibid.

177 Hobbes, *Leviathan*, p. 338.

Christ.[178] This would appear to be an extreme instance of the 'outward conformity can be compatible with inward integrity' argument.

Once more, it has the effect of relegating conscience very much to an internal, private sphere. As for conscience in the civil arena, that is a matter of the sovereign's commands. Thus, not surprisingly, Hobbes identifies as one of a number of 'weak and false principles' which are 'contrary to the peace of mankind' the notion 'that men shall judge of what is lawful and unlawful, not by the law itself, but by their own consciences (that is to say, by their own private judgments)'.[179] This is, of course, consistent with his identification of peace as the primordial imperative of natural law: the whole point of the establishment of the commonwealth is to maintain peace; thus, obedience to the sovereign is the primary obligation of conscience. This leaves private conscience as a subjective thing, with very little or no role to play at the public level. The public conscience may be subjective as well—subjective to the sovereign—but once expressed it becomes the measure to which all else must bend. The implication for the Chancellor is not necessarily that there is no role for conscience. However, to the extent that he is concerned with conscience, it is to articulate what is implicit in the sovereign's commands but not yet explicit in the positive law. It would thus appear to entail equity in the sense of getting at the intent of the positive law, not of correcting it or modifying it according to moral criteria.

Hobbes's position can hardly be said to have been conventional wisdom in his own time—if it ever has been. But it is indicative of the kinds of pressures bearing upon the concept of conscience, and the tendency for the private-public split to become more pronounced, with the effect that conscience as an independent criterion of public judgment becomes more and more tenuous, or even superfluous.

Some of the problems are suggested in Cudworth's tendentious and (as we might say) reactionary response to Hobbes's position, which he summarizes in the following words: '*That Private Judgment of Good and Evil, is Contradictious to Civil Sovereignty, and a Body Politick, this being One Artificial Man, that must be all Governed, by One Reason and Will.* But Conscience is Private *Judgment of Good and Evil, Lawful and Unlawful, &c.*[180] Cudworth is concerned that this position operates on the assumption that there is *'nothing in Nature*, of a *Publick* or *Common Good*, Nothing of *Duty* or *Obligation*, but all are *Private Appetite*, and *Utility* …' (p. 898). On this view, private conscience—if it can be called conscience at all—is radically subjective and self-serving. Hence, too, it is radically incompatible with the idea of the commonwealth. Only a conscience 'of a *Publick* and *Common Nature*' 'can *Naturally Consociate Mankind* together … and take away that *Private Will* and *Judgment* according to mens *Appetite* and *Utility*, which is Inconsistent with the [body politic]' (p. 898). Cudworth vigorously

178 Ibid.

179 Ibid., p. 225.

180 Cudworth, *True Intellectual System*, p. 898.

repudiates the radical dissociation—indeed, opposition—between private and public conscience that this entails.

Indeed, he says that the idea of a 'Publick Conscience' is '*Nonsense* and *Ridiculous*' (p. 898). Conscience is essentially and necessarily private: 'particular Persons must make a *Judgment* in *Conscience* for themselves' (p. 898). But the fact that conscience is private does not make it subjective, relative, or arbitrary. The private judgment that it entails is always subject to an objective rule, 'either the *Natural* and *Eternal Laws* of *God*, or else his revealed *Will*, things more *Publick*, than the *Civil Laws* of any Country, and of which others also may Judge' (p. 899). What makes conscience common, and—as importantly—commonly accessible, is its being subject to some eternal, and external, rule. On this view, private conscience is not discontinuous with 'public' conscience; they are the same thing. The obligation in conscience to obey the lawful commands of the sovereign arises from divine command, not from a bartering of one's personal inclinations for the promise of security. On this view as well, the insights of private conscience can coherently be said to complement the civil law, not just by discerning the sovereign's intention, but by making the law more complete. Civil law and conscience are not radically at odds, or at odds at all.

The Decline of Casuistry

One last phenomenon which I want to mention at this point is the decline of casuistry towards the end of the seventeenth century. This, in fact, is not a separate tendency, but a consequence of some of the other developments in thinking about conscience that I have been discussing. So, for example, Leites, observing that by the early eighteenth century, casuistry 'was no longer an important force in the religious, intellectual, and moral life of Protestant England',[181] attributes this partly to the rise of the concept of 'a truly moral will'.[182] That casuistry declined, of course, does not mean that the significance of conscience declined.[183] But a different emphasis entailed a departure from the premises upon which casuistical practice was founded. If the focus of one's ethical life was the possession of such a 'moral will', as opposed to applying a method of intellectual analysis to determine whether particular actions are right or wrong, one can see that a science defined in terms of the latter will suffer abatement. As some of what Cudworth says indicates, one kind of moral discernment involves deliberation about objective principles

181 Leites, 'Casuistry and Character', p. 119. Compare Thomas, 'Cases of Conscience', p. 52.

182 Leites, ibid., p. 120.

183 So, for example, John Sharp, who arguably emphasized the volitional character of conscience, nevertheless could maintain that '[t]o have a good Conscience, is the greatest Duty, and the greatest Felicity in the World …' (*Sixteen Casuistical Sermons*, p. 362; ECCO image CW3319329214:371).

that are both accessible to reason and communicable by rational discourse. Or, as Leites puts it, 'casuists tried to reach the will of the individual via the route of his judgment'.[184] A conception of conscience that diminished the role of judgment, that instead privileged the sincere will, would tend to make the special contribution that casuistry claimed to be able to make rather otiose. Thus, the decline of casuistry is largely just evidence of the growing departure from the traditional view of conscience. This decline, in so far as it evidences the end of an era, is perhaps another reason for ending a study like this one in the late seventeenth century.

Conclusion

We have noticed already John Sharp's observation that '[t]here is nothing more in our Mouths than *Conscience*'.[185] This assertion attests to the continuing preoccupation with conscience into the later seventeenth century, and reminds us of the rhetorical power of the word. Conscience was invoked regularly and often. At the same time, the assertion reminds us of the diversity of views of conscience: the word is in *everyone's* mouth, it seems. Earlier, Henry Hammond had complained that conscience is 'worship't in so many corporeous shapes, that there is … scarce any thing so vile … but hath the favour or lucke to be mistaken for *Conscience*, and receive all the respect, that I say, not adoration, that belongs to it'.[186]

Sharp claims that, in spite of its being so frequently invoked, conscience is poorly understood—and he, like others, purports to explain it. But 'it is not understood' is a kind of cipher for 'there is no agreement as to what it means'. The implication of the stance taken by a number of writers is that, if only people could correctly understand conscience, then all the disagreement would dissipate. The position taken by orthodox writers was that conscience was an objective concept, having a unity of meaning and a coherence of application that tended to be defined in terms of their view of the matter. But the multifariousness of the understandings of conscience and its implications made this orthodox view increasingly problematic. The diversity of perspective was too insistent. The result was that, in spite of gallant attempts to preserve the integrity of the concept, and to continue its appropriation by the established institutions of religion (and, indeed, of law), both dissidents and the orthodox came to associate conscience more and more with the private, the internal, the spiritual—in other words, with the individual—in a more radical sense than it had been before. Whether this made conscience 'subjective' is debatable: those who invoked conscience probably thought that they were applying objective moral principles. But the decision about where to find those principles and what they were became an increasingly individual activity. These tendencies further compromised the cogency of conscience as a juristic principle.

184 Leites, 'Casuistry and Character', p. 129.

185 Sharp, *Discourse*, p. 1; EEBO image 37553:3.

186 Hammond, p. 1; EEBO image 123411:2.

Not only was conscience—or what conscience dictated—radically variable, but the sphere in which conscience operated was increasingly distinguished from the sphere in which civil law operated. Conscience increasingly was separated from the magistrate's sphere of concern, rather than being seen as somehow informing it.

Chapter 8
Later Seventeenth-Century Equity and Lord Nottingham

Introduction

Conscience continued to be very much a part of the discourse of equity throughout the seventeenth century. In his chapter 'Of the Chauncerie', William Sheppard (1595–1674) equates equity and conscience, writing, 'Conscience or Equity (as our Law takes it) is said to bee *Tacitum animi infallibileq[ue] facti nostri judicium, à communi Justitiæ formula quam Deus insculpsit omnibus hominibus productum, per quod accusatur res mala, & defenditur bona …*'.[1] This observation, apparently copied from William West without attribution,[2] is noteworthy not only for presenting the conventional chancery/equity/conscience nexus, but also for ascribing to conscience the usual characteristics: it is infallible; it relates to principles of common justice; it is in all of us and is the same for all of us. Sheppard goes on to explain that this conscience, 'being aided and assisted by the Laws of God, Nature, Nations, Reason, and our Country', provides the 'Rule' by which courts of equity operate 'to allay, qualifie, and temper the rigor, severity, and sharpnesse of the Common Law' in particular cases.[3]

The connection between Chancery and conscience continues to be made in ways with which we are familiar. For one thing, as the quotation from Sheppard indicates, conscience continues to be regarded as a criterion of judgment in equity. This point is made in a variety of related ways. Thomas Fuller (1608–61) says that the 'principal imployment' of the Chancellor is 'to mittigate the rigour of the Common Law with Conscientious qualifications';[4] Thomas Blount (1618–79)

---

1 William Sheppard, *The Faithful Councellor: or the Marrow of the Law* (London, 1651), p 596; EEBO image 48696:204. (Roughly, 'The silent infallible judgment of our soul and of our deed from the common formula of justice which God has inscribed in all men, by which the evil matter is accused and the good defended'). Sheppard repeats this statement in *An Epitome of All the Common & Statute Laws of this Nation* (London, 1656), p. 193; EEBO image 101814:108.

2 William West, 'Of the Chauncerie' in *Three Treatises of the Second Part of Symbolæography* (London, 1594), sig. B1r; EEBO image 29131:41, citing Johan Oldendorp.

3 Sheppard, p. 596; EEBO image 48696:204.

4 Thomas Fuller, *The History of the Worthies of England* (London, 1662), p. (second of two numbered) 16; EEBO image 54862:12.

allows the Chancellor 'absolute power to moderate the Written Law, governing his Judgment by the Law of Nature and Conscience';[5] the compiler of *Reports of Cases Taken and Adjudged in the Court of Chancery* observes that English monarchs have, since the separate central courts were established, 'justiced and relieved their Subjects from the Rigor and Extremity of Law by the Rules of Equity and Conscience';[6] and William Brown (*fl.* 1671–1705) notes that '*Matters of Equity, or Conscience*' are determined by the Chancellor.[7] Similarly, Chancery is commonly referred to as a 'Court of Conscience'.[8] Further, it is seen, or the Chancellor is seen, as distributing the sovereign's conscience—a point made both while the monarchy was in abeyance[9] and while it was in place.[10]

Just as writers on Chancery continue to assume the virtual equation of conscience with equity, so too does conscience continue to figure routinely in Chancery pleadings throughout this period, as is attested by the various manuals of Chancery practice published in the later seventeenth century.[11] These manuals display continuity with earlier works of the genre, so that, for example, Brown's dedication[12] to *The Clerk's Tutor* acknowledges West's *Symbolæography*,

---

5 Thomas Blount, *Nomo-Lexikon: A Law-Dictionary* (London, 1670) under 'Chancellor'; EEBO image 57644:32. In the same entry, he says that the Chancellor judges according to 'Conscience and Equity'.

6 'The Jurisdiction of the Court of Chancery Vindicated' in *Reports of Cases Taken and Adjudged in the Court of Chancery* (London, 1693), p. 10; EEBO image 29452:177.

7 William Brown, *Praxis Almæ Curiæ Cancellariæ* (2nd edn, 2 vols, London, 1705), vol. 2, p. 47; ECCO image CW106378798:54. The first edition is dated 1694, and purports to relate to 'Causes of the greatest Moment (wherein Equity hath been allowed) which have been Commenced in the High Court of Chancery, For more than 30. Years last past'.

8 See, for example, Sheppard, p. 597; EEBO image 48696:204, Edward Leigh (1602–71), 'Epistle Dedicatory' (to John Lisle (1610–64), one of the Lords Commissioners of the Great Seal during the Commonwealth), *A Philologicall Commentary: or, an Illustration of the Most Obvious and Useful Words of the Law* (London, 1658), sig. A5v; EEBO image 170016:5 (Leigh presumes to admonish Lisle, '[l]et conscience bear sway in all your publike and private determinations'), and Walter Williams, *Jus Appellandi ad Regem Ipsum a Cancelaria* (London, 1684), pp. 6, 121 EEBO images 36889:9, 66.

9 See *Considerations Touching the Dissolving or Taking away the Court of Chancery* (London, 1653), where Chancery is described as 'the *conscience* of the *Supreme Authority*' (p. 4; EEBO image 61188:5).

10 See, for example, John Hacket, *Scrinia Reserata: A Memorial offer'd to the Great Deservings of John Williams, D.D.* (London, 1693), p. 56; EEBO image 49492:30 and *The Practice of the High Court of Chancery* (London, 1672), p. 38; EEBO image 33548:24 ('the Lord Chancellour judgethe as by the kings own Conscience').

11 Among them, *The Compleat Clark* (3rd edn, London, 1671), William Brown's *The Clerk's Tutor in Chancery* (London, 1688) and his *Praxis Almæ Curiæ Cancellariæ.*

12 To Lord Chancellor Jeffreys (1645–89); sig. A2r, EEBO image 98107:3. The third edition (1705) is dedicated in essentially the same terms to Lord Keeper Sir Nathan Wright.

remarking that, while the latter was pretty comprehensive for its time, it no longer adequately reflects the machinations of 'subtle Contrivers of Fraud'.

To document all the references to conscience in these productions would be long and repetitive. They appear over and over again.[13] But one can identify typical, even formulaic, elements. So, customarily, after detailing the facts, the petitioner, or 'orator', will allege that the acts of the defendant (or the defendant and his confederates) are 'contrary to all Equity and good Conscience'.[14] Fairly typically, the petitioner will then assert that he has no means of redress by the strict course of the common law—meaning, usually, that he does not have access to the kind of proof that the common law requires. He will allege that there were clandestine dealings and/or that witnesses are dead or have gone 'over the seas'. Thus, it is necessary for the defendant to be examined under oath. For example, in one case, the petitioner says that he 'cannot prove the Premisses in so exact and strict a manner as is required by the Common Law', and that he will be remediless 'unless by the aid and assistance of this Honourable Court your Orator may have a particular discovery ... by the Oath of the [defendant] who well knows, and is satisfied in his Conscience of the truth of all and singular the Premisses before herein set forth'.[15] Assuming that the truth will thus be discovered the petitioner prays to be relieved according to 'equity and good conscience' or, sometimes, 'according to the rules of Equity and good Conscience'.[16]

As I have intimated, there is something *pro forma* and uncritical about these allusions to conscience in the context of equity—not just in the forms of pleadings, but also in the commentators' continuing characterization of Chancery as a court of conscience.

At the same time, there are indications in the materials, especially some cases, which suggest a more substantive engagement with conscience as a live issue. For example, in *Lord Cornbury* v. *Middleton*, Justice Wyld, who was assisting Lord Keeper Bridgman (1606–74), affirms: 'This is a case in Equity and in Conscience,

---

[13] So, for example, one can find such references on the following pages of Brown's *Praxis Almæ Curiæ Cancellariæ*, vol. 1, pp. 202, 211, 214, 218, 221, 235, 247, 252, 257, 261, 269, 271, 279, 284, 285, 286, 290, 305, 315, 318, 335, 341, 347, 355, 362, 368, 376, 383, 384, 403, 406, 410, 413, 414, 438, 451, 459, 460, 470 and 476; EECO images CW106378798:209, 218, 221, 225, 228, 242, 254, 259, 264, 268, 276, 278, 286, 291, 292, 293, 297, 313, 323, 326, 343, 349, 355, 363, 370, 376, 384, 391, 392, 411, 414, 418, 421, 432, 446, 459, 467, 468, 498, and 484, respectively.

[14] Or some variant, such as 'against all Justice, Right, Equity and good Conscience' (ibid., p. 368; EECO image CW106378798:376).

[15] Ibid., p. 214; ECCO image CW106378798:221. Geoffrey Gilbert (1674–1726), in *The History and Practice of the High Court of Chancery* (2 vols, Dublin, 1758) observes that 'proper interrogatories' are 'put to the conscience of the defendant upon the fact and circumstances' (vol. 1, p. 94; ECCO image CW102104288:95).

[16] See, for example, *Compleat Clark*, p. 282; EEBO image 48193:148.

and this Court is to help that side that hath Conscience'.[17] He proceeds to analyse the issue of conscience in terms of notice, finding it 'against good Conscience' that a party with notice should succeed, and reiterates: 'the Court must judge with Conscience, and not against Conscience'.[18] Similarly, counsel in *Searle* v. *Lane*, another case involving the issue of notice, argue that '*that* rigour of the law, ought not to be carried on against conscience, in a court of equity', and that their client (an administrator who had paid the deceased's lower-order debts unaware that a decree had been entered for those of a higher order) 'had no notice of the decree, and could not divine that there was any debt owing of a superior nature'; therefore, 'it would be against conscience to charge him with it'.[19]

My objective in this chapter is to consider materials which might permit a more searching analysis of the concept of the conscience of equity, and particularly the implications of Lord Nottingham's very deliberate distinction between private conscience and political or 'civil' conscience, the latter presumably being proper to equity.

The Political Challenge to Chancery

Before getting to that, however, I wish to highlight two matters. One of these I have already discussed at length in Chapter 7: that is, the increasing destabilization of conscience as a result of religious controversy and the apparent realization that the idea of a uniform, objective conscience was difficult to sustain. The other relates specifically to political challenges to the Chancery itself, for, during the period of the Civil War and the Commonwealth, the continued existence of the Court had been more seriously threatened than ever before,[20] and, indeed, in 1653 Parliament voted to abolish the Chancery,[21] although this vote was not carried into effect.

---

17 *Lord Cornbury* v. *Middleton* (1671) 1 Ch. Cas. 208 at 209, 22 ER 765 at 766.

18 Ibid.

19 *Searle* v. *Lane* (1688) 2 Vern. 88 at 88, 23 ER 667 at 667. The Chancellor, however, determines that the decree for the debt is itself notice. Compare *Lee* v. *Boles* (1682) 2 Ch. Cas. 95 at 97, 22 ER 863 at 864, where counsel argues that, though 'in Strictness of Law' an agreement is not effective, 'yet in natural Justice it is all one as to the Conscience of the Parties, where there is no Fraud or Practice, nor Surprize in obtaining it '.

20 'Introduction', *Lord Nottingham's 'Manual of Chancery Practice' and 'Prolegomena of Chancery and Equity'*, ed. D.E.C. Yale (Cambridge, 1965), p. 7.

21 Among contemporary tracts relating to this issue are L.D., *An Exact Relation of the Proceedings and Transactions of the Late Parliament* (London, 1653) (purporting to describe the proceedings, but attacking the dilatoriness and expense of Chancery), Henry Robinson, *Certaine Proposals in Order to a New Modelling of the Lawes, and Law-Proceedings* (London, 1653) (arguing for the abolition of Chancery as a separate court), *Considerations Touching the Dissolving or Taking Away the Court of Chancery* (London, 1653) (arguing against the abolition of Chancery, largely on the basis that its functioning is integral to the ordinary courts), and Edward Leigh, *Second Considerations Concerning*

Unlike the challenge involved in the Coke-Ellesmere controversy of the early years of the century, which could be characterized as largely legal and jurisdictional, this later challenge was more radical and political, going to certain of the fundamental features of the Court as a court of law, namely, its ostensible absoluteness and arbitrariness. In so far as its definition of its jurisdiction in terms of conscience can be identified with these features, the Chancery had at least in some measure to re-invent itself in ways which rendered these features less obvious *foci* of criticism. Correspondingly, its status as a court of conscience needed to be qualified.

As we have noticed elsewhere, it was customary during this early period to remark upon the 'two-fold Power' of the Chancery. Thus, Sheppard observes that, while common-law judges proceed '*Secundum potestatem ordinariam*', the Chancellor proceeds '*Secundum potestatem absolutam*', and then goes on to say that in fact the Chancery has both an ordinary power and 'another Power that is more arbitrary and unlimited', that is, the equitable jurisdiction *per se*.[22] Similarly, Walter Williams (d. 1708) says that Chancery consists of two courts, 'one Ordinary, wherein the Lord Chancellor or Lord Keeper ... proceeds according to the right line of the Law', and

> the other is Extraordinary, wherein the Chancellor ought to proceed according to the Rule of Equity, which according to what it is now taken, is what is according to the Chancellor's single Conscience ...; it is (say some) an absolute Power without controul ... and spreadeth it self most largely without any Limitation ....

Moreover, it renders the judgments of the other courts 'vain and ineffectual, *durante bene placito*, of the Chancellor or Keeper ...'.[23] These observations encompass a number of matters of concern to Chancery critics: the court exercises uncontrolled power; it is bound to no other rule than the conscience of the Chancellor for the time being; and it interferes with the ordinary course of the common law. Thus, critics are wont to characterize it pejoratively as 'a back doore for the Kings Arbitry'[24] or as '*an absolute Prerogative Royall*'.[25] For such critics, 'conscience' is regarded as a rhetorical subterfuge, putting a benevolent face upon what they regard as an abuse of law. Thus, Nathaniel Bacon (1593–1660) says that the court has, historically, augmented its powers 'under the colours of Equity, Honor, Conveniency, and Conscience',[26] and the Leveller John Warr (*fl.* 1648–49), whom one might admittedly expect not to be particularly temperate,

---

the High Court of Chancery, and the Most Excellent Ordinance for the Regulation and Limitation of that Court (London, 1658).

22 Sheppard, p. 656; EEBO image 48696:234.

23 Williams, pp. 43–4; EEBO image 36889:27–8.

24 Nathaniel Bacon, *The Continuation of an Historicall Discourse of the Government of England* (London, 1651), p. 35; EEBO image 165805:31.

25 Robinson, p. 4; EEBO image 62328:4.

26 Nathaniel Bacon, p. 35; EEBO image 165805:31.

complains that Chancery has 'doubled and trebled' wrongs upon the populace 'under pretence of equity, and a Court of Conscience', and that, again, 'under a pretence of Conscience' has 'devolve[d] all causes upon meer will'.[27]

Of the components of this negative complex—arbitrariness, unlimitedness, and interference with regular law—associated with Chancery, conscience was particularly linked to the evil of arbitrariness. One polemicist writes that '[e]very one will, or at the least will seem, to detest Arbitrarie Autoritie in Judicatories',[28] and attributes this character to Chancery, which, he says, unlike the other courts of Westminster, whose judgments 'are given according to the Rules of Law', 'is not tied unto Rules'.[29] An implication is that people cannot know why, for example, 'their Lands and Goods [might be] taken from them', except that it is 'becaus the Judges in their opinions think it to bee equitie'.[30] As we have already noticed, Williams (whose thesis is that there should be an appeal from the Chancery to the King himself) criticizes the Court because the 'Rule of Equity' it applies is supplied by 'the Chancellors single Conscience': 'what Rules or General Notions the Lord Chancellor or Lord Keeper ... doth assign unto himself for Limitation of Equity, and direction of his Conscience, those lie hid and concealed in his own Breast ...'.[31]

One of the most sustained critiques of Chancery in these (and other) terms is that of Robert Atkyns (1621–1709).[32] Although it appeared late in the century, it is perhaps representative of attitudes that arose much earlier and persisted. In his view, the common law is 'the true Natural and Original Law of *England*', and not 'any new Rules devised ... at the Discretion of any one Man, tho never so Great, or Wise, or Learned'.[33] He repeatedly disparages a jurisdiction involving the discretion of a single person. Shall the common laws, he says, 'be all made Subject to the Sudden and Arbitrary Opinion of any one Man ... under a pretence of Equity …?'[34] How can a person 'Prognosticate, what [will] be the Opinion ... of One single Person upon [his] Case, who is not so tied to Rules as the Judges are' but judges 'according to his Discretion, by an Absolute and Arbitrary, and

---

27 John Warr, *A Brief Survey of the English Laws, and, Their Unsoundness and Corruption Discovered* (London, 1653), p. 14; EEBO image 151437:11.

28 *Reasons Against the Bill, Intituled, An Act for Countie-Registers, Wills and Administrations* (London, 1653), p. 2; EEBO image 133365:3.

29 Ibid., pp. 11, 12; EEBO images 133365:7–8.

30 Ibid., p. 11; EEBO image 133365:7.

31 Williams, pp. 47–8; 36889:29–30. We may recall that even Chancery proponents like Robert Snagg and Ellesmere acknowledge this ultimate fact.

32 Robert Atkyns, *An Enquiry into the Jurisdiction of the Chancery in Causes of Equity* (London, 1695).

33 Ibid., pp. 11, 12; EEBO images 57482:8–9. We may recall that Chancery partisans customarily emphasize that the Chancellor is chosen for his learning and integrity.

34 Ibid., p. 28; EEBO image 57482:17.

Dictatorian Power'?[35] Because cases in Chancery 'depend upon the sole Opinion and Conscience of one single Person', are decided solely 'by the Rules of his own Conscience', his powers are 'Absolute and Arbitrary'.[36]

To be sure, criticisms of conscience as being too arbitrary to be tenable as a juristic principle are not a new phenomenon in the mid-seventeenth century. We have noticed examples going back at least to the early sixteenth century in observations that different Chancellors may have more strict or more lax consciences. But, with the constitutional crisis of the seventeenth century, the challenge to the legitimacy of 'Arbitrary Autoritie in Judicatories' became much more pervasive, radical, and political. In some measure, Chancery's survival depended upon its being able to respond to such criticisms, upon its being able to present what it dispensed as being more like *regular* law. Clearly, this enterprise must engage its character as a 'court of conscience', because the criterion of conscience was perceived to be a fundamental feature of its variability, or irregularity.

Lord Nottingham and the Regularization of Equity

The jurist conventionally and particularly associated with the early regularization of equity was Heneage Finch, Lord Nottingham, who held the Great Seal, first as Lord Keeper and then as Lord Chancellor, from 1673 to 1682. He was not the first Chancellor to attempt to make Chancery jurisdiction more law-like: we have seen evidence of this impulse in, for example, Lord Ellesmere and Lord Keeper Coventry. Nor was he the last. Nor was he the only one of his own time to do so. But because he is commonly regarded as the father of modern or systematic equity[37] and because he addressed the issue of the conscience of equity directly (albeit not in any great analytical detail), he is the obvious focus for this part of my study.

---

35 Ibid., p. 30; EEBO image 57482:18.

36 Ibid., p. 31; EEBO image 57482:18.

37 See, for example, D.E.C. Yale, 'Introduction' to *Lord Nottingham's Chancery Cases* (2 vols, London, 1957), vol. 1, p. xlv: 'the whole tendency of Lord Nottingham's work was towards a scientific arrangement of equity; he was the father of systematic equity'. Not everyone has applauded Nottingham's approach. Roger North (1653–1734), brother of Nottingham's successor Francis North, Lord Guilford (1637–85), characterizes it as follows: 'he was Formalist … Supposing that, if he split the Hair, and, with his Gold Scales, determined reasonably on one side …, Justice was nicely done' (*The Life of the Right Honourable Francis North, Baron Guilford* [London, 1742], p. 198; ECCO image CW103613479:212). North prefers his brother's approach, 'having no content in any Thing but the Substance of Justice' (ibid.). Similarly, he criticizes Nottingham's judgment in *Howard* v. *Duke of Norfolk*, again preferring the approach of his brother—'knowing no Rule but his Judgment of the Law, and Conscience in Equity'—in reversing Nottingham's decree (ibid., p. 208; image 222).

Nottingham directly and explicitly responded to concerns about equity's arbitrariness. In the *Prolegomena*, he asserts that 'if equity be tied to no rule … everything becomes arbitrary',[38] a point which he reiterates in the case of *Earl of Feversham* v. *Watson*:

> But yet Justice is a severe thing and knows no compliance nor can bend itself to any man's conveniences, and equity itself would cease to be Justice if the rules and measures of it were not certain and known. For if conscience be not dispensed by the rules of science, it were better for the subject there were no Chancery at all than that men's estates should depend upon the pleasure of a Court which took upon itself to be purely arbitrary.[39]

'Rules', 'measures' and 'science' are by-words of his preoccupation with making equity more regular and law-like than it was frequently perceived to be.

At the same time, he did not abandon conscience as a touchstone of equity; indeed, he appears to have referred to it as, or more, frequently than his predecessors.[40] Thus, he continues to speak of Chancery as a 'court of conscience';[41] he refers to the 'conscience of this Court'[42] or to 'conscience' as if it were synonymous with the court[43] or with equity;[44] he observes that 'all courts which hold plea in equity … administer the conscience of the King';[45] he asserts that 'though rights in law are governed by rules of law, yet rules in equity are governed only by conscience'[46] so that what accords with 'good conscience' is to

---

38 Nottingham, *Prolegomena*, p. 194.

39 *Earl of Feversham* v. *Watson* (1678), *Lord Nottingham's Chancery Cases*, ed. D.E.C. Yale (2 vols, London, 1961), vol. 2, p. 639.

40 It is, of course, impossible to be certain about this because of the incompleteness of the records. Indeed, we have a more complete record of Nottingham's reasoning in equity than of his predecessors.

41 See, for example, *Burges* v. *Skinner* (1673/74), *Nottingham's Chancery Cases*, vol. 1, p. 31; *Wyvell* v. *Beckwith* (1676), ibid., vol. 2, p. 451; *Hatchett* v. *Bindon* (1677), ibid., vol. 2, p. 566; *Coke* v. *Bishop* (1677), ibid., vol. 2, p. 570; *Staples* v. *Stone* (1679), ibid., vol. 2, p. 740.

42 See, for example, *Nurse* v. *Yerworth* (1674), ibid., vol. 1, p. 119 and *Lord Mordant* v. *Earl of Peterborough* (1674/75), ibid., vol. 1, p. 142.

43 See, for example, *Danby* v. *Read* (1675), ibid., vol. 1, p. 156: 'conscience will not suffer extortion to continue by craft or engine'.

44 See, for example, *Bateman* v. *Tidcomb* (1676), ibid., vol. 1, p. 347: 'the Court will consider the conscience of the award …'.

45 *Lenthall* v. *Waring* (1676), ibid., vol. 1, p. 333. See also Nottingham, *Prolegomena*, p. 185.

46 *Cox* v. *Quantock* (1674), *Nottingham's Chancery Cases*, vol. 1, p. 102. Compare *Norcliffe* v. *Worsly* (1674), ibid., vol. 1, p. 86, *Salsbury* v. *Bagott* (1677), ibid., vol. 2, p. 503, *Barkly* v. *Penn* (1680/1), ibid., vol. 2, p. 863, *Coulston* v. *Gardner* (1680/1), ibid., vol. 2, p. 871.

be approved,[47] what is 'against conscience' is to be reproved,[48] and standing upon legal rights may be unconscientious.[49] Conscience is the judge in equity[50] and equities are "to be governed as Conscience directs this Court [Chancery] …'.[51]

Given, on the one hand, Nottingham's concern to forestall arbitrariness and, on the other, his continuing invocation of conscience, the question becomes: 'How does he reconcile the ostensible vagaries of the latter with his project of developing a ruled, measured, scientific system of equity?' Or, putting the question slightly differently: 'How does he understand or limit the notion of conscience so as to make it compatible with the regular equity which he espoused?'

Conscientia civilis and *conscientia interna*

A crucial distinction for Nottingham in this regard is that between, ostensibly, private conscience and public conscience. In the *Prolegomena*, he says that 'there is a twofold conscience, *viz. conscientia politica et civilis, et conscientia naturalis et interna*' and that '[m]any things are against inward and natural conscience, which cannot be reformed by the regular and political administration of equity'.[52] He makes the point again in 'the great case' of *Cook* v. *Fountain*: '[w]ith such a conscience which is only *naturalis et interna* this Court hath nothing to do; the conscience by which I am to proceed is merely *civilis et politica*, and tied to certain measures …'.[53] As Yale points out, this kind of distinction was not new with Nottingham.[54] It corresponds, at least roughly, with the venerable distinction between the *forum internum* and the *forum externum*, and we will recall Francis

---

47 See, for example, *Albermarle* v. *Cutler* (1676/7), ibid., vol. 2, p. 470, *Hyde* v. *Seymour* (1678), ibid., vol. 2, p. 709, *Williams* v. *Day* (1680), ibid., vol. 2, p. 821 ('let the mother be charged no further than in good conscience she ought to be and not according to niceties of law'), *Gibson* v. *Kenvyn* (1682), ibid., vol. 2, p. 931.

48 See, for example, *Burges* v. *Skinner* (1673/4), ibid., vol. 1, p. 31, *Hinckly* v. *Hinckly* (1674), ibid., vol. 1, p. 76, *Bowyer* v. *Birds* (1675), ibid., vol. 1, p. 193, *King* v. *Hatchett* (1676), ibid., vol. 1, p. 344, *Gawdy* v. *Marriot* (1676/7), ibid., vol. 2, p. 476, *Lawrence* v. *Berney* (1677), ibid., vol. 2, p. 513, *Nance* v. *Cook* (1677), ibid., vol. 2, p. 560 (plea), *Butcher* v. *Hinton* (1677), ibid., vol. 2, p. 578, *Duke of Newcastle* v. *Heathcott* (1677/8), ibid., vol. 2, p. 612 (plea), *Moor* v. *Hinton* (1677/8), ibid, vol. 2, p. 619, *Huntingdon and Scarsdale* v. *Greenville* (1682), ibid., vol. 2, p. 921 (plea).

49 See, for example, *Anon.* (1674), ibid., vol. 1, p. 63, *Rosser* v. *Evans* (1675), ibid., vol. 1, p. 221, *Wyvell* v. *Beckwith* (1676), ibid., vol. 2, pp. 450–51, *Brend* v. *Brend* (1682), ibid., vol. 2, p. 920.

50 *Hickson* v. *Wytham* (1675) 1 Ch. Cas. 248 at 249, 22 ER 784 at 784.

51 *Norcliffe* v. *Worsly* (1674) 1 Ch. Cas. 234 at 236, 22 ER 777 at 778.

52 Nottingham, *Prolegomena*, p. 194.

53 *Cook* v. *Fountain* (1676), *Nottingham's Chancery Cases*, vol. 1, p. 371.

54 Yale, 'Introduction', *Nottingham's Chancery Cases*, vol. 1, p. xlvi. George Spence maintains that, in making this distinction, Nottingham 'was not making a rule but declaring

Bacon's allusion to Justice Fenner's distinction between a party's 'private conscience' and 'the general conscience of the realm, which is Chancery',[55] as well as Ellesmere's between *lex conscientiæ politicæ* and *lex conscientiæ Divinæ*.[56] Yale claims that '[t]he novelty resides in [Nottingham's] application ... of this antithesis to equity in a general form'.[57]

It should be remembered that the antithesis, at least in some versions, did not go unquestioned. We have noticed that, in a work dedicated to Nottingham, Ralph Cudworth rejected the notion of a 'Publick Conscience' as '*Nonsense* and *Ridiculous*'.[58] Conscience is inevitably private, although not arbitrary or subjective, but rather subject to God's laws. Of course, Cudworth here is responding to certain of Hobbes's propositions, and is not considering the private/public dichotomy in the same context as is Lord Nottingham. We will recall that Lord Clarendon—who criticizes Hobbes in rather similar terms[59]—deplores Bishop Williams's invocation of the antithesis in advising Charles I in the case of Strafford that he should, as King, follow a 'publick' conscience, whatever his private conscience as a man should tell him.[60] Again, however, one must be mindful of the context of this critique. Clarendon may simply be criticizing the cloaking of *realpolitik* in the flattering garb of conscience rather than flatly rejecting the idea of a conscience whose sphere of application is the public as opposed to simply the private realm.[61] Since I shall be relying heavily on Lord Nottingham's distinction, I did want to

---

what had become the established doctrine of the Court' (*The Equitable Jurisdiction of the Court of Chancery* (2 vols, Philadelphia, 1846), vol. 1, p. 417.

55 Francis Bacon, *Reading on the Statute of Uses*, in *The Works of Francis Bacon*, eds J. Spedding, R.L. Ellis and D.D. Heath (14 vols, London, 1857–74), vol. 7, p. 401.

56 Thomas Egerton (Lord Ellesmere), *Certaine Observations Concerning the Office of the Lord Chancellor* (London, 1651), p. 48; EEBO image 51543:29.

57 Yale, 'Introduction', *Nottingham's Chancery Cases*, vol. 1, p. xlvii.

58 Ralph Cudworth, *The True Intellectual System of the Universe* (London, 1678; reprinted Stuttgart, 1964), p. 898.

59 Like Cudworth, he responds to Hobbes's assertion that one of the '*diseases*' of a commonwealth is the doctrine that '*every private man is Judg of good and evil actions*', noting that 'throughout the whole new Testament the conscience is made the Judg of all we do'. He does resile somewhat from the implications of this position, however, saying that the private conscience does owe obedience to the civil law (Edward Hyde [Lord Clarendon], *A Brief View and Survey of the Dangerous and Pernicious Errors to Church and State, in Mr. Hobbes's Book, Entitled Leviathan* (Oxford, 1676), pp. 161–2; EEBO images 60912:85–6).

60 Edward Hyde (Lord Clarendon), *The History of the Rebellion and Civil Wars in England* (3 vols, Oxford, 1704), vol. 1, pp. 275, 202; ECCO images CW102710855:295, 224. Clarendon also wrote an essay, 'On Conscience', published in *A Compleat Collection of Tracts, by that Eminent Statesman the Right Honourable Edward, Earl of Clarendon* (London, 1747), pp. 162–7; ECCO images CW122271120:173–8, but he does not explicitly address the issue of private *versus* public conscience.

61 In 'On Conscience', he rather sarcastically suggests that 'conscience' perhaps should 'be expunged out of all Discourses of Religion and Honesty' and 'assigned and

flag the facts that the idea of a public conscience was contested and that it might have different implications in different contexts.

It bears remarking too that Nottingham himself did not invariably adhere to the distinction. Sometimes his own conscience is very much in the foreground in his judicial functions. So, for example, in *Howard* v. *Duke de Norfolk*, he defends his decision by saying 'it is my Decree, I must be saved by my own Faith, and must not decree against my own Conscience and Reason'.[62] To be sure, he is not applying a private conscience whose criteria are more comprehensive than some kind of public conscience. But nor is he positing a judicial conscience that is radically discontinuous from his own personal conscience. In *Lawrence* v. *Berney*, he elaborates, at least implicitly. There, he distinguishes a decree of a predecessor which can be executed 'by the ordinary Process and Forms of the Court' from one 'where the common Process of the Court will not serve'.[63] In the former case, 'whatever the Iniquity of the first Decree may be', the Court is bound to assist it', 'for in all this, the Conscience of the present Judge is not concerned, because it is not his Act'.[64] But, where a new decree is required for the execution of the earlier one, 'there this Court desired to be excused, in making it its own Act, to build upon such ill Foundations, and charging his own Conscience with promoting an apparent Injustice'.[65] While one might be tempted to say that judicial consistency is an aspect of public conscience, Nottingham clearly would not follow this line of reasoning to its inevitable conclusion. *His* conscience is involved.

One other point meriting emphasis at the outset is that the expression 'twofold conscience' may be misleading. Nottingham's use of the word 'twofold' and Yale's (and my) use of the word 'antithesis' could be taken to suggest two mutually-exclusive parallel categories, two separate divisions within a larger concept. But the relationship may be vertical rather than lateral, so to speak. That is, *conscientia naturalis et interna* may in some sense comprehend *conscientia politica et civilis*. John Norman describes 'the object of Conscience' as 'whatsoever is morally operable'—'whether external or internal; … whether toward God, or toward man', and whether 'concerning holiness or honesty'.[66] One can conceive of all objects of

appropriated to the Politicians, to cover their Reason of State with ...' (ibid., p. 165, image 176).

62 *Howard* v. *Duke de Norfolk* (1682) 3 Ch. Cas. 40 at 47, 22 ER 955 at 959; he repeats the sentiment at 3 Ch. Cas. 52, 22 ER 962. In the 'Preface to the Reader', the compiler of *The Second Part of Reports of Cases Taken and Adjudged in the Court of Chancery* (London, 1694) quotes Nottingham's words to explain that one reason why Chancery decrees are often reversed by subsequent chancellors is their perceived need to follow the dictates of their own consciences (sig. A3r; EEBO image 33203:4).

63 *Lawrence* v. *Berney* (1677–78) 2 Ch. Rep. 127 at 127, 21 ER 636 at 636.

64 Ibid.

65 Ibid.

66 John Norman, *Cases of Conscience Practically Resolved* (London, 1673), pp. 25, 24; EEBO image 46170:17.

conscience, whatever is 'morally operable', as a large circle, the outer portions of which do not engage the court of equity. But, within that large circle of conscience generally is a smaller circle containing objects of conscience having sufficient additional characteristics (whatever they are) to engage the attention of equity. The residue is the area of purely private conscience. Something like this picture is, I think, implicit in Nottingham's saying 'God forbid, a man should use no better conscience than the Chancery can compel him, however the rule must always hold, that 'tis not fit for a court of equity to do everything that is fit to be done'.[67] What is legally cognizable is only a part of what conscience might require.

A possible qualification of this picture would be *adiaphora*, matters that are morally or spiritually indifferent but that are regulated by positive civil law. Conscience would require us to obey the law, but the particular law would not be an instantiation of a higher-order moral imperative that would bind in any event. Such would be an example of a purely political or civic conscience. But the more problematic area is where equity purports to supplement the law by an appeal to some higher-order law—of reason, or of God. In such a case, the decree of equity would be a legal instantiation of a higher law of conscience. Although I shall continue to invoke the two categories, it is important to keep this picture of their likely relationship in mind. One implication is that clear demarcation is made more difficult, since political or public conscience is continuous with private conscience, almost certainly sharing its basic character.

Normative and Factual Dimensions of Conscience

In essaying to ascertain what Lord Nottingham meant by *conscientia politica et civilis* we must again remember that conscience involves both a normative and a factual, or evidentiary, element. In the conventional account, *synderesis* allows us to apprehend precepts from which we can derive the rules by which we should govern our conduct; this knowledge is applied to the facts we know about ourselves by virtue of that aspect of conscience that serves as 'a thousand witnesses'. As we have seen, the Chancery was not confined by the ordinary rules of proof; it had relatively unfettered means of finding facts. Hence, it could 'examine' the conscience of a defendant, to try to determine what that person alone knew. This did not, of course, involve inquiry as to what norms his or her *synderesis* dictated, but getting at information that conscience afforded. Indeed, it would have been rather meaningless to speak of a particular person's *synderesis* since we know that *synderesis* theoretically involves knowledge that is common to all. We have noticed as well that the Chancellor was commonly said to have been chosen for the quality of his conscience—meaning, presumably, his heightened awareness of relevant norms and his ability to apply those norms to facts otherwise made manifest. Thus, for example, when Nottingham alludes to the practice of ordering

[67] Nottingham, *Prolegomena*, p. 194.

a trial of the facts 'in order to the satisfaction of the conscience of this Court',[68] he is speaking of establishing the minor, factual, premise in the syllogism of conscience. The 'conscience of the court' is ambiguous: it entails not only the application of rules that are ostensibly more finely morally calibrated than those of the common law, but also the possession of more complete information.[69] The source of that information may be the parties' consciences; once ascertained, it becomes the factual basis upon which the court's conscience operates.

As I have just intimated, a way of thinking about this is to recall the 'two syllogisms' often said to comprise the operation of conscience. 'The first, it will be remembered, involves the application of a first principle given by *synderesis* to a minor premise, also normative in substance, to derive a normative conclusion. That conclusion, in turn, becomes the major premise of a second syllogism, the minor of which is some fact about the specific situation in issue, followed by a conclusion about the appropriateness of the conduct entailed by that fact. The major premise of the first syllogism and that of the second are normative elements in conscience and constitute the 'rules' which a court of equity applies. The minor premise of the second syllogism is the factual element in the process, involving the court's information-accessing function. I would say that, in the great majority of cases, when Nottingham refers to 'conscience', he is speaking of the normative dimension. The facts, he generally accepts or assumes, are adequately known. It is the norms implicit in conscience, and in terms of which the facts are being assessed, that he ordinarily means to refer to when he uses expressions such as 'it is against conscience' or 'rules in equity are governed only by conscience'.

My emphasis in what follows will be on this normative dimension of conscience. That is, the general form of my question will be: how does Nottingham limit the normative scope of *conscientia politica et civilis*? In other words, can we identify at least provisional criteria which indicate what categories of conduct and/or psychological states will be beyond the pale of the conscience of equity? At the same time, I do want to take explicit account of the factual element, for at least two reasons. First, in some contexts, it may define what is public as opposed to what is private. That is, 'public conscience' may refer to knowledge available by regular judicial procedures (albeit broader than those of the common law); 'private conscience' would then refer to what is not so known, to what remains secreted in the heart of the individual person. The second reason—closely related, but I think conceptually distinct—would be to say that what is known only to private conscience defines the normative reach of a court of conscience. We might say, for example, that that which is known only to a person and God, though engaging

68 *Lord Mordant* v. *Earl of Peterborough* (1674/75), *Nottingham's Chancery Cases*, vol. 1, p. 142.

69 For an intimation of Nottingham's attitude in this regard, see *Earl of Leicester* v. *Sidney* (1680/81), ibid., vol. 2, p. 856: he claims to have looked closely at the evidence 'as a man that studies to find out the truth and will always take it for the greatest obligation in the world to be better informed'.

private conscience, should not be the concern of equity, not just because it is hard to know, but because it is intrinsically private. So, it might be argued, a plausible place to draw the line between *conscientia naturalis et interna* and *conscientia politica et civilis* is between 'inward things' and overt acts. I shall return to this possibility.

The point I have been making might be illustrated by returning again to *Cook* v. *Fountain*, the case in which Nottingham makes the *conscientia interna*/*conscientia civilis* distinction. The question in that case had to do with the existence of a 'secret trust'. This itself is an ambiguous term. In some contexts a secret trust is a trust not evidenced by certain forms of proof:[70] for example, a trust created by parol outside the express terms of a will. But 'secret trust' can also mean just that—an unknown or unevidenced trust. It appears that Nottingham is using the expression in the latter sense, for he observes that there is *no* effective evidence for the trust: 'no bill charges, no proof can make out, and the defendant denies upon oath'.[71] Having noted this absence or inaccessibility of information, Nottingham says that the existence of the trust is a matter 'between a man and his confessor' and then makes the statement which we have already seen: '[w]ith such a conscience which is only *naturalis et interna* the Court hath nothing to do'.[72]

A plausible reading of this could be that 'public conscience' involves those matters of fact which ordinary procedures of inquiry disclose, and private conscience relates to what one knows about oneself after those ordinary (or, in the case of Chancery, 'extraordinary') procedures have been exhausted. That is, Nottingham may be doing no more than making the fairly obvious point that a tribunal like Chancery can act only on facts proven in the public forum and not on the basis of surmising what really is the case, on the basis of what a party might know but has not revealed. This reading is reinforced, I believe, by his subsequent statement that 'it is infinitely better for the public that a trust, security or agreement, which is wholly secret, should miscarry than that men should lose their estates by the mere fancy and imagination of a chancellor'.[73] The 'fancy and imagination' of the Chancellor presumably would not apply to the enforcement of a proven trust, but rather to his finding facts supporting a trust on the basis of flimsy evidence or conjecture.

---

[70] Thus, for example, whereas 'the Law looks only to the outward assurance' the Court of Chancery will enforce 'the inward, and secret trust' (*Practice of the High Court of Chancery*, p. 45; EEBO image 33548:27). Here, apparently, while the common law is satisfied only with a formal 'outward assurance', equity will accept other proof of the trust.

[71] *Cook* v. *Fountain*, *Nottingham's Chancery Cases*, vol. 1, p. 371. He says as well: 'God forbid that such proofs which are not convincing should take away any man's estate' (p. 370).

[72] Ibid., p. 371.

[73] Ibid.

Yale implicitly endorses this reading when he relates Nottingham's words to the 'idea of a private conscience contrasted with the limits of judicial knowledge' found in the 'great mass of medieval literature upon this difference of public and private knowledge in a judge and of his public and private conscience'.[74] Unlike this case, where Nottingham does not have private knowledge of the trust, although he may have suspicions, the conundrum addressed in the literature to which Yale refers is the situation where a judge does have knowledge of material facts in his private or personal capacity, but those facts have not been evidenced judicially in the public forum. So, for example, if A is being tried for murder, and facts are adduced against him in court, but the judge, in his private capacity, knows that A was nowhere near the crime scene at the relevant time, should the judge, or should he not, take into account his private knowledge? Yale suggests, *dubitante*, that Nottingham may have had this literature directly in mind.

He need not, however, have gone so far back to encounter the controversy. It appears in the casuists who were his contemporaries. Taylor devotes some space to the question, ultimately taking issue with the argument that a judge, as a private person, 'must proceed upon the notices and persuasions of his conscience', but, 'as he is a judge, he is to do the office of a judge, and to receive information by witnesses and solemnities of law, and is not to bring his own private conscience to become the public measure'.[75] He goes on to say that although a judge is normally 'tied … to proceed according to allegation and proof, ordinarily and regularly', if he has 'a surer way of evidence', then he is to proceed according to that.[76] He questions the 'two consciences' account:

> If the judge had two consciences, and two real persons, then it were to be granted that they were to be served and attended in their several callings; but it is not so, they are but two persons in fiction of law, but materially, and to all real events, the same: it is the same conscience ministering to divers duties: and therefore as the judge is always that man, so his conscience is the conscience of that man; … the judge is still that man ruled by that conscience.[77]

---

74 Yale, 'Introduction', *Nottingham's Chancery Cases*, vol. 1, p. xlvii.

75 Jeremy Taylor, *Ductor Dubitantium* in *The Whole Works of the Right Rev. Jeremy Taylor D.D.*, ed. A. Taylor (10 vols, London, 1883), vol. 9, p. 104. That Taylor uses the expression 'notices and persuasions of his conscience' perhaps indicates that he is not contemplating only what facts a person knows, but also what rules he believes should apply.

76 Ibid., p. 113. A related point is that factual conclusions dictated by presumptions must yield to the truth otherwise known. As Lord Keeper Bridgman, citing St. German, puts it in *Vanbrough* v. *Cock* (1671) 1 Ch. Cas. 200 at 201, 22 ER 761, 'A Law grounded on a Presumption, if the Presumption be untrue is not to be holden in Conscience …'.

77 Taylor, vol. 9, pp. 114–15.

This appears to have been an ongoing issue. Superficially, it seems that Taylor and Nottingham were on different sides in the debate, but such a conclusion would have to be qualified, for several reasons. For one thing, as has been observed, Nottingham is commenting on a situation in which he has no certain knowledge, while Taylor's argument is based on the premise that the judge has 'a surer way of evidence'. Moreover, as we have noticed, it is not clear that Nottingham always left his 'private' conscience out of account. Though he customarily referred to the conscience of equity as a kind of disembodied, objective entity, his private conscience did sometimes come to the forefront, albeit apparently not in relation to factual knowledge.[78] Finally, Taylor (like Ames earlier) appears to say that his argument, requiring the judge to act on his private knowledge, applies only where life is at stake, and not necessarily in cases involving property interests, such as those typically coming before the Chancellor.

Criteria for the 'Normative' Conscience of Equity?

It is thus evident that, in making the distinction between internal and political conscience, Nottingham is thinking in terms that comprehend factual knowledge. But the distinction obviously can have a wider reach, as for example his expression of the point in the *Prolegomena* suggests. There, we will recall, he says that ''tis not fit for a court of equity to do everything that is fit to be done' and that '[m]any things are against inward and natural conscience, which cannot be reformed by the regular and political administration of equity'.[79] Thus, if 'for example, a man swears off a true debt by wager of law … no court of conscience can help these cases. Yet the party is bound to restitution *sub periculo animæ*'.[80] Here, what is 'fit to be done' fairly clearly involves the normative scope of the court of conscience. That is to say, not all the norms applicable to private conscience will or should be enforced in the public forum. The question then becomes, 'What kinds of criteria are or may be relevant to sorting the kinds of norms that are appropriately enforced in Chancery from those that should be left to operate on private conscience only?'

Inward dispositions and outward acts

One obvious candidate—suggested by the expression *conscientia interna*—is the dichotomy between internal psychological dispositions and overt acts. That is,

---

78 That is, he is doing what he believes is right; he does not purport to be acting on information he has acquired in his personal capacity, although he may be relying on his appreciation of what the proven facts imply.

79 Nottingham, *Prolegomena*, p. 194.

80 Ibid. Compare the argument of the Attorney General in *Negus* v. *Fettiplace* (1674) 1 Ch. Cas. 239 at 239, 22 ER 779 at 780: even though 'the whole Truth was known', 'it was in *foro conscientiæ*'. That is, even though there was no more information to be gleaned, the substantive question (he argues) is one for private conscience.

one might argue that the court of conscience should limit itself to the latter. As we have seen elsewhere, it was common for writers on conscience to emphasize this distinction. So, for example, Sanderson observes that some virtues and vices are internal, such as '*acts* of the *Will* … and the movings of the affections … and … other cogitations, and intentions of the heart, and mind', and some external, 'of which sort are all the commanded acts of the will, and the indeliberate motions of the affections, which are exercised by *bodily Organs* …'.[81] The laws of men 'only bind the external motions of the body to an external Conformity, from the knowledge and command whereof, all internal motions, and several hammers that strike upon the clocks of the *mind*, and *Conscience*, are altogether to be exempted'.[82] Sanderson offers three rationales for this 'exemption'—two ostensibly related to the competence of human tribunals, and one more to what today would probably be called 'policy'. So, he observes, 'First … an external Court cannot understand, nor judge of inward actions'.[83] This is close to the evidentiary point that I have already made: since only God and the person involved can know 'inward actions', it is incoherent to speak of a human tribunal judging these things. 'And secondly', Sanderson continues, 'it were a vain thing to command or prohibit that by a Law which when it is committed we are not able to punish.'[84] The point of this observation is that human commands cannot operate directly upon the conscience: all that a human tribunal can do is to provide a remedy binding outward things—the body of the person (by imprisonment) or the person's property (by, for example, sequestration). When a judge in equity says that (a court of) 'conscience binds a person', he cannot mean that the person's conscience itself is bound, for, as we have seen elsewhere, the court may require a person to make restitution, but cannot force that person to do so with a generous heart. Sanderson's third reason is that 'the external operation of good works, and the external declination of evil ones doth suffice to the outward felicity of a Republick'.[85]

It might be tempting to leave the matter there and say: equity does not concern itself with internal dispositions, but only with outward manifestations. Having eliminated the former from the purview of the court of conscience, one could then explore what further distinctions, relating now only to outward manifestations, *conscientia politica et civilis* might entail. Unfortunately, the proposition that internal dispositions are simply 'exempted' needs to be qualified.

Jeremy Taylor reminds us that there are at least two salient dimensions to this issue—one evidentiary and the other substantive—and that human law may be concerned in each. So, he tells us, '[s]ome things are secret or private in their own

---

81 Robert Sanderson, *Ten Lectures on the Obligations of Humane Conscience* (1647), trans. Robert Codrington (London, 1660), p. 317; EEBO image 154344:176.

82 Ibid., p. 114; image 154344:69.

83 Ibid., p. 318; image 154344:177.

84 Ibid.

85 Ibid.

nature'—for example, 'the thoughts of the heart'—while '[o]thers are secret, but yet are they such only by accident, and for want of proof …'.[86]

Regarding the second, what he has to say is unremarkable. Some acts are done in secret, and until they become known, they are not justiciable. But this is just a matter of obtaining the evidence: '[t]hose actions which were done in secret … when they are brought to judgment change their nature, and become publick …'.[87] This is rather commonplace: the law cannot act in the absence of evidence upon which judicial knowledge may be founded. On one reading, Nottingham is not saying much more than this in *Cook* v. *Fountain*: there is simply no evidence upon which the conscience of equity can proceed to judgment.

With respect to the first—'things … secret or private in their own nature'—Taylor at first says that they are 'such as are only the prerogative of God to judge of',[88] but then appears to backtrack. For one thing, respecting only unevidenced secret acts, he observes that one way of proving them is by *confession*, a man's 'own witness against himself' being 'as good as ten thousand'.[89] If confession can be evidence of hidden actions,[90] so, presumably, can it be evidence of inward dispositions. One of the persons (the other being God) who can know those dispositions is attesting to them. Taylor does not make this point explicitly. Rather he goes on to explore the question '[w]hether Humane Laws can command or forbid inward acts', to which his answer (in spite of what is 'generally taught by Divines') is 'yes'.

He offers two examples from penal law. One is the law of attempts:

> The law that punishes the criminal before he hath acted the evil, punishes the internal principally: for in the address and first preparations nothing is done but the discovery of the thought; but when the thought is so discovered, and the action is not done, if the man be punished, it is not for the action, but for the thought.[91]

Here, the law is addressed (according to Taylor) to an internal disposition, a thought or intention. If it remains only a thought or intention, it is unreachable by the law. But if there is some overt 'address and … preparations', this is only evidence ('discovery') of the thought, which is what is 'principally' condemned.[92] The other

86 Taylor, vol. 10, p. 48.

87 Ibid.

88 Ibid.

89 Ibid., p. 49.

90 So, referring to Chancery jurisdiction, Gilbert tells us that 'fraud is properly conusable in a court of equity, because it lies in the dark, and is discoverable principally from the oath of the defendant himself' (vol. 1, p. 95; ECCO image CW102104228:96).

91 Taylor, vol. 10, pp. 51–2.

92 The word 'principally' is probably critical here: presumably a confession of the thought will not suffice, although Taylor's treatment of the inchoate action as evidence,

example involves the degrees of *mens rea* that distinguish the different varieties of homicide, that is, murder, manslaughter, or 'chance-medley'. The distinctions again manifest the fact that 'the action [is] wholly differenced by the thought of the heart'.[93] So, while for both substantive (the internal tends not to affect others) and evidentiary (the internal tends to be difficult to prove) reasons the internal is recalcitrant to human laws, a proposition so broad as to exclude the internal altogether from the purview of such laws is untenable.

One kind of internal disposition that played—and continues to play—a role in some doctrines of equity is awareness, advertence, or 'knowledge'. The moral—and hence equitable—quality of certain actions is determined by what the actor knows.

As we have seen, casuists, in considering conscience *per se* or 'private' conscience, paid heed to ignorance, or the absence of relevant awareness. Broadly, they distinguished want of knowledge into two categories: ignorance (leading to error) which was 'invincible and innocent' and that which was 'vincible' or corrigible and which therefore did not excuse error.[94] Taylor offers the striking example of a mother who as a result of a clandestine sexual tryst is impregnated by her own son. Realizing her state, she sends the son abroad. Returning after many years, he falls in love with the beautiful young woman (his own daughter) whom he finds living in his mother's house. Despite the mother's strenuous remonstrances (which do not include telling him the truth), he marries the young woman. The mother, afflicted in conscience, consults a counsellor as to whether she should apprise them of the facts. The determination (which Taylor seems to approve) is that she should not. The son and daughter, ignorant of the true state of affairs, were living together 'innocently', and to reveal the facts to them would be to 'change that into a known sin, which before was an unknown calamity'; they were left to live 'under the protection of a harmless, though erring and mistaken conscience'.[95]

So, too, equity recognizes lack of awareness as affording protection to the conscience in some circumstances. Usually, what is in issue is ignorance of a salient fact which would provide the minor premise in the second syllogism of conscience. However, Nottingham does appear, at least occasionally, to take into account ignorance—or at least doubt—respecting the applicable norms. In *Butler v. Harrison*, for example, he affirms that he will not concern himself with 'the scandal of [a plaintiff's] second marriage' after divorce on the grounds of his wife's adultery, but will leave him to 'consider that between God and his own conscience'

rather than a substantive element in the offence, and his giving the example of a crime defined by the thought alone leaves this unclear.

93 Taylor, vol. 10, p. 52.

94 See, for example, Richard Baxter, *A Christian Directory or a Sum of Practical Theology, and Cases of Conscience* (London,1678), Bk. 1, p. 113; EEBO image 58467:75, and Taylor, vol. 9, p. 148.

95 Taylor, vol. 9, p. 149.

and will confine himself to his proper 'business' of seeing to the 'just performance of agreements'.[96] This seems to be another instance of Nottingham's demarcating the spheres of private conscience and regular equity. He purports to leave the moral quality of the plaintiff's conduct to *conscientia interna*. Nevertheless, admitting to being affected by 'pity of such a marriage which some casuists hold lawful',[97] he makes an order which in effect recognizes the marriage.[98] There is no ignorance of the facts here: Dr. Butler (and his second wife) know that he was married before, that he was divorced, and that he has purported to re-marry. But, apparently, Nottingham believes that he merits indulgence because of the uncertain major premise of the second syllogism of conscience here. That is, he does not *know* that such a re-marriage is wrong. Indeed, he seems to be adopting something like a probabilistic position here: since some (not all) authorities think that such a second marriage might be permissible, indulgence is warranted.

More usually, however, equity might be indulgent in cases of ignorance of fact. The typical instance is the purchaser of legal title to property who takes without notice of an existing equity,[99] an issue that Nottingham not unexpectedly addresses in a number of cases.[100] One observation that must be made about this doctrine is that it arguably does not involve an internal state at all. That is, 'notice'

---

96 *Butler* v. *Harrison* (1677), *Nottingham's Chancery Cases*, vol. 2, pp. 549–50.

97 Ibid., p. 550. For examples of such casuists, see Baxter, Bk. 2, p. 56; EEBO image 58467:244, and Joseph Hall, *Cases of Conscience Practically Resolved* (3rd edn, London, 1654), pp. 311ff.; EEBO images 47748:170ff. See also 'Mr. Cottrington's Case of Divorce' in Thomas Barlow, *Several Miscellaneous and Weighty Cases of Conscience* (London, 1692), pp. 1ff., EEBO images 64424:81ff., for a casuistical analysis of an analogous situation.

98 Gilbert's account of this case is instructive, partly because it does not disclose Nottingham's ambivalence in coming to the conclusion he reaches: 'If a man is divorced from his wife for adultery and marries another, and enters into an agreement upon such marriage, a Court of Equity will specifically perform it, because it is a marriage according to the christian Law; and therefore such agreements as are made upon such marriage ought to be established in *foro conscientiæ*. For tho' such a marriage be a nullity by the Common Law, upon political reasons, yet since they are not against the law of God, such agreements upon such marriages are not contrary to natural justice, nor *mala in se*, and therefore they ought to be established in a Court of Conscience' (vol. 2, pp. 3–4; ECCO images CW3301899608:4–5).

99 The doctrine was a longstanding one. Recall that Francis Bacon, in his *Reading on the Statute of Uses*, says that what makes the conscience of a person taking land subject to a prior equity 'corrupt' is his *knowing* about that equity (p. 405). The protection arising from lack of notice does not apply where the purchaser takes only an equitable interest, as Lord Nottingham observes in *Mirfield* v. *Morley* (1676/7), *Nottingham's Chancery Cases*, vol. 2, p. 475: 'Ignorance mends no man's title'.

100 See, for example, *Botham* v. *Townsend* (1674), *Nottingham's Chancery Cases*, vol. 1, p. 100, *Green* v. *Gardner* (1675), ibid., vol. 1, p. 170, *Salsbury* v. *Bagott*, ibid., vol. 2, p. 504, and *Jennings* v. *Gorges* (1677), ibid., vol. 2, p. 543.

is merely the outward act of communicating, or bringing to a person's attention, regardless of whether the recipient has internalized that communication as actual knowledge. Thus, in *Salsbury*, the reading of a document in the recipient's hearing was treated as constituting 'full and conclusive notice',[101] and in *Jennings*, notice of a will naming executors was regarded as notice of 'the trust affixed to that executorship'.[102] Moreover, it appears that actual, personal, subjective knowledge—or even notice—is not necessary, so that in *Green* notice to an agent is treated as notice to the principal, on the basis not so much of the actual condition of the principal's conscience, but of the need to protect third-party rights. Conversely, actual notice might *not* burden a person's conscience as far as equity is concerned: thus, in *Salsbury* we are told that a subsequent recipient with notice will take free of the prior equity if the initial recipient did not have notice.[103] Again, some other factor besides the subjective state of knowledge of a defendant is being taken into account.

At the same time, it seems evident—at least some of the time—that the real, underlying concern *is* with what the recipient knows,[104] even if that may be made subject to a presumption in the presence of certain kinds of evidence. In *Green*, Nottingham is concerned to buttress the deemed notice *via* an agent by looking as well at the principal's psychological state: there was 'wilful ignorance' on his part.[105] And, in *Botham*, although the recipient actually had personal notice, he was 'innocent'. Nottingham explains: '[f]or a purchaser without notice is only favoured because he is innocent, but if he that hath notice be equally innocent, as here he is, he ought to be equally favoured'.[106] This is reminiscent of equity's approach elsewhere. Whatever forms of evidence the law presumes, generally, to

---

101 *Salsbury* v. *Bagott*, ibid., vol. 2, p. 505.

102 *Jennings* v. *Gorges*, ibid., vol 2, p. 543.

103 *Salsbury* v. *Bagott*, ibid., vol. 2, p. 504.

104 The subjective moral dimension may be reinforced by Nottingham's use of the expression 'infected with notice' in some of these cases (see *Salsbury*, ibid., vol. 2, pp. 504, 507, and *Bovey* v. *Smith* (1676), ibid., vol. 2, p. 470).

105 *Green* v. *Gardner*, ibid., vol. 1, p. 170. Compare *Finch* v. *Hawtry* (1673), ibid., vol. 1, p. 17. 'Wilful ignorance' presumably aligns, although not exactly, with the casuists' vincible or corrigible ignorance. I say 'not exactly' because Nottingham seems to apply a looser test to the converse, 'invincible ignorance', than the casuists would have. In *Salsbury*, one kind of evidence of notice brought forward was an ambiguous message advising the recipient of the prior interest. Nottingham dismisses this as being 'no direct or intelligible notice'. Although it put the recipient 'upon the inquiry', the inquiry (requiring a trip to Wales) would have been impracticable. On this basis, he is treated as not having received notice on these facts. So Nottingham appears prepared to preserve a party's conscience intact on the basis of less than incorrigible ignorance. We will recall Ellesmere's similar refusal to treat as notice a third party's allegation of an equitable interest—ostensibly in the name of economic practicality.

106 *Botham* v. *Townsend*, ibid., vol. 1, p. 100. Here, the defendant/recipient of notice had compelling reason to believe that the plaintiff's 'pretense' was unfounded.

be determinative, they must yield in particular cases to more compelling proof of the real state of facts, for example, of what the party actually *knew*.

Thus, while we might be tempted to say that, generally, the conscience of equity will not concern itself with internal dispositions, this is not always true. Indeed, what often imparts the relevant moral quality to outward actions—in the contemplation of law and equity—is what is in a person's mind, if not his heart. Of course, saying that the internal disposition accompanying an outward state of affairs colours the moral and hence at least sometimes the legal status of that state of affairs is far different from saying that an internal disposition pure and simple and corresponding to no outward manifestation will ever be the concern of human laws. A cankered heart may be unconscientious, but if it is given no outward expression a court, even of conscience, will presumably not interfere.

'Spirituals' versus 'civils'

Another perhaps significant distinction is highlighted in a Robert Eyre sermon preached before members of the Bench at Winchester, in which he opines that 'the Exercise of a Good Conscience' is 'the Rule by which all Civil, as well as all Moral and Religious Actions, ought to be directed'.[107] 'Civil' ostensibly corresponds to one part of Nottingham's dichotomy, *conscientia civilis*; perhaps the other, 'Moral and Religious', or spiritual, corresponds in some way to the other, *conscientia interna*.[108] The argument would be that what is 'merely' spiritual is beyond the purview of a court of conscience, which should restrict itself to 'civils'.

Two preliminary points should be made. First, there might be a temptation to equate the spiritual exclusively with the internal, as I have discussed it. So, the anonymous author of *The True Magistrate*, who explicitly invokes the distinction between 'civils' and 'spirituals', defines the latter as the 'inward workings in our spirits' and observes that these are things 'meerly relating to conscience'.[109] But, as I have already intimated, I am using the word to include not only faith, but outward conduct in the religious sphere. So one possible basis for, or element

---

107 Robert Eyre, *A Discourse Concerning the Nature and Satisfaction of a Good and Inoffensive Conscience* (London, 1693), pp. 1–2; EEBO images 62636:4–5.

108 See also Thomas Hall (1610–65), 'Men are Gods, or the Dignity of Magistracy' in *The Beauty of Magistry* (London, 1660), distinguishing 'spirituals' (respecting which only God can bind the conscience) from 'external policy' (p. 197; EEBO image 96886:112), John Warr, *Administrations Civil and Spiritual* (London, 1648), and Anthony Cade, *Conscience, its Nature and Corruption* (London, 1661), speaking of the unredeemed post-lapsarian conscience which suffices 'for performance of outward morall, civill, and some religious duties for preservation of humane societie and common life' but not for the attainment of 'the knowledge of the mysteries of saving religion' (p. 12; EEBO image 54332:11). The dichotomies of these writers are not all congruent with each other, but suggest general lines of distinction.

109 *The True Magistrate* (London, 1659), p. 8; EEBO image 119150:5.

in, distinguishing the objects of public and private conscience is whether we are facing merely spiritual or religious issues.

Second, we must distinguish *objects* of assessment by conscience from *kinds* of conscience themselves. In some ways, one defines the other: that is, the spiritual conscience is that which addresses itself to spiritual matters. Indeed, much of what I have said so far has involved the implicit definition of conscience in terms of the objects to which it relates. But many writers speak of different *kinds* of conscience prior to or apart from their objects. We have noticed before that William Ames for example distinguishes '*Naturall*' conscience from 'that which is *Inlightened*';[110] and John Jackson similarly speaks of 'the distinction of Conscience *naturall* and *illuminated*'.[111]

There is a terminological ambiguity here, for we will recall that Nottingham's categories are *conscientia naturalis et interna* and *conscientia politica et civilis*. Do both 'natural' and 'enlightened' conscience fall within the first of these categories, so that we can assume that Ames and Jackson are simply leaving out of account political and civil conscience? If their categories are in fact comprehensive, then clearly enlightened conscience, concerned with spiritual or religious things, would be outside the conscience of equity as Nottingham conceives it, leaving natural conscience (or part of it) to operate by default in the secular sphere. For example, Sanderson distinguishes conscience which obliges people not only 'to the performance of their duties, as they are men, but to believe the mysteries of Faith ... as they are Christians'.[112] So, again, we might assume that natural conscience suffices as a guide for ordinary, perhaps civic, duties.

Henry Hammond offers a rather more complex classification: '… Conscience of duty in any particular action is to be ruled by that law which is proper to that action; as for example: The *Christian law* is the rule of Conscience for Christian actions; the *law of reason*, or morall law, for morall, the *law nationall*, municipal, or locall, for civill ...'.[113] Further, he says, 'it is very irregular, and unreasonable to measure any action by a rule that belongs not to it'.[114] There are different kinds of conscience appropriate to different kinds of objects, and they ought to be kept in their proper spheres. A problem is that equity is ostensibly part of the 'nationall' law. Is it then, determined by that law? Well, yes and no. Nottingham himself said that '[i]n suits in equity… the Lord Chancellor must order his conscience after the rules and grounds of the laws of this realm'.[115] At the same time, equity undeniably

110 William Ames, *Conscience with the Power and Cases Thereof* (Leyden and London, 1639), p. 5; EEBO image 15139:7.

111 John Jackson, *The Booke of Conscience Opened and Read* (London, 1642), p. 14; EEBO image 103990:13.

112 Sanderson, p. 28; EEBO image 154344:26.

113 Henry Hammond, *Of Conscience* (Oxford, 1645), pp. 10–11; EEBO image 123411:7.

114 Ibid., p. 11.

115 Nottingham, *Prolegomena*, p. 200. Yale, 'Introduction', *Nottingham's Chancery Cases*, vol. 1, p. lii observes that Nottingham 'deliberately and … constantly' turned to the

did extend the ordinary law. One common way of understanding equity, as is well known, was that it 'supplied the wants' of the strict law, or the common law. So, in some sense, it appealed to another kind of authority. One formulation of this was that equity rendered the positive law more perfect by making its operation more completely conformable to reason.[116] So we might say that the conscience of equity extends to the conscience dictated by natural reason, but that the dividing line has to be between that and conscience as further dictated by religious revelation.

Even this distinction is complicated, however. For one thing, as I have outlined in Chapter 2, historically the conscience of equity was importantly 'spiritual'. We will recall A.W.B. Simpson's observation that, for the medieval chancellors conscience 'connoted ... the moral law *as it applied to particular individuals for the avoidance of peril to the soul through mortal sin*'.[117] And, indeed, we have discerned remnants of this attitude in Ellesmere, for example.

One might be tempted to say that what Nottingham did, at least, was to relegate this spiritual conscience to the sidelines as far as equity is concerned. Indeed, his leaving certain matters to a person and that person's confessor seems to involve just this point, which he appears to make in other ways. So, in the passage from the *Prolegomena* which I have already cited, he says that 'no court of conscience can help [certain] cases', although 'the party is bound to restitution *sub periculo animæ* ...';[118] the fact that a person's soul might be in jeopardy does not mean that equity will act. Elsewhere, he observes that a plea against a plaintiff that he is precluded by his own bad conscience from succeeding must not relate to 'collateral matters' 'else no sinner should be relieved in equity'.[119] That a person is generally sinful, or sinful in relation to other matters, will not bar that person from relief—although unconscientiousness directly related to the matter in issue may

common law 'to aid him in constructing rules of equity'.

116 Recall, for example, St. German's Doctor's definition of equity as 'a [ryghtwysenes] that consideryth all the pertyculer cyrcumstaunces of the dede/the whiche also is temperyd with the swetnes of mercye. And [such an equytye] must alway be obseruyd in euery lawe of man' (*St. German's Doctor and Student*, eds.T.F.T. Plucknett and J.L. Barton [London, 1974], p. 95 [brackets present in source text]). See also Edward Stillingfleet (1635–99), *A Discourse Concerning Bonds of Resignation of Benefices* (London, 1695), p. 24; EEBO image 55952:20, citing Coke: '*Equity is the Reason of the Law*'. Incidentally, he makes the familiar distinction between equity as 'a Reasonable Construction of Law' and equity as filling gaps in the common law, the latter being 'the true foundation of the *Court of Equity* in *Chancery*' (p. 23; image 55952:19).

117 A.W.B. Simpson, *A History of the Common Law of Contract: The Rise of the Action of Assumpsit* (Oxford, 1975), p. 398.

118 Nottingham, *Prolegomena*, p. 194.

119 Ibid., p. 305. This is not, of course, the same as the general point, but it does evidence an impulse to set 'sin' to one side. And see *The Practice of the High Court of Chancery*, p. 49; EEBO image 33548:29, where we are told that among suits denied help in Chancery are those involving 'houses of iniquity'—presumably *ipso facto* repugnant to equity.

engage the 'clean hands' doctrine. In the case of *Whitchcott* v. *Mekins* Nottingham cautions that 'articles to displace an officer ought to be such as do concern his breach of trust in execution of his office, not such as concern the piety of his life ...'.[120] Such observations seem to indicate that the *forum internum*, 'concerned with the individual's spiritual health, and the avoidance of sin',[121] is co-extensive with the *conscientia interna* that Lord Nottingham brackets as non-justiciable.

Although it would be convenient if we could leave the matter there, another complication is that Lord Nottingham does not consistently maintain the separation. His was a sensibility, common enough at the time, that tended to see things, ultimately, in religious terms. Joseph Parkes offers a striking illustration in a letter Nottingham penned to his chaplain, John Sharp, charging him to provide diligent advice respecting 'ecclesiastical preferments' within the Chancellor's disposition: 'I ... charge it upon your conscience, as you will answer to Almighty God, that ... you … give me the best advice you can ... which if you neglect to do, the guilt will be entirely yours, and I shall deliver my own soul.'[122]

This tendency is evident as well in forensic contexts. In his speech to Serjeant Scroggs on the latter's accession to the Court of Common Pleas, he expressed the view that '[t]he administration of justice is ... so divine and so sacred an employment that he who enters upon it may in some sense be said to enter into religion'.[123] Echoing Ellesmere three-quarters of a century earlier,[124] he gives, in *Howard* v. *Duke of Norfolk*, as the primary reason for objecting to perpetuities the fact that they 'fight against God'.[125] Elsewhere, in *Grey* v. *Grey*, Nottingham, disagreeing with Coke, says that the reason that trusts of land do not ascend (that is, from son to father) is 'not ... from natural philosophy, *quia gravia deorsum*, but from moral philosophy, *quia amor descendit non ascendit*, and from divinity, because fathers are bound to provide for their children'.[126] Moreover, although he does observe

120 *Whitchcott* v. *Mekins* (1675), *Nottingham's Chancery Cases*, vol. 1, p. 246.

121 Simpson, p. 381.

122 Joseph Parkes, *A History of the Court of Chancery* (London, 1828), p. 213.

123 Lord Nottingham, Speech to Serjeant Scroggs on the latter's accession to the Court of Common Pleas (October 23, 1676), *Nottingham's Chancery Cases*, vol. 1, p. 436.

124 *Anon.* (1599), Cary 9, 21 ER 5.

125 *Howard* v. *Duke of Norfolk* (1681/82), *Nottingham's Chancery Cases*, vol. 2, p. 908. In the *Prolegomena*, p. 222, he cites Ellesmere for this proposition. See also *The Practice of the High Court of Chancery*, p. 49. Another example of his linking a rule of law to the law of God occurs in *Clerk* v. *Perryer* (1679/80), *Nottingham's Chancery Cases*, vol. 2, pp. 783–4: this rule 'is grounded upon the law of God, for Jacob did make good to Laban all that was lost or stolen …'. For this reason and others, he says that 'a wise and a just man might well decree this case for the plaintiff'. However, he goes on to outline countervailing equitable factors which would make it 'very hard' to decree against a defendant who 'hath acted according to the best of his skill without fraud or covin'.

126 *Grey* v. *Grey* (1676/77), ibid., vol. 2, p. 484. In a footnote, Yale states that 'Finch Co. Litt. has in margin at f. 10b: The true reason is … from Moral Philosophy, and from the

that a decedent's mortgage debt 'doth more nearly concern the executors than the heir, and was antiently thought to concern the soul'[127]—suggesting that this is an obsolete attitude—he invokes the same kind of reasoning himself. Thus, in *Hickson* v. *Wytham*, which involved a question of priority between legacies and a testator's debts, he uses language reminiscent of a medieval chancellor: '[p]ayment of debts oblige [*sic*] the conscience but legacies concern not the soul of the defunct'; not to prefer debts 'were to expound the testator's will so as to die in mortal sin'; and then he invokes the maxim *nemo præsumitur immemor æternæ salutis*.[128] And, in *Nurse* v. *Yerworth*, a case involving, broadly, the question whether a posthumous child should be understood as included in the terms of a testator's will, one of the reasons he gives for an affirmative answer is that the alternative would be 'contrary to piety and good manners', and would make 'a good Christian die worse than an infidel'.[129] It appears, then, that at least sometimes Nottingham was prepared to invoke 'spirituals' as criteria for conscience in equity, or at least as factors in applying that conscience.[130]

Does this make nonsense of the ostensible distinction between *conscientia interna* and *conscientia civilis*? Probably not. One might attribute these deviations, if that is what they are, to inadvertence: Nottingham was heir to doctrines that often originated in this kind of thinking, and it would be asking too much—indeed, it might be perverse—to expect him to have superseded the attendant discourse.

Law of Nature … and Law of God, 2 Cor. 12, v. 14 '.

[127] Nottingham, *Prolegomena*, p. 283 (my emphasis).

[128] *Hickson* v. *Wytham* (1674/75), *Nottingham's Chancery Cases*, vol. 1, p. 137. Yale's footnote tells us that Nottingham apparently said elsewhere that he 'would not let a man sin in his grave' (1 Eq. Ca. Ab. 141 B(3)). See also *Foly* v. *Paston* (1679/80), *Nottingham's Chancery Cases*, vol. 2, p. 793. In *Hickson* v. *Wytham*, it is not clear what the testator intended, so the court resolves the question in favour of giving priority to debts. Where the testator himself gives priority to legacies over debts, however, Nottingham says that Chancery will not intervene, for the court cannot make him die with a better conscience than he expressed (p. 137). A possible departure from this latter principle appears to have occurred in *Hele* v. *Hele* (1682) 2 Ch. Cas. 87. A testator failed to perform a covenant during his lifetime and in his will left all his estates to a third party. Nottingham, in decreeing that the amount covenanted for should be paid out of the lands devised, observes: 'the Court shall do what in Conscience he ought to have done' (p. 91).

[129] *Nurse* v. *Yerworth*, *Nottingham's Chancery Cases*, vol. 1, p. 117. Compare *Hyde* v. *Seymour* (1678), ibid., vol. 2, p. 709 where Nottingham says that a will ought to be construed so as to 'stand with the good conscience of a dying father'.

[130] Further, he appears to acknowledge that some well-recognized doctrines of equity may have moved from the sphere of private to that of public conscience. In the *Prolegomena*, referring to the issue of whether one joint tenant has a right 'in conscience' to half the whole profits taken by the other joint-tenant, he observes that *Doctor and Student* considers the matter as 'a case between a man and his confessor, *viz*. that he is bound to reform it if he will save his soul', but that '[n]ow equity construes all receipt to the common profit, and that without great strain' (pp. 213–14).

Perhaps more important, in each of the instances cited, 'divinity' is one of the reasons given, but not the only one, and not necessarily a sufficient one. For example, in *Nurse* v. *Yerworth*, he provides a list of reasons, among them that a disinheriting construction would be 'against natural and universal justice',[131] and in connection with the 'ascent' of trusts of land, he invokes moral philosophy and, apparently, the law of nature as well as the law of God. Thus, if something were *only* against the Christian law, or the spiritual law, he might not have seen it as sanctionable in equity. So, in spite of these ostensible counter-examples, one helpful line of demarcation may still be that between Hammond's '*law of reason* or morall law' and 'Christian law', although this does not mean that the dictates even of the former apply comprehensively.

Thus, mindful of the qualifications presented in the preceding discussion, one might say that seventeenth-century legal conscience, in contrast to conscience *per se*, evinced a bias toward the external and the secular or 'civil'. The rationale for this is implicit in Sanderson's third reason for limiting the former to outward manifestations: 'the external operation of good works, and the external declination of evil ones doth suffice to the outward felicity of a Republick'.[132] The concern is what will conduce to public order—or even 'felicity'. As we have seen, however, even some internal states—for example, awareness and intention—are regarded by the law as incompatible with that order. Moreover, Sanderson (and many others) would certainly have regarded certain spiritual states and actions as inconsistent with it. So, on the one hand, the category 'external and secular' is probably too narrow as a delimitation of the sphere of operation of the conscience of equity. Conversely, the category 'external and secular' is too broad: the conscience of equity does not reach all outward, civil actions. Indeed, much of what conduces to the 'outward felicity of a Republick'—what we have seen William Perkins describe as 'that externall and civil peace which is betweene man and man'—resides in non-legal normative principles. The question thus becomes whether there are general criteria for distinguishing social interactions that are subject to regulation by the conscience of equity from those that are not.

We have already noticed in Nottingham some intimation of where lines might be drawn: recall that in *Butler* v. *Harrison*, he disclaims judicial concern with the 'scandal' of a party's second marriage. Similarly, in *Masters* v. *Strode*, a case involving the giving of a bond for the resignation of a clerical living,[133] although he 'reprove[s] the taking of bonds for resignation as a thing that looks ill, was once

131 *Nurse* v. *Yerworth*, *Nottingham's Chancery Cases*, vol. 1, p. 117.

132 Sanderson, p. 318; EEBO image 154344:177. Similarly, Taylor appears to approve Francisco Suarez's (1548–1617) argument 'that virginity [apparently both "spiritual" and private, if not "internal"] should be kept is a work of supererogation, that has no necessary conjunction with the end of any public good; and therefore cannot be enjoined by a human law' (vol. 10, p. 45).

133 For a nearly-contemporaneous discussion of the issues involved in these cases, see Stillingfleet, *Discourse Concerning Bonds of Resignation of Benefices*.

held to be void for simoniacal pravity, and still sounds in scandal',[134] he purports to find for the plaintiff on other grounds. It appears that conduct's merely being scandalous or disreputable[135] will not in itself engage the conscience of equity—although Nottingham's foregrounding it in the way that he does perhaps suggests that it is affecting his judgment at some level.

Another instance—perhaps related loosely to scandal—is obligations due in 'honour', which, though not the same thing as private conscience, is, as a kind of extra-legal normativity, analogous to it. In *Honywood* v. *Bennett*, Nottingham observes of a promise to pay another's debts that if it 'were voluntary and without consideration, though it did bind the son in honour and private conscience, with which I had nothing to do, it could not bind him in legal and regular equity'.[136] Once again, much of the civility that promotes social order lies outside the purview of the court of conscience.

The point is again complicated by Nottingham's failure consistently to exclude matters of honour or propriety from his discourse. Sometimes he alludes to them merely, and beside the legal issue, to upbraid a litigant. But, sometimes, 'honour' seems like the basis of, or an important ingredient in, his reasoning. In *Shipton* v. *Tyrrell*, for example, he says that the residue of a testator's personal estate 'ought in honour and conscience to be made as beneficial to [a legatee] as possible'.[137] And, in *Earl of Leicester* v. *Sidney*, one of the factors in his decision is that 'there was some consideration …, not a legal and meritorious consideration in strictness of law, but a very just and honourable motive and inducement between families of ... great quality'.[138] Again, one might see these as nothing more than *per incuriam* departures from what would appear to be his more central position—that conduct that is just 'dishonourable' and nothing more does not suffice to attract equity's intervention.

---

134 *Masters* v. *Strode* (1677/78), *Nottingham's Chancery Cases*, vol. 2, p. 604. Simony is trafficking in sacred things, notably the purchasing of religious preferment.

135 Although 'scandal' in Nottingham's time had something like the connotation that it has today, it also had meanings with distinctly religious overtones: see, for example, Henry Hammond, *Of Scandall* (Oxford, 1644). One of these is conduct respecting some 'indifferent thing' which the actor 'in Conscience is inform'd to be perfectly lawfull for him to do' but which might 'occasion another mans sinne by doing that after him which he is not resolv'd to be lawfull' (p. 8; EEBO image 123414:6).

136 *Honywood* v. *Bennett* (1675), *Nottingham' Chancery Cases*, vol. 1, p. 214. Compare *Clishold* v. *Backwell* (1681), ibid., vol. 2, p. 891: 'I dismissed the bill, for the husband was never bound in law or equity but only in honour' (p. 891). Conversely, on the appeal of *Earl of Feversham* v. *Watson*, to the House of Lords, Lord Privy Seal distinguished 'the latitude of their consciences', by which the Lords might judge, from 'rules of equity', and opined that 'this Court might judge on grounds of honour as well as equity' (ibid., vol. 2, p. 648).

137 *Shipton* v. *Tyrrell* (1675/76), ibid., vol. 1, p. 273.

138 *Earl of Leicester* v. *Sidney* (1680/81), ibid., vol. 2, p. 860. See also *Duke of Newcastle* v. *Clayton* (1676), ibid., vol. 1, p. 442 where Nottingham considers the fact that 'the Duke had so honourably acquitted himself' (p. 443).

Charity versus justice

Another—perhaps more central—distinction that may afford insight into which outward actions will engage the conscience of equity is that of 'charity' as opposed to 'justice'. For my purposes, 'charity' can be taken as referring broadly to acts of simple generosity and related concepts such as gratitude, forgiveness and compassion, while 'justice' will generally involve obligations based on some kind of reciprocity, or *quid pro quo*. Fairly evidently, both categories involve 'conscience' in some sense, but the former, calling for responses not based on the kind of mutual obligation implicit in the doctrine of consideration, apparently makes more extreme demands. So the question is whether the conscience of equity limits itself to the demands of justice, or whether Chancery will ever require persons to be conscientious by being generous, grateful,[139] forgiving, or compassionate.[140] In reflecting upon this issue we should be mindful that equity, as well as being associated with the more finely-attuned 'justice' of which Aristotle speaks, was not uncommonly understood to involve 'the sweetness of mercy'.

The distinction between charity and justice regularly appears in the commentaries on conscience. For example, Richard Baxter tells us that 'the Law of Nature forbiddeth ... three sorts of sins: 1.Those that are against *Piety* to God: 2. Those that are against our own welfare. 3. Those that are against our Neighbours good ...'.[141] Apparently, 'sins ... against our Neighbours good' are external actions implicating public order, or felicity. Baxter further subdivides sins against our neighbours into those '1. Against Justice: 2. Against Charity'. Although they might not draw the line in the same place as Baxter, other writers invoke the 'charity'/ 'justice' distinction.[142]

As usual, the dichotomy I am invoking here requires nuancing. Hall suggests that charity might be in some way 'ever inseparable from Justice', and Baxter

[139] Barlow observes that ingratitude, 'though certainly a crime against the Law of Nature', is generally not susceptible to legal regulation. The main reason for this, he says, is that it is 'very hard to know when a man was ingrateful, and the measure of his ingratitude' (pp. 33–4; EEBO images 64424:20–21). In other words, the problem is one of proof.

[140] The Court of Chancery did assume jurisdiction over charitable uses or trusts, of course. But that jurisdiction assumed that such trusts had already been constituted, or evaluated whether they had been so constituted. The question I am considering here is whether, apart from a specific donative act, the Court would impose generosity on litigants.

[141] Baxter, Bk. 4, p. (erroneously paginated) 208; EEBO image 58467:452.

[142] See John Sheffeild, *A Good Conscience the Strongest Hold* (London, 1650), distinguishing for example between 'Debts of *Justice*' and 'debts of *charitie*' (p. 199; EEBO image 169447:116), and Joseph Hall, p. 3; EEBO image 47749:13 ('with those that are truly ... conscionable, the bond of gratitude is no lesse strong then that of law and justice'), p. 10; image 47749:17 ('[t]he maximes of Traffique [commerce] are almost infinite; onely Charity (but ever inseparable from Justice) must make the application of them'), p. 12; image 47749:18 ('Rigour and excesse ... equally crosses the law of commutative Justice, equally crosses the law of Charity'), and elsewhere.

says that '*the two great principles of Justice*'—love of one's neighbour and self-denial, are reducible to one precept: '[*t*]*he loving of your neighbour as your self*'[143]—that is, in terms that perhaps more appropriately suggest 'charity'. At one point, Sanderson identifies charity with things that are 'spiritual' and 'directed to a *supernatural end*'.[144] On this view, we would already have 'done' charity in our 'spirituals'/'civils' discussion. Sheffeild in fact analyses charity into '*Ecclesiasticall*, or spirituall and Christian' and '*Externall*, or Civill'—the latter involving beneficence to the poor, benevolence to one's neighbour and forgiveness of one's enemies.[145] For present purposes, we can probably set aside 'spirituall' charity; the question remains whether beneficence, benevolence and forgiveness are bases of obligations cognizable by Chancery as a court of conscience.

Broadly, the answer is 'No'. Nottingham does sometimes refer to charity and justice in ways that make their relative status ambiguous. In *Solly* v. *Whitfield*, he revives an extinguished rentcharge because there is precedent for so doing 'where it tends to advancement of justice ... or of charity'.[146] This could be taken as treating 'charity' as an independent ground of decision.[147] And, in *Powell* v. *Morgan* he determines that the defendant should not 'take advantage of [a] legal accident' and that 'justice and charity both require that [the] will should take effect'.[148] Here charity is not an independent basis for the decision, but arguably an extra-legal reason gratuitously added to the real reason, justice. Occasionally, Nottingham appears to acknowledge ingratitude (perhaps related to charity) as a factor affecting his view of a case.[149] However, in cases where he actually has to decide between issues of charity and justice, Nottingham tends to exclude the former—albeit not just in these terms. Recall *Hickson* v. *Wytham*, where he says that a testator's debts were to be paid before legacies, because 'justice is to [be] preferred before bounty'.[150] And, in *Thornborough* v. *Baker*, he dismisses a point as being 'an argument of compassion, not of right'.[151]

143 Baxter, Bk. 4, p. 97; EEBO image 58467:446.

144 Sanderson, p. (erroneously paginated) 221; EEBO image 154344:72.

145 Sheffeild, p. 195; EEBO image 169447:114.

146 *Solly* v. *Whitfield* (1675/76), *Nottingham's Chancery Cases*, vol. 1, p. 288.

147 However, the case cited in *Solly* v. *Whitfield* as authority for the proposition that charity can be a ground for decision, *Earl of Dorset* v. *Hospital of East Grinstead*, is complicated in that it involved a 'charitable use', giving rise to special considerations.

148 *Powell* v. *Morgan* (1680), *Nottingham's Chancery Cases*, vol. 2, p. 837.

149 See *Stowbard* v. *Wingfield* (1676), ibid., vol. 1, p. 342: the suit was 'unjust and indeed … ungrateful' (p. 343); and *Rodd* v. *Ryer* (1676), ibid., vol. 2, p. 468: 'this seemed to me the most ingrateful suit that could be'. In *Forth* v. *Wade* (1675), ibid., vol. 1, p. 206, he takes account of the fact that 'continual kindness and confidence … made the defendant rest quiet as to his own demand' until a limitations period ran out.

150 *Hickson* v. *Wytham*, ibid., vol. 1, p. 137 [brackets in source].

151 *Thornborough* v. *Baker* (1675), ibid., vol. 1, p. 204. In another case, however, he seems to regard compassion as reinforcing equity: 'all the equity and compassion was on the

The distinction may be illustrated by comparing religious writers' approach with Nottingham's. Hall, for example, states that 'a sure rule' for 'all humane and civill acts of Commerce' is 'our *Charity*'.[152] He then identifies charity with the Golden Rule: '[l]ooke what you could wish to be done to you by others, doe but the same to others, you cannot be guilty of the breach of Charity'.[153] As we have seen, it is commonplace for these writers to identify this Rule as *the* rule of general equity: Sheffeild, citing Lactantius, calls it 'the very root and foundation of all equity';[154] John Tillotson describes it as '*[t]he great rule of equity in all our dealings with men*';[155] John Warr calls it 'the Beauty of *Equity* stamped upon the Soul'.[156] In one assize sermon Michael Thomas characterizes it as 'the grand rule of Equity', and 'the first law which God wrote in the heart of Mankind',[157] and in another Nicholas Stratford observes that it is 'indelibly ... engraven in our Consciences'.[158]

Baxter routinely invokes the Rule in his discussion of cases of conscience. Even non-religious writers make the same kind of point. Lord Somers (1651–1716), in his extra-judicial *A Discourse Concerning Generosity*, in which he distinguishes generosity from matters of reward and punishment, says of both positive and negative[159] formulations of the Rule that 'they contain the Sum of Natural Justice and Equity', and that they 'serve to guide us by the Rules of Equity and Mercy' as well as by 'the ordinary Rules of Justice'.[160]

For these authors, this Rule is a basic moral precept, of the kind given by *synderesis*. Thus, at least in so far as 'dealings between men' are concerned, it

---

other side', *Cheke* v. *Lord Lisle* (1673/4), ibid., vol. 1, p. 23. And, somewhat paradoxically, in *Nurse* v. *Yerworth*, ibid., vol. 1, p. 117, he speaks of 'that legal compassion due to all dying men who are *inopes consilii*'.

152 Joseph Hall, p. 9; EEBO image 47749:16. Compare Samuel Clarke, *Medulla Theologiæ: or the Marrow of Divinity* (London, 1659), containing a section on '*Questions, and Cases of Conscience about Charity*' (pp. 229ff.; EEBO images 64964:137ff). He identifies three 'principall' ways of expressing charity: '1. in giving. 2. In forgiving. 3. In lending.' (p. 240; image 64694:144).

153 Joseph Hall, p. 10; EEBO image 47749:17.

154 Sheffeild, p. 124; EEBO image 169447:79.

155 John Tillotson, 'Wherein lies that exact Righteousness, which is required between Man and Man?' in *The Morning-Exercise at Cripplegate: or, Several Cases of Conscience Practically Resolved, by sundry Ministers*, ed. Samuel Annesley (London, 1664), p. 217; EEBO image 105033:113.

156 John Warr, *Administrations Civil and Spiritual* (London, 1648), p. 2; EEBO image 65034:6.

157 *Two Assize Sermons* (London, 1659), p. 17; EEBO image 170373:16.

158 *A Sermon Preached at the Assizes Held at Chester* (London, 1681), p. 6; EEBO image 100328:6.

159 'Do *not do* unto others what you would *not* have them do unto you.'

160 John Somers (Lord Somers), *A Discourse Concerning Generosity* (2nd edn, London, 1695), pp. 88–9; EEBO image 150297:57.

would constitute the major premise of the first syllogism of conscience, from which secondary or lower-order principles, and even specific rules for particular situations, are to be derived.[161]

One may compare this radical and comprehensive approach with Nottingham's approach (which, presumably, was also the Chancery's approach) to 'generosity'. While some of what Lord Somers says might suggest the conventional distinction between strict law and Chancery equity,[162] Nottingham makes it clear that enforcing generosity is not a part of Chancery law. In *Sarten* v. *Darcy*, for example, he observes:

> ... the strictness which the defendant uses in this case does very much resemble that of the ill servant in the Gospel who, when his master had forgiven him many talents, would not forgive his fellow servant a few pence. But yet a court of regular equity can oblige no man to forgive what is justly due to him or quit any advantage which the law gives him so long as he comes to that advantage without any fraud or circumvention ....[163]

As a convinced Anglican, Nottingham unquestionably would have regarded the defendant's position as inconsistent with Christian charity, but the court of conscience has no jurisdiction to compel people to be generous. This is close to a statement that the Golden Rule, in its more altruistic dimensions, is not enforceable in Chancery.

A few specific examples of the kind of reasoning the religious writers employ with respect to some typical 'legal' questions will highlight the distinction. Baxter addresses a range of such issues in his chapter 'General Directions and particular Cases of Conscience, about Contracts in general, and about Buying and Selling, Borrowing and Lending, Vsury, &c. in particular'. One question he asks is whether one, entering a contract, must try to ensure that the other party '*may be a gainer by the bargain as well as I*'. The answer, is 'Yes, if you ... be in the like condition. But if he be very poor, and you be rich, Charity must be so mixt with Justice, that you must endeavour that it be more to his commodity than yours ...'.[164] So, generally, you must ensure that the advantage is to the other party as well as to yourself, but sometimes you should favour the other party. Thus, if you buy a 'durable thing' for less than market value from a necessitous person, since Charity must be exercised as well as Justice, you should treat the transaction as a mere pledge, allowing

---

161 See, for example, Tillotson, 'Exact Righteousness', pp. 30–32; EEBO images 105033:20–21.

162 'Generosity … restrains Men from doing many things, which according to human Laws or the ordinary Rules of Justice, may appear lawful, and enclines them oftentimes, as the circumstances of things may be, to do more than those ordinary Rules in strictness require ...' (Somers, p. 89; EEBO image 150297:57).

163 *Sarten* v. *Darcy* (1677/78), *Nottingham's Chancery Cases*, vol. 2, p. 601.

164 Baxter, Bk. 4, p.103; EEBO image 58467:449.

the seller to redeem the thing later, so as to sell it for a higher price to someone else.[165] And, if between making the contract and payment by the purchaser the commodity is 'casually' lost or destroyed, although 'rigorous Justice will allow the purchaser nothing', 'common humanity, which all good men use in bargaining, which tempereth Justice with Charity, will teach men [sellers] to bear part of the loss; because they must do as they would be done by'.

Equity in the juridical sense, although it sometimes—for example, where there is a constituted fiduciary relationship—will demand selfless behaviour, is not so generally inclined to decree beneficence. In *Maynard* v. *Moseley*, Nottingham expresses the view that '*Caveat emptor* is a very needless advice if the Chancery ... can establish another rule instead of it by declaring that equity must suffer no man to have an ill bargain'.[166] In other words, Chancery will not enforce the rule of charity that requires contractors, in conscience, to seek the equal advantage of the other party. In another case between the same parties, Nottingham characterizes a failure to give notice that was not strictly required as 'an unkindness, but ... no injustice'.[167]

Nottingham's reluctance to save parties from 'ill bargains' perhaps should remind us again that, although *Deus* may be *procurator fatuorum*, Chancery is not. I addressed this point at some length in Chapter 6. The question is, broadly, whether equity should be so compassionate as to relieve persons from the consequences of their own foolishness. Or, from another perspective, does a party's gaining an advantage from another's folly engage the former's conscience in a way that should concern equity? The religious writers' response, based on the Golden Rule, is that we are bound in conscience to look out for the interests of those with whom we transact. In the passage from *Maynard* v. *Moseley*, Nottingham appears to take the opposite view. He expresses a similar attitude elsewhere: thus, he says, 'it was … folly' for a plaintiff not to ascertain the terms of a lease, 'and equity

---

165 Ibid., Bk. 4, p. 104; image 58467:450. This is in fact somewhat analogous to how equity re-characterizes a mortgage of land, converting a transfer of title into a security for repayment of a debt (see, for example, *Thornborough* v. *Baker*, *Nottingham's Chancery Cases*, vol.1, p. 202: 'in natural justice and equity the principal right of the mortgagee is to the money, and his right to the land is only as a security for the money ...'). But in those cases, equity purports to discern the real substance of the transaction, not to impose charitable conduct on the 'purchaser'.

166 *Maynard* v. *Moseley* (1676), *Nottingham's Chancery Cases*, vol. 1, p. 345. Of the doctrine of *caveat emptor*, Baxter says that it should not be the rule 'among Christians, nor Infidels who profess either truth or common honesty' (Bk. 4, p.104; EEBO image 58467:450).

167 *Maynard* v. *Moseley* #2 (1676), ibid., vol. 1, p. 401. In *Ayloffe* v. *Thomson* (1673), ibid., vol. 1, p. 10, remarking that a promise 'was purely voluntary and without consideration', he says that 'no equity would oblige [the party] to stand to his kind word'—although, if it had induced reliance, that would have been different. Compare *Butcher* v. *Hinton* (1677), ibid., vol. 2, p. 578, again regarding equity's reluctance to enforce 'any voluntary condescension'.

cannot relieve … negligent or careless persons'.[168] He was, perhaps, not entirely consistent in this regard. In another case, in which a testator had given his widow the discretion to distribute his assets among their children, he is concerned that this puts not only the children but the testator's reputation in the widow's power. '[N]ow it will depend very much upon the wife's discretion whether the husband died like a wise man or a fool.'[169] Observing that such clauses should be 'executed ... with equity and good conscience', he orders an equal division.[170] Generally, however, he seems to require more—*suggestio falsi* or *suppressio veri*[171] or at least 'surprise'[172]—before the conscience of equity will be roused.

Although matters of charity clearly engage *conscientia interna*, they appear not to have been part of the *conscientia civilis* that the Court of Chancery was concerned with. At best, some shadow of the rule 'Do unto others as you would have them do unto you'—at least in its full-blown form—persisted in the Court's enforcement of selfless conduct where certain kinds of obligations had been undertaken and, perhaps, in an attenuated form in the Court's insistence that 'he who seeks equity must do equity'.[173] But even this latter envisages an actual *quid pro quo*, and not the merely hypothetical one that the Golden Rule contemplates.

Simplex Conscientia and *Regulata Conscientia*

Thus far, I have been focusing on what might be described as the *substantive* character of *conscientia civilis*. That is, I have been attempting to distinguish its proper sphere on the basis of the kinds of subject-matter to which it might relate. I want now to return to the procedural or methodological dimensions of the question. Arguably, what characterizes *conscientia civilis* is not—at least not only—the subject-matter it deals with, but *how* it approaches that subject-matter. This takes us back to observations such as Nottingham's that equity must adhere to 'certain and known' 'rules and measures', that it must be dispensed according to the strictures of 'science',[174] or that the conscience by which he is to proceed must be 'tied to certain measures'.[175] The 'regular and political administration of

---

168 *Hill* v. *Bowyer* (1675/6), ibid., vol. 1, p. 312.

169 *Gibson* v. *Kenvyn* (1682), ibid., vol. 2, p. 931.

170 Ibid.

171 *Boys v. Wilkinson* (1679/80), *Nottingham's Chancery Cases*, vol. 2, p. 806.

172 *Gravenor* v. *Cartwright* (1679), ibid., vol. 2, p. 758.

173 Invoked by Nottingham, in some form or another, in several cases: see, for example, *Hatton* v. *Long* (1673), ibid., vol. 1, p. 10, *Knight* v. *Coke* (1673), ibid., vol. 1, p. 16, *Godfry* v. *Lloyd* (1675/6), ibid., vol. 1, p. 260, *Botham* v. *Farrington* (1676), ibid., vol. 1, p. 348, and *Jarvis* v. *Midleton* (1680/1), ibid., vol. 2, p. 856.

174 *Earl of Feversham* v. *Watson*, ibid., vol. 2, p. 639.

175 *Cook* v. *Fountain*, ibid., vol. 1, p. 371. I take 'certain' here to be used in the sense of 'determined, fixed; not variable' (*Shorter Oxford English Dictionary*).

equity'[176] or 'legal and regular equity'[177] to which he refers may speak as much to order and consistency of process as to substantive parsimony.

Once again, this concern is hardly new with Nottingham. We will remember, for example, Robert Snagg's distinction, during the Elizabethan period, between '*Simplex Conscientia*' and '*Regulata Conscientia*'—ostensibly between conscience at large and conscience applied in a consistent, regulated way. We will recall as well the distinction between the Chancery's *Potentia Ordinaria* and its postulated *Potentia Absoluta*, which the author of *Praxis Almæ Curiæ Cancellariæ* articulates in procedural terms. 'Potentia Ordinaria', we are told, is '*where a certain Order is observed, as in the Law Positive, whereby the Lord Chancellor ... proceedeth .... according to the Course and Method of Proceedings at the Common Law*', whereas 'Lex Naturæ non habet certum Ordinem, *but by whatsoever means the Truth may be found ...* . Et ideo dicitur Processus Absolutus ...'.[178] As we have noticed, an important characteristic of Chancery was that it did not regard itself as subject to the procedural constraints of the common law courts. In arguing that equity should be more regular, Nottingham was not, of course, saying that common law procedural rules should apply, but he was saying that equity should follow *some* rules, presumably both procedural and substantive. Even the latter involve a procedural dimension: while the content of the rule is substantive, the requirement that it be consistently applied—or even that it is understood as a *rule*—is a matter of method or process.

The issue is highlighted in the House of Lords' discussion in *Earl of Feversham* v. *Watson*, which focuses on the question whether equity as administered there need be as constrained as that administered in the Chancery. One view is represented by the Earl of Shaftesbury (1621–83)[179] ('Law and equity stand upon rules and are not arbitrary'[180]) and Lord Holles ('our power here is by rules of law or rules of equity, for though we are above forms, yet certainly we are not above rules'[181]); the other by Lord Fretchville ('I do not think we are tied up here by the rules of legal equity'[182]), by Lord Privy Seal ('This Court is not tied to the rules below but hath a right to use the latitude of their consciences'[183]), and by Lord George Berkeley ('we are not tied to judge as the Lord Chancellor must do, but may go on equity at large'[184]). Two points require emphasis here. First, the Lords make a distinction between Chancery equity and equity generally or, to use the Lord Treasurer's words, between 'the King's conscience limited to rules' and 'his

176 Nottingham, *Prolegomena*, p. 194.

177 *Honywood* v. *Bennett*, *Nottingham's Chancery Cases*, vol. 1, p. 214.

178 Brown, *Praxis*, p. 46; ECCO image CW3306379434:53.

179 Anthony Ashley-Cooper, Earl of Shaftesbury; himself Lord Chancellor (1672–73).

180 *Earl of Feversham* v. *Watson*, *Nottingham's Chancery Cases*, vol. 2, p. 646.

181 Ibid., p. 648.

182 Ibid., p. 647.

183 Ibid., p. 648.

184 Ibid.

conscience administered with more latitude'.[185] Second, whatever their views on equity in the House of Lords, they all appear to agree that Chancery equity, or the conscience of Chancery, is regulated or ruled. In other words, there is a sense in which Chancery equity, although less strictly ordered than the common law, by this time is far from being simply '*Potesta Absoluta*'.

Not surprisingly, Nottingham regularly invokes 'rules'—certainly preferring them to the compassion, if not to the justice, of a case. So, for example, in *Coles* v. *Hancock*, he appears unwilling to accept a litigant's argument based on the broad equity that it would be 'against natural Right and Conscience, that her Father leaving a very considerable Estate, she should have nothing of it',[186] preferring to adhere closely to the wording of the deed and will in question.[187] And, *Bluck* v. *Crisp*, he observes that, by coming into Chancery, a litigant submits himself 'to the standing rules of legal equity', and, although he 'reprove[s] Bluck for so rigorous an exaction of a debt', he feels that he is 'tied up to rules' from which he cannot depart.[188]

Yale remarks Nottingham's dedication to constructing rules, noting particularly his regular resort to the common law for patterns of such rules.[189] In the *Prolegomena*, Nottingham himself, citing St. German, says that 'the Lord Chancellor must order his conscience after the rules and grounds of the laws of this realm',[190] and in many cases he does just that.[191]

But one must be careful not to overstate Nottingham's following the law in constructing rules of equity. Recall that, in *Earl of Feversham* v. *Watson*, he says that what is required is that conscience should be dispensed according to 'rules of science'. 'Science' here connotes among other things consistency, system, and reason, not simply imitation of the common law. Frequently the 'reason' underlying rules of equity is not the same as that of the common law. As we have seen, Nottingham makes observations such as 'though rights in law are governed by rules of law, yet rules in equity are governed only by conscience'.[192] Explicitly,

---

185 Ibid.

186 *Coles* v. *Hancock* (1680–81) 2 Ch. Rep. 210 at 211, ER 659 at 659.

187 He does, however, appear to make some concession to her argument when he divides the proceeds of the testator's real estate, which the latter apparently wanted added to his personal estate left to his four other children, among all five children.

188 *Bluck* v. *Crisp* (1673/74), *Nottingham's Chancery Cases*, vol. 1, p. 35.

189 Yale, 'Introduction', ibid., vol. 1, p. lii.

190 Nottingham, *Prolegomena*, p. 200.

191 See, for example, *Thornborough* v. *Baker*, *Nottingham's Chancery Cases*, vol. 1, p. 202, where he says that 'there ought … to be some certain rule. And the best rule is to come as near the rule and reason of the Common Law as may be'. Compare *Tabor* v. *Tabor* (1679), ibid., vol. 2, p. 769.

192 *Cox* v. *Quantock* (1674), ibid., vol. 1, p. 102. Compare *Salsbury* v. *Bagott*, ibid., vol. 2, p. 503, *Barkly* v. *Penn* (1680/81), ibid., vol. 2, p. 863, and *Coulston* v. *Gardner* (1680/81), ibid., vol. 2, p. 871.

conscience can be a *source* of rules. He regularly contrasts common law rules with the rules given by conscience: 'whatever the law be in that case, I held it good conscience to charge the husband';[193] a 'title, though good in law, is against conscience';[194] a party should 'be charged no further than in good conscience she ought to be and not according to niceties of law'.[195] He sometimes even implicitly disparages common law rules by juxtaposing them with 'natural and universal justice'.[196] Elsewhere, he envisages that a measured alternative to that offered by 'the rules of Common Law' is 'the rules of natural and universal justice'.[197] Whatever the rules of equity might be, they do not simply mimic the rules of common law.

Indeed, one should be cautious in emphasizing that Lord Nottingham consistently insists on the primacy of established rules or prior judicial decisions. Recall that in *Lawrence* v. *Berney*, he refuses to accept a decree issued by his predecessor on the basis that he 'will never charge [his] conscience with promoting an apparent injustice',[198] a position that he adopts again in *Moor* v. *Hinton*: citing 'the manifest partiality and injustice of [an order]', he declares that 'a court of conscience will never confirm ... an award against conscience'.[199] Elsewhere, invited by counsel to accept the limits defined by an earlier case—'where will you stop if you do not stop at *Child & Baylie's case*?'—he declines to do so: 'I answer, I will stop everywhere where any inconvenience appears, nowhere before.'[200] Indeed, Walter Williams reports that Nottingham once said that 'he would leap over Hedge and Ditch' to come at justice, and specifically relates this attitude to Chancery's absolute power, including a power to re-hear cases.[201] While Nottingham undoubtedly enterprised to make equity more 'measured', his position in this respect—especially regarding the source of the 'measure'—must be nuanced.

One aspect of the process of making equity more rule-bound is, of course, the recognition of precedent. In this context, the well-known exchange between

---

193 *Dux Albermarle* v. *Cutler* (1676), ibid., vol. 2, p. 470.

194 *Rosser* v. *Evans* (1673), ibid., vol. 1, p. 221.

195 *Williams* v. *Day* (1680), ibid., vol. 2, p. 821.

196 *Nurse* v. *Yerworth*, ibid., vol. 1, p. 117. He goes on to observe that the law's narrow approach 'would be laughed at in any other part of the world'.

197 *The East India Company* v. *Blake* (1674), ibid., vol. 1, p. 61. Here he is referring to the instance of 'an infidel's country where no ordinary justice can be had' (pp. 60–61).

198 *Lawrence* v. *Berney*, ibid., vol. 2, p. 584.

199 *Moor* v. *Hinton* (1677/78), ibid., vol. 2, p. 619.

200 *Howard* v. *Duke of Norfolk* (1681/82), ibid., vol. 2, p. 914. Here the more basic principle seems to be 'convenience', rather than conscience or natural justice. As we have noticed previously, the word 'convenient' at that time had more of a connotation of 'fitting' or 'appropriate' than it does now.

201 Williams, p. 121.

Vaughan C.J. (1603–74)[202] and Lord Keeper Bridgman in *Fry* v. *Porter*[203] is instructive. The former—perhaps reflecting a common lawyer's perception of equity—expresses surprise at Keeling C.J.'s (c. 1607–71)[204] 'citing of Presidents [precedents] in matter of Equity, for ... Equity is an universal Truth, and there can be no President in it'.[205] If the precedent accurately reflects 'universal Truth', it is superfluous; if it does not, it should not be followed. The Lord Keeper replies that 'Presidents are very necessary and useful to us, for in them we may find the reasons of the Equity to guide us ... and it would be very strange and very ill, if we should disturb and set aside what has been the course for a long *Series* of time and ages'.[206] There are, it should be noted, two kinds of arguments in this response. One is that precedents help judges to understand the underlying equity, which presumably is the critical point. The second is more formalistic, suggesting that what has been done before (at least for a period of time) should be done again. According to at least one late seventeenth-century case, ''Tis nothing but Precedent that consecrates Half the Decrees in Equity'.[207]

Further comment on the issue of precedent in equity appears in 'The Preface' to a late seventeenth-century compilation of Chancery cases. The compiler, having cited the above exchange, acknowledges that '*Equity and right Reason in it self is an universal thing*'; neither '*Climates nor Cases, Persons or Things .... can alter the proper and intrinsick Notions of Truth, Right and Justice*'.[208] At the same time, '*Mens Judgments, especially in Politicks or Morals, can seldom be said to amount to Mathematical Decisions: No one can imagine himself to have such refined Powers of Soul as to decree* Æquitatem ad pondus'.[209] The reference to 'Mathematical Decisions' reminds us—or reminds me—of Nottingham's 'certain measures'. Presumably, one kind of 'certain measure' would be a mathematical assessment of 'intrinsick … Truth, Right and Justice'. But, says the compiler of the *Reports*, such precision is hard, if not impossible, to achieve. Moreover, there will inevitably be '*some little ... Inclinations (no ways guided by any Interest or Prejudice) which will turn the Scale ... something of a Mans Temper which*

---

202 Sir John Vaughan, Chief Justice of the Court of Common Pleas (appointed 1668).

203 *Fry* v. *Porter* (1670) *Modern Reports* (1682) 300.

204 Sir John Keeling, Chief Justice of the Court of King's Bench (appointed 1665).

205 *Fry* v. *Porter*, p. 307.

206 Ibid.

207 *Countess of Radnor* v. *Vandenbendy* (1697) Shower 69 at 71–72, 1 ER 48 at 49. The attitude is illustrated by Lord Keeper North's expression of surprise in *Edmunds* v. *Povey* (1683) 1 Vern. 187 at 188, 23 ER 404 at 404 that, although a practice might be 'very disputable', 'counsel laid their shoulders to a point, that had been so long since settled, and received as the constant course of Chancery'.

208 *Reports of Cases Taken and Adjudged in the Court of Chancery*, sig. A4r; EEBO image 29452:4.

209 Ibid., sigs. A4r–A4v; images 29452:4–5.

will insensibly mingle and slide into his best formed Notions and Designs'.[210] Careful attention to precedents permits a judge to constrain such inclinations, thus '*secur[ing] himself from making Orders and Decrees totally Arbitrary*'.[211] Recognizing the binding nature of precedents may forestall that arbitrariness which Chancery critics denounced and which Chancery apologists like Nottingham acknowledged to be threats to regular justice.

Nottingham's own attitude towards precedent was, at least, ambivalent. As we have seen, in places he speaks of being tied to rules, and in one case he observes that the law has for so long condemned something that it is no longer necessary to give any reason other than the rule itself.[212] Such observations suggest a process to which I have previously alluded: while general principles—of, say, justice or conscience—might have been the basis for original decisions in equity, once those decisions have been made, they become themselves the rule for subsequent like cases, obviating the need to return to basic concepts. In other words, while the judgment in a case entirely new might involve beginning with a primary principle given by *synderesis* and working from that through two or more linked syllogisms, whereby the conclusion of each higher-order syllogism becomes the major premise of the next, once the specific major premise which applies to the particular case is ascertained, it becomes a rule. So, in the next case, all that is necessary is to go to that lowest level syllogism and apply the specific rule to the new facts. As more and more cases are decided, more and more rules are generated and there is correspondingly less and less need to resort to the basic precepts of conscience. When Nottingham says that he is tied to rules, he is essentially acknowledging the consequences of this process, albeit not in these terms.

But his position seems not to have involved total acquiescence in this process. An illustrative case is *Thornborough* v. *Baker*. The issue in the case was whether money paid to redeem a mortgage should go to the deceased mortgagee's executor as personal property or to his heir as real property. Nottingham offers a number of reasons for choosing the former—among them, as we have seen, that 'in natural justice and equity the principal right of the mortgagee is to the money'.[213] Having presented reasons, he proceeds to examine the precedents. This clearly indicates that he took prior decisions seriously. But he did not take them uncritically. One of the precedents he approves; one he distinguishes; but others he disapproves and does not follow. In other words, there is arguably a certain rule given by cases

210 Ibid., sig. A4v; image 29452:5.

211 Ibid. We will recall that Hacket, commenting on Lord Keeper Williams, made the point that 'Equity according to Decrees and Precedents foregoing' was necessary 'to keep the Keeper from Exravagancies of his own Fancies and Affections, and so to hold him really to Conscience ...' (p. 57; EEBO image 49492:30).

212 *Knight* v. *Knight* (1674), *Nottingham's Chancery Cases*, vol. 1, p. 104.

213 *Thornborough* v. *Baker*, ibid., vol. 1, p. 202.

decided by his predecessors.[214] But the fact of there being previous decisions is not the ultimate criterion. The precedent he approves he calls 'right and just'.[215] Conversely, one he disapproves because the court invoked an incorrect 'measure of justice'.[216] That is, the court considered the fact that, while the executors already had assets, 'the heir had no other provision'. It is in this context that Nottingham remarks that this is irrelevant to the justice of the case, because '[d]isherison of the heir [is] an argument of compassion, not of right'.[217] However we might identify counter-examples, in this case and many others Nottingham evinces a habit of mind in which higher-order principles of justice remain the touchstone against which 'rules' emerging from particular cases are to be assessed.

That is, when he speaks of the need for 'certain measures', he does not mean only positive rules. In *Thornborough* he says specifically that the *measure* of justice is not whether a person already has assets or not. Although specific rules may frequently, or even usually, be a good measure of what a court should do, they are themselves subject to being measured by something more fundamental. Correspondingly, 'science' for equity is not comprehended by an encyclopedic knowledge of recognized rules and previous cases, although both of these are important aspects of that science. But, for Nottingham, the science of equity involves the *reasons*, in 'natural right and common justice',[218] 'natural justice',[219] 'natural equity',[220] 'natural honesty',[221] or even mathematical truth[222] that support the rule.[223] Equity can be 'scientific' without merely applying, unsearchingly, 'rules'.

As we have seen, Nottingham in more than one place tells us that equity is governed by 'rules of conscience'. These rules may correspond to common law rules, but they frequently do not. Moreover, he insists that conscience must be dispensed by 'the rules of science'. So both conscience and, by extension, equity must be constrained by 'science'. But 'science' here is intensely ambiguous. For

---

214 One of the cases he disapproves, *Tilly* v. *Egerton* (1660), 2 Freeman 125, 1 Ch. Rep. 181, 22 ER 1102, was decided by *two* of his predecessors, Lord Clarendon, then Chancellor, and Bridgman C.J. In another, *Martin* v. *Hall* (1661), he was himself counsel for the successful heir.

215 *Thornborough* v. *Baker*, *Nottingham's Chancery Cases*, vol. 1, p. 204.

216 Ibid.

217 Ibid. (Second set of brackets in text.)

218 *Weaver* v. *Woodyear* (1680), *Nottingham's Chancery Cases*, vol. 2, p. 832.

219 See, for example, *Boys* v. *Wilkinson* (1679/80), ibid., vol. 2, p. 806.

220 See *Nurse* v. *Yerworth*, ibid., vol. 1, p. 119.

221 *Hatchett* v. *Bindon* (1677), ibid., vol. 2, p. 565.

222 *Furner* v. *Lane* (1677), ibid., vol. 2, p. 539, ruling that children 'of the half blood are equally capable of administration with them of the whole blood. And the reason of it is mathematical, for *quod tangit in puncto æque tangit ac si tetigesset toto latere*'.

223 Yale observes that Lord Nottingham was 'a pioneer in equity in providing reasons for his rules' ('Introduction', ibid., vol. 1, p. cxxi).

one thing, as we well know, the conventional view of conscience emphasized that an essential element of the word itself is 'science', meaning knowledge. In this view, conscience was necessarily 'scientific' in the sense of involving accurate knowledge of rules and facts, and logical derivation of conclusions. Not only religious controversialists, but also politico-legal writers continued to make this point. Thus, to cite only two further examples, Sir Edward Coke is reported to have said '*Ubi non est scientia, non est conscientia*'[224] and Lord Clarendon, in a rather different context, says that 'there is some Science necessary to be supposed, where there is a Pretence to Conscience'.[225] If science is essential to conscience in any event, is Nottingham's endeavour to constrain the operation of conscience by science merely tautological?

For it not to be, he must either be contemplating that there is a kind of conscience—*conscientia interna*—that is not scientific, that is subjective or intuitive, or he must be thinking of 'science' in terms narrower than those in which the casuists regarded it in relation to conscience. The first possibility, that Nottingham thought of private conscience as 'unscientific' is plausible, but unlikely: one would assume that, if asked, he would have adopted the conventional position that there are absolute moral principles, probably grounded in the law of God, that are knowable. Even Hobbes has one of his interlocutors in *A Dialogue Between a Philosopher and a Student*, which in some ways recalls St. German's *Doctor and Student*, argue that bishops should be chancellors because they are 'the most able and rational men, obliged by their profession to Study Equity, because it is the law of God', and because 'they are the Doctors in Cases of Conscience'.[226] I doubt that Nottingham would have maintained that 'practical divinity' is not scientific, although he might have maintained that it was not the proper science to be exercised in the Court of Chancery. So this leaves us with the likelihood that he was contemplating 'science' of a different, more circumscribed kind when he spoke of the science of conscience in relation to equity.

How to define that narrower science in coherent general terms is not self-evident. The fact that it was systematic, for example, does not really distinguish it from the science of the casuists. If anything, that science forms a system more comprehensive and intricately inter-linked than the law. Nor was Nottingham's 'science' of equity the science of Baconian induction, as opposed, say, to scholasticism. Although

224 Cited in *Reasons Against the Bill*, p. 3; EEBO image 133365:3.

225 Clarendon, 'On Conscience', p. 163; ECCO image CW332271293:174.

226 Thomas Hobbes, *A Dialogue Between a Phylosopher and a Student of the Common-Laws of England* (London, 1681), p. 84; EEBO image 54911:129. Alan Cromartie says that Hobbes made the suggestion 'mischievously' ('General Introduction' to *A Dialogue Between a Philosopher and a Student of the Common Laws of England*, in *Thomas Hobbes: Writings on Common Law and Hereditary Right*, eds Alan Cromartie and Quentin Skinner (Oxford, 2005), p. xxxiii.

Nottingham sometimes speaks disparagingly of 'scholastic' reasoning,[227] his mode of thinking regularly involved deduction from first principles of 'natural justice'. This corresponds to the casuists' reasoning from basic precepts given, ostensibly, by *synderesis*, and, indeed, in an unelaborated assertion, Lord Campbell suggests that Nottingham's mode of judicial reasoning 'remind[s] one of the resolution of cases of conscience by the schoolmen'.[228] To be sure, Nottingham did employ the kind of inductive or analogical reasoning involved in looking closely at precedents and at particular circumstances, but it is not clear that he developed general principles from these 'particulars' rather than assessing the particulars in terms of more general, perhaps even *a priori*, principles.

What Nottingham might have been getting at, although not explicitly, was that the 'science' of equity was the science of a particular discipline, the discipline of the law as opposed to the discipline of, say, practical theology. So, referring to Chief Justice Hale, he says that he was an 'absolute … master of the whole science of the Common Law', clearly referring to his knowledge of 'even ... the most abstruse and hidden parts of it'.[229] This seems to be the essence of the response of Hobbes's lawyer to the philosopher's suggestion that ecclesiastics should be 'Judges in a Court of Equity'. That is, although they are 'able and rational', although they are specialists in matters of conscience, they are not learned in the civic law. Indeed, one can find in religious writers instances of diffidence about commenting on the actual law, albeit they seem quite assured about the moral or spiritual dimensions of an issue. Thus, for example, Tillotson, although he purports to describe '*What that exact Righteousness is ... in matter of Contracts*', admits that it is a question 'to be handled very modestly, by such as acknowledge themselves unacquainted with the affairs of the world, and the necessities of things, and the particular and hidden reasons of some kinde of dealings'.[230] We will recall, too, that Hacket criticizes the view that 'an unexpert Man' might be 'the chief Arbiter in a Court of Equity', that it is enough to 'Bring Reason and Conscience with you, the good stock of Nature'.[231] So, although it is not clear, a significant dimension of the 'science' to which Nottingham refers is the knowledge of the *law* and of the processes of the law.

A problem with making 'science' refer to a distinction between disciplines is, of course, that still in Nottingham's time, that distinction was not always

---

[227] See, for example, *Earl of Feversham* v. *Watson*, *Nottingham's Chancery Cases*, vol. 2, p. 647, referring to the reasoning of the Bishop of Chester (John Pearson [1612–86]).

[228] John Campbell, *The Lives of the Lord Chancellors and Keepers of the Great Seal of England*, ed. J.A. Mallory (10 vols, Toronto, 1876), vol. 4, p. 226.

[229] Lord Nottingham, Speech to Serjeant Rainsford on the latter's accession to the seat of Chief Justice of the King's Bench, in *Nottingham's Chancery Cases*, vol. 1, p. 319.

[230] Tillotson, 'Exact Righteousness', p. 229; EEBO image 105033:119.

[231] Hacket, p. 57; EEBO image 49492:30.

clearly demarcated. Although he might not have gone as far as Baxter who says that 'it is most easy to see that he that will be a good *Lawyer* must first be a *Divine*',[232] he would almost certainly have found it difficult to maintain a strict separation between the sacred and the secular. We have already noted instances of his invoking 'the law of God' as at least part of his reasoning in many cases. But we have seen as well that his reasoning is eclectic in many ways—he brings into consideration not only the law of God, but also the laws of natural phenomena, the insights of mathematics, moral philosophy, natural justice, and so on. In spite of his announced desire to confine equity to strictly 'legal' limits, the sources of legal knowledge were, for him, various. The boundaries between disciplines were porous, and 'leakage' appears to have been inevitable.

Conclusion

Yale observes that '[i]t would be wrong ... to look to Lord Nottingham or any other practising lawyer of his day for a philosophical analysis of justice'.[233] Similarly, it is in some ways perverse to look to him for a coherent philosophical analysis of conscience in the juridical sense. His distinction between *conscientia interna* and *conscientia civilis* temptingly suggests such an analysis, but an examination of his practice reveals considerable uncertainty about the parameters of each. Again, this is partly because conscience *per se* comprehends any sub-set of conscience, so what we have is a continuum rather than really separate categories. And it is partly because conscience at that time was a spiritual and moral criterion: excluding these dimensions would have been inconsistent with its understood character. Nottingham indeed represents an important point in the regularization of equity, but he has not really become the 'modern' that he is sometimes made out to be. If the conscience of equity became more distinct as a result of his efforts, it was probably not so much because he had developed a coherent theory as because he more fully established the kinds of particular situations to which that conscience would extend—and to which it would be limited.

232 Baxter, Bk. 4, p. 36; EEBO image 58467:416.

233 Yale, "Introduction," *Nottingham's Chancery Cases*, vol. 1, p. cxxiii.

Chapter 9
Conclusion

Discourse depicting conscience as a defining feature of equity persisted throughout the period I have been examining—as, indeed, it still does today. But that discourse tends to be formulaic, or at least re-iterative. The same expressions recur; often, one author simply repeats what others have said. In the available materials, it is difficult to discern much analysis of the concept, at least in general terms. At the same time, equity—and, presumably, the role of conscience as well—were evolving from something 'praetorian' to something more systematic. We encounter the same words and expressions—formulæ—used as if they are describing what they always described, but what they relate to has been undergoing gradual and more or less subtle changes. To some extent what we witness is a verbal *stasis* accompanied by a conceptual evolution. This is common enough in the history of words: referents change, so that old words have new meanings. What is perhaps noteworthy about conscience as definitive of equity is that the evolution of the referent tends to compromise it as a juristic concept. Attempts to preserve its meaning in this context—for example by positing a notion of 'public conscience'—are a kind of implicit acknowledgement of this diminishing appropriateness. At the same time they tend to introduce elements rather antithetical to what the word comes primarily to mean.

To be sure, there was what might be called an 'official' account of conscience which presented it in terms consistent with what we expect of a juristic principle. That account, more immediately associated with divinity than with law but arguably a culturally paradigmatic account, was developed by medieval scholastics and persisted, with modifications, well into the seventeenth century. It can be characterized as offering a picture of conscience as objectively authoritative. The notion of objectivity would appear to be crucial to conscience as a principle of judicial decision. Otherwise, conscience would be a variable standard, ostensibly incongruous with the imperatives of the 'rule of law'. As long as conscience can be understood as subject to uniform overarching rules and as involving processes of rational inference, it reproduces what are conventionally regarded as typical legal processes. It can at least be rationalized as being non-subjective and non-arbitrary. As long as it is objective in these ways, we can comfort ourselves with the view that the same conscience might be applied by different persons. But to the extent that that objective account becomes attenuated, conscience becomes less compelling (except, perhaps, rhetorically) as a basis for judgment, at least where consistency and certainty are privileged features of judicial activity.

In observing that there was a conventional account of conscience that *portrayed* it as objective, I am not, of course, saying that it ever 'really' was. It may be that what we call conscience always has been some kind of subjective intuition, a *mélange* of feelings, familial conventions, personal experiences, prejudices, and so on. All I am saying is that, if the concept of conscience is constructed in a certain way, that might make it more or less congruent with a prevalent concept of law. Therefore, it at least makes sense, in terms of that construction, to invoke it as a basis for judicial decision. Where, on the other hand, the received account of conscience constructs it as essentially subjective, and indeed extols that subjectivity, then conscience is more difficult to reconcile with what we may understand legal judgment to entail. At least its role has to be explained in a very different way: for example, we may admire judges who have a strong sense of (subjective) conscience, or we may make respect for individual and implicitly subjective conscience a deep element in the rules we apply, so that 'freedom of conscience' becomes a fundamental right, defining a space into which the law may not intrude. But this is a far cry from saying that conscience can identify and declare what substantive legal norms should be. What I argue is that, while the official view was still recognizable well into the seventeenth century it was becoming modified in significant ways that made its reconciliation with law increasingly awkward.

Perhaps the major change, wrought in large part by the Reformation, was the growing individualization of conscience. Theoretically, at least at first, individualization did not necessarily mean subjectivization. Although determinations of conscience became a matter for the individual, the measure of conscience was still thought to be, or depicted as, objective, so that every person's conscience, governed by the same ultimate rule and rightly instructed, should reach the same conclusion. In other words, there were still thought to be uniquely right answers, although it was now for the individual to seek those answers, rather than to have them dictated by an external, traditionally ecclesiastical, authority. But a virtually inevitable concomitant of the individualization of conscience is its diversification.

Several inter-related aspects of this individualization of conscience can be identified. One, perhaps the broadest, is captured by the expression 'every man his own casuist'. That is, in cases of conscience, rather than deferring to the authority of an expert (or simply of someone higher up in a given hierarchy), each person could—and indeed, must—take responsibility for him or herself. The precise role of the specialist was, of course, not as clear-cut as this implies, for Protestant casuists were undoubtedly still offering advice about specific cases. Thus, Wood points out that Taylor recognized that there was often a need for 'a spiritual guide', that Sanderson, while cautioning against reliance 'upon another man's judgment', acknowledged that deference was due to 'the authority of learned men', and that Hall deprecated not only the alleged Roman Catholic tendency to make their priests 'either oracles or idols', but also that of some Protestants to make 'cyphers' of theirs.[1] But, ultimately, for Protestants it was for the individual to draw conclusions of conscience.

Besides privileging the role of the individual in applying rules to personal circumstances, the process of individualization which affected conscience also had the effect of making the rules themselves increasingly unstable. As we have seen, for the seventeenth century Christian, the rule of conscience was the will of God, manifested in more than one way, but ultimately in Scripture.[2] But the Protestant emphasis upon each person's access to, and reading of, the sacred text created the potential for diversity of interpretation. Thus not only the particular conclusions of conscience from an agreed rule were individualized but so too was the rule itself. We have noticed that a lawyer like Edward Hake, for example, can argue that non-ecclesiastics are, after the Reformation, as qualified as ecclesiastics to administer conscience, because they have ready access to the source of the rules of conscience. He may be assuming that all qualified readers will understand the rules similarly. But implicit in his acknowledgement of an increased number of authoritative readers of the rules is the possibility of an indefinite number of such readers who will not necessarily all read in the same way. The notion of a limited body of authoritative readers of a generally inaccessible text has been replaced by that of a democracy of readers engaging with an open and contested text. If not fully in the seventeenth century, this process leads ultimately to that stage in the development of the concept of conscience which C.S. Lewis describes as follows: '[h]ence we have *consciences* in the plural, not meaning those different conscirings which different men must obviously have but those different inner laws they acknowledge'.[3]

Coupled with these individualizing tendencies there was a deep concern to maintain the authority of conscience. Perhaps even more than their Catholic predecessors, the Protestant casuists wrestled with the conundrum of the erroneous, but authentic, conscience. Sharp, as we have seen, is a late example. He specifically addresses the question of the '*Authority of Conscience*', that is, '*how far a Man is Obliged to follow or be guided by his Conscience in his Actions*'.[4] Where the conscience is correct in its conclusion, this issue is unproblematic. The difficulty arises where our conviction 'in our Judgment' is that we should do or refrain from doing something 'because we believe that God hath Commanded it',[5] but where that conviction (or the judgment upon which it is based) may be, according to some 'absolute' criterion, *wrong*. Like many others before him, Sharp

---

[1] Thomas Wood, *English Casuistical Divinity During the Seventeenth Century* (London 1952), pp. 54–5.

[2] See, for example, Robert Eyre, *A Discourse Concerning the Nature and Satisfaction of a Good and Inoffensive Conscience* (London, 1693), p. 8; EEBO image 62636:8.

[3] C.S. Lewis, *Studies in Words*, (2nd edn, Cambridge, 1967), p. 199.

[4] John Sharp, *A Discourse Concerning Conscience* (London, 1687), p. 17; EEBO image 37553:11.

[5] Ibid.

says that it is sinful not to follow one's conscience. But, if one's conscience has 'mispersuaded'one what is done remains *objectively* sinful. Sharp acknowledges the harshness of this doctrine, implying as it does that in these circumstances one cannot help but sin. He ultimately takes the position, with many qualifications, that if a person has done all that is in his power to inform his conscience aright he will not be culpable if he acts according to his conscience. The sincere individual conscience, and not necessarily the correctness of judgment, becomes an ultimate measure of one's actions.

At the same time, granting that the sincere individual conscience has this kind of authority has potentially far-reaching implications. Notably, it creates the potential for social and political disunity. As we have seen, this was a serious preoccupation for Sharp and for others. Indeed, an important paradox of conscience is that it pulls in opposite directions. As Sharp puts it,

> A strange thing this is; that *Conscience*, which among other ends, was given to Mankind for a Preservative, and Security of the Publick Peace; for the more Effectually Obliging Men to Unity, and Obedience to Laws; yet should be a means of setting them at distance, and prove a Shelter for Disobedience, and Disorder.[6]

Such an observation anticipates by three centuries Lowell Gallagher's thesis that while, officially, conscience was supposed to be a principle of social cohesion and even control, because of the dimension that focuses on personal judgment, even aberrant judgment, it was inherently destabilizing.[7]

This authentication of individual conscience leads to a perceived need to hive off its sphere of operation. Possible responses to the apprehended threat include Sharp's: posit very stringent criteria for what constitutes sincere or authentic conscience, and insist that the dissenter accept, quietly, the social consequences of non-conformity. That is, broadly, confine such aberrant, but nevertheless valid, conscience. A more comprehensive way of confining such consciences is to push conscience into the realm of the private. Obviously, conscience operates in those who do conform, but the *assertion* of conscience, and hence to a large extent its foregrounding, tends to become associated with those who do not. To the extent that conscience tends to be identified with dissent, it has to be isolated if it is to be validated. Such isolation must involve displacing the *special* sphere of operation of conscience from the public order, where it might be disruptive. As Edward Bagshaw puts it in a letter—framed, incidentally, as a plea for equity—to Lord Clarendon, 'difference in Opinion about *Religious Matters*, may easily

---

6 Ibid., p. 2; EEBO image 37553:4.

7 Lowell Gallagher, *Medusa's Gaze: Casuistry and Conscience in the Renaissance* (Stanford, 1991).

be reconciled to a candid pursuance of the same *Civil Interests*'.[8] This may be true, but, paradoxically, it could be that the reconciliation may be achieved only by division, by the separation of the particular sphere of conscience ('*Religious Matters*') from the civil arena.

We have noticed as well other aspects of the response to conscientious dissent that had the tendency to make it private. So, for example, there were those who distinguished liberty of conscience from liberty of practice, arguing that, since conscience is essentially a matter of inner conviction, it can be separated from outward conformity. Liberty of conscience, some argued, can be maintained while adhering, in outward practice, to the demands of social, political or ecclesiastical order. Conversely, there were those who argued that the norms of at least the political order should not touch the inward or the spiritual, the special sphere of conscience. Although used by different camps in the debate, each of these positions had the effect of pushing conscience toward the private. In this connection we should recall as well the Protestant emphasis on the radical unknowability, except by oneself and God, of what the conscience knows.

All of these tendencies would, I suspect, have encouraged the privatization or interiorization of conscience and a corresponding association of conscience typically with the private alone. Thus, apart from observations such as Cudworth's that the idea of a public conscience is internally contradictory, wider processes in the re-characterization of conscience would have had the effect of confining it more to one's personal judgment and persuasion. Gradually, whatever the theory might be, conscience is moved in the direction of the subjective.

Other phenomena might be seen as reinforcing this process. Wood suggests that the development of what he calls Jesuit 'legalism' resulted, in Roman Catholicism, in 'the drawing of a distinction between "moral" theology and "ascetic' theology"'.[9] The former is concerned with 'the minimum that can be required to secure the observance of the commandments of God and the precepts of the Church'.[10] Crudely, one might say that this is a matter of knowing and following the rules. Ascetic theology, on the other hand, seeks 'to train men in the way of Christian perfection'[11]—that is, presumably, not just to adhere to external strictures, but to cultivate the internal disposition of righteousness. Wood goes on to argue that the thrust of Protestant practical divinity was, ultimately, to lead people 'to the Christian ideal of holiness'.[12] That is, the 'whole' tendency of Protestant casuistry was something like that of Catholic 'ascetic' theology. We have encountered this kind of claim before, for example in observations that for at least some Protestants the point of examination of the conscience was not so much

---

[8] Edward Bagshaw, *A Letter to the Right Honourable, Edward Earl of Clarendon, Lord High Chancellour of England* (London, 1662), p. 9; EEBO image 52251:6.

[9] Wood, p. 64.

[10] Ibid.

[11] Ibid.

[12] Ibid., p. 65.

to determine particular instances of conduct as to assess the spiritual condition of the person as a whole. So, for example, Samuel Clarke (1599–1682) defines conscience as 'a prime faculty of the reasonable soul, there set to give notice of its spirituall estate in what terms it stands with God'.[13] We have qualified this generalization by pointing to Protestant casuists' significant concern with assessing what is to be done in specific situations. Even then, as Wood argues and as we have seen elsewhere, the Protestant approach was somewhat tentative, concerned less with offering catalogues of detailed rules or answers than with teaching a method, with explaining and proving "Propositions concerning … *Conscience* in Thesi, and in general ...'.[14] In this regard, we will recall Robert Eyre's observation (cautiously qualified) that, even if 'a Mans Conscience … misguide him'[15] that conscience may still be '*Good and Inoffensive*' if he is 'diligent and industrious to know and understand his Duty' and is 'sincere and hearty in the performance of it'.[16] What is important is what kind of person one is, rather than always doing the correct thing in particular situations.

The significance of this for a theory of conscience in equity is that Protestant casuistry, if not at first, at least at some point tended to make inquiry into matters of conscience less of a law-like activity. Indeed, as Wood observes, that casuistry, to the extent that it involved seeking rules, involved 'rules intended to lead men onwards … to a spiritual condition in which the rules themselves would be no longer necessary'.[17] Again, one must be very wary of accepting this at face value: it may imply something of a caricature of the Roman Catholic position and it may be a rather too optimistically spiritualized account of the Protestant. However, to the extent that it is accurate, it suggests that the realm of conscience in the Protestant conception was in some sense radically separate from the realm of law. If conscience relates, more or less exhaustively, to one's whole spiritual condition, to whether one is in a state of grace or not, then it fits awkwardly with a concept of law as essentially general, externally-dictated rules.

This does not, of course, mean that conscience has nothing to do with the social. In a way, given the basic precept, 'Do unto others as you would have others do unto you', it has everything to do with the social, although not necessarily with the legal. One would hope that the laws of the social order, if not informed by principles generated from conscience, should at least correspond to those principles. And, in general, we are obliged in conscience to observe them. But if we have achieved the condition Wood identifies, then in order to be good we do

---

13 Samuel Clarke, *Medulla Theologiæ: or the Marrow of Divinity* (London, 1659), p. 430; EEBO image 64694:239. Compare Henry Carpenter, *The Deputy Divinity* (London, 1657), p. 18; EEBO image 170295:16.

14 Wood, p. 51, quoting Thomas Barlow, *Directions for the Choice of Books* (Oxford, 1700), p. 41; EEBO image 171143:26.

15 Eyre, p. 14; EEBO image 62636:11.

16 Ibid., p. 20; EEBO image 62636:14.

17 Wood, p. 66.

not need the law: in a sense we do what is right independently of what the law prescribes.

There is, of course, a paradox here, for we know that the Protestant casuists more or less uniformly insist that conscience must have a rule, and that rule is the law of God. But we do not follow it under compulsion; we follow it because it is what we want. In the social sphere, being conscientious entails that we are heartily better than any law compels us to be. For the genuinely conscientious person, civic laws, at least apart from those that are merely for convenience, are superfluous.

There is another dimension to this. If, on the one hand, we are obliged to obey society's laws but, on the other, private conscience has a kind of ultimate validity, there may be pressure to make those laws neutral—or perhaps even minimal with respect to their impact on conscience. The tendency, one might expect, would be to limit the law at least in so far as it impinges on controverted insights of conscience. Something of this process is evident in the 'Preface' to the (revised) 1662 version of the *Book of Common Prayer*, which is significant because it is an 'official' document. The compilers' 'general aim', they say, was 'to do that, which … we conceived might most tend to the preservation of Peace and Unity in the Church'.[18] Doing this involved, among other things, making such modifications 'as should be thought requisite for the ease of tender Consciences'.[19] History no doubt offers intimations of how successful, or otherwise, this endeavour was. But what was intended is evident: in matters of public conformity, concessions must be made to 'tender Consciences'. Again, one thing this entails is that, as much as possible, provisions for public order must be restrained so as to accommodate—or at least not interfere with—private conscience.

Clearly, in explicitly religious matters, this restraint may not be great. But, where the matter is purely social, political, or 'civil', one might expect the restraint to be more extensive. To go back to Wood's observation, we might expect public law (or even 'public conscience') to involve 'the minimum … required' to secure social order or unity. The role of this law is not to impose virtue, but to maintain cohesion and stability. Correspondingly, conscience as the spring of virtue tends to be seen as something else, perhaps even in some ways antithetical to law. On this view, 'private conscience' becomes simply 'conscience', and 'public conscience' is the general law. What was, ostensibly, a three-fold classification—'confessional' conscience, conscience that will engage equity, and law—tends increasingly to look like a dichotomy—private conscience on the one hand and law on the other, the latter comprehending the rules of equity.

The foregoing is rather conceptual, perhaps even speculative. There were other factors at work that probably reinforced the tendencies I have been discussing, or at least operated in concert with them.

---

[18] Church of England, 'Preface', *Book of Common Prayer* (London, 1662), sig. b6r; EEBO image 137235:15.

[19] Ibid., sig. b5v; EEBO image 137235:15.

One category of such other factors might be called 'political'. An early example is St. German himself for, as we will recall, a significant part of his project was to 'nationalize' equity. That is, he resisted the foreign provenance of principles of conscience in what might be called 'papal law' and stressed the ways in which conscience was congruent with the home-grown common law. Again, although his concern was not so much to examine Chancery jurisdiction specifically, his work did impact on conscience in equity. This it did partly by arguing that equity was already in the general law, if that law were understood aright, and partly by arguing that the common law was a reliable indicator of conscience, at least in many cases. This had the effect both of limiting the ambit of equity, and of suggesting that the common law could be a pattern for equity. In some ways this can be seen as the precursor of Lord Nottingham's frequent, but far from invariant, modelling of equity on common law rules.

Then, too, we have seen that, particularly in the seventeenth century, as part of a broader political agenda, Chancery was robustly criticized. Some critics emphasized its ostensibly alien origins in civil and canon law. The concern was intensified by the perception that Chancery was subversive of the Englishman's (*sic*) 'birthright',[20] 'the true Natural and Original Law of *England*'[21]—that is, the common law, with its time-proven particular rules, procedural regularity, factual determinations according to the consciences of juries, and so on. Some emphasized Chancery's supposed connection with the prerogative, that is, with what was seen as arbitrary power. The perceived arbitrariness of Chancery was a particular focus of attack, the arbitrariness arising from the fact that the bases of judgment were hidden in the breast of one man, the Chancellor. This arbitrariness was associated with conscience, but the attack tended not to be so much on conscience *per se*, but on alleged arbitrary *fiat* dressed up in the flattering garb of conscience. Although conscience itself was not deplored so much as what was regarded as the rhetorical deployment of 'conscience', the cure for the problem was to make equity more like regular law and hence to circumscribe conscience as a creative source of Chancery decisions.

Lord Nottingham's insistence that he was administering 'legal and regular equity' can be seen as a direct response to these criticisms. At the same time, his continuing characterization of Chancery as a court of conscience is not wholly inconsistent with that insistence, since it is not conscience but arbitrary judgment that is objectionable. What 'conscience' describes in this context is less vulnerable to criticism, because the positive word 'conscience' is related to an institution whose perceived evils have become attenuated. The difficulty is that what it describes is less distinctively captured by the word. It may be a court of conscience, but the conscience it administered has become rather diluted.

---

20 See Robert Atkyns, *An Enquiry into the Jurisdiction of the Chancery in Causes of Equity* (London, 1695), p. 30; EEBO image 57482:18.

21 Ibid., p. 11; EEBO image 57482:8.

Apart from political pressures, there were economic factors militating against anything like a full-blooded concept of conscience being the criterion of judgment in equity. Thus, for example, W.J. Jones suggests that security of contract was becoming an increasingly important objective,[22] one with which implicit qualifications such as those imposed by equity might not be a good fit. One can discern judicial recognition of this fact in Lord Nottingham's insistence on the doctrine of *caveat emptor* and on implying trusts only when absolutely necessary. Similarly, Wood observes that 'rapid economic changes' 'produced a direct challenge to the seventeenth-century casuists'.[23] We have seen already that several of these casuists devoted considerable space to the application of conscience to commercial transactions, and we noted again considerable, and probably increasing, discrepancies between the perceived demands of pure or absolute conscience and the perceived realities of the marketplace.

As an illustration of the process, one might refer, briefly, to the way usury, or the taking of interest on money loaned, was treated by some of the casuists. Joseph Hall, for example, remarking that, generally, 'Conscience must be the Clarke of the Market',[24] asserts that 'all usury, which is an absolute contract for the meere loane of money, is unlawfull both by law naturall, and positive, both divine and humane'.[25] He does qualify his position, allowing interest to be charged, but only in very narrow circumstances, where the criteria dictated by *charity* are satisfied. Similarly, Richard Baxter considers the issue in terms of the 'Law of Nature', which dictates, broadly, that we should be both just and charitable to others. Asking whether 'all Usury be against Justice or Charity to our Neighbour', he concludes that 'There is a Usury which is against Justice and Charity. There is Usury which is against Charity, but not against meer Justice: And there is an Usury which is against neither Justice nor Charity'.[26] Baxter is, in fact, trying to justify some kinds of usury in terms of conscience. But, like Hall, in making charity one, if not the only, criterion, he maintains a test that is impracticable for commercial relations. At the very least, he bifurcates conscience into matters of charity and matters of justice, and in so doing identifies a large and perhaps essential area of conscience—charity—which is subject to differential treatment. This, I think, tends to reinforce the distinction between what the law, including equity, can impose and what conscience essentially demands. As Wood puts it, the 'total result' of developments such as these was the 'taking economic questions more and more out of the direct influence of theology'.[27] We will recall, for example,

22 W.J. Jones, *The Elizabethan Court of Chancery* (Oxford, 1967), p. 448.

23 Wood, p. 101.

24 Joseph Hall, *Cases of Conscience Practically Resolved* (3rd edn, London, 1654), pp. 16–17; EEBO image 47749:20.

25 Ibid., p. 5; EEBO image 47749:14.

26 Richard Baxter, *A Christian Directory* (London, 1678), p. (erroneously paginated) 208; EEBO image 58467:452.

27 Wood, p. 101.

John Tillotson's diffidence about insisting on the application of his pure casuistical analysis of contracts to the 'real' commercial world. Prudence and pragmatism tend to supplant the ambitious morality that conscience would impose.

In other words, conscience as a criterion for law tends to be further circumscribed, and its relevance correspondingly diminished. That aspect of conscience which implicates justice still applies, but what it dictates may be ascertained in terms that do not really require the distinctive insights offered by conscience. Concepts of justice alone will generally suffice. What are most characteristically or distinctively matters of conscience tend to be relegated to the non-juridical sphere.

Apart from these 'external' factors—evolution of the concept of conscience, political pressures, and changing economic expectations with which some traditional constraints of conscience fit awkwardly—there were institutional developments within Chancery itself tending to neutralize conscience as an active juristic principle. These included such things as the regularization of procedure and the availability of more reliable case reports. But probably the most important was the proliferation of Chancery case law itself.

As I have noted in more than one place in this study, although conscience may be an original and creative source of decision in a new case, once that case is decided, it becomes the 'rule' for subsequent like cases. Indeed, as we have also seen, one of the early modern meanings of 'equity' in the judicial context was the deciding of similar cases in the same way. In a sense, this dimension of equity is in competition with the meaning of equity which has been the preoccupation of this study, that is, the deciding of extraordinary cases according to conscience. As soon as an extraordinary case is determined in this way, it is no longer extraordinary in the sense of not being subject to any previously-articulated rule. As more and more cases are decided, more and more cases become 'ordinary'. Rather than resort to the basic principles of conscience being necessary, reference to precedent becomes the way decisions are made. Moreover, reference to precedent becomes another way of justifying the jurisdiction of equity as systematic and regular. This, we may recall, is a large part of the argument of the compiler of the late seventeenth-century *Reports of Cases Taken and Adjudged in the Court of Chancery*.[28] The process is mutually reinforcing: because there are precedents, it is easier to be consistent; because consistency is regarded as desirable, precedent tends to be increasingly foregrounded.

One important consequence of these developments is that 'conscience' comes to be defined not 'intensionally', but 'extensionally'. A word's intension, roughly, is the set of criteria for its application, the essential elements that must be present for the word to apply. Much of my project has involved an inquiry into the 'intension' of conscience, in the sense of asking the question, 'What are the key elements in the meaning of (juristic) 'conscience'—or, more narrowly, of Lord Nottingham's *conscientia civilis et politica*?' So, I have wondered whether that conduct might not be defined in terms of outward conduct (as opposed to inward dispositions),

[28] *Reports of Cases Taken and Adjudged in the Court of Chancery* (London, 1694).

'civils' (as opposed to 'spirituals'), justice (as opposed to charity), and so on. But perhaps it is impossible to formulate a definition of juristic conscience in terms of general criteria.

Arguably, what the conscience of equity became was simply the sum of all the individual cases which the Chancellor decided. That is, the meaning of 'conscience' is its extension, all the particular instances to which it refers, or was made to refer. Conscience is case A, case B and case C, but not cases E and F. But there is no general test for distinguishing the two categories or predicting into which category unadjudicated case G will fall. Perhaps we have some indication of this process in William West's observation that Chancery is understood by the common people to be a court of conscience.[29] This would be a way of describing it in general terms, terms having a positive connotation. But what it entails, its actual meaning, resides in all the details of the innumerable causes it has determined. This meaning, because it consists of myriad single instances, is accessible only to legal experts. It may be ironical that the court of conscience should become more legitimate as a court of law by becoming more specialized and inaccessible.

All these developments, I suspect, had the effect of compromising whatever vitality conscience might ever have had as a juristic principle. One should not, however, exaggerate the stage which the process had reached by, say, Lord Nottingham's time. As we have seen, Nottingham is in many ways an ambiguous figure in this regard. True, he did emphasize the importance of equity becoming systematic and regular. True, he did distinguish between *conscientia naturalis et interna* and *conscientia civilis et politica*, ostensibly limiting equity to the latter. But, at the same time, he was a traditionalist. He understood conscience in religious terms; he evinced a concern for litigants' spiritual well-being as a dimension of what equity was about; he regarded, at least at times, the judgment and persuasion of his own conscience as a counterpoise to what had been done before. In many ways, he stood as much at the end of one era as he did at the beginning of another one. In spite of the developments I have outlined and his response to them, it still made some sense for him to continue to refer to Chancery as a court of conscience, for conscience was still explicable in terms of a theory that aimed to accord it objective coherence—although that theory was in the process of coming apart. It probably makes much less sense for those who today see conscience as a continuing informing principle in equity, long after the theory has disintegrated into a perhaps inevitable subjectivism.

[29] William West, 'Of the Chauncerie', *Three Treatises, of the Second part of Symbolæographie* (London, 1594), sig. B1r; EEBO image 29131:141.

Bibliography

CASES

Cited to Reporters

Anonymous (1599), Cary 9, 21 ER 5.
Clench v. *Tomley* (1603), Cary 23, 21 ER 13.
Coles v. *Hancock* (1680–81), 2 Ch. Rep. 210, 21 ER 659.
Corbet's Case (1600), I Co. Rep. 83b, 76, ER 187.
Cotton v. *Causton* (1579) Cary 79, 21, ER 42.
Countess of Radnor v. *Vandenbendy* (1697), Shower 69, 1 ER 48.
The Earl of Oxford's Case (1615), 1 Ch. Rep. 1, 21 ER 485.
Edmunds v. *Povey* (1683), 1 Vern. 187, 23 ER 404.
Fry v. *Porter* (1670), Mod. Rep. 300, 86 ER 898.
Hele v. *Hele* (1682), 2 Ch. Cas. 87, 22 ER 859.
Howard v. *Duke de Norfolk* (1682), 3 Ch. Cas. 40, 22 ER 955.
Lacy v. *Anderson* (1581–82), Choyce Cases in Chancery 155, 21 ER 91.
Lawrence v. *Berney* (1677–78), 2 Ch. Rep. 127, 21 ER 636.
Lee v. *Boles* (1682), 2 Ch. Cas. 95, 22 ER 863.
Lord Cornbury v. *Middleton* (1671), 1 Ch. Cas. 208, 22 ER 765.
In re Montagu's Settlement Trusts, [1987] 1 Ch. 264.
Mynn v. *Cobb* (1604), Cary 25, 21 ER 14.
Negus v. *Fettiplace* (1674), 1 Ch. Cas. 239, 22 ER 779.
Searle v. *Lane* (1688), 2 Vern. 88, 23 ER 667.
Shelley's Case. Wolfe v. *Shelley* (1581), 1 Co. Rep. 93b, 76 ER 206.
Stone v. *Withepoole* (1588), Owen 94, 71 ER 924.
Tilly v. *Egerton* (1660), 2 Freeman 125, 1 Ch. Rep. 181, 22 ER 1102.
Vanbrough v. *Cock* (1671) 1 Ch. Cas. 200, 22 ER 761.

In Other Collections

Cary, George. *Reports or Causes in Chancery* (London, 1665).
Cases Concerning Equity and the Courts of Equity 1550–1660, ed. W.H. Bryson (2 vols, London: Selden Society, 2001.) [Publications of the Selden Society, vol. 117].
Allen's Case (c. 1610), case 174, vol. 1, pp. 387–91.
Anon. (C.P. 1594), case 70, vol. 1, p. 139.

Anon. (Ch.), item 119 (Cases in Tempore Egerton [Ch. c. 1598 x c. 1602]), case 179, vol. 1, pp. 299–300.
Anon. (Ch.), item 119, case 123, vol. 1, p. 290.
Anon. (Ch.), item 119, case 150, vol. 1, p. 294.
Anon. (Ch.), item 120 (Cases in Tempore Egerton [Ch. c. 1599 x c. 1604]), case 91, vol. 1, p. 334.
Anon. (Ch.), item 119, case 210, vol. 1, p. 305.
Anon. (Ch.), item 119, case 46, vol. 1, p. 284.
Anon. (Ch.), item 120, case 49, vol. 1, p. 326.
Anon., item 119, para. 152, vol. 1, pp. 294–5.
Anon., item 167 (Notes and Cases [c. 1608 – 1620]), case 576, vol. 1, pp. 380–81.
Anon. (1612), case 189, vol. 2, p. 398.
Anon. (Ch. c. 1629), case 327, vol. 2, 598–599.
Anon. (Ch. 1631), case 363, vol. 2, p. 628.
Arden v. *Darcy* (Ex. 1610–14), case 218, vol. 2, pp. 431–3.
Attorney-General v. *Abington* (Ex. 1613–19), case 210, vol. 2, pp. 408–22.
Clifton v. *Basset* (Ch. 1584), item 117 (Richard Powle's Reports [Ch. 1579 x 1600]), case 29, vol. 1, pp. 175–6.
Crudge v. *Lower* (Ch. 1581–82), item 118 (Cases and Notes [Ch. c. 1580 x c. 1600]), case 98, vol. 1, p. 244.
Damery v. *Woston* (Ch. 1594), item 118, case 152, vol. 1, p. 252.
Earl of Northumberland v. *Bowes* (Ch. 1621), case 261, vol. 2, pp. 489–91.
Earl of Shrewsbury's Case (Ch. c. 1573), case 11, vol. 1, p. 100.
Finch v. *Finch* (Ch. 1597), item 120, case 87, vol. 1, p. 333.
Finch's Case (Ch. 1579–87), case 22, vol. 1, p. 107.
Glanville's Case (K.B. 1615), case 230, vol. 2, pp. 440–47.
Giles v. *Gesling* (Ch. 1631), case 351, vol. 2, pp. 618–19.
Hurd v. *Dodington* (Ch. 1598), item 118, case 273, vol. 1, p. 266.
Kettleby v. *Kettleby* (Ch. 1599), item 118, case 319, vol. 1, p. 272.
Lister v. *Lee* (Ch. 1604), item 120, case 71, vol. 1, p. 330.
Mainwaringe v. *Lovelace* (Ch. 1612), item 167, case 254, vol. 1, p. 376.
Martin v. *Marhsall* [*sic*] (C.P., 1615), case 231, vol. 2, pp. 444–7.
Matthews v. *Askwill* (Ch. 1604), item 120, case 67, vol. 1, p. 329.
Morris v. *Morris* (Ch. after 1580), case 25, vol. 1, pp. 108–10.
Omer v. *Ashley* (Ch. 1599), item 118, case 298, vol. 1, p. 269.
Orrell v. *Eccleston* (Ch. 1601), item 119, case 222, vol. 1, pp. 307–8.
Peck v. *Davis* (Ch. 1600), item 117, case 366, vol. 1, p. 229.
Pomery v. *Ford* (Ch. 1600), item 118, case 341, vol. 1, p. 275.
Ragland v. *Wildgoose* (Ch. 1596), item 118, case 199, vol. 1, p. 258.
Ramsay v. *Goslin* (Ch. 1631), case 349, vol. 2, p. 617.
Sheffield v. *Lopton* (Ch. 1598), item 118, case 201, p. 258.
Smallman v. *Pollard* (Ch. 1600), case 91, vol. 1, p. 159.
Tufton v. *Waller* (Ch. 1598), item 119, case 12, vol. 1, pp. 278–9.

Vendal v. *Harvey* (Ch. 1633), case 377, vol. 2, pp. 639–41.
Ward v. *Fulwood* (Ch. 1597), item 118, case 201, vol. 1, p. 258.
Willoughby v. *Paramore* (Ch. 1596), case 78, vol. 1, pp. 146–7.
Witham v. *Waterhouse* (Ch. 1596,), case 80, vol 1, pp. 148–51.

Lord Nottingham's Chancery Cases, ed. D.E.C. Yale (2 vols, London: Selden Society, 1957). [Publications of the Selden Society vol. 73].
Anon. (1674), case 108, vol. 1, p. 63.
Albermarle v. *Cutler* (1676/7), case 617, vol. 2, p. 470.
Ayloffe v. *Thomson* (1673), case 21, vol. 1, pp. 10–11.
Barkly v. *Penn* (1680/1), case 1077, vol. 2, p. 863.
Bateman v. *Tidcomb* (1676), case 488, vol. 1, pp. 347–8.
Bluck v. *Crisp* (1673/74), case 72, vol. 2, pp. 34–5.
Botham v. *Farrington* (1676), case 489, vol. 1, p. 348.
Botham v. *Townsend* (1674), case 150, vol. 1, p. 100.
Bovey v. *Smith* (1676), case 618, vol. 2, p. 470.
Bowyer v. *Birds* (1675), case 285, vol. 1, pp. 192–3.
Boys v. Wilkinson (1679/80), case 1008, vol. 2, pp. 805–6.
Brend v. *Brend* (1682), case 1153, vol. 2, pp. 920–21.
Burges v. *Skinner* (1673/74), case 66, vol. 1, p. 31.
Butcher v. *Hinton* (1677), case 761, vol. 2, pp. 577–8.
Butler v. *Harrison* (1677), case 730, vol. 2, pp. 549–50.
Cheke v. *Lord Lisle* (1673/4), case 45, vol. 1, p. 23.
Clerk v. *Perryer* (1679/80), case 992, vol. 2, pp. 782–4.
Clishold v. *Backwell* (1681), case 1123, vol. 2, p. 891.
Coke v. *Bishop* (1677), case 753, vol. 2, p. 570.
Cook v. *Fountain* (1676), case 500, vol. 1, pp. 362–71.
Coulston v. *Gardner* (1680/1), case 1090, vol. 2, pp. 869–72.
Cox v. *Quantock* (1674), case 155, vol. 1, pp. 102–3.
Danby v. *Read* (1675), case 220, vol. 1, p. 156.
Duke of Newcastle v. *Clayton* (1676), case 576, vol. 1, pp. 442–3.
Duke of Newcastle v. *Heathcott* (1677/8), case 802, vol. 2, pp. 611–12.
Dux Albermarle v. *Cutler* (1676), case 617, vol. 2, p. 470.
Earl of Feversham v. *Watson* (1678), case 823, vol. 2, pp. 637–49.
Earl of Leicester v. *Sidney* (1680/81), case 1075, vol. 2, pp. 856–62.
The East India Company v. *Blake* (1674), case 105, vol. 1, pp. 59–61.
Finch v. *Hawtry* (1673), case 38, vol. 1, p. 17.
Foly v. *Paston* (1679/80), case 997, vol. 2, pp. 792–3.
Forth v. *Wade* (1675), case 295, vol. 1, p. 206.
Furner v. *Lane* (1677), case 715, vol. 2, pp. 538–40.
Gawdy v. *Marriot* (1676/7), case 629, vol. 2, p. 476.
Gibson v. *Kenvyn* (1682), case 1165, vol. 2, p. 931.
Godfry v. *Lloyd* (1675/6), case 382, vol. 1, p. 260.
Gravenor v. *Cartwright* (1679), case 962, vol. 2, pp. 757–9; case 972, pp. 764–5.

Green v. *Gardner* (1675), case 246, vol. 1, pp. 170–71.
Grey v. *Grey* (1676/77), case 643, vol. 2, pp. 481–6.
Hatchett v. *Bindon* (1677), case 749, vol. 2, pp. 565–6.
Hatton v. *Long* (1673), case 19, vol. 1, pp. 9–10.
Hickson v. *Wytham* (1674/75), case 188, vol. 1, pp. 136–7.
Hyde v. *Seymour* (1678), case 890, vol. 2, p. 709.
Hill v. *Bowyer* (1675/6), case 448, vol. 1, p. 312.
Hinckly v. *Hinckly* (1674), case 123, vol. 1, pp. 75–6.
Honywood v. *Bennett* (1675), case 307, vol. 1, pp. 214–15.
Howard v. *Duke of Norfolk* (1681/82), case 1145, vol. 2, pp. 904–15.
Huntingdon and Scarsdale v. *Greenville* (1682), case 1154, vol. 2, pp. 921–2.
Jarvis v. *Midleton* (1680/1), case 1073, vol. 2, pp. 855–6.
Jennings v. *Gorges* (1677), case 720, vol. 2, pp. 543–4.
King v. *Hatchett* (1676), case 483, vol. 1, p. 344.
Knight v. *Coke* (1673), case 35, vol. 1, p. 16.
Knight v. *Knight* (1674), case 157, vol. 1, pp. 103–4.
Lawrence v. *Berney* (1677), case 679, vol. 2, pp. 512–13; case 767, pp. 581–4.
Lenthall v. *Waring* (1676), case 466, vol. 1, p. 333.
Lord Mordant v. *Earl of Peterborough* (1674/75), case 200, vol. 1, pp. 141–2.
Masters v. *Strode* (1677/78), case 790, vol. 2, pp. 603–4.
Maynard v. *Moseley* (1676), case 484, vol. 1, pp. 344–5.
Maynard v. *Moseley* (re-hearing) (1676), case 537, vol. 1, pp. 399–401.
Mirfield v. *Morley* (1676/7), case 627, vol. 2, pp. 474–5.
Moor v. *Hinton* (1677/8), case 809, vol. 2, p. 619.
Nance v. *Cook* (1677), case 741, vol. 2, pp. 559–61.
Norcliffe v. *Worsly* (1674), case 130, vol. 1, pp. 85–6.
Nurse v. *Yerworth* (1674), case 121, vol. 1, pp. 70–73; case 173, pp. 114–20.
Powell v. *Morgan* (1680), case 1048, vol. 2, pp. 836–7.
Rodd v. *Ryer* (1676), case 611, vol. 2, pp. 467–8.
Rosser v. *Evans* (1675), case 321, vol. 1, p. 221.
Salsbury v. *Bagott* (1677), case 671, vol. 2, pp. 501–9.
Sarten v. *Darcy* (1677/78), case 786, vol. 2, pp. 599–602.
Shipton v. *Tyrrell* (1675/76), case 212, vol. 1, p. 150.
Solly v. *Whitfield* (1675/76), case 415, vol. 1, p. 238.
Staples v. *Stone* (1679), case 938, vol. 2, pp. 740–41.
Stowbard v. *Wingfield* (1676), case 480, vol. 1, pp. 342–3.
Tabor v. *Tabor* (1679), case 978, vol. 2, pp. 768–70.
Thornborough v. *Baker* (1675), case 291, vol. 1, pp. 201–5.
Whitchcott v. *Mekins* (1675), case 363, vol. 1, p. 245.
Weaver v. *Woodyear* (1680), case 1040, vol. 2, p. 832.
Williams v. *Day* (1680), case 1029, vol. 2, p. 821.
Wyvell v. *Beckwith* (1676), case 584, vol. 2, pp. 450–51.

Reports of Cases Decided by Francis Bacon, Baron Verulam, Viscount St. Albans, Lord Chancellor of England, in the High Court of Chancery (1617–21), ed. John Ritchie (London: Sweet, 1932).
Carter v. *Scoble* (1618, 1619), pp. 140–41.
Chapman v. *Emery and Porter* (1617, 1618), pp. 77–80.
Dodson v. *Lutterford* (1617), pp. 62–3.
Eldred v. *Rawleigh* (1618), pp. 82–3.
Freeman v. *Blagrave* (1616, 1617), pp. 11–13.
Goodfellowe v. *Morris* (1618), pp. 131–3.
Helme v. *Conham* (1617), pp. 21–3.
Hoskett v. *Hellier* (1619–20), pp. 196–200.
Hunt v. *Bancroft* (1617–9), pp. 65–9.
Moreton v. *Briggs* (1618), pp. 133–6.
Parke v. *Wannell* (1619), pp. 143–4.
Rolt v. *Smith* (1617), pp. 53–4.
Simeon v. *Dean and Cannons of Windsor* (1617), pp. 49–53.

Reports of Cases Taken and Adjudged in the Court of Chancery (London, 1693). Early English Books Online. British Library. http://gateway.proquest.com/openurl?ctx_ver=Z39.88-2003&res_id=-xri:eebo&rft_id=xri:eebo:image:29452.[1]
Arrundel v. *Trevillian*, 10 Car. I, p. 87.
Atkins v. *Temple*, 1 Car. I, pp. 13–15.
Carpenter v. *Tucker*, 10 Car. I, pp. 78–9.
Havers v. *Burton*, 4 Car. I, pp. 26–7.
Herbert v. *Lowns*, 3 Car. I, pp. 22–5.
Isham v. *Cole*, 15 Car. I, pp. 127–8.
Kennedy v. *Vanlore*, 9 Car. I, pp. 70–76.
Lake v. *Phillips*, 9 Car. I, pp. 69–70.
Levington v. *Wooton*, 7 Car. I, pp. 52–5.
Mayor of London v. *Bennet*, 6 Car. I, pp. 44–5.
Middleton v. *Jackson*, 5 Car. I, pp. 33–4.
Petty v. *Styward*, 7 Car. I, pp. 57–8.
Pool v. *Pool*, 1 Car. I, p. 18.
Revet v. *Rowe*, 10 Car. I, pp. 50–53.
Roberts v. *Wynn*, 15 Car. II, pp. 236–41.
Scott v. *Wray*, 10 Car. I, pp. 84–6.
Tuphorne v. *Gilbie*, 5 Car. I, pp. 39–40.
Winchcomb v. *Hall*, 5 Car. I, pp. 40–41.
Wiseman v. *Roper*, 21 Car. I, pp. 158–60.
Yate v. *Southby*, 3 Car. I, p. 25.

[1] All the works from Early English Books Online have the same url, apart from the starting image number. Hereafter, I shall use the short form: EEBO, location of original, starting image number.

The Reports of Sir John Spelman, ed. J.H. Baker (2 vols, London: Selden Society, 1978) [Publications of the Selden Society vol. 94].

Rolle, Henry, *Un Abridgment des Plusieurs Cases et Resolutions del Common Ley* (London, 1668) EEBO. Cambridge University Library. 103278.

Rolle, Henry, *Un Continuation des Reports de Henry Rolle* (London, 1676). EEBO, Huntington Library. 53314.

The Second Part of Reports of Cases Taken and Adjudged in the Court of Chancery (London, 1694). EEBO. British Library. 33203.

Select Cases in Chancery A.D. 1364 to 1471, ed. William Paley Baildon (London: Quaritch, 1896) [Publications of the Selden Society vol. 10].

Statham's Abridgment of the Law, trans. Margaret C. Klingelsmith (Boston: Boston Book Company, 1915).

Statham, Nicholas, *Abridgment des libres annals* (Rouen, 1490). EEBO. British Library. 1984.

Year-Books of Edward II, vol. 1, 1 & 2 Edward II, A.D. 1307–1309, ed. F.W. Maitland (London: Quaritch, 1903) [Publications of the Selden Society, vol. 17].

OTHER SOURCES

Early Works

An Anthology of Chancery English. Electronic Text Center, University of Virginia. http://etext.lib.virginia.edu/toc/modeng/public/AnoChan.html.

Ames, William, *Conscience, with the Power and Cases thereof* (Leyden and London, 1639). EEBO. Cambridge University Library. 15139.

Andrewes, Lancelot, 'A Sermon Preached at Whitehall, November 26th, 1606', 'Certaine Sermons Preached at sundry times, upon severall occasions', in *XCVI Sermons* (London, 1629). EEBO. Cambridge University Library. 7203.

Annesley, Samuel, 'How may we be universally and exactly conscientious' in *The Morning-Exercise at Cripplegate: or, Several Cases of Conscience, Practically Resolved, by sundry Ministers* (London, 1664). EEBO. Huntington Library. 105033.

Aquinas, Thomas, *Debated Questions on Truth 16–17*, trans. T.C. Potts, in T.C. Potts, *Conscience in Medieval Philosophy* (Cambridge: Cambridge University Press, 1980).

Aristotle, *Rhetorica*, trans. W. Rhys Roberts, in W.D. Ross (ed.), *The Works of Aristotle Translated into English* (12 vols, Oxford: Clarendon Press, 1908; reprint 1946), vol. 11.

Ashe, Thomas, *Epieikeia* (London, 1609). EEBO. Library of Congress. 382.

Atkyns, Robert, *An Enquiry into the Jurisdiction of the Chancery in Causes of Equity* (London, 1695). EEBO. Huntington Library. 57482.

Bacon, Francis, *The Advancement of Learning* in *The Works of Francis Bacon*, eds. J. Spedding, R.L. Ellis and D.D. Heath (14 vols, London: Longmans, 1857–74; reprinted New York: Garrett Press, 1968), vol. 3.

Bacon, Francis, *The Confession of Faith* (London, 1641). EEBO. Harvard University Library. 55866.

Bacon, Francis, 'The Effect of that which was spoken by the Lord Keeper of the Great Seal of England, at the taking of his Place in Chancery', in *The Works of Francis Bacon*, eds J. Spedding, R.L. Ellis and D.D. Heath (14 vols, London: Longmans, 1857–74; reprinted New York: Garrett Press, 1968), vol. 13.

Bacon, Francis, 'Epistle Dedicatorie' to Queen Elizabeth, *Maxims of the Common Law* (1597), published in *The Elements of the Common Lawes of England* (London, 1630). EEBO. Huntington Library. 447.

Bacon, Francis, 'Example of a Treatise on Universal Justice or the Fountains of Equity, by Aphorisms', appended to Book 8 of *De Augmentis* (1623), in *The Works of Francis Bacon*, eds J. Spedding, R.L. Ellis and D.D. Heath (14 vols, London: Longmans, 1857–74; reprinted New York: Garrett Press, 1968), vol. 7.

Bacon, Francis, *Reading on the Statute of Uses* (1600), in *The Works of Francis Bacon*, eds J. Spedding, R.L. Ellis and D.D. Heath (14 vols, London: Longmans, 1857–74; reprinted New York: Garrett Press, 1968), vol. 7.

Bacon, Francis, *Three Speeches of the Right Honorable, Sir Francis Bacon* (London, 1641). EEBO. Huntington Library. 51155.

Bacon, Nathaniel, *The Continuation of an Historicall Discourse of the Government of England* (London, 1651). EEBO. Harvard University Library. 52042.

Bagshaw, Edward, *A Letter to the Right Honourable Edward Earl of Clarendon, Lord High Chancellor of England* (London, 1662). EEBO. Union Theological Seminary. 52251.

Bagshaw, Edward, *The Second Part of the Great Question Concerning Things Indifferent in Religious Worship* (London, 1661). EEBO. Huntington Library. 54584.

Barlow, Thomas, *Autoschediasmata, de studio theologiæ, or, Directions for the Choice of Books in the Study of Divinity* (Oxford, 1700). EEBO. Bodleian Library. 171143.

Barlow, Thomas, *Several Miscellaneous and Weighty Cases of Conscience* (London, 1692). EEBO. British Library. 64424.

Barnes, Barnabe, *Foure Bookes of Offices* (London, 1606). EEBO. Cambridge University Library. 7337.

Barnes, Thomas, *The Court of Conscience* (London, 1623). EEBO. Bodleian Library. 15204.

Baxter, Richard. *A Christian Directory* (London, 1678). EEBO. Bodleian Library. 58467.

Bernard, Richard, *Christian See to Thy Conscience* (London, 1630). EEBO. British Library. 14165.

Blount, Thomas, *Nomo-Lexikon: A Law-Dictionary* (London, 1670). EEBO. Harvard Law School Library. 57644.

Bodin, Jean, *The Six Bookes of a Commonweale*, trans. Richard Knolles (London, 1606; reprinted Cambridge: Harvard University Press, 1962).
Bourne, Immanuel, *The Anatomie of Conscience* (London, 1623). EEBO. Folger Shakespeare Library. 7186.
Brown, William, *The Clerk's Tutor in Chancery* (London, 1688). EEBO. Cambridge University Library. 98107.
Brown, William, *Praxis Almæ Curiæ Cancellariæ* (2nd edn, 2 vols, London, 1705). Eighteenth Century Collections Online. Bodleian Library. http://galenet.galegroup.com/servlet/ECCO. Document No. CW106378798.[2]
Burges, Cornelius, *A New Discouery of Personal Tithes* (London, 1625). EEBO. Cambridge University Library. 14242.
Burnet, Gilbert, *History of the Reformation of the Church of England, the Second Part* (London, 1681). EEBO. Huntington Library. 65548.
Burroughs, Edward, *The Case of Free Liberty of Conscience in the Exercise of Faith and Religion* (London, 1661). EEBO. Huntington Library. 58212.
Cade, Anthony, *Conscience, Its Nature and Corruption* (London, 1661). EEBO. Bodleian Library. 54332.
Calamy, Benjamin, *A Discourse About a Scrupulous Conscience* (2nd edn, London, 1683). EEBO. Huntington Library. 54114.
Calamy, Edmund, 'The Epistle to the Reader'. in William Fenner. *The Sovles Looking-glasse, Lively representing its Estate before God: With A Treatise Of Conscience* (Cambridge, 1640). EEBO. Cambridge University Library. 15425.
Calvin, John, *Institutes of the Christian Religion*, trans. H. Beveridge (Peabody, Mass.: Hendrickson Publishers, 2008).
Carpenter, Henry, *The Deputy Divinity or Inferiour Deity and Subordinate God in the World, Conscience* (London, 1657). EEBO. British Library. 170295.
Carpenter, Richard, *The Conscionable Christian* (London, 1623). EEBO. Folger Shakespeare Library. 8100.
Cavendish, George, *The Life and Death of Thomas Woolsey, Cardinal* (London, 1667). EEBO. Huntington Library. 64261.
Church of England, 'Preface', *Book of Common Prayer* (London, 1662).
Clarke, Samuel, *Medulla Theologiæ or the Marrow of Divinity* (London, 1659). EEBO. Union Theological Seminary. 64694.
The Compleat Clark (3rd edn, London, 1671). EEBO. Harvard Law School Library. 48193.
Considerations Touching the Dissolving or Taking Away the Court of Chancery (London, 1653). EEBO. Huntington Library. 61188.
Coventry, Thomas, Speech to accused in *The Arraignment and Conviction of Mervin Lord Audley, Earl of Castlehaven* (London, 1642). EEBO. Thomason Collection. 120643.

[2] In subsequent citations of texts from Eighteenth Century Collections Online, I shall use the following format: ECCO, location of original text, document number.

Crompton, Richard, *L'Avthoritie et Ivrisdiction des Covrts de la Maiestie de la Roygne* (London, 1594). EEBO. Huntington Library. 9565.

Crook, John *et al.*, *Liberty of Conscience Asserted* (London, 1661). EEBO. University of Texas Library. 61615.

Cudworth, Ralph, *A Treatise Concerning Eternal and Immutable Morality* (London, 1731). ECCO. Harvard University, Andover-Harvard Theological Library. Document No. CW119071315.

Cudworth, Ralph, *The True Intellectual System of the Universe* (London, 1678; reprinted Stuttgart: F. Frommann, 1964).

Culverwell, Nathaniel, *An Elegant and Learned Discourse of the Light of Nature*, eds R.A. Greene and H. MacCallum (Toronto: University of Toronto Press, 1971).

D., L., *An Exact Relation of the Proceedings and Transactions of the Late Parliament* (London, 1653). EEBO. British Library. 112863.

Dan Michel's Ayenbite of Inwit, or, Remorse of Conscience, ed. Richard Morris (London: Early English Text Society, 1866).

Davies, John, 'A Preface Dedicatory', *Le Primer Report des Cases & Matters en Ley resolues & adiudges en les Courts del Roy en Ireland* (Dublin, 1615). EEBO. Folger Shakespeare Library. 7771.

Deguileville, Guillaume, *Pèlerinage de l'Ame* (1355–58), ed. J.J. Stürzinger (London: Nichols and Sons, 1893).

Dickson, David, *Therapeuta Sacra, Shewing briefly The method of healing the diseases of the Conscience, concerning Regeneration* (Edinburgh, 1664). EEBO. Bodleian Library. 40880.

Doderidge, John, *The English Lawyer, Describing a Method for the Managing of the Lawes of this Land* (London, 1631). EEBO. Huntington Library. 10306.

Doderidge, John (attributed), *The Lawyers Light* (London, 1629). EEBO. Huntington Library. 10308.

Donne, John, *Pseudo-Martyr* (1610), ed. Anthony Raspa (Montreal and Kingston: McGill-Queen's University Press, 1993).

Donne, John, *The Sermons of John Donne*, eds George R. Potter and Evelyn M. Simpson (10 vols, Berkeley and Los Angeles: University of California Press, 1953–59).

Dugdale, William, *Origines juridicales* (London, 1666). EEBO. Huntington Library. 58205.

Dyke, Jeremiah, *Good Conscience, or, a Treatise Shewing the Nature, Meanes, Markes, Benefit, and Necessitie Thereof* (6th edn, London, 1635). EEBO. Cambridge University Library. 17557.

Eburne, Richard, *The Royal Law: or the Rule of Equitie Prescribed by Ovr Saviour* (London, 1616). EEBO. Bodleian Library. 18996.

Egerton, Thomas, Lord Ellesmere, *Certaine Observations Concerning the Office of the Lord Chancellor* (London, 1651). EEBO. British Library. 51543.

Egerton, Thomas, Lord Ellesmere, *The Priviledges and Prerogatives of the High Court of Chancery* (London, 1641). EEBO. Huntington Library. 93844.

Egerton, Thomas, Lord Ellesmere, *The Speech of the Lord Chancellor of England, in the Eschequer Chamber, touching the Post-nati* (London, 1609). EEBO. British Library. 336.

Eyre, Robert, *A Discourse Concerning the Nature and Satisfaction of a Good and Inoffensive Conscience* (London, 1693). EEBO. Yale University Library. 62636.

Finch, Heneage, Lord Nottingham, *Prolegomena of Chancery and Equity*, in D.E.C. Yale (ed.), *Lord Nottingham's 'Manual of Chancery Practice' and 'Prolegemona of Chancery and Equity'* (Cambridge: Cambridge University Press, 1965; reprinted Holmes Beach: Gaunt, 1986).

Finch, Heneage, Lord Nottingham, 'Speech to Serjeant Scroggs on the latter's accession to the Court of Common Pleas' (23 October 1676), in *Lord Nottingham's Chancery Cases*, ed. D.E.C. Yale (2 vols, London: Selden Society, 1961), vol.1, pp. 435–7.

Finch, Henry, *Law or a Discourse thereof, in Four Books* (London, 1627). EEBO. British Library. 22891.

Forsyth, James, *The Great Day of Chancery* (London, 1619). EEBO. Huntington Library. 5984.

Fowler, Edward, *Libertas Evangelica: or, a Discourse of Christian Liberty* (London, 1680). EEBO. Bodleian Library. 100709.

Fuller, Thomas, *The History of the Worthies of England* (London, 1662). EEBO. Huntington Library. 54862.

Garey, Samuel, *Ientaculum iudicum: or, a Breake-fast for the Bench* (London, 1623). EEBO. British Library. 2978.

Gerson, Jean, *On Mystical Theology: The First and Speculative Treatise* (1408), trans. and ed. B.P. McGuire, *Jean Gerson: Early Works* (New York: Paulist Press, 1998).

Gerson, Jean, *Treatise Against 'The Romance of the Rose'*, trans. and ed. B.P. McGuire, *Jean Gerson: Early Works* (New York: Paulist Press, 1998).

Gilbert, Geoffrey, *The History and Practice of the High Court of Chancery* (2 vols, Dublin, 1758), vol. 1. ECCO. Harvard University Law Library. Document No. CW102104288.

Goodman, John, *A Discourse Concerning Auricular Confession* (London, 1684). EEBO. Huntington Library. 54888.

Goodman, John, *The Golden Rule, or, the Royal Law of Equity Explained* (London, 1688). EEBO. Cambridge University Library. 60390.

Hacket, John, *Scrinia Reserata: A Memorial Offer'd to the Great Deservings of John Williams, D.D.* (London, 1693). EEBO. Bristol Public Libraries. 49492.

Hake, Edward, *Epieikeia: A Dialogue on Equity in Three Parts*, ed. D.E.C. Yale (New Haven: Yale University Press, 1953).

Hale, Matthew, *Contemplations Moral and Divine* (first published 1676, London, 1705). ECCO. British Library. Document No. CW119804003.

Hale, Matthew, *A Discourse of the Knowledge of God, and of our Selves* (London, 1688). EEBO. University of Illinois. 94495.

Hall, Thomas, *The Beauty of Magistry* (London, 1660). EEBO. Union Theological Seminary Library. 96886.

Hall, Joseph, *Cases of Conscience Practically Resolved* (3rd edn, London, 1654). EEBO. Harvard University Library. 47749.

Hammond, Henry, *Of Conscience* (Oxford, 1645). EEBO. British Library. 42068.

Hammond, Henry, *Of Scandal* (Oxford, 1644). EEBO. British Library. 154183.

Harris, Robert. *S. Paul's Confidence* (London, 1628). EEBO. Folger Shakespeare Library. 3976.

Harris, Robert, 'St. Paul's Exercise', in *Sixe Sermons of Conscience* (2nd edn, London, 1630). EEBO. Folger Shakespeare Library. 6263.

Harrison, William, *An Historicall Description of the Iland of Britaine*, in R. Holinshed *et al.*, *The First and Second Volumes of Chronicles* (London, 1587). EEBO. Huntington Library. 183967.

Hatton, Christopher (attributed), *A Treatise Concerning Statutes, or Acts of Parliament, and the Exposition thereof* (London, 1677). EEBO. Cambridge University Library. 98014.

Herbert, Edward, Lord Herbert of Cherbury, *The Ancient Religion of the Gentiles* (1643) (London, 1711). ECCO. British Library. Document No. CW123338156.

Herbert, Edward, Lord Herbert of Cherbury, *The Life and Reign of King Henry VIII* (London, 1741). ECCO. British Library. Document No. CW100151570.

Herbert, Edward, Lord Herbert of Cherbury, *De la verité en tant qu'elle est distinct de la Révélation* (3rd edn, n.p., 1639). EEBO. Harvard University Library. 14.

Hobbes, Thomas, *A Dialogue Between a Phylosopher and a Student of the Common-Laws of England*, in *The Art of Rhetoric, with a Discourse of the Laws of England* (London, 1681). EEBO. British Library. 54911.

Hobbes, Thomas, *The Elements of Law Natural and Politic*, ed. J.C.A. Gaskin (Oxford: Oxford University Press, 1999).

Hobbes, Thomas, *Leviathan*, ed. Edwin Curley (Indianapolis: Hackett, 1994).

Hooker, Richard, *Of the Laws of Ecclesiastical Polity*, ed. Christopher Morris (2 vols, London: Everyman, 1907; reprinted 1963).

Howesoun, John, *A Short Exposition … Containing a very Profitable Discourse of Conscience* (Edinburgh, 1600). EEBO. British Library. 17063.

Hughes, John, *St. Pavls Exercise, or, a Sermon of Conscience* (London, 1622). EEBO. British Library. 4483.

Huit, Ephraim, *The Anatomy of Conscience* (London, 1626). EEBO. Harvard University Library. 27800.

Hyde, Edward, Earl of Clarendon, *A Brief View and Survey of the Dangerous and Pernicious Errors to Church and State, in Mr. Hobbes's Book, Entitled Leviathan* (2nd impression, Oxford, 1676). EEBO. Huntington Library. 60912.

Hyde, Edward, Earl of Clarendon, *The History of the Rebellion and Civil Wars in England* (3 vols, London, 1704). ECCO. British Library. Document No. CW102710855.

Hyde, Edward, Earl of Clarendon, 'On Conscience', in *A Compleat Collection of Tracts, by that Eminent Statesman the Right Honourable Edward, Earl of Clarendon* (London, 1747). 162–7. ECCO. British Library. Document No. CW122271120.

Jackson, John, *The Booke of Conscience Opened and Read* (London, 1642). EEBO. Bodleian Library. 103990.

James I, *Basilikon Doron* (Edinburgh, 1599). EEBO. British Library. 1192.

James I, *His Maiesties Speech in the Starre-Chamber the XX of June Anno 1616* (London, 1616). EEBO. Harvard University Library. 26198.

Jeanes, Henry, *A Treatise Concerning a Christians Carefull Abstinence from all Appearance of Evill* (Oxford, 1640). EEBO. Union Theological Seminary Library. 3506.

Jones, Andrew, *The Black Book of Conscience or Gods High Court of Justice in the Soul* (6th edn, London, 1658). EEBO. British Library. 34792.

'The Jurisdiction of the Court of Chancery Vindicated', in *Reports of Cases taken and adjudged in the Court of Chancery* (London, 1693). EEBO. British Library. 29452.

Lambard, William, *Archion, or, a Comentary upon the High Courts of Ivstice in England* (London, 1635). EEBO. British Library. 8665.

Langland, William, *Piers the Ploughman*, trans. J.F. Goodridge (Harmondsworth: Penguin, 1968).

Leigh, Edward, *A Philologicall Commentary: or, an Illustration of the Most Obvious and Useful Words in the Law* (2nd edn, London, 1658). EEBO. Huntington Library. 65537.

Leigh, Edward. *Second Considerations Concerning the High Court of Chancery, and the Most Excellent Ordinance for the Regulation and Limitation of that Court* (London, 1658). EEBO. Bodleian Library. 65747.

Lipsius, Justus, *Sixe Bookes of Politickes or Civil Doctrine*, trans. William Jones (London, 1594). EEBO. Folger Shakespeare Library. 180969.

Lloyd, David, *State-worthies, or, the Statesmen and Favourites of England Since the Reformation* (London, 1766). ECCO. British Library. Document No. CW104918924.

Lydgate, John, *The Pilgrimmage of the Life of Man*, eds. F.J. Furnivall and Katherine B. Locock (London: Early English Text Society, 1899–1904).

Mason, Henry, *The Tribvnall of the Conscience: or, a Treatise of Examination* (London, 1626). EEBO. British Library. 12751.

Moore, Francis, *Letter to Bishop John Williams*, 1621, Cambridge University Library MS. Gg 2.31, f. 298, reproduced in *Lord Nottingham's 'Manual of Chancery Practice' and 'Prolegomena of Chancery and Equity'*, ed. D.E.C. Yale (Cambridge, 1965; reprinted Holmes Beach: Gaunt, 1986), pp. 78–80.

Morton, Thomas, *A Defence of the Innocencie of the Three Ceremonies of the Church of England* (London, 1618). EEBO. Bodleian Library. 13224.

Morton, Thomas, *The Necessity of Christian Subjection* (Oxford, 1643). EEBO. Huntington Library. 62522.

Nalson, John, *The True Liberty and Dominion of Conscience* (2nd edn, London, 1678). EEBO. Union Theological Seminary Library. 56946.

Norman, John, *Cases of Conscience Practically Resolved* (London, 1673). EEBO. Bodleian Library. 46170.

North, Roger, *The Life of the Right Honourable Francis North, Baron Guilford* (London, 1742). ECCO. British Library. Document No. CW103613479.

The Paston Letters, A.D. 1422–1509, ed. James Gairdner (6 vols, London: Chatto and Windus, 1904; reprinted New York: AMS Press, 1965).

Pecock, Reginald, *The Reule of Crysten Religioun*, ed. W.C. Greet (London: Oxford University Press for Early English Text Society, 1927). [Early English Text Society Series no. 171.]

Penn, William, *The Great Case of Liberty of Conscience* (London, 1670). EEBO. Huntington Library. 98352.

Perkins, William, *A Discourse of Conscience* (Cambridge, 1596). EEBO. Huntington Library. 10898.

Perkins, William, *Epieikeia, or a Treatise of Christian Equity and Moderation*, ed. Ian Breward, in *The Works of William Perkins* (Abingdon, Berkshire: Sutton Courtenay Press, 1970).

Perkins, William, *The Whole Treatise of the Cases of Conscience* (Cambridge, 1606). EEBO. Cambridge University Library. 14434.

Pett, Peter, *A Discourse Concerning Liberty of Conscience* (London, 1661). EEBO. Bodleian Library. 109702.

Philip the Chancellor, *Treatise on Conscience* (1235), trans. Timothy C. Potts, in Timothy C. Potts, *Conscience in Medieval Philosophy* (Cambridge: Cambridge University Press, 1980).

Philips, Ambrose, *The Life of John Williams* (Cambridge, 1700). EEBO. Huntington Library. 98394.

Pickering, Thomas, 'Epistle Dedicatorie' to William Perkins, *The Whole Treatise of the Cases of Conscience* (Cambridge, 1606). EEBO. Cambridge University Library. 14434.

Pierce, Thomas, *A Decad of Caveats to the People of England* (London, 1679). EEBO. Union Theological Seminary Library. 65411.

The Practice of the High Court of Chancery Unfolded (London, 1672). EEBO. Bodleian Library. 33548.

'The Preface to the Reader', *The Second Part of Reports of Cases Taken and Adjudged in the Court of Chancery* (London, 1694). EEBO. British Library. 33203.

Reasons Against the Bill, Intituled an Act for Countie-Registers, Wills and Administrations (London, 1653). EEBO. William Andrews Clark Memorial Library, University of California. 133365.

The Replication of a Serjeant at the Laws of England, in *Christopher St. German on Chancery and Statute*, ed. J.A. Guy (London: Selden Society, 1985). [Selden Society Supplementary Series vol. 6.]

Reynoldes, Edward, *A Treatise of the Passions and Faculties of the Soule of Man* (London, 1640). EEBO. Huntington Library. 16360.

Rivius, Johannes, *De conscientia* (Leipzig, 1541).

Robinson, Henry, *Certaine Proposals in Order to a New Modelling of the Lawes, and Law-Proceedings* (London, 1653). EEBO. Yale University Library. 62328.

Rolle, Richard, *The Pricke of Conscience*, ed. Richard Morris (Berlin: A. Asher, 1863).

Roper, William, *The Life of Sir Thomas More*, in R.S. Sylvester and D.P. Harding (eds), *Two Early Tudor Lives* (New Haven: Yale University Press, 1962).

Ross, Alexander, *The Picture of Conscience Drawne to the Life, by the Pencell of Divine Truth* (London, 1646. EEBO). British Library. 119965.

Rous, Francis, *The Ancient Bounds, or Liberty of Conscience* (London, 1645). EEBO. British Library. 158553.

Sanderson, Robert, 'Ad magistratum', in *Twelve Sermons* (3rd edn, London, 1637). EEBO. British Library. 17135.

Sanderson, Robert. *Ten Lectures on the Obligation of Humane Conscience* (1647), trans. Robert Codrington (London, 1660). EEBO. Folger Shakespeare Library. 154344.

Scot, Thomas, *Christ's Politician, and Salomon's Puritan* (London, 1616). EEBO. Union Theological Seminary Library. 164.

Scot, Thomas, *God and the King* (Cambridge, 1633). EEBO. Union Theological Seminary Library. 141.

Selden, John, *Table Talk of John Selden*, compiled by Richard Milward, ed. Frederick Pollock (London: Quaritch, 1927).

Sharp, John, *A Discourse Concerning Conscience* (London, 1687). EEBO. Huntington Library. 62035.

Sharp, John, *Sixteen Casuistical Sermons Preached on Several Occasions* (4th edn, London, 1748). ECCO. Harvard University Houghton Library. Document No. CW119328844.

Sheffeild, John, *A Good Conscience the Strongest Hold* (London, 1650). EEBO. British Library. 169477.

Sheppard, William, *An Epitome of All the Common & Statute Laws of this Nation* (London, 1656). EEBO. Huntington Library. 101814.

Sheppard, William, *The Faithful Counsellor: or the Marrow of the Law* (London, 1651). EEBO. Huntington Library. 48696.

Smith, Thomas, *The Commonwealth of England* (London, 1635). EEBO. Huntington Library. 7893.

Smith, Thomas, *De Republica Anglorum* (London, 1583). EEBO. Huntington Library. 18192.

Snagg, Robert, *The Antiquity & Original of the Court of Chancery, and Authority of the Lord Chancellor of England* (London, 1654. EEBO). Bodleian Library. 152381.

Somers, John, Lord Somers (attributed), *A Discourse Concerning Generosity* (2nd edn, London, 1695). EEBO. British Library. 150297.

Sparrow, Anthony, *Confession of Sins, and the Power of Absolution* (London, 1704). ECCO. British Library. Document No. CW122804330.

Spenser, Edmund, *Edmund Spenser: The Faerie Queene*, eds Thomas P. Roche, Jr. and C. Patrick O'Donnell, Jr. (New Haven: Yale University Press, 1978).

St. German, Christopher, *Christopher St. German on Chancery and Statute*, ed. J.A. Guy (London: Selden Society, 1985) [Selden Society Supplementary Series, vol. 6].

St. German, Christopher, *St. German's Doctor and Student*, eds T.F.T. Plucknett and J.L. Barton (London: Selden Society, 1974) [Publications of the Selden Society, vol. 91].

Stillingfleet, Edward, *A Discourse Concerning Bonds of Resignation of Benefices. In Point of Law and Conscience* (London, 1695). EEBO. Huntington Library. 55952.

Stratford, Nicholas, *A Sermon Preached at the Assizes Held at Chester* (London, 1681). EEBO. Union Theological Seminary. 100328.

Taylor, Jeremy, *Ductor Dubitantium*, ed. A. Taylor *The Whole Works of the Right Reverend Jeremy Taylor, D.D.* (10 vols, London: Longman, Green and Co., 1883), vols 9 and 10.

'Theophilus Philanax Gerusiphilus Philalethes Decius', *An Answer to the Lord George Digbies Apology for Himself ... Put into the Great Court of Equity, otherwise Called the Court of Conscience* (London, 1643). EEBO. British Library. 125909.

Thomas, Michael, *Two Assize Sermons* (London, 1659). EEBO. British Library. 170373.

Tillotson, John, *The Rule of Faith* (London, 1688). EEBO. Huntington Library. 107805.

Tillotson, John, 'Wherein lies that exact Righteousness, which is required between Man and Man?' in *The Morning-Exercise at Cripplegate or, Several Cases of Conscience Practically Resolved, by sundry Ministers, September 1661*, ed. Samuel Annesley (London, 1664). EEBO. British Library. 105033.

The True Magistrate, or the Magistrates Duty and Power in matters of Religion, or In things meerly relating to Conscience (London, 1659). EEBO. British Library. 119150.

Vincent, Nathanael, *A Heaven or Hell upon Earth, or, a Discourse Concerning Conscience* (London, 1676). EEBO. Bodleian Library. 44406.

Warr, John, *Administrations Civil and Spiritual* (London, 1648). EEBO. Bodleian Library. 65034.

Warr, John, *A Brief Survey of the English Laws, and, Their Unsoundness and Corruption Discovered* (London, 1653). EEBO. British Library. 151437.

West, William, 'Of the Chauncerie', in *Three Treatises, of the Second part of Symbolæographie* (London, 1594). EEBO. Cambridge University Library. 29131.

Whitelocke, Bulstrode, *Memorials of the English Affairs* (London, 1682). EEBO. Huntington Library. 49724.
Wigmore, Michael, *A Dissection of the Braine: A Sermon Preached at the Assizes in Lincoln* (London, 1641). EEBO. Thomason Collection. 93539.
Wilde, Robert, *The Arraignment of a Sinner at the Bar of Divine Justice* (London, 1656). EEBO. Union Theological Seminary Library. 54555.
Wilkins, John, *Of the Principles and Duties of Natural Religion: Two Books* (London, 1695). EEBO. Rutgers University Library. 62179.
Williams, Walter, *Jus Appellandi ad Regem Ipsum a Cancelaria* (London, 1684). EEBO. Bodleian Library. 36889.
Wolseley, Charles, *Liberty of Conscience* (London, 1668). EEBO. Huntington Library. 95413
Woolton, John, *Of the Conscience* (London, 1576). EEBO. Folger Shakespeare Library. 6659.
Worship, William. *The Christians Iewell, or, the Treasvre of a Good Conscience* (London, 1617). EEBO. Union Theological Seminary Library. 14830.
Yorkshire Writers: Richard Rolle of Hampole and his Followers, ed. C. Horstmann (London: Swan Sonnenschein and Co., 1895–96).

Modern Secondary Sources

Adams, George Burton, *Council and Courts in Anglo-Norman England* (New Haven: Yale University Press, 1926). [Yale Historical Publications, no. 5.]
Alford, John, 'Literature and Law in Medieval England', *PMLA*, 92/5 (1977): 941–51.
Allen, Carleton Kemp, *Law in the Making* (6th edn, Oxford: Clarendon Press, 1958).
Avery, M.E, 'The History of the Equitable Jurisdiction of Chancery Before 1460', *Bulletin of the Institute of Historical Research*, 42 (1969): 129–44.
Baker, J.H., 'The Common Lawyers and the Chancery: 1616', in J.H. Baker, *The Legal Profession and the Common Law: Historical Essays* (London: Hambledon Press, 1986).
Baker, J.H., *An Introduction to English Legal History* (4th edn, London: Butterworths, 2002).
Baker, J.H., 'Introduction' to *The Reports of Sir John Spelman*, ed. J.H. Baker (2 vols, London: Selden Society, 1978). [Publications of the Selden Society vol. 94.]
Baker, J.H., *The Oxford History of the Laws of England, Volume VI 1483–1558* (Oxford: Oxford University Press, 2003).
Baker, J.H., *Readers and Readings in the Inns of Court and Chancery* (London: Selden Society, 2000).
Barbour, Willard T, *The History of Contract in Early English Equity* (New York: Octagon, 1974). [Oxford Studies in Social and Legal History, vol. 4.]

Barbour, Willard T, 'Some Aspects of Fifteenth-Century Chancery', *Harvard Law Review*, 31/6 (1918): 834–59.

Barton, J.L., 'Equity in the Medieval Common Law', in R.A. Newman (ed.), *Equity in the World's Legal Systems* (Brussels: Émile Bruylant, 1973), pp. 139–59.

Baylor, Michael G., *Action and Person: Conscience in Late Scholasticism and the Young Luther* (Leiden: E.J. Brill, 1977). [Studies in Medieval and Reformation Thought, vol. 20, series ed. Heiko A. Oberman.]

Behrens, Georg, 'An Early Tudor Debate on the Relation Between Law and Equity', *Journal of Legal History*, 19/2 (1998): 143–61.

Behrens, Georg, 'Equity in the *Commentaries* of Edmund Plowden', *Journal of Legal History*, 20 (1999): 25–50.

Beilby, Mark, 'The Profits of Expertise: The Rise of the Civil Lawyers and Chancery Equity', in Michael A. Hicks (ed.), *Profit, Piety and the Professions in Later Medieval England* (Gloucester: A. Sutton, 1990): 72–90.

Berman, Harold, 'Conscience and Law: The Lutheran Reformation and the Western Legal Tradition', *Journal of Law and Religion*, 5/1 (1987): 177–202.

Berman, Harold, 'The Origins of Historical Jurisprudence: Coke, Selden, Hale', *Yale Law Journal*, 103/7 (1994): 1651–1737.

Birks, Peter, 'Annual Meigunyah Lecture: Equity, Conscience and Unjust Enrichment', *Melbourne University Law Review* 23/1 (1999): 1–29.

Bosco, David, 'Conscience as Court and Worm: Calvin and the Three Elements of Conscience', *Journal of Religious Ethics*, 14/2 (2001): 333–55.

Brown, Meg Lota, *Donne and the Politics of Conscience in Early Modern England* (Leiden: E.J. Brill, 1995). [Studies in the History of Christian Thought, vol. 61, series ed. Heiko A. Oberman.]

Bryson, W.H., 'Introduction', in W.H. Bryson (ed.), *Cases Concerning Equity and the Courts of Equity 1550–1660* (London: Selden Society, 2000). [Publications of the Selden Society vol. 117.]

Campbell, John, Lord Campbell, *Lives of the Lord Chancellors and Keepers of the Great Seal of England*, ed. J.A. Mallory (10 vols, Toronto: Carswell, 1876).

Coing, Helmut, 'English Equity and the *Denunciatio Evangelica* of the Canon Law', *Law Quarterly Review*, 71 (1955): 223–41

Coquillette, Daniel, *Francis Bacon* (Stanford: Stanford University Press, 1992). [Jurists: Profiles in Legal Theory, series eds. William Twining and Neil MacCormick.]

Cromartie, Alan, 'General Introduction' to *A Dialogue Between a Philosopher and a Student of the Common Laws of England*, in *Thomas Hobbes: Writings on Common Law and Hereditary Right*, eds Alan Cromartie and Quentin Skinner (Oxford: Oxford University Press, 2005).

Dickinson, John W, 'Renaissance Equity and "Measure for Measure"', *Shakespeare Quarterly*, 13/3 (1962): 287–97.

Dobbins, Sharon K 'Equity: The Court of Conscience or the King's Command, the Dialogues of St. German and Hobbes Compared', *Journal of Law and Religion*, 9/1 (1991–92): 113–49.

Doe, Norman, *Fundamental Authority in Late Medieval English Law* (Cambridge: Cambridge University Press, 1990; reprinted Holmes Beach: Gaunt, 2000).

Drewes, J.B., 'Zinderises, Hell's Public Prosecutor: Origin, Name and Function', *Neophilologus*, 53/1 (1969): 257–60.

Endicott, Timothy A.O., 'The Conscience of the King: Christopher St. German and Thomas More and the Development of English Equity', *University of Toronto Faculty Law Review* 47/2 (1989): 549–70.

Fortier, Mark, *The Culture of Equity in Early Modern England* (Aldershot: Ashgate Publishing, 2005).

Gallagher, Lowell, *Medusa's Gaze: Casuistry and Conscience in the Renaissance* (Stanford: Stanford University Press, 1991).

George, Charles H. and Katherine George, *The Protestant Mind of the English Reformation 1570–1640* (Princeton: Princeton University Press, 1961).

Gilmore, Myron P, 'The Jurisprudence of Humanism', *Traditio*, 17 (1961): 493–501.

Gray, Charles M, 'The Boundaries of the Equitable Function', *American Journal of Legal History*, 20/3 (1976): 192–226.

Greene, Robert A, 'Synderesis, the Spark of Conscience, in the English Renaissance', *Journal of the History of Ideas*, 52/2 (1991): 195–219.

Guy, J.A., 'The Development of Equitable Jurisdictions 1450–1550', in *Law, Litigants, and the Legal Profession*, E.W. Ives and A.H. Manchester (eds) (London: Royal Historical Society, 1983), pp. 80–86. [Royal Historical Society Studies in History, no. 36.]

Guy, J.A., 'Introduction' to *Christopher St. German on Chancery and Statute*, ed. J.A. Guy (London: Selden Society, 1985). [Selden Society Supplementary Series vol. 6.]

Halliwell, Margaret, *Equity and Good Conscience in a Contemporary Context* (London: Old Bailey Press, 1997).

Haskett, Timothy S., 'The Medieval English Court of Chancery', *Law and History Review*, 14/2 (1996): 245–313.

Holdsworth, W.S., *A History of English Law* (9 vols, Boston: Little, Brown, 1924).

Holmes, P.J., *Elizabethan Casuistry* (Catholic Record Society, 1981).

Janda, Richard, 'Legal Architecture, Equity and Christopher St. German' in John E.C. Brierley *et al.* (eds), *Mélanges offerts par ses collègues de McGill à Paul-André Crépeau* (Cowansville: les Editions Yvon Blais Inc., 1997), pp. 373–416.

Jones, W.J., *The Elizabethan Court of Chancery* (Oxford: Clarendon Press, 1967).

Keenan, James F., 'Was William Perkins' *Whole Treatise of Cases of Conscience* Casuistry?: Hermeneutics and British Practical Divinity', in H.E. Braun and E. Vallance (eds), *Contexts of Conscience in Early Modern Europe 1500–1700* (Basingstoke: Palgrave Macmillan, 2004), pp. 17–31.

Klinck, Dennis R., 'Imaging Equity in Early Modern England', *Canadian Bar Review*, 84/2 (2005): 217–47.

Klinck, Dennis.R., 'Lord Nottingham and the Conscience of Equity', *Journal of the History of Ideas*, 67/1 (2006): 123–47.

Klinck, Dennis R., 'The Nebulous Equitable Duty of Conscience', *Queen's Law Journal*, 31/1 (2005): 206–58.

Klinck, Dennis R., 'The Unexamined "Conscience" of Contemporary Canadian Equity', *McGill Law Journal*, 46/3 (2001): 571–614.

Knafla, L.A., 'Conscience in the English Common Law Tradition', *University of Toronto Law Journal*, 26/1 (1976): 1–16.

Langdell, C.C., 'The Development of Equity Pleading from Canon Law Procedure', in *Select Essays in Anglo-American Legal History* (Boston: Little, Brown, 1908), vol. 2, pp. 753–78.

Lefebvre, Charles, 'Natural Equity and Canonical Equity', trans. Jeanne Rodes, *Natural Law Forum* 8 (1963): 122–36.

Leites, Edmund, 'Casuistry and Character', in Edmund Leites (ed.), *Conscience and Casuistry in Early Modern Europe* (Cambridge: University Press, 1988), pp. 119–33.

Lewis, C.S., 'Conscience and Conscious', *Studies in Words* (2nd edn, Cambridge: Cambridge University Press, 1967), pp. 181–213.

Macnair, Mike, 'Equity and Conscience', *Oxford Journal of Legal Studies*, 47/4 (2007): 659–81.

Merrill, Thomas F., *William Perkins, 1558–1602, English Puritanist; His Pioneer Works on Casuistry: 'A Discourse of Conscience' and 'The Whole Treatise of Cases of Conscience'* (Nieuwkoop: B. De Graaf, 1966).

Metzger, Franz, 'The Last Phase of the Medieval Chancery', in *Law-Making and Law-Makers in British History,* Alan Harding (ed.) (London: Royal Historical Society, 1980), pp. 79–89. [Royal Historical Society Studies in History Series no. 22.]

Meyjes, G.H.M. Posthumus, *Jean Gerson Apostle of Unity: His Church Politics and Ecclesiology*, trans. J.C. Grayson (Leiden: Brill, 1999).

Nelson, Benjamin, 'Conscience and the Making of Early Modern Cultures: "The Protestant Ethic" Beyond Max Weber', *Social Research*, 36/1 (1969): 5–21.

Palmer, Robert C., *English Law in the Age of the Black Death, 1348–1381* (Chapel Hill: University of North Carolina Press, 1993).

Park, John James, *What Are Courts of Equity?* (London, 1832).

Parkes, Joseph, *A History of the Court of Chancery* (London, 1828).

Pierce, C.A., *Conscience in the New Testament* (London: SCM Press, 1955). [Studies in Biblical Theory no. 15.]

Pike, L.O., 'Common Law and Conscience in the Ancient Court of Chancery', in *Select Essays in Anglo-American Legal History* , Association of American Law Schools (ed.) (3 vols, Boston: Little, Brown, 1908), vol. 2, pp. 722–36.

Plucknett, T.F.T. *A Concise History of the Common Law* (Boston: Little, Brown and Co., 1956; reprinted Union, N.J.: The Lawbook Exchange, 2001).

Plucknett, T.F.T. and J.L. Barton, 'Introduction' to Christopher St. German, *Doctor and Student*, eds T.F.T. Plucknett and J.L. Barton (London: Selden Society, 1974). [Publications of the Selden Society vol. 91.]

Post, J.B., 'Equitable Resorts Before 1450' in E.W. Ives and A.H. Manchester (eds), *Law, Litigants and the Legal Profession* (London: Royal Historical Society 1983), pp. 68–79. [Royal Historical Society Studies in History No. 36.]

Potts, Timothy C., 'Conscience', in *The Cambridge History of Later Medieval Philosophy*, N. Kretzmann, A. Kenny and J. Pinborg (eds) Cambridge: Cambridge University Press, 1982), pp. 687–704.

Potts, Timothy C., *Conscience in Medieval Philosophy* (Cambridge: Cambridge University Press, 1980).

Pronay, Nicholas, 'The Chancellor, the Chancery, and the Council at the End of the Fifteenth Century', in *British Government and Administration*, H. Hearder and H.R. Loyn (eds) (Cardiff: University of Wales Press, 1974), pp. 87–103.

Radin, Max, 'The Conscience of the Court', *Law Quarterly Review*, 48 (1932): 506–20.

Rueger, Zofia, 'Gerson's Concept of Equity and Christopher St. German', *History of Political Thought*, 3/1 (1982): 1–30.

Russell, Bertrand, *Wisdom of the West* (London: Macdonald, 1959).

Shapiro, Barbara J., *Probability and Certainty in Seventeenth-Century England* (Princeton: Princeton University Press, 1983).

Siegel, Stephen A., 'The Aristotelian Basis of English Law 1450–1800', *New York University Law Review*, 56/1 (1981): 18–59.

Simpson, A.W.B., *A History of the Common Law of Contract: The Rise of the Action of Assumpsit* (Oxford: Clarendon Press, 1975).

Skulsky, Harold, 'Pain, Law, and Conscience in *Measure for Measure*', *Journal of the History of Ideas*, 25/2 (1964): 147–68.

Slights, Camille Wells, *The Casuistical Tradition in Shakespeare, Donne, Herbert and Milton* (Princeton: Princeton University Press, 1981).

Slights, Camille Wells. 'The Conscience of the King: Henry V and the Reformed Conscience', *Philological Quarterly*, 80/1 (2001): 37–55.

Slights, Camille, 'Ingenious Piety: Anglican Casuistry of the Seventeenth Century', *Harvard Theological Review*, 63/3 (1970): 409–32.

Slights, Camille Wells, 'Notaries, Sponges, and Looking-glasses: Conscience in Early Modern England', *English Literary Renaissance*, 28/2 (1998):231-46.

Sokol, B.J. and M. Sokol, 'Shakespeare and the English Equity Jurisdiction: *The Merchant of Venice* and the Two Texts of *King Lear*', *Review of English Studies*, 50 (1999): 417–39.

Sommerville, Johann, 'Conscience, Law, and Things Indifferent: Arguments on Toleration from the Vestiarian Controversy to Hobbes and Locke', in *Contexts of Conscience in Early Modern Europe 1500–1700*, H.E. Braun and E. Vallance, (eds) (Basingstoke: Palgrave Macmillan, 2004), pp. 166–79.

Spence, George, *The Equitable Jurisdiction of the Court of Chancery* (2 vols, Philadelphia, 1846).

Spivak, Carla, 'The Conscience of the Queen: Lady Macbeth, Queen Elizabeth, and the Transparent Female Body in Jacobean England'. bepress Legal Series, Paper 558 (2005). http://law.bepress.com/expresso/eps/558.

Stone, M.W.F., 'Scrupulosity and Conscience: Probabilism in Early Modern Scholastic Ethics', in *Contexts of Conscience in Early Modern Europe, 1500–1700*, H.E. Braun and Edward Vallance (eds) (Basingstoke: Palgrave Macmillan, 2004), pp. 1–16.

Story, Joseph, *Commentaries on Equity Jurisprudence* (Boston: 1836).

Tentler, Thomas N., 'The Summa for Confessors as an Instrument of Social Control', in *The Pursuit of Holiness in Late Medieval and Renaissance Religion*, C. Trinkhaus and H.A. Oberman (eds) (Leiden: Brill, 1974), pp. 103–25. [Studies in Medieval and Reformation Thought, vol. 10.]

Thomas, G.W., 'James I, Equity and Lord Keeper John Williams', *English Historical Review*, 91/360 (1976): 506–28.

Thomas, Keith, 'Cases of Conscience in Seventeenth-Century England', in *Public Duty and Private Conscience*, J. Morrill, P. Slack and D. Woolf (eds) (Oxford: Clarendon Press, 1993), pp. 29–56.

Thorne, Samuel E., 'Preface' to Edward Hake, *Epieikeia: A Dialogue on Equity in Three Parts*, ed. D.E.C. Yale (New Haven: Yale University Press, 1953). [Yale Law Library Publications No. 13.]

Traver, Hope, *The Four Daughters of God* (Philadelphia: Bryn Mawr College Monographs, 1907).

Tucker, P., 'The Early History of the Court of Chancery: A Comparative Study', *English Historical Review*, 115/463 (2000): 791–811.

Tully, James, 'Governing Conduct', in *Conscience and Casuistry in Early Modern Europe*. Edmund Leites (ed.) (Cambridge: Cambridge University Press, 1988), pp. 12–71.

Ullmann, Walter, *The Medieval Idea of Law as Represented by Lucas de Penna* (London: Methuen, 1946).

Underhill, Norman, *The Lord Chancellor* (Suffolk: Terence Dalton Ltd., 1978).

Van Leeuwen, Henry G., *The Problem of Certainty in English Thought 1630–1690* (The Hague: Nijhoff, 1963).

Vinogradoff, Paul, 'Reason and Conscience in Sixteenth-Century Jurisprudence' in *The Collected Papers of Paul Vinogradoff* (Oxford: Clarendon Press, 1928; reprint London: Wildy and Sons, 1964), vol. 2, pp. 190–204.

Walsham, Alexandra, 'Ordeals of Conscience: Casuistry, Conformity and Confessional Identity in Post-Reformation England', in *Contexts of Conscience in Early Modern Europe 1500–1700*, H.E. Braun and E. Vallance (eds) (Basingstoke: Palgrave Macmillan, 2004), pp. 32–48.

Watt, Gary, *Equity Stirring: The Story of Justice Beyond Law* (Oxford: Hart Publishing, 2009).

Witte, John Jr., *Law and Protestantism: The Legal Teachings of the Lutheran*

Reformation (Cambridge: Cambridge University Press, 2002).
Wood, Thomas, *English Casuistical Divinity During the Seventeenth Century* (London: SPCK, 1952).
Yale, D.E.C., 'Introduction' to Edward Hake, *Epieikeia: A Dialogue on Equity in Three Parts* (New Haven: Yale University Press, 1953).
Yale, D.E.C., 'Introduction' to *Lord Nottingham's Chancery Cases* (2 vols, London: Selden Society, 1957), vol. 1. [Publications of the Selden Society vol. 73.]
Yorke, Philip C., *The Life and Correspondence of Philip Yorke, Earl of Hardwicke, Lord High Chancellor of Great Britain* (Cambridge: Cambridge University Press, 1913; reprinted New York: Octagon Books, 1977).

Index